Re-inventing the Italian Right

Following his third election victory in 2008, the Italian Prime Minister Silvio Berlusconi was the most controversial head of government in the EU. This is a cogent examination of the Berlusconi phenomenon, exploring the success and development of the new populist right-wing coalition in Italy since the collapse of the post-war party system in the early 1990s.

Carlo Ruzza and Stefano Fella provide a comprehensive discussion of the three main parties of the Italian right: Berlusconi's Forza Italia, the xenophobic and regionalist populist Northern League and the post-fascist National Alliance. The book assesses the implications of this controversial right for the Italian democratic system and examines how the social and political peculiarities of Italy have allowed such political formations to emerge and enjoy repeated electoral success.

Framed in a comparative perspective, the authors:

- explore the nature of the Italian right in the context of right-wing parties and populist phenomena elsewhere in other advanced democracies, drawing comparisons and providing broader explanations.
- locate the parties of the Italian right within the existing theoretical conceptions of right-wing and populist parties, utilising a multi-method approach, including a content analysis of party programmes.
- highlight the importance of political and discursive opportunities in explaining the success of the Italian right, and the agency role of a political leadership that has skilfully shaped and communicated an ideological package to exploit these opportunities.

Giving an excellent insight into a key European nation, this work provides a thoughtful and stimulating contribution to the research on the Italian right, and its implications for democratic politics.

Carlo Ruzza is Professor of Sociology at the University of Leicester and has previously taught at the Universities of Surrey, Essex and Trento.

Stefano Fella writes on British and Italian politics, has taught European politics at London Metropolitan University and previously co-ordinated research projects at the University of Trento.

Routledge Studies in Extremism and Democracy

Edited by Roger Eatwell, *University of Bath,*
and Cas Mudde, *University of Antwerp-UFSIA*

This new series encompasses academic studies within the broad fields of 'extremism' and 'democracy'. These topics have traditionally been considered largely in isolation by academics. A key focus of the series, therefore, is the (inter-)*relation* between extremism and democracy. Works will seek to answer questions such as to what extent 'extremist' groups pose a major threat to democratic parties, or how democracy can respond to extremism without undermining its own democratic credentials.

The books encompass two strands:

Routledge Studies in Extremism and Democracy includes books with an introductory and broad focus that are aimed at students and teachers. These books will be available in hardback and paperback. Titles include:

Understanding Terrorism in America
From the Klan to al Qaeda
Christopher Hewitt

Fascism and the Extreme Right
Roger Eatwell

Racist Extremism in Central and Eastern Europe
Edited by Cas Mudde

Political Parties and Terrorist Groups (2nd edition)
Leonard Weinberg, Ami Pedahzur and Arie Perliger

Routledge Research in Extremism and Democracy offers a forum for innovative new research intended for a more specialist readership. These books will be in hardback only. Titles include:

1. Uncivil Society?
Contentious politics in post-Communist Europe
Edited by Petr Kopecky and Cas Mudde

Re-inventing the Italian Right

Territorial politics, populism and 'post-fascism'

Carlo Ruzza and Stefano Fella

LONDON AND NEW YORK

First published 2009
by Routledge
2 Park Square, Milton Park, Abingdon, Oxfordshire OX14 4RN

Simultaneously published in the USA and Canada
by Routledge
711 Third Avenue, New York, NY 10017

Routledge is an imprint of the Taylor & Francis Group, an informa business

First issued in paperback 2010

Typeset in Times New Roman by
Taylor & Francis Books

British Library Cataloguing in Publication Data
A catalogue record for this book is available from the British Library

Library of Congress Cataloging in Publication Data
Ruzza, Carlo.
Reinventing the Italian right : territorial politics, populism and "post-
fascism" / Carlo Ruzza and Stefano Fella.
    p. cm. – (Routledge studies in extremism and democracy)
Includes bibliographical references.
    1. Italy–Politics and government–1994- 2. Right and Left (Political
science) 3. Fascism–Italy–History–21st century. 4. Populism–Italy–History–
21st century. 5. Political parties–Italy–History–21st century. 6. Berlusconi,
Silvio, 1936- I. Fella, Stefano. II. Title.
    JN5452.R89 2009
    324.245'023–dc22
                    2008054184

ISBN13: 978-0-415-34461-6 hbk
ISBN13: 978-0-415-66602-2 pbk

From Carlo to Lina and Carletto
From Stefano to Simon and the Howden family

Contents

Illustrations

Series Editors' Preface

For much of the 'short twentieth century', history was characterized by the clash of great ideologies, internal violence and major wars. Although most catastrophic events took place outside the Western world, Europe and the USA were not immune from the turmoil. Two world wars and a series of lesser conflicts led to countless horrors and losses. Moreover, for long periods Western democracy – especially in its European form – seemed in danger of eclipse by a series of radical forces, most notably communist and fascist.

Yet by the turn of the 1990s, liberal democracy appeared destined to become the universal governmental norm. Dictatorial Soviet communism had collapsed, to be replaced in most successor states by multi-party electoral politics. Chinese communism remained autocratic, but in the economic sphere it was moving rapidly towards greater freedoms and marketization. The main manifestations of fascism had gone down to catastrophic defeat in war. Neo-fascist parties were damned by omnipresent images of brutality and genocide, and exerted little appeal outside a fringe of ageing nostalgics and alienated youths.

In the Western World, political violence had disappeared, or was of minimal importance in terms of system stability. Where it lingered on as a regularly murderous phenomenon, for instance in Northern Ireland or Spain, it seemed a hangover from the past – a final flicker of the embers of old nationalist passions. It was easy to conclude that such tribal atavism was doomed in an increasingly interconnected 'capitalist' world, characterized by growing forms of multi-level governance that were transcending the antagonism and parochialism of old borders.

However, as we move into the new millennium there are growing signs that extremism even in the West is far from dead – that we celebrated prematurely the universal victory of democracy. Perhaps the turn of the twenty-first century was an interregnum, rather than a turning point? In Western Europe there has been the rise of 'extreme right' and 'populist' parties such as Jean-Marie Le Pen's Front National, which pose a radical challenge to existing elites – even to the liberal political system. In the USA, the 1995 Oklahoma mass-bombing has not been followed by another major extreme right attack, but there is simmering resentment towards the allegedly over-powerful state among a miscellany of discontents, who appear even more dangerous than the militias which emerged in the 1990s. More generally across the West, new forms of green politics, often linked by a growing hostility to globalization-Americanization, are taking on more violent forms (the issue of animal rights is also growing in importance in this context).

In the former Soviet space, there are clear signs of the revival of 'communist' parties (which often masquerade as 'socialists' or 'social democrats'), whose allegiance to democracy is (in varying degrees) debatable. In Latin America, there remain notable extremist movements on the left, though these tend not to be communist. This trend may well grow both in response to globalization-Americanization and to the (partly-linked) crises of many of these countries, such as Argentina. This in turn increases the threat to democracy from the extreme right, ranging in form from paramilitary groups to agro-military conspiracies.

The rise of Islamic fundamentalism has been an even more notable feature of recent years. This is not simply a facet of Middle Eastern politics. It has had an impact within some former Soviet republics, where the old nomenklatura have used the Islamic threat to maintain autocratic rule. In countries such as Indonesia and India, Muslims and other ethnic groups have literally cut each other to pieces. More Al-Qaeda bombings of the 2002 Bali type threaten economic ruin to Islamic countries which attract many Western tourists.

It is also important to note that growing Islamic Fundamentalism has had an impact within some Western countries. The terrorist attacks on the World Trade Center and elsewhere in the USA on September 11, 2001 are perhaps the most graphic illustration of this impact. But in democracies generally, the rise of religious and other forms of extremism pose vital questions about the limits of freedom, multiculturalism, and tolerance. This is especially the case in countries which have experienced notable Islamic immigration and/or which face the greatest threat of further terrorist attack.

Democracy may have become a near-universal shibboleth, but its exact connotations are being increasingly challenged and debated. As long as the 'evil empire' of communism existed, Western democracy could in an important sense define itself by the 'Other' – by what it was not. It did not have overt dictatorial rule, censorship, the gulags, and so on. But with the collapse of its great external foe, the spotlight has turned inward (although Islam is in some ways replacing communism as the 'Other'). Is (liberal-Western) democracy truly democratic? Can it defend itself against terrorism and new threats without undermining the very nature of democracy?

These general opening comments provide the rationale for the *Routledge Series on Extremism and Democracy*. In particular, there are three issues which we seek to probe in this series:

- Conceptions of democracy and extremism
- Forms of the new extremism in both the West and the wider world
- How democracies are responding to the new extremism

Given all the commotion following the installation of the Austrian ÖVP-FPÖ government in 2000, it is often forgotten that the first postwar government in Europe that included a populist radical right party was constituted in Italy in 1994. It consisted of an odd mix of new and old parties, most notably Silvio Berlusconi's brand new *Forza Italia* (FI), Umberto Bossi's relatively new *Lega Nord* (LN), and Gianfranco Fini's old *Movimento Sociale Italiano/Alleanza Nazionale* (MSI/AN).

Maybe part of the lack of outrage can be explained by the difficulties that many commentators had with categorizing the parties. FI was so new and based upon the personality of its leader that it was almost impossible to determine whether it stood for anything other than Berlusconi's corporate and personal self-interest. The LN was notorious for its leader's antics and volatile programmatic positions, which initially included the breakaway of the prosperous north of Italy ('Padania') from the rest. And the MSI/AN was in the process of transformation from a clearly neo-fascist party into a yet to be defined new party.

While the government was short-lived, the three parties would come together again in 2001, and this time their coalition government would survive for a full term (a unique accomplishment in postwar Italian politics). But while the parties became better known and established, debate remained within and outside academia about their ideological profiles. This book is the first to systematically analyze the ideologies of all three parties and compare and contrast them. It shows that much remains vague and uncertain, given the parties' dependency on their highly idiosyncratic leaders (though less so for the AN, which in 2009 merged into the People of Freedom (PdL), which had emerged from FI in 2008). They are all right-wing, that much is clear. All are also populist, although in the case of the AN, this seems to have been a matter of strategy rather than ideology.

In addition to analyzing the parties' ideologies and categorizing them within broader party and political families, this book also provides a clear and concise overview of the fundamental political changes that have taken place in Italy since the period of scandals and transformations in the early 1990s. Drawing upon a wealth of mostly secondary sources the authors show how the right-wing parties, mostly for their own motives but also as a result of a form of competitive cooperation, used clever and sometimes cynical strategies to fill the political void left by the implosion of the main parties of the Italian 'First Republic', most notably the *Democrazia Christiana* (DC). It is no surprise that their new identity, even if more constructed than real, and populist rhetoric were so successful at a time that almost half of the members of the lower house of parliament were under criminal investigation for fraud and other crimes.

But the book also provides lessons for the study and understanding of populism in other countries. Among the most important points it makes are that the populist (radical) right (1) is not simply a successor of the traditional right and (2) is an active actor in its own success. Moreover, it provides findings that go against some of the main theories in the literature on the populist radical right. For example, contrary to the broadly held belief that populist parties fare badly under majoritarian electoral systems, the Italian Right actually profited from a change away from proportionality and towards a more majoritarian electoral system. A possible explanation for this atypical finding is that most literature on the populist (radical) right assumes that it is shunned by other political parties. However, as has also been the case in various countries in postcommunist Eastern Europe (e.g. Poland, Romania, and Slovakia), when the populist (radical) right is part of larger political block, often in a two-block-party system, it can profit from electoral majoritarianism and political polarization.

In short, *Reinventing the Italian Right* is, first and foremost, the ultimate study of the three main contemporary parties of the Right in Italy. It provides an original ideological analysis and a broad overview of the history and explanations of their electoral and political successes. As such, it is a must read for all students of contemporary Italian politics. However, scholars with an interest in general populist politics will find much to reflect on too. This will hopefully help make the remarkable Italian case a more central part of comparative studies on populist (radical) right parties in Europe.

Roger Eatwell and Cas Mudde

Acknowledgments

We are grateful to the many people who have helped us in different ways in producing this book. We discussed individual chapters with several colleagues. Conversation with Jens Rydgren and Mark Gilbert gave us interesting insights on Italian populism. Special thanks to the series editors, Cas Mudde and Roger Eatwell for their invaluable comments and suggestions. Thanks to Pino Gangemi for his valuable comments on the Northern League. We are also very grateful to Piergiorgio Corbetta and to the Istituto Carlo Cattaneo for access to the Itanes (Italian National Data Election Studies) data set.

The Cinefogo (Civil Society and New Forms of Governance in Europe - the Making of European Citizenship) network of excellence – supported by the EU 6th framework programme - sponsored a set of conferences on populism and related topics which helped us refine and present our findings. We wish to thank its director Thomas Boje and the executive council. Thanks to all the participants in the conferences, particularly Alessandro Pizzorno, Paul Taggart, Ephraim Nimni, Tim Bale and Duncan McDonnell who shared their expertise with us

Work for this book began when the two authors were working together at the University of Trento. We are especially grateful to the team at Trento who assisted us with the frame analysis. In particular, we would like to thank Paolo Pasi, Mara Dalmonech and Giulia Bigot for their work in collating and analysing the party documents and elaborating the data. Thanks also to Enzo Loner for his help with the methodology and Lella Pileri who helped us with referencing, translation and text editing.

Carlo taught a course on right-wing politics and movements at the University of Trento and would like to thank all the students who attended this course and provided insightful comments. He would like to thank Hans Joerg Trenz who stimulated him to work on relationships between civil society and the right. He is also particularly grateful to the Institute for Migration, Diversity and Welfare at Malmo for hosting him on a Willy Brandt Guest Professorship in 2008, while work on the book was being finalised (and revised due to an early general election in Italy). In particular, he would like to thank its director Björn Fryklund, and its staff and graduate students. The Institute provide a quiet and intellectually stimulating environment for the completion of the book. Finally he would like to thank Lella without whose support and patience this book would not have been possible.

Stefano would like to thank the UK Political Science Association Italian politics specialist group for providing a stimulating forum in which to discuss various aspects of his research on the Italian right, through the panels staged at the PSA conferences from 2004–2007, and particularly James Newell for convening this group.

Finally, we would like to thank the editorial and production team at Routledge for their assistance in guiding our manuscript through the final production phase.

Abbreviations

AD	*Alleanza Democratica*	
	Democratic Alliance	
AN	*Alleanza Nazionale*	
	National Alliance	
AS	*Alternativa Sociale*	
	Social Alternative	
CCD	*Centro Cristiano Democratico*	
	Christian Democratic Centre	
CdL	*Casa delle Libertà*	
	House of Freedoms	
CISNAL	*Confederazione Italiana Sindacati Nazionali dei Lavoratori*	
	Italian Confederation of National Unions of Workers	
CNEL	*Consiglio Nazionale dell'Economia e del Lavoro*	
	National Council for the Economy and Labour	
CDU	*Cristiani Democratici Uniti*	
	United Christian Democrats	
DC	*Democrazia Cristiana*	
	Christian Democracy	
DE	*Democrazia Europea*	
	European Democracy	
DS	*Democratici di Sinistra*	
	Left Democrats	
FdG	*Fronte della Gioventù*	
	Youth Front (MSI)	
FI	*Forza Italia*	
	Come on Italy!	
FN	*Front National*	
	National Front (France)	
FPO	*Freiheitliche Partei Österreichs*	
	Austrian Freedom Party	
FUAN	*Fronte Universitario d'Azione Nazionale*	
	University Front of National Action (MSI)	
IDV	*Italia dei Valori*	
	Italy of Values	

LN	*Lega Nord*
	Northern League
MPA	*Movimento per l'Autonomia*
	Movement for Autonomy
MSI-DN	*Movimento Sociale Italiano – Destra Nazionale*
	Italian Social Movement – National Right
ON	*Ordine Nuovo*
	New Order
PD	*Partito Democratico*
	Democratic Party
PDCI	*Partito dei Comunisti Italiani*
	Party of Italian Communists
PDS	*Partito Democratico della Sinistra*
	Democratic Left Party
PLI	*Partito Liberale Italiano*
	Italian Liberal Party
PPI	*Partito Popolare Italiano*
	Italian Popular Party
PRI	*Partito Repubblicano Italiano*
	Italian Republican Party
PSDI	*Partito Socialista Democratico Italiano*
	Italian Social Democratic Party
PSI	*Partito Socialista Italiano*
	Italian Socialist Party
RC	*Rifondazione Comunista*
	Communist Refoundation
REP	*Die Republikaner*
	The Republicans (Germany)
RI	*Rinnovamento Italiano*
	Italian Renovation
RRP	Radical Right Party
RSI	*Repubblica Sociale Italiana*
	Italian Social Republic
SDI	Socialisti Democratici Italiani, Italian Democratic Socialists
SVP	*Südtiroler Volkspartei*
	South Tyrol Peoples Party
Udeur	*Unione Democratici per l'Europa*
	Union of Democrats for Europe
UEN	Union for Europe of the Nations
UGL	*Unione Generale del Lavoro*
	General Union of Labour
UKIP	United Kingdom Independence Party
UPE	Union for Europe
UQ	*Fronte dell'Uomo Qualunque*
	Common Man's Front

1 Introduction

The charismatic and controversial leadership of Silvio Berlusconi and the pasts and presents of his government coalition partners have placed the Italian political system, particularly following Berlusconi's electoral successes in 2001 and 2008, in the international spotlight. The centre-right government over which Berlusconi presided between 2001 and 2006 could lay claim to the considerable achievement (in Italian terms) of managing to remain in office for a full parliamentary term, and indeed in the meantime, setting a record for longevity in office for a post-war Italian government. It also did considerably better than the short-lived government led by Berlusconi in 1994, which lasted eight months. Although the centre right was defeated by the narrowest of margins in the 2006 general election, the collapse of the centre-left government in early 2008 paved the way for Berlusconi's third general election victory and return as prime minister in April.

The success of the centre-right coalition over this period was all the more remarkable when one considers the history and nature of the political forces that constituted it. In 2008, Berlusconi headed the Popolo della Libertà (PdL, People of Freedom) electoral list, which brought together his own Forza Italia (FI) party, the post-fascist National Alliance (Alleanza Nazionale, AN) and other disparate centre-right and right-wing groupings. FI was a party founded from scratch by Berlusconi in the early 1990s, when he was better known as a successful entrepreneur who owned Italy's three main private TV stations as well as its leading football club, AC Milan. It was a party whose leadership and policy direction was dominated by Berlusconi and viewed by many as his personal vehicle. The AN emerged out of the MSI (Movimento Sociale Italiano, Italian Social Movement), which presented itself until the early 1990s as the unashamed guardian of Italy's fascist legacy. In 2008, the PdL list was allied with the Northern League (Lega Nord, LN), a regionalist populist party that has at times advocated the break-up of Italy and is often categorised as part of the family of new xenophobic radical right-wing populist parties (RRP) or extreme right populists in Europe. The PdL–LN alliance in essence reproduced the House of Freedoms (CdL, Casa delle Libertà) coalition, through which the AN, the LN and FI together fought the 2001 and 2006 elections. The difference in 2008 was that the fourth party of the CdL coalition, the centrist Christian Democrat UDC, this time ran separately, having refused to join the PdL list. This accentuated the right-wing character of the coalition which, in contrast to 2001-6, would not contain this prominent moderating centrist element. Although the PdL also included some smaller Christian Democrat groupings, it also included a group of unreconstructed fascists led by Alessandra Mussolini (grand-daughter of Italy's fascist dictator) who had previously quit the AN in protest at its leader Gianfranco Fini's disavowal of aspects of the fascist regime.

The nature of this coalition and its success over a number of Italian elections raises a number of broader questions for observers of party change, party systems and representative democracy. The degree to which Berlusconi, his party and coalition partners have benefited from his ownership and control of a swathe of the Italian mass media raises general questions regarding the relationship between the media and politics and the potential conflict of interests that can arise in this regard. In addition, the political style of Berlusconi lends itself to interpretations based on the importance of communications and personal image in politics. More broadly, the three main parties of the coalition provide excellent examples of the role of leadership in politics, the increasing personalisation of politics and the tendency towards leadership centralisation in parties, both in Italy and more globally. Moreover, the LN and FI, in particular, provide interesting examples of the global phenomenon of populism and rare European examples of how new populist movements behave in government and reconcile their anti-establishment and anti-political discourse with the trappings of office. Furthermore, AN provides a remarkable case of how a political force that was until recently associated with Europe's old neo-fascist right has been able to re-invent itself as a legitimate political actor, viewed across the political spectrum in Italy as a democratic force, albeit one with authoritarian conservative tendencies.

These phenomena need to be understood in the wider context of party system change, in relation to which Italy also presents itself as an extreme case, at least in the western European context. Between 1992 and 1994, the major governing parties in Italy imploded, notably the Christian Democrat (DC), which had been present in government as the largest party continuously since 1947, and its main coalition partner, the Italian Socialist Party (PSI). This collapse was precipitated by the *mani pulite* (clean hands) investigations, which implicated a large number of parliamentarians and sections of the leadership of both parties in a complicated web of corruption: the so-called *tangentopoli* (kickback city) scandal. Some of the minor parties, such as the PSDI (Social Democrats) and PLI (Liberal party), that had frequently been present in the DC-led coalitions were also brought down by the scandal. A new centre-left coalition led by the reformed former communist Democratic Left party (PDS) – previously excluded from government because of its association with Soviet communism – appeared likely to profit from the political vacuum created by the collapse of the DC and its allies, and win government office in 1994. This was until the decision by Silvio Berlusconi to enter the fray at the head of his newly created Forza Italia party, knitting together a coalition that also included the AN and the LN. Making full use of the media and financial resources at Berlusconi's disposal, the new coalition achieved a stunning election victory. The government formed in 1994 was viewed by many observers as a break with Italy's anti-fascist consensus (a principle around which the post-war republican constitution was organised), given that it included a number of ministers from the MSI–AN. Although differences within the coalition meant that the government was short-lived (collapsing at the end of 1994 after the withdrawal of the LN), the three parties have since remained the principal players on the centre right in Italy, returning to government in coalition again in 2001 and this time remaining in office for the full parliamentary term, only to lose office by the narrowest of margins in 2006, before returning to government again in 2008. Following this latest election victory, the leaderships of both FI and the AN signalled their intention to dissolve their parties into a new PdL party.

The success of the centre-right coalition in remaining in power for the length of the 2001–6 parliamentary term and returning to government again in 2008 needs to be considered in a number of contexts, notably the history of the post-war Italian republic in which government executives were marked by a seemingly congenital fragility, as demonstrated by the impressively large number of governments that came and went since the end of the second world war (fifty-eight from 1945 to 2001). However, the maintenance of this alliance was all the more remarkable when one considers the history and nature of the political forces that constituted it and, moreover, when one considers the apparent irreconcilability of some of the key constituent parties, straddling as they do a number of the key cleavages that shape Italian political culture, including those relating to the north–south divide, the secular–catholic division in politics and conflicting interpretations regarding the role of the state and the free market (see Pasquino 2003a).

In order to understand the rapid rise of these parties, a broader understanding of the remarkable political changes that have taken place in Italy since the 1990s is required. In essence, a whole new electoral marketplace has been created in Italy, creating new political opportunities for innovative political parties and imaginative party leaders.

Although the opportunity to carve out new political space was created by the collapse of the DC and its allies, the adoption of a new set of rules to govern the electoral marketplace, i.e. a new predominantly majoritarian electoral system, was also central to the development of the new party system. This meant that, while carving out different political spaces for themselves, these parties had to co-operate if they wished to achieve electoral success and enter government. The nature of this coalition has been highly controversial, not least because of the personal political style and 'conflict of interests' of its leader, Berlusconi, and because of the nature of its leading party, Forza Italia – the personal creation of Berlusconi. However, the participation of both the LN and the AN raised concerns for differing reasons, the AN because of its recent past as the neo-fascist MSI, in which all of its key leaders received their political formation, and the LN because of a populist exclusionist discourse often labelled as xenophobic.

The principal aim of this book is to provide an understanding of the nature of these new and re-invented political forces on the Italian right, explaining their growth and development and exploring how the social and political peculiarities of Italy have allowed such controversial political formations to emerge and conquer the electorates of an advanced European democracy.

The book seeks to explain the success of the right with reference to a combination of factors. In relation to these, it must be stressed – as explained in the next chapter – that the success of the right has taken place in a state of continuing political turmoil – the transition to the much trumpeted 'second Italian republic' has never quite reached its destination. The unsettling effects on political institutions, on the economic performance of the country and on the efficiency of the state have contributed to a continuing popular dissatisfaction with the conduct of politics. We posit that the right has been better able to govern this continuing state of transition and the turmoil that has ensued.

To explain the superior performance of the right, we will emphasise ideological factors, the changing structural characteristics of Italian society and the resources at the disposal of political actors. We will posit that, following the traumatic events of *tangentopoli*, the right could re-invent itself in a fashion that was more suited to the changes that Italian society was undergoing, while the left remained fragmented and anchored to old ideological schemes. Conversely, the right has been able to innovate ideologically and to an extent find common ideological elements to mask persisting divisions. The book will document the process of re-invention of the Italian right through an empirical analysis of its ideology. It will stress in particular the accord between the socially conservative values of a dominant institution such as the catholic church in Italy and the right, and the success of the right in interpreting a variety of anti-political sentiments through ideological statements but also through markers such as a distinctive use of the language of politics and political symbolism. In terms of its better ability to respond to societal changes, we will emphasise the impact of de-industrialisation and the necessity of responding to the interests of the self-employed and young job-seekers thorough promises such as reduction of the tax burden and more flexibility in the job market, which were crucial in distinguishing the right from the left and contributed significantly to its success at several points in time. In terms of resources, we will point to those that Silvio Berlusconi has had at his disposal through a never resolved conflict of interest resulting in synergies between his dual role of wealthy entrepreneur and powerful political actor. His media skills and his control of the private television networks have been particularly relevant.

To these variables, we should add the role of personal charisma – or rather, the various ways in which charismatic domination can be achieved and utilised. The leaders of these three parties, Gianfranco Fini of the AN, Umberto Bossi of the LN and Silvio Berlusconi of FI, have proved particularly skilful and adept in using distinctive leadership styles to exploit the opportunities provided by the changing political circumstances of Italy since the early 1990s. Hence this book will pay special attention to the leadership of these three key figures. Through a process of ideological re-invention and fine tuning that differed among the three parties and required distinctive leadership styles, these parties have moved to carve out particular niches and broader spaces within the new Italian political landscape.

In order to assess the success, continuing appeal and long-term prospects of the Italian right, while placing it in a broader global context, an understanding is required of the nature, strategies and constituencies of its component parties. Just a cursory examination of the political cultures and agendas of two of these political forces, the AN and the LN, suggests a lack of compatibility which points to a future of instability and division and difficulties in maintaining a united centre-right pole, either in government or in opposition. The AN has a centralising, statist tradition, places a priority on the maintenance of the values and integrity of the Italian nation-state and draws its support mainly from the south. The LN favours autonomy for the north of the country (and has occasionally threatened northern secession from the rest of the Italy) and, as the name suggests, its constituency lies almost exclusively in the north. One could argue that a lack of compatibility in terms of constituencies, values, programmatic goals and broader strategies threatens the continuing viability of these parties as an electoral and governing coalition. Alternatively, one could argue that, particularly in a bipolar political system, the distinctiveness of these political forces is an advantage, in that each can reach a part of the electorate that its competitors–allies cannot, thus contributing to the construction of the broad church representing diverse political interests and constituencies that is essential to conquer power in an advanced liberal democracy.

The experience of the second Berlusconi government of 2001–6 also provides an opportunity to assess the ability of these parties to deliver in office, as they sought to combine a continuing appeal to their political constituencies with their institutional role. Both the LN and the FI leaderships have been characterised by the use of a populist discourse which juxtaposes a pure honest common people against a corrupt self-serving political elite, characterised by cynical political parties, led and staffed by 'professional' politicians. Thus, Berlusconi has made great play of his background as a political outsider, Italy's most successful entrepreneur who reluctantly entered politics in the midst of the political crisis in the early 1990s to save Italy from the peril represented by the recycled former communists and professional politicians of the centre left. Bossi, as leader first of the Lombard League in the 1980s, and then of the Northern League, broke the mould of Italian politics with his populist attacks on the Italian state, Rome and the south in the late 1980s and early 1990s. The LN's political discourse has also taken on an ethno-populist form that was also unprecedented in the history of the Italian republic, in which first southern Italian migrants were scapegoated for bringing social and economic problems to the north of Italy, and then later (when the LN's participation in a national electoral coalition required it to moderate this discourse) the non-EU migrant became the 'other' against which the LN's imagined community of honest hard-working northern Italians was juxtaposed. The AN, given its fascist antecedents, has had to tread a more careful path. In seeking to reassure sections of the Italian population, and the international community, of its new democratic credentials, the use of populist demagoguery would have been counter-productive. Thus its leader, Gianfranco Fini, has presented a more moderate and prudent political image. Nevertheless, the MSI–AN benefited in the early 1990s from its exclusion from the governing system and the constitutional arch of potential governing parties, as well as its previous critique of Italy's corrupt *partitocrazia* (rule by parties) and advocacy of institutional reforms (such as direct presidential elections). Moreover, this anti-party ethos was combined with continued references to the Italian national community, tough (although recently moderated) positions on immigration control and a valorisation of traditional catholic conceptions of family life and morality, which also sometimes lend themselves to populist interpretations.

Thus, one may ask, how did these new and recycled parties, which had no experience of government prior to 1994 (and in 2001 only the short and abruptly ended period of office in 1994 to refer back to) cope with the demands of government office? How were populist and anti-political positions reconciled with the assumption of government responsibility? Moreover, how were the distinct political identities and different electoral constituencies that these parties were elected to represent reconciled in government office?

One other grouping on the centre right should also be mentioned here: the UDC is a catholic centrist grouping that developed out of conservative splinters from the former DC. However, given these antecedents, its involvement in government between 2001 and 2006 was far less controversial. In this period, it sought to distance itself from the other centre-right forces, particularly FI and the LN, and the 'populist' nature of the coalition in general. Following the defeat of the coalition in 2006, the UDC took a number of positions independent of the rest of the CdL, before leaving the alliance and finally deciding to run separately from the PdL in 2008. It is notable in this context that the UDC refuses to don the centre-right label. Like the DC before it, it insists on presenting itself as a centrist political force. Given these various considerations, the focus of this book will be on the FI, LN and AN, i.e. the new and re-invented right and the interactions within it, rather than the UDC, although the UDC will often be discussed in terms of the relationship of these parties to it.

Structure and general approach of book

The next chapter will examine in more detail the nature of the political system of the post-war republic and the reasons for its collapse, exploring the way in which right and centre right found expression within the post-war party system and seized the initiative following its collapse in the early 1990s.

The interaction between the three parties and their behaviour from the first Berlusconi government to the third will be assessed in order to provide the background for the more detailed interpretations and analysis of each of the parties that will come in Chapters 4–6. Following on from this, Chapter 3 will provide a broader conceptual framework for the book, by examining the social, cultural and political processes that have led to the emergence of new populist movements throughout Europe and shaped the trajectory and successes of the right, explaining their relevance for Italy. Chapters 4–6 will then examine the nature, political culture, strategy, programme and constituency of the LN, FI and AN within the context of the discussion and conceptual framework presented in Chapters 2 and 3. Chapter 7 will present conclusions as to the reasons for the success of the Italian right, drawing from the findings of the party chapters and seeking to answer the questions posited by these introductory comments as to the appeal of the Italian right and the nature of the new political styles it has heralded. The final chapter will seek to place the Italian right within the broader literature on right-wing and populist political parties, examining its success in comparison with other European polities and its implications for democratic politics in general. It will stress the role of political and cultural opportunities in explaining the differing levels of success of the right in Europe.

Throughout this book, specific reference will be made to the ideology of the different political forces on the Italian right and the role played by the party leaders in shaping their ideological trajectories. This will draw from analysis of party programmes. While a variety of studies of Italian politics, or some of its parties, in the 1990s have examined aspects of the trajectory of the right and often included in their examination references to the communication strategies of the coalition and of its parties, these references often consist of marginal notations supported by examples usually focusing on one or other party. At other times, the centrality and innovative character of the political discourse of this coalition is asserted but without systematic study of its features and changing traits. We posit that effective political communication has been a central element of the success of the right and that the creation of new and persuasive ideological frames represents one of the successful accomplishments of the centre-right coalition. For this reason, the role of ideology in the different parties is studied in detail. The production and diffusion of ideological frames is examined through a variety of methods and constitutes a central element of the analysis. We will return to the technical aspects of our methodology in more detail in Chapter 3. But here some introductory comments are useful.

Different authors give varying attention to ideology and often define it differently. For some, ideology mainly consists of rhetorical window-dressing. Others conceptualise it as the narrative that justifies specific policy preferences and relates them to one another. For some, it merely reflects an elaboration of underlying economic interests. For others, ideologies are part of a long and complex process of continuous definitions and re-definitions of interests and related policy preferences that is substantially influenced by interpersonal communication or by media dynamics. Authors studying the extreme or radical right often emphasise both the picturesque element and the threatening aspect of right-wing ideologies and relate them to concepts such as 'cultural protectionism' or 'ethnic rivalry', which are in turn explained by general socio-political themes such as globalisation or the changing functions of the state (Betz 1994; Kitschelt and McGann 1995; Zaslove 2004). We posit that, although there is mileage in these approaches, it is necessary to be specific in their use. It is necessary to be precise in the identification of the ideological production of parties and in the identification of the reasons why they change over time. A precise documentation of the ideological content of these parties helps in addressing issues such as the relationship between the economic interests, policy orientations and cultural views of the electorate. Thus we strive to examine in detail processes of ideological production and adaptation.

Ideology is differently reflected in different arenas – it emerges differently in media texts, party programmes and oral statements. We have examined various forms of ideological production through interviews with party activists, and monitoring of media reports, party literature and speeches, and we have performed a content analysis of party programmes. The content analysis of party programmes is particularly relevant for several reasons. They are the 'official voice' of the parties. Much discussion and negotiation has been put into their preparation. Thus, in analysing them, a researcher can be assured of the importance and representativity of the material. They lend themselves to systematic comparisons over time and across parties. They are distributed as a source of inspiration to party activists and incumbents and therefore have a socialising intent and reflect chosen strategies of political communication. Of course, parties often know that they have to speak with different voices to different audiences, and programmes are only one such voice. But they are more important in several ways than other formalised public expressions, as parties can be held accountable to them in ways than do not apply to other voices and arenas. For these reasons, we devoted substantial time and effort to analysing them. Through the analysis of these and other texts, we will argue that the success of the Italian right in recent years can be attributed to the intersection of a set of differentiated and often opposing right-wing discourses that have resonated with different groups of the population, with inconsistencies and incompatibilities disguised by a common emphasis on conservative values and the unifying discourses of populism.

Only a few years ago, a book on the Italian right would have started with references to Italy's fascist past and the difficult transition of the post-war years. Today, however, one cannot write about the political right without an immediate reference to populism. Populism as the condemnation of professional politicians and the proclamation of the intrinsic dignity, honesty and moral rectitude of ordinary people and as the source of inspiration in the conduct of political affairs is what unifies and distinguishes the Italian right. The virtues of 'the people' are asserted in opposition to a corrupt political class to which the right presents itself as the main opponent. Populism is thus an ideology that shapes its collective identity and political rhetoric. While the fascist legacy is arguably still present in the Italian right, what characterises it today is its unique political communication and the ownership of a media empire by the leader of the right-wing coalition's strongest party – FI – and also the distinctly bombastic rhetoric style of the LN. Even AN strives to portray itself in more appealing 'post-fascist' terms, eschewing traditional right-wing platforms in favour of a more complex and nuanced ideological mix. The parties of the Italian right, at the turn of the century, differ substantially from one another in terms of their structure, constituency, tactics and strategies, but have all been framed in the literature as populist parties. Populism as a political category has been used frequently and widely in political analyses, and has been considered to be somewhat overused. A clarification of its meaning and its function is necessary to show that the use of this interpretive category is appropriate in reference to such different formations as FI, AN and LN, and will be accomplished through analysis of their texts.

As with all complex political concepts, 'populism' focuses attention on a range of issues while playing down others. It identifies 'the people' as a foundational political category – as a self-evident source of legitimacy – and it implicitly plays down all the institutional mechanisms that come between 'the people' and public decision-making. In this juxtaposing of the virtuous people and the corrupt elite and in siding with the people – we will argue – lies a key element of the success of the Italian right.

2 Right and centre right in the post-war party system

> In Italy, the political struggle is so specific that a right wing of a classic traditional type, that is, a respectable, law abiding right, is unthinkable because it would be soon labelled as fascist.
>
> De Felice (1975: 97)

Until the 1990s, the musings of the renowned historian of Italian fascism, Renzo De Felice, as to the difficulties of establishing a legitimate right-wing political force in post-war Italy appeared to hold true. The right-wing label was associated with extremism and anti-democratic sentiment and regarded as a 'taboo' in Italian politics (Pasquino 2005; Sidoti 1992: 155). This perception had been fuelled by the historical role played by the Italian right and notably the multiple connections between the conservative and fascist right in Italian history. Since the foundation of the modern Italian state in the second half of the nineteenth century, the traditional conservative right had been easily swayed by authoritarian and anti-democratic tendencies, with a substantial section of it generally being rather suspicious of democratic norms. This was illustrated by the accommodations reached by the conservative right and the fascist right in the early 1920s. The Italian conservative right generally shared the fascist distrust of liberal institutions, as well as the fascists' virulent anti-communism. It eased the path to power of the fascists, believing that it could manipulate them in order to preserve and promote its own interests. As Roland Sarti notes, Italian conservatives showed very little 'Burkean respect for institutions and processes received from the distant past' (Sarti 1990: 14). Conservative forces in Italy have always been rather more attached to traditional symbols of authority such as family and church than to political institutions. Conservatives in Italy have supported authoritarian dictatorships when they felt that they could get away with it (prior to 1945 at least – although much the same could also be said of most European countries), or democratic constitutionalism where they felt they could maintain their interests or at least manage an inevitable change in conditions favourable to them. In the aftermath of the Second World War, the changed political climate meant that most conservatives saw the Christian Democratic (DC) party as a convenient vehicle for the promotion of their interests. The mass mobilisation against fascism and the new international order, in which Italy was placed very much within the US sphere of influence, meant that a democratic system would prevail in the post-war period, the precise procedures of which were established by the new republican constitution drawn up by the constituent assembly in 1946–47. Most conservatives were content to work within the newly constituted liberal democratic system, in which the exclusion of the communist left from power became the unwritten first article.

Christian Democracy and the post-war centre right

The DC was a confessional party founded towards the end of the Second World War by leaders of the pre-fascist Catholic Popular party and various Catholic associations, trade unionists and anti-fascist groups. Although it presented itself as a 'centrist' political force, it occupied at least partially the political space occupied by centre-right parties in other advanced western democracies, attracting the support of conservative forces. Indeed, as Robert Leonardi and Douglas Wertman suggest in their study of Italian Christian Democracy, the DC was constructed on the basis of a:

> coalition of interests, individuals and ideas forged in the heated political atmosphere of the immediate post-Second World War period, during which the party became the instrument for the achievement of a number of political objectives such as, for example, safeguarding the role of the Catholic Church in the country and serving as a bulwark against radical social change and the rise to power of Marxist parties.
>
> Leonardi and Wertman (1989: 4)

However, the same authors suggest that the DC could not, despite attempts to depict it as such, be viewed as 'a conservative bourgeois party in the classical European sense', because a number of the important socio-economic clea- vages that generally separate such parties from their opponents, e.g. developed versus under-developed areas, city versus countryside, agriculture versus industry, and workers versus owners, cut through the DC (Leonardi and Wertman 1989: 10). The DC generally portrayed itself as a broad church, 'catch-all', inter-class party of the centre. It avoided presenting itself as right wing, although some of its factions were. As Hine explains, it had 'an ideological self image substantially different from north European conservatism, or even from German Christian Democracy' (Hine 1993: 129).

The varied and sometimes opposing interests that made up the DC were reflected in the various factions that made for an often uneasy power balance within the party. Although generally united by catholic social doctrine and an aversion to communism, these factions ranged from the staunchly con- servative to the progressive social reformist. The latter involved leftist groupings associated with the catholic trade union movement and thinkers such as Dossetti who favoured radical reform options (in the immediate post-war context) as regards the organisation of society and the economy. Nevertheless, the left factions of the DC were always in a minority within the party, which was generally dominated by a coalition of forces occupying the centre of the party, encapsulated in the immediate post-war period by the leadership of Alcide De Gasperi.

Moreover, while disposed to experiment with new social and economic ideas, the centre of gravity within the DC represented by De Gasperi and his successors remained firmly grounded in a conservative vision of society and the economy (Leonardi and Wertman 1989: 22). Indeed, the intensifying cold war climate of the late 1940s and 1950s contributed to a dilution of the DC's originally progressive instincts, and the perception that it was the party that represented conservative interests, enjoying the support, as it did, of big business, landed interests and, of course, the church. The DC enjoyed a close relationship with *Confagricoltura*, the association of large landowners, and with *Confindustria*, the industrial business association. At the same time, it enjoyed a closely intertwined relationship with the *Coldiretti*, the association of small landowners (Bardi and Morlino 1994).

Pre-dating fascism, the Italian Liberal party (PLI) had traditionally been the party of big business and bourgeois interests. However, attempts to revive it as the main rallying point for conservative forces after the war were unsuccessful. As Paul Ginsborg notes, the Liberals 'never managed to adapt to the changed conditions of post-war Italy', in the main thinking it sufficient to return to the liberalism of the pre-fascist constitutional monarchy (Ginsborg 1990: 75). Although the PLI would intermittently take conservative votes from the DC, for example in relation to resentment towards the agrarian reform of the 1950s and the DC's increasing predilection for an expanded role of the state in the economy, its share of the vote would not rise again above a few percentage points (it peaked at 7 per cent in 1963, following the DC's decision to form a centre-left coalition with the Socialists). Instead, it remained an occasional coalition ally of the DC, located to its right on questions related to the relationship between state and economy. The PLI's lay secularism and its *laissez-faire* approach, which extended to the private activities of individuals as well as the economy, however meant that it was frequently more progressive than the DC on matters related to catholic morality.

As the PLI become more embedded in the systemic clientelism that marked the post-war republic until the 1990s, it was notable that many of the business interests that had previously backed it switched their support to the Republican Party (PRI), which came to be viewed as a modern liberal and (more importantly) relatively clean pro-business party in the 1980s. Indeed, while it retained a close relationship with elements of the DC, *Confindustria* would increasingly channel its views through PRI ministers and spokespersons (Morlino 2001). Nevertheless, the PRI's share of the vote would generally hover around the 2–3 per cent mark, and *Confindustria* and major economic interests would also continue to enjoy privileged ties with the DC, or at least influential elements within it.

The MSI and the extreme right

Before discussing the main party of the post-war Italian extreme right, the MSI, mention should be made of the Fronte dell'Uomo Qualunque (the Common Man's Front, UQ), which emerged in the immediate aftermath of the Second World War and contested the first post-war democratic election in 1946 – the election for the constituent assembly that drew up the republican constitution. UQ was led by a playwright – Guglielmo Giannini – and took an anti-political stance against the anti-fascist governing parties (which at the time included the PCI and PSI as well as the DC) and the allied occupation. It polled 5.3 per cent of the vote – over a million voters – mainly in the south in 1946, providing an outlet for southern notables and former fascists who had been denied entry into the PLI (Ginsborg 1990: 99–100).

Fascist sympathisers were particularly attracted by its anti-communism and the position it took against the anti-fascist purges of the state apparatus (although these had rather limited effects). The party would quickly fade away, after having aligned itself with the DC in 1947 when the PCI was expelled from government. UQ disappeared at the 1948 elections, with most of its voters switching to the triumphant DC. Many of its original backers would however later find a home in the MSI. Its main legacy was the term *qualunquismo* – a label that opponents would attach to the new populist parties that emerged in Italy in the 1990s – denoting an anti-political populist stance.

Given the preference of Italian conservatives of a democratic disposition for the centrist label, the right-wing label was, in the post-war party system, associated predominantly with the MSI, a political party originally formed by veterans of the fascist Italian Social Republic (RSI),[1] which unashamedly assumed the fascist mantle. Its historical associations clearly conflicted with the official anti-fascist consensus that provided a foundation for the construction of the Italian republic following the defeat of fascism in 1945. Thus, the MSI was excluded from the small circle of political parties deemed as legitimate participants in government during the first republic, as was the much larger and more influential Italian Communist Party (PCI).

The PCI's association with Soviet communism would disqualify it from government from the onset of the cold war in 1947 until the fall of the Berlin wall in 1989, despite its central role in the anti-fascist resistance and its influential role in the constituent assembly that designed the republican constitution. The principal beneficiary of the exclusion of these two polar opposites from government was the DC, which remained in office throughout the period, usually in coalition with one or more of the smaller non-Marxist lay parties that continued to flourish under Italy's proportional electoral system. Nevertheless, while the official republican consensus was one of anti-fascism, it was anti-communism that became the abiding principle of the Italian republic in the cold war period, to the extent that the MSI was considered as a potential political ally by the DC in the late 1950s until mass protests and social unrest triggered by the Tambroni government's reliance in 1960 on MSI support in order to maintain its parliamentary majority forced it to rethink its coalition-building strategy. While the MSI was forced back into its political ghetto, the DC was obliged to expand its circle of potential coalition partners to also include the Italian Socialist Party (PSI), a former ally of the PCI that had moved away from its previous Marxist vocation. Indeed, the PSI was more often than not present in government from the 1960s until the early 1990s, allowing the ruling coalition sometimes to be portrayed as one of the centre left (although such a description became increasingly spurious as the PSI's appetite for the clientelistic practices that marked the governing parties grew and its leftism waned).

Dissatisfaction with the DC's centrism and its openings to the left in the 1960s and 1970s occasionally brought the rather dubious democratic credentials of elements of the Italian conservative right out into the open. For example, disgruntlement regarding the DC's apparent appeasement of the left signalled by the 'centre-left' coalition in the 1960s resulted in various subterfuges, in which traditional conservatives and neo-fascist groups connived in order to replace the democratic republic with some form of conservative authoritarian dictatorship. One incident involved the then commander of the carabinieri (later to become an MSI deputy), General Giovanni De Lorenzo, in 1964, who apparently plotted with the support of reactionary industrialists and politicians to use the carabinieri to arrest the leaders of the left-wing parties and other supposed subversives. Following on from this, evidence suggests that conservative forces within the Italian state orchestrated a 'strategy of tension' in the late 1960s and 1970s, motivated first by the opening to the PSI in the 1960s, and then by the growing popular support for the PCI in the 1970s as well as the increasing prominence of the extra-parliamentary left following the social unrest of the late 1960s. These forces were backed by elements of the armed forces, and used radical neo-fascist groups as their foot soldiers. While the precise role of these groups and their leaders remains unclear, among the groups involved in the radical right maelstrom was Ordine Nuovo (ON), an offshoot of the MSI formed by Pino Rauti. Although he would later return to and briefly lead the MSI, Rauti had quit the party in the 1960s in frustration at a parliamentary strategy that had led only to political marginalisation (Ignazi 1994a: 32–36).

Members of ON and more radical offshoots from it, as well as other radical right groups such as Avanguardia Nazionale, would be linked to various coup attempts and bombing campaigns in the period (Caprara and Semprini 2007). It has been suggested that the shady P2 Masonic lodge (consisting of conservative figures from business, politics, the police and the armed forces) was also involved in orchestrating some of the interconnected incidents that marked these years (Ginsborg 1990: 423). All involved were united by paranoia about an imminent communist coup. The strategy was to exacerbate the general climate of social unrest, marked by left-wing protest, through the unleashing of terrorist outrages, to be blamed on the left, in order to cultivate an increased climate of fear, pushing moderate public opinion to the right, and therefore encouraging an authoritarian solution (Ferraresi 1988: 88; Weinberg and Eubank 1987: 137).

Given the links between some of its past and present members with the violent extra-parliamentary strategies referred to above, as well as the less sinister street-fights with the extra-parliamentary left, the MSI tended to suffer from guilt by association during this period. Nevertheless, the adoption of the *destra nazionale* (national right) strategy by its historic leader, Giorgio Almirante, in 1972 led to a brief revival in its fortunes. Almirante – who had led the MSI following its foundation in the late 1940s – was previously associated with a more radical opposition to the conservative authoritarian leadership that had dominated the MSI in the 1950s and 1960s. Although the founders of the MSI (such as Almirante and Rauti) took their original inspiration from the radical variant of fascism embodied in the RSI, i.e. a violent, socialising, revolutionary republicanism, which, it was claimed, reflected fascism's early origins as a movement, its leaders in the 1950s and 1960s period, De Marsanich and Michelini (who took over in 1956) were rather suspicious of the radical 'socialisers'. They were determined to steer the MSI towards the traditional, clerical and monarchical right, attempting to conclude political alliances and avoid confrontation. These leaders had pursued a strategy of *inserimento* (insertion), which was to become a recurring theme in the political strategy of the MSI. Despite its anti-system rhetoric, the MSI sought to work within the liberal democratic constitutional system. It participated in day-to-day parliamentary politics, and in several municipal coalitions in the south, with the DC and sometimes with the Monarchists and PLI (Ignazi 1994a: 21–29). Disillusionment with this strategy had led to the formation of groups such as Rauti's ON, particularly after the apparent failure signalled by the collapse of the Tambroni government in 1960.

Almirante reassumed the leadership of the MSI in 1969 following the death of Michelini. Encouraged by this, and also by fears provoked by the threat of leftist subversion, which they perceived as running through the 'hot autumn' of worker and student revolt, Rauti and other ON leaders rejoined the MSI. Almirante launched a double-pronged (and rather contradictory) strategy. While renewing links with the militants and reaffirming the radical vocation of the MSI, Almirante attempted to reconstruct an image of a respectable conservative party, a bulwark against the left. This was a renewal of the *inserimento* strategy of the 1950s, which Almirante had previously been prominent in opposing. Ferraresi writes: 'The ability of this respectable party, if need be, to call its militants into the street ... was all the more reassuring to conservatives frightened by generalised social unrest' (Ferraresi 1988: 88). In 1972, the MSI-Destra Nazionale (DN) was launched. This merged the monarchists into the MSI, and also aimed to attract other conservative figures such as right-wing Christian Democrats and Liberals (Ginsborg 1990: 336). Almirante sought to present the MSI as the fulcrum of a broader conservative right-wing front, although this stimulated debates within the MSI with some factions disputing the right-wing label attributed to their fascism (aligning themselves with a revolutionary 'fascism in movement'[2]).

Almirante's strategy brought early success. The MSI–DN polled its highest ever (until 1994) vote in the 1972 general election: 8.7 per cent. The MSI benefited from presenting itself as the party of 'law and order'. It also capitalised on southern protest. It orchestrated a wave of protest in Reggio Calabria, after another Calabrian city, Catanzaro, was chosen ahead of it as the seat of the new regional government (although the MSI had opposed the recent institution of regional governments in Italy). The contradictions in the MSI's approach soon became apparent. As Caciagli writes, the MSI 'defended the violent actions of young people and the revolts in the Mezzogiorno; it certainly kept in contact with sectors of "black (right-wing) terrorism" and with the organisations that inside and outside the state apparatus formulated plans for a coup' (Caciagli 1988: 21). These associations all served to damage the public credibility of the Destra Nazionale strategy. In the 1976 national election, the MSI vote fell back to 6.1 per cent.

A faction within the MSI, made up of ex-monarchists and other moderates, frustrated in their aspirations to turn the MSI into a conventional democratic conservative party, broke away and formed their own party Democrazia Nazionale (National Democracy) in 1976, accusing Almirante of keeping contact with right-wing terrorism and of being unable to follow a parliamentary strategy. They sought to construct a national right-wing force more clearly distinct from the fascist heritage and the association with political violence. Despite taking with it half the MSI's parliamentary representation and nearly all the party's public finance, Democrazia Nazionale was obliterated at the 1979 national election. The small grassroots electorate of the MSI stayed loyal to it. However, the MSI remained isolated, a situation exacerbated by the polarised ideological climate of the 1970s, which the MSI itself had helped to create. Ignazi sums up the weakness of the Destra Nazionale strategy as 'a superficial and not very sincere ideological revision, and an inability to control the often violent radical right-wing groups and even some fringes of the party's own youth organisation' (Ignazi 1993: 82).

The political system of the post-war republic

For much of the post-war period, indeed until the 1990s, Italy was regarded as having a 'blocked political system' with no proper alternation of government – a situation that fostered stagnation and corruption. The pure system of proportional representation for parliamentary elections exacerbated the problem of a fragmented party system and thus militated against strong stable government. However, perhaps more of a problem was the way in which party alignments were organised with the deliberate intention of keeping the PCI out of government.[3] Its exclusion created a serious distortion, in allowing the DC to remain permanently in government until 1994. Italy would become the only major western democracy in which there was no alternation in government (Furlong 1991; Hine 1993).

Although permanently in government, the proportional electoral system and fragmented party system required that the DC generally ruled in coalition with other smaller parties. Initially, following the expulsion of the PCI and PSI from government in 1947, its preferred coalition partners were the PLI, PRI and Social Democrats (PSDI). The latter had broken away from the PSI in 1946 in opposition to its subordination to the PCI and Soviet communism. Following the violent reaction to the Tambroni government's moves to bring the MSI into the governing majority in 1960, the vast majority of the DC became convinced that the centre-left strategy – including the PSI in government – was the best way forward to avoid polarising the country and to maintain a firm grip on power. However, by the middle of the 1970s, the PCI was polling around a third of the share of the vote at national and regional elections, and there were fears that it would soon overtake the DC to become the leading party in terms of vote share. The PCI leader, Enrico Berlinguer, called for a 'historic compromise' between the PCI and DC in order to forestall a possible seizure of power by the right in the fevered and violent political climate. DC leaders also gradually came around to the idea of such a compromise with the left.

In 1976, the 'national solidarity' phase was launched when the PCI gave indirect support to the government of Giulio Andreotti (despite his association with the DC right), abstaining on its parliamentary vote of confidence and winning the presidency of the chamber of deputies and various parliamentary committees in return. In 1978, the DC leader, Aldo Moro, appeared to have convinced his party to allow the PCI to enter into the government's parliamentary majority. However, Moro's kidnapping by the Red Brigades on the day on which the vote of confidence in this 'national solidarity' government was due to take place, and his subsequent murder, put paid to closer PCI–DC collaboration. The 1980s witnessed the return to the government fold of the PSI and its increased ascendancy under the leadership of Bettino Craxi, who held the office of prime minister from 1983 to 1988. Craxi's appointment as prime minister came shortly after that of the Republican, Giovanni Spadolini, who became the first non-DC prime minister since 1945. However, the DC remained the dominant force in government in both cases. Government in this period (until the 1990s) was generally based on the five-party (*pentapartito*) coalition, involving the PSDI, PRI and PLI as well as the DC and PSI.

The political system thus displayed a remarkable continuity despite the appearance of instability given by the high turnover of government administrations. The DC remained a permanent fixture in government as did certain personnel. The likes of Andreotti had been involved in government in some capacity since the 1940s (Andreotti performed seven separate stints as prime minister). Governments were replaced by near-identical governments often with exactly the same personnel. So-called government crises (and there were many) were simply means to temporarily resolve internal disagreements.

Although the 1980s and early 1990s were marked by the increased strength of the PSI, and occasional talk of it becoming the focal point of a new social democratic 'left alternative' to the DC under Craxi's leadership, for many observers the involvement of the PSI in government had, over time, somewhat blurred the distinction between it and the DC. As had occurred in relation to the other minor coalition partners, the behaviour of the PSI in government had come to resemble that of the dominant party, in terms of its enthusiastic embrace of a complacent clientelism. DC dominance of the levers of government and the absence of alternation had led to a practice similar to that which had been observed in the pre-fascist Liberal Italy, i.e. a transformism (*trasformismo*), in which new parties were co-opted into the governing apparatus, giving them a share of the spoils of office and binding them into the system (Pasquino 2005: 178). While some parties may have entered the ruling coalition with good intentions, they soon ended up behaving like the others. Thus, while the PSI first entered government in the 1960s with a strong social democratic work-erist ideology, it would over time become absorbed into the system, eventually rivalling the DC as a skilled practitioner in the clientelistic system that became entrenched in the 1950s as the ruling parties exploited the expansion of the public sector, and the establishment of various public agencies and special funds (for example for the development of the south of Italy) (Bardi and Morlino 1994: 250–52). The sharing of spoils, known as *lottizzazione*, involved key posts and fiefdoms within Italy's public sector being divided among the ruling parties.

The way in which parties colonised the public administration and, through an extensive network of state intervention, extended their reach into civil society was referred to as the *partitocrazia* (partyocracy) – the rule of the parties. Parties organised their supporters not on the basis of policy pro-grammes, but through exclusive subcultures in which political loyalty was rewarded through preferment in employment in the bloated state sector or the award of lucrative contracts to undertake public works. Often the intervention of party contacts was required in order to make the inefficient public admin-istration function. Policies were bargained between the various parties and factions in government, bearing little relation to policy preferences expressed by electoral demand. Substantive change was frequently prevented by the breadth of the coalition of interests needed to take decisions and hence the likely existence of a veto group within it. Major policy initiatives took years to materialise, the adoption of legislation enabling the establishment of regional governments being a prime example[4] (Bull and Newell 2005; Hine 1993: 4–12). The clientelistic system meant that the delivery of public goods that were supposed to be universal (such as certain welfare benefits) was often depen-dent on political favours (at the basic minimum, this meant electoral support for a particular party or faction), as were jobs in the public sector, including the myriad of public agencies that mushroomed in the post-war period. Not to take part in such exchanges was to risk having requests for jobs, services and goods in the public sector disappear into an unresponsive state bureau-cracy. This meant that the system enveloped a large swathe of the population, particularly voters for the parties of the *pentapartito*. Moreover, this system also involved the PCI and its supporters, given its governing role at the local level, and its involvement in a consociational system at the national level, whereby legislation was often passed by committees in which it played a key role (the adoption of such legislation required a broader consensus, making the involvement and support of the PCI necessary in certain cases). In addition to clientelism, more straightforward corruption was endemic. The two appeared to operate side by side, as described by Donald Sassoon:

> Corruption involved entrepreneurs funding political parties in exchange for state contracts and other business-related favours. Clienteles involved political parties funding citizens (jobs, privileges, undeserved benefits) in exchange for votes. Thus political parties were at the centre of the flow of transactions. The precondition which makes everything else possible is the de facto continuous control and possession of the state by the ruling parties. Corruption and clientelism contribute to this continuous control. Thus the system is self perpetuating.
>
> Sassoon (1995: 135–36)

The decline of the old party system

The *partitocrazia* and the parties that were central to it, notably the DC and the PSI, came crashing down in the course of the political crisis of 1992–94. Although a number of circumstantial factors were central to this collapse – notably the *tangentopoli* scandal and the linked adoption of a new electoral system – a number of longer term factors also contributed to a decline of the old party system and perhaps softened it up, to the extent that, while it appeared to be still firmly entrenched at the beginning of 1990s, it was blown away with astonishing ease and rapidity by the events that subsequently unfolded. Moreover, the shift towards a bipolar system of electoral alliances and the collapse of the DC-dominated centre was aided by a number of factors that served to legitimise the formerly excluded forces of the right and the left and facilitated the emergence of new political movements that challenged the old order.

Bardi and Morlino (1994) suggest that, while the events of the early 1990s may have accelerated the process of party transformation, there was evidence of a much longer trend towards party organisational decline going back to the late 1960s. The need to expand the governing coalition, notably in the 1960s with the inclusion of the PSI, also created greater competition among the parties in government for a share of the spoils, requiring an expansion of the clientelistic system. This partly explained the gradual expansion of the public sector to the point where it became unsustainable. At the same time, the relationship between the main parties and the dominant societal subcultures (the catholic one in the case of the DC, the Marxist one in the case of the PCI) was gradually being eroded. In the case of the DC, this came about through a gradual secularisation of society, particularly since the 1960s, diminishing the importance of its relationship with catholic organisations, and requiring it to mobilise more through the conventional apparatus of political parties and conventional appeals to political preferences. Moreover, whereas the DC's privileged relationships within the agricultural sector (for example through its close ties to *Confagricoltura* – the association of land-owners – and its hegemonic role *vis-à-vis* the *Coldiretti* – the association of small landowners) and industrial sector (through its strong influence within *Confindustria*) had been central to its earlier dominance, the decline of both these sectors (and the expansion of the service sector in their place) eroded the importance of these, as did the diminishing sense of cultural identity within these sectors. Data from Mannheimer and Sani (1987) showed that the proportion of opinion voters (those who vote on the basis of preferences regarding political issues and programmes) had steadily increased at the expense of those voting on the basis of party identification (on the basis of ideology or, as often was the case with the DC, on the basis of a shared catholicism). The combination of these various (and linked) changes in civil society enmeshment, the structure of the economy and party identification had a corrosive effect on the DC's hold on Italian society and its organisational strength (Bardi and Morlino 1994; Mannheimer and Sani 1987).

The MSI, despite little movement in its national share of the vote, benefited from a de-radicalisation of the political climate in the 1980s, as the terrorism and political violence of both right and left slowly petered out. This was notable in the wake of the massacre at Bologna train station in 1980, in which eighty-five people lost their lives at the hands of a bomb planted by right-wing terrorists. There were 173 episodes of political violence in 1982 compared with 2,039 in 1979 (Ignazi 1994a: 66). The familiar MSI strategy of *inserimento* (the attempt to develop links across the conservative right) began to bear some fruit through the issues of institutional reform and political morality. The MSI organised and participated in discussions on these questions with members of the other parties. Following the 1983 national election, the new (and first socialist) prime minister, Bettino Craxi, expressed in his inaugural speech a desire to establish a constructive dialogue with all opposition forces within parliament, and pledged to put an end to the existence of political ghettoes (Tassani 1990: 127). He addressed these remarks directly towards the MSI. Craxi and the PSI strongly supported a revision in Italy's constitution and, in particular, a move to a presidential republic, i.e. one where the president (preferably Craxi himself) would be directly elected. This coincided with a central plank of MSI policy. In this period, the end of the MSI's official political isolation became a reality with its inclusion in the *lottizzazione* system with *missini* appointed to a number of public posts, and involvement in an all-party parliamentary commission on institutional reform. In relation to the latter, the MSI proposed an entirely new constitution involving a corporatist political system based on compulsory trade unions, direct election of the head of state, with strong executive powers, and a limit to the role of political parties (Tassani 1990: 129). The latter was symbolic of Almirante's repositioning of the MSI's stance to one of protest against the *partitocrazia*. The MSI also continued to champion conservative causes, demanding tougher measures on law and order, such as the restoration of the death penalty, and campaigning against drugs.

The slow process of de-radicalisation of political conflict in Italy was paralleled and partially aided by a 'historicisation' of the fascist period. A less demonised vision of the fascist period emerged. There was a more neutral historical approach to the analysis of fascism, characterised by the work of Renzo De Felice. De Felice claimed that the fascist period was a unique and closed period, which should therefore be studied historically, rather than as part of a continuing struggle. His interpretations sparked a broader debate about the fascist period (and denunciations from the left and catholic centre) (Bosworth 1993: 131–41). Thus, Fascism became a more relativised phenomenon, to be judged in historical rather than political terms.

The MSI was also aided in the early 1990s by interventions in the political debate by the president of the republic, Francesco Cossiga (Buffachi and Burgess 2001: 22–27).[5] Cossiga began to openly denounce the *partitocrazia*, and called for institutional reform in the direction of presidentialism. These statements coincided with similar positions being taken by Fini, and there was a clear appreciation of each other's positions (Valentini 1994). Nevertheless, despite the opportunities offered by the changing political climate, the MSI appeared to be making no real headway with the Italian electorate at the beginning of the 1990s. Indeed, in 1992, as the *tangentopoli* scandals began to unfold, the MSI managed to poll only 5.4 per cent. Despite the openings afforded to the MSI by the changing political climate of the 1980s and early 1990s, it remained 'constrained by its nostalgic recall of old authoritarianism and its support for unfashionable solutions' (Furlong 1992: 352). Meanwhile, the new Leagues in the north were capitalising on the eruption of discontent at Italy's failing political class (Ruzza and Schmidtke 1992). New movements in the south, such as Leoluca Orlando's Sicilian-based, catholic, anti-mafia Rete (network) party, were also benefiting at the expense of the MSI. While the Leagues were exploiting demands for greater autonomy, decentralisation and de-regulation from the corrupt tentacles of Rome, the MSI was still calling for a stronger centralisation of the same corrupt Italian state, and the abolition of regional government.

The foundation of the League and the re-discovery of the centre–periphery dimension

The main economic cleavage in Italy has historically been and remains the north–south one.[6] This can also be defined in terms of the concept of centre–periphery cleavage if one considers that Rome, the political capital, is only to an extent the source and location of power that the concept of centre implies. Industrial and financial power and the many types of social power that this implies have remained firmly situated in the north, engendering a structural juxtaposition between Rome and the large industrial areas of the north. This can be traced back to the unification of Italy in the 1860s and a process of internal colonisation when the comparatively economically advanced northern Savoy monarchy based in Piedmont annexed the south. The problem of southern under-development and societal ambivalence towards state structures has been a constant in the history of modern Italy. The post-war period saw an 'economic miracle' in the north of Italy, integrating it into the modern capitalist economies of the industrialised world, while the south was left behind and contributed mainly through massive migration of its populations to the north. The dependency on the state and north–south fiscal transfers became more pronounced with the institution of mechanisms such as the *Cassa per il Mezzogiorno* (development fund for the south), the latter also becoming a tool for the clientelistic practices of the DC-dominated party system. What was initially framed as a 'southern question', i.e. the need to address southern underdevelopment, would in the 1980s be reframed as a 'northern question' by the Leagues, i.e. an unfair transfer of resources from the productive north to the unproductive south, characterised by clientelistic practices and overseen by a corrupt Rome-based elite.

Other centre–periphery cleavages that concerned linguistic and cultural issues were earlier considered politically salient and led to the establishment of five special autonomy regions following the Second World War (Sardinia, Sicily, Friuli–Venezia–Giulia, Valle d'Aosta and the Trentino–South Tyrol). However, issues of economic and cultural regionalism would later begin to gain political voice in new areas of the north that were not border areas and without a strong linguistic specificity (Ruzza and Schmidtke 1992). The 'Leagues', which initially included the Veneto League (Liga Veneta) and later the Lombard League, were the most relevant voices of this kind of regionalism. Other smaller formations also emerged and included the Arnassita Piemonteisa in Piedmont. The Lombard League – the politically most relevant of these formations – emerged in 1982. Various leagues would unite under Bossi's leadership in 1991, forming the new Northern League. The League's main objective was to address what it perceived as a state-driven and inequitable redistribution of resources between the north and the south of the country.

In founding the Lombard League in 1982, Bossi was inspired by the leader of a small and established independence movement: the Union Valdotaine of Valle d'Aosta. More broadly, the Leagues emerged at a time when there was a general revival of ethnic identities that in a European context made regions a plausible alternative to nation-states. The idea of regional autonomy was gaining currency, being discussed throughout the European media. On the basis of economic grievances and a new ethno-territorial awareness, the Lombard League acquired some visibility in 1985, when it first competed in the electoral arena. Initially, it participated in a few local elections and obtained 2.5 per cent of the valid votes in the province of Varese. In 1987, it participated in the Lombardy regional election and was chosen by 2.7 per cent of registered voters. This figure grew to 6.5 per cent in the European election of 1989 and to 16.4 per cent in the regional elections of 1990.

If the main cleavage was an economic one, it came to be associated with a set of other dimensions, which the League proposed as distinctive differences between the northern part of the country and the centre–south. The depth of ethno-nationalist sentiments might be questionable – some observers see the League's nationalist claims as mainly a justification for bourgeois egoism and see the activities of symbolic state-building as a superficial justification for essentially economically motivated behaviour (Harvie 1994). Others have interpreted northern Italian nationalism as the result of processes of symbolic construction that address identity needs derived from a collapse of local communities emanating from social dynamics connected to processes of secularisation and urbanisation (Ruzza 1996). In any event, the fact that this party utilised much later than elsewhere claims typical of the process of national formation – claims of ethnic and historical distinctiveness – made it a significant focus of academic and media attention. The rapid transformations in its ideology, the broad oscillations of electoral support and the flamboyant character and bombastic statements of its undisputed leader, Umberto Bossi, received much attention from political and academic commentators (Biorcio 1997; Diamanti 1996; Mannheimer 1991; Ruzza 2004).

The political crisis of the 1990s and the collapse of the party system

Although long-term trends help to explain the vulnerabilities of the old party system and the gradual legitimisation of the old Italian right, and may have eventually effected a change in the party system over time, it is unlikely that they alone would have caused the spectacular collapse of the system that occurred from 1992 to 1994 had it not been for a number of more circumstantial political factors shaped by external events, most notably the collapse of communism in central and eastern Europe in 1989 and the decision to adopt a European single currency in 1991. The former helped to legitimise the Italian left as a governing alternative, while the latter required the Italian state to adopt greater fiscal discipline in order to meet the necessary convergence conditions required to participate. The legitimising of the Italian left was greatly facilitated by the decision of the PCI to formally shed its communist identity, changing its name to the Democratic Party of the Left (PDS) in 1991 and presenting itself as a conventional European social democratic party (Bull 1991; Fouskas 1998). This in a sense robbed the *pentapartito* system of its *raison d'être*. The DC-dominated apparatus had been justified in terms of the need to protect Italy from the communist threat and thus deny the PCI a role in government. The majority of Italian voters had given consent to this system through support for governing parties at general elections, partly because of concerns about the likely communist alternative. However, the removal of the communist menace meant that Italian voters were more likely to be more discerning in their electoral choices and less tolerant of the corrupt and inert system presided over by the DC. They would also be more likely to vote for new parties, less fearful as to the potential this had to destabilise the system, possibly to the communists' advantage. This occurred in 1992, when for the first time the governing parties combined failed to win the endorsement of the majority of voters. However, rather than the PDS, the real beneficiary of this was the newly unified Northern League (LN). The LN proved attractive to disgruntled voters in the DC's former heartlands in the northeast of the country, who continued to be hostile towards the other main alternative to the DC, that is the former communists (Ruzza and Schmidtke 1992). The LN won 8.7 per cent of the national vote – 17.3 per cent in the northern regions in which it stood.

Although the DC-led coalition was able to retain a parliamentary majority in 1992, it was clear that the old partitocratic system was living on borrowed time. The political deficiencies of the system were being exacerbated by economic pressures, which were heightened by the fiscal constraints created by the convergence conditions required in relation to European monetary union (EMU) necessitating a reduction in public debt. The Italian clientelistic system was thus becoming increasingly unaffordable. Initially, some political figures sought to address this by demanding more and increasingly intolerable amounts of money from their clienteles, leading some of the latter to begin to speak out against the system. This contributed to the unravelling of the *tangentopoli* scandal – in which the initial denunciations of corrupt political individuals snowballed to implicate an entire political class. Moreover, attempts to increase revenue by cracking down on tax evasion and increasing the tax burden in general created further discontent among those who took umbrage at having to finance such an inefficient system. The vulnerability of the governing parties demonstrated by the 1992 election result also served to embolden a group of publicly minded magistrates once the chance to launch a widescale investigation into the corrupt practices of the political class arose (Sassoon 1995).

The *mani pulite* magistrates uncovered a series of corrupt arrangements whereby private and public enterprises financed politicians and political parties in exchange for favours including the passage of special legislation and the awarding of public contracts. The sums collected by the parties were used to bribe more people to obtain further financial and political support or were used, quite simply, to sustain the lifestyle of the politicians and their cronies. There was evidence that all parties (including the PCI) to an extent participated in this system, but the main protagonists were the DC and PSI. *Mani pulite* led to the arrest of 2,000 people and the investigation of some of the country's most powerful politicians, among them Craxi, Andreotti and the DC leader Arnaldo Forlani. One-third of those elected in 1992 were placed under investigation (Buffachi and Burgess 2001: 62–68).

The period 1992–1994 thus saw a haemorrhaging in the support of the ruling parties, while support for the LN surged upwards. Popular disgust with the state of affairs had one outlet in the successful referendum campaign in 1993 promoted by a Christian Democrat reformist politician, Mario Segni.[7] The referendum of April 1993 – in which 82.7 per cent of the electorate voted for the proposal – had concentrated on removal of the proportional element in senate elections. However, it resulted in a popular de-legitimisation of the entire electoral system and obliged moves for a wider electoral reform, involving the chamber of deputies as well as the senate.[8]

Such was the impact of the 1993 electoral reform on the underlying philosophy of the constitution that many commentators began to speak of a Second Republic. The wider impact of the political crisis and the implications of the reforms led to broader discussions about institutional reform. Under the new electoral rules for the chamber of deputies approved in August 1993, 75 per cent of seats in the chamber were to be elected in first-past-the-post, single-member constituencies, while the remaining 25 per cent were allocated by a proportional representation (PR) method. A similar system would apply for the senate. The new majoritarian system created a logic whereby parties were forced to co-operate in electoral alliances in order to stand a chance of winning seats. The new system had the effect of polarising the contest, eventually leading to the formation of rival electoral blocs to fight the single-member constituency elections – replacing the multi-party competition that flourished before with a bipolar system (Buffachi and Burgess 2001: 128–40). The new electoral system, together with the realignments in the party system it would help to engender, would pave the way for a transition of the Italian party system from one of consensual democracy – whereby the government emerges out of negotiation among the political parties following an election – to one based on competitive democracy, in which the government emerges directly out of the electoral process (Fabbrini 2006: 150–53).

A new electoral system for local elections was also put in place in 1993 (the government legislated for this ahead of a proposed referendum). Elections under this system at the end of 1993 demonstrated the likely effects of a general election under the majoritarian system. A new PDS-led centre-left coalition (also including La Rete and the Greens) won the mayoralty in a number of big city elections at the end of 1993. This centre-left coalition initially looked better placed to exploit the new system at the national level, given the political vacuum on the centre-right that had been illustrated all too clearly in the 1993 local elections. In these elections, the DC vote collapsed, leaving the LN as the main electoral rival to the centre-left in the north, and the MSI as its main rival in the south. In seeking to purify and re-invent itself, the DC returned to its social catholic roots, and renamed itself the Popular party (PPI). This harked back to the old Catholic Popular Party, of pre-fascist Liberal Italy. This movement towards its left wing had been paralleled by the exit of a part of its right wing, which formed the Christian Democratic centre (CCD), and would later form a part of Berlusconi's Polo della Libertà. However, this re-invention could not arrest the slide, and the DC–PPI would be squeezed between the new centre-left pole and the disparate forces of the right.

The 1993 elections proved a turning point for the MSI, benefiting from the skilful leadership of Fini who exploited to the full the MSI's extraneousness from the *mani pulite* inquiry. Indeed, while the investigations had decimated all of the governing parties, and even contaminated to a certain extent the PDS (given that it had had its own share of the spoils in the old system), the only one of the old parties totally excluded from this was the MSI, which had been only marginally included in the spoils system. Thus, the MSI was able to manifest itself as the immaculate opponent of the First Republic, and the fact that it had previously been championing some rather old-fashioned and undemocratic solutions to the Republic's ills hardly seemed to matter any more, such was Italian public anger with the governing parties. MSI local councillors appeared to be among the best informed accusers of corrupt politicians. At the national level, Fini seized the initiative in order to capitalise on the disarray of the DC. While the DC fielded low-profile candidates in the major Italian cities in the mayoral elections of November 1993, the MSI fielded the highest possible profile candidates. Fini stood in Rome and achieved 46.9 per cent of the vote in the run-off with the left-backed Green candidate Francesco Rutelli, while Alessandra Mussolini, the grand-daughter of *Il Duce*, polled 43.4 per cent in Naples. The MSI's good performance in these elections was generally overlooked in the euphoria of the left's successes in the major cities. Yet the MSI won nineteen mayorships, including those of four provincial capitals in the south. The MSI also profited from the endorsement of Silvio Berlusconi. He proclaimed that, if he was a Roman, he would choose Fini as mayor. This was considered to be an indiscretion on Berlusconi's part at the time. That perhaps Italy's most influential entrepreneur and proprietor of much of its media was prepared to give Fini his endorsement was a major boost to his legitimacy, and to his claims to represent a popular and modern conservative force (Ignazi 1994a: 105–8).

Fini had already been mooting the idea of creating a broader conservative front – a National Alliance – around the MSI, which could better capitalise on the political space on the centre-right created by the collapse of the DC. Cossiga had been touted as a possible figurehead for such a front. The good result in the November local elections, combined with the endorsement of Berlusconi, provided the critical momentum to push forward with this project. Berlusconi replaced Cossiga as the likely interlocutor for it. Berlusconi's endorsement was perhaps decisive in the legitimisation of the MSI–AN. Following the 1993 election results, it was clear that the MSI had to be included in any centre-right pole, if it were to be capable of defeating the centre left. Fini's great personal success in 1993 allowed him to assume firm control over the MSI's direction, and he was now able to press on with the construction of the National Alliance with his authority massively strengthened (Ignazi 1994a: 106). The National Alliance was ratified at the January 1994 assembly of the MSI, with no real opposition to Fini. At this stage, the AN did not exist as an autonomous organisation. It remained an electoral front, controlled totally by the MSI and involving a few outsiders such as the political science professor, Domenico Fisichella, and a small number of former Christian Democrats.

Berlusconi enters the field and the right enters government

The creation of the AN coincided with the entrance on to the political field of Berlusconi himself, at the head of his personal creation Forza Italia. Silvio Berlusconi's decision to form his own political movement was very much conditioned by the circumstances of the political crisis. Indeed, Berlusconi's decision related to his alarm at the collapse of the old party system, which had facilitated his rise to prominence as Italy's leading media mogul, and at the likelihood that this would lead to the election of a centre-left government. Berlusconi feared this new political environment would be antagonistic towards his business interests in general and, more specifically, towards his media empire's dominance of Italy's private television networks. Although he would later present himself as a political outsider, Berlusconi and his business interests had benefited from his close relationship with the political elites brought down by the *tangentopoli* scandal. In particular, he had a close relationship with Bettino Craxi, prime minister between 1983 and 1988, and leader of the PSI, whose political career would be left in ruins by the *mani pulite* investigations. Craxi helped Berlusconi secure his hold over Italy's private television stations and was godfather to one of Berlusconi's children. He would later die in exile in Tunisia, a fugitive from Italian justice (Ginsborg 2004: 33–38).

Prior to Berlusconi's dramatic entrance, the smart money still appeared to be on the centre left winning the first national election to be held under the new majoritarian system, given the seeming incompatibility between the LN and the nationalist and predominantly southern MSI and the lack of a credible unifying national centre-right force. However, the sudden materialisation of Forza Italia as such a force, and Berlusconi's deft knitting together of two separate electoral alliances, one with the AN in the south and one with the LN in the north, enabled the incompatibility issue to be sidestepped until after the 1994 general election was won. The centre-right alliances were also extended to smaller entities such as the CCD and the ex-Liberal Union of the Centre.

Berlusconi was able to concentrate his huge media resources on highlighting the imagined perils of the communist threat. This was despite the fact that the PDS had shed both its communist name and identity, although it was not helped by the inclusion in the centre-left coalition of the unreconstructed Communist Refoundation (Rifondazione Communista, RC) formed by the sizeable minority of the PCI that had refused to go along with the new PDS project. Berlusconi was able to frame the contest as one between liberty and totalitarianism (of the communist variety). The centre right was also successful in presenting itself as a new and vibrant force, while the left was associated with the failed forces of the First Republic.

With the financial and propaganda resources of Berlusconi's media empire behind it, the centre-right pole was able to win a resounding victory in the 1994 general election. Forza Italia itself became the leading party in Italy with 21 per cent of the vote, while the MSI–AN's vote leapt to 13.5 per cent and the LN polled 8.4 per cent of the national vote. In May 1994, a new government was formed based around these new and re-invented political forces. Controversy surrounded the inclusion for the first time in the government of a modern European democracy of 'neo-fascists'. Israel declined to send its customary congratulations to the new Italian government. The inclusion of a number of MSI–AN ministers in the cabinet had seemingly put an end to the anti-fascist consensus in Italy[9] (Sznajder 1995).

Given its attacks on the unity of the Italian state, its previous anti-southern stance and the radical departure it offered from the form of politics hitherto employed in the post-war republic, the LN's inclusion in government was equally as remarkable as that of the MSI. Indeed, Bossi's fulminations against the political establishment also involved his new partners in government. His outspoken attacks against both Berlusconi and Fini (he continued to describe the latter and his party as fascists) continued while the government was being formed and during its short period of office.

Bossi continued to attack Berlusconi's conflict of interests, given his media ownership and the broader economic interests of his Fininvest company, as well as the attempts made by Berlusconi in government to curb the power of the judiciary in corruption investigations (Katz and Ignazi 1996: 22). In this short first period as prime minister, Berlusconi forced the resignation of the board of the state television broadcasters, RAI, and intervened in the selection of the replacement board to ensure it was favourable to him. Over the course of the year, investigations into corruption by Fininvest had gathered speed, and judicial proceedings also began against Berlusconi's brother. The government's proposed response to this had been a decree to curb the power of judges in corruption cases. A public outcry, as well as the threat of resignation by the prosecuting magistrates and open dissent from the LN, meant that the government was forced to drop the decree (Katz and Ignazi 1996: 29).

The difficulties the LN had in reconciling its populist character with the demands of government led to its exit from the governing coalition at the end of 1994, precipitating its collapse. The immediate context for the LN's withdrawal from government was the corruption investigations launched by the Milan magistrates against Berlusconi himself towards the end of 1994. There were also accusations of broken promises on federalist reforms and economic liberalisation. However, the concerns of Bossi and his party that FI was successfully colonising the LN's anti-state pro-de-regulation constituency in the north was perhaps the major factor in its withdrawal.

The right in opposition – consolidation and radicalisation

Following the collapse of the first Berlusconi government, a caretaker government led by Lamberto Dini was put in place, lasting until early 1996 when new elections took place. The decision by the LN to run separately – and against the AN and FI, who maintained their electoral alliance – was instrumental in securing a victory for the centre-left coalition led by Romano Prodi.

In this period, the LN adopted a secessionist stance, advocating the independence of the northern part of Italy. Through this stance, the LN was seeking to distinguish itself from the new political consensus on decentralisation and attempting to ensure that the impressive levels of popular mobilisation that it enjoyed prior to 1994 would be retained and built upon and its anti-establishment image reinforced. At the same time, this allowed Bossi to re-establish his supremacy over his party, given the popularity of the secessionist idea among activists.

Whereas the LN's actions in government reflected concerns about its identity being compromised in government and a fear that FI was stealing its populist clothes and its northern middle-class electorate, the MSI–AN was content to consolidate its new-found legitimacy and centrality to the new centre-right pole. In many ways, its entrance into government could be interpreted as the culmination of its historic strategy of *inserimento*, according to which it sought to conclude alliances with conservative forces and participate in day-to-day democratic politics (Ignazi 1994a). Thus, in practice, it had generally adopted policy positions that one would associate with the conservative right, despite its anti-system rhetoric and fascist nostalgia. Its entry into government therefore required that it drop the anti-system discourse while retaining a continuity in terms of past policy positions and the general alignment with the conservative right that had been cultivated by Fini. This worked well provided discussions of the past – and perceptions of the fascist regime – were avoided. Previous proposals, such as that for a corporatist parliament, were now deemed unnecessary in the new political context, i.e. the collapse of the old *partitocrazia* which the MSI had previously railed strongly against. The fall of the post-war system meant that it could now abandon its previous anti-system stance – thus its previous attacks on the liberal democratic system were retrospectively recast as an opposition to the rule by parties which characterised the 'First Republic' (Fella 2006).

In opposition from 1995 onwards, and more so following the election defeat of 1996, the centre-right parties underwent a process of re-organisation and re-evaluation. The MSI was dissolved into the new AN party at the Fiuggi Congress in January 1995. The refusal of a group led by the veteran neo-fascist revolutionary, Pino Rauti, to accept the transformation, instead forming a breakaway party, Movimento Sociale – Fiamma Tricolore (Social Movement – Tricolour Flame, MS–FT), served to reinforce the impression that the AN represented a fundamental break with the past. Following on from this, the AN sought to consolidate its new-found legitimacy and modify its positions further in order to present itself as a modern European centre-right party. The LN, on the other hand, moved to a more radical separatist position. However, by pleasing its radical activists and its small town electorate with the new secessionist stance, the LN put off its urban moderate electorate. In this period, a significant exodus took place of people who had previously thought that the LN would become 'respectable' and could be used for personal and social advancement. By the end of 1998, it was clear to the

LN that secession was a controversial slogan with only limited support in the population and, after much internal debate, the issue was left unresolved and gradually dropped. Other issues became more important. The development of anti-European and anti-American attitudes – combined with an increasing focus on anti-immigration rhetoric – would be illustrative of attempts to pander to popular anti-cosmopolitan sentiments while finding common ground to unite the LN's radical activists with its more institutional face evident in its prominent role in local government in the north (Ruzza 2004).

While the LN found itself isolated from 1995 onwards, Fini used the period of renewed opposition to consolidate the AN's new democratic credentials further, for example through participation in the failed bicameral parliamentary commission on constitutional reform (*Bicamerale*) and entrance into the Gaullist UPE grouping in the European Parliament. In this period, the AN was also re-emphasising its traditional role as a guardian of national identity – a logical reaction to the antics of the LN at the time – organising counter-demonstrations in defence of the Italian nation (Fella 2006). Growing discontent within the AN regarding its subordination to the FI, and dislike and distrust of Berlusconi within the party, led to calls for a clearer differentiation from FI, and led Fini to make renewed overtures to the catholic centre and centre right. In this period, the AN sought to challenge the ascendancy of FI within the centre-right pole. It adopted a number of pro-market positions at its 1998 Verona Congress, hoping that, by stealing FI's neo-liberal pro-market clothes, it could win over some of its supporters. In the 1999 European elections, the AN stood on a joint list with the Patto Segni – with which it had also allied itself in the failed referendum campaign to eliminate the remaining proportional quotient of the electoral law.[10] The joint list polled 10.3 per cent (as opposed to the AN's share of 15.7 per cent in the 1996 general elections). The LN performed equally badly, polling 4.5 per cent (having polled 10.1 per cent in 1996). The FI, on the other hand, recovered its strength and centrality to the Italian centre right, polling 25.2 per cent (Daniels 2000).

This period also witnessed an internal re-organisation of Forza Italia, as it sought to set down deeper institutional and territorial roots, with internal elections involving party members. However, it remained a party heavily dominated by its leader. Despite the unpromising circumstances he found himself in at the end of 1994 – under formal investigation for corruption and his period as prime minister ending in abject failure – Berlusconi was able to revive his own reputation in this period, casting himself as a victim of a politically biased judicial plot, and as having been denied his rightful chance to govern by political betrayal. His political rehabilitation was aided by the leader of the PDS, Massimo D'Alema, who engaged him in talks on a possible broader understanding among the main parties to bring constitutional reform. This prompted Berlusconi to abandon his constant demands for fresh elections at the end of 1995 and declare support for a new interim government that would oversee reform (Maraffi 1996: 123). Although this plan was thwarted – the AN in particular was strongly opposed – Berlusconi initially co-operated with the bicameral parliamentary commission overseen by D'Alema following the centre-left election victory in 1996. While there appeared to be consensus within the committee on proposals for a shift to a French-style semi-presidential system, as supported by both Berlusconi and Fini, Berlusconi later withdrew support for this reform attempt, much to the chagrin of Fini, who hoped that his party's participation in defining a new constitutional settlement would cement its democratic legitimisation.

Following the poor electoral performances in 1999, a new phase was evident in both the AN and the LN with their respective leaderships reappraising their previous strategies. For the AN, this meant a shift back towards more traditional positions. Themes such as identity, law and order and security were emphasised, and the free market euphoria of Verona dropped. In order to distinguish itself from its competitor-allies, Fini opted for marketing the AN as 'the socially advanced wing of the centre-right' placing a renewed emphasis on the concept of the social market economy (Tarchi 2003b: 163–65).

Bossi, for his part, engineered a fundamental transformation of the LN's approach, declaring that the epoch of uncompromising separatism had to end. Alliances had to be accepted, even if unpalatable to base militants. The new approach led to the LN joining the right-wing coalition that competed successfully in the 2000 regional elections. Nevertheless, the LN's stance on the issue of greater autonomy for Padania would remain uncompromising. The price of participation in the coalition would be the delivery of devolution reforms to enhance the power and status of the Italian regions (the new emphasis on 'devolution' rather than federalism or independence seemed to be a nod to the successful enactment of devolution in Scotland).

The CdL and the second Berlusconi government

In the 2001 general election, the centre right was able to capitalise on popular dissatisfaction with the performance of the centre left, and in particular an apparent return to the instability and behind-the-scenes manoeuvring that characterised the First Republic. The Prodi government had fallen in 1998 (as a result of a withdrawal of support from RC), and was replaced by another centre-left government led by the PDS leader, Massimo D'Alema, which itself lasted until 2000 when it was replaced by another centre-left variation led by Giuliano Amato. However, the centre-left candidate in 2001 would be none of these figures. Instead, Francesco Rutelli, who had been untainted by this apparent failure, was selected to fight against Berlusconi in a campaign that would be focused around the latter's personality and fitness or not to lead Italy.

This was reflected in the glossy book on Berlusconi's life, *Una Storia Italiana* (an Italian story), mailed to millions of Italian households, and also Berlusconi's 'contract with the Italian people' signed live on television. The contract committed Berlusconi to realising four out of five policy objectives within the 5-year parliamentary term (promising to withdraw from the subsequent election if he failed to do this). These involved income tax cuts for low and high earners, a crime reduction plan, an increase in the minimum pension, the creation of 1.5 million new jobs and the initiation of a 10-year plan for major public infrastructure works. More generally, alongside devolution of key policies (such as health, education and policing) to the regions, the CdL manifesto promised cuts in bureaucracy and the freeing of business from 'useless and inappropriate burdens', restrictions on immigration and the tackling of clandestine immigration in particular, and privatisation of public utilities within a broader framework of market liberalisation. (Edwards 2005: 229–30).

The election resulted in a clear victory for the CdL, and a strong performance for Forza Italia in particular, which seemed to vindicate the focus on Berlusconi's leadership of the coalition. Forza Italia itself won 29.4 per cent of the vote, a large increase on its vote in the elections of 1994 and 1996. However, this increase came partly at the expense of its coalition allies, the AN dropping to 12 per cent and the LN's vote plummeting to 3.9 per cent. The former Christian Democrat CDU and CCD parties (which would later merge to form the UDC) together polled 3.2 per cent. The new government drew from all these parties, and also saw the appointment of non-party figures such as the former World Trade Organization (WTO) head Renato Ruggiero as foreign minister. Other notable appointments included Fini as deputy prime minister and Bossi as minister for constitutional reform.

As it had done in 1994 and during the 2001 general election campaign, the question of Berlusconi's conflicts of interests was raised repeatedly in government. By 2001, this related not only to the conflict between Berlusconi's leadership of the government and his business affairs, but also to the various judicial proceedings against him for corruption and financial irregularities. The nature of a number of laws passed by the Berlusconi government in its first few years exacerbated these concerns, given that these laws appeared to be designed primarily to resolve Berlusconi's personal and business problems. These laws, labelled *ad personam* laws by Berlusconi's detractors, included one on international requests for judicial assistance (*rogatorie*), making evidence obtained in this way inadmissible unless documents were originals or authenticated individually (thus obstructing prosecutors who had used Swiss bank records in the SME case where it was alleged that Berlusconi and his close associate, Cesare Previti, were involved in bribing judges), and another that decriminalised certain forms of false accounting and cut the statute of limitations for prosecution (thus getting Berlusconi off the hook on one such charge). In 2002, a law was passed enabling defendants to appeal for their cases to be moved to a different court on the grounds of prosecutors' bias against them (Berlusconi and Previti unsuccessfully attempted to have the SME trial moved from Milan). Following on from this, a law was adopted in 2003 exempting the holders of the five highest political offices in Italy from judicial prosecution, thereby effectively halting the ongoing corruption proceedings against Berlusconi (a law later overturned by the constitutional court). Two of Berlusconi's own private lawyers, who had been elected as FI deputies, sat on the judicial affairs committee that was involved in the drafting of some of these laws (Hopkin 2005: 110–11). One other law that could be characterised as *ad personam* was the Gasparri law in 2004 (named after the minister for communications who piloted it, Maurizio Gasparri of the AN). The law effectively reversed a constitutional court order for Berlusconi's Mediaset company to divest itself of one of its three terrestrial national TV channels. It also altered laws on general media ownership in a flexible direction, thus allowing Mediaset to extend its holdings in other forms of media. The president of the republic, Carlo Azeglio Ciampi, initially refused to give his assent to the law, sending it back to the government for modifications.

It was striking that parties such as the AN and the LN, both of which had made such political capital out of the attacks on the corrupt Italian political establishment in the 1990s, were happy to go along with such laws. Indeed, in general, Berlusconi – despite occasional attacks on recycled First Republic politicians (aimed at both the opposition and also his erstwhile allies in the UDC and AN) – appeared to favour a rehabilitation of the political class brought to its knees by the *mani pulite* investigations. He repeatedly denounced the 'politically motivated' or 'leftist' magistrates who led the investigations and sought to curb judicial power in this area, going as far as to suggest that 'you had to be mad to be a judge' and also comparing the magistrates unfavourably with the fascist regime. In relation to this, a notable element of the government's reform programme was its controversial reform of the judiciary, piloted by the LN justice minister, Roberto Castelli. This involved a reform of the selection procedures and career patterns of judges, which was eventually adopted in 2005.

A departure from the focus on *ad personam* laws was the law passed on immigration in 2001, which increased immigration controls, notably by tying the issuing of immigration visas to the possession of employment contracts (Zincone 2002). The law was notable for the collaboration between the AN and the LN that took place on it, symbolised by the naming of the law, the Bossi–Fini law, after the two party leaders who co-sponsored the bill. This appeared to reflect an attempt by the main parties of the centre right to find common ground on issues on which their identity was particularly strong. This was also evident in the tough positions adopted within the ruling coalition as regards the policing of the G8 summit in Genoa in July 2001. Another early initiative by the government was the attempt to liberalise the labour market, focusing on the rather symbolic reform of article 18 of the worker's statute (preventing firms employing more than fifteen people from sacking workers without 'just cause'). This aroused mass protest from the trade unions and the left, and proved to be an early rallying point for opposition to the government. The government was forced to back down on this point, although a milder labour market reform was later adopted to make it easier for firms to hire temporary workers (Accornero and Como 2003).

Despite the government's large majority, and its unprecedented longevity, progress on achieving the promised economic miracle, involving the heady mix of liberalisation, tax cuts, job creation and grandiose public works projects, proved rather patchy. Aside from the apparent preoccupation with *ad personam* laws, this partly related to factors beyond the government's control, such as the slow growth and tight fiscal constraints of the eurozone, and the turbulent international situation in the wake of the September 11 attacks, which proved a distraction from domestic affairs and also had an effect on international economic developments. In relation to the first point, leading government figures did not hesitate to blame 'Prodi's euro' for Italy's economic difficulties. Berlusconi would also blame obstruction within his own government for the failure to make progress – 'they don't let me govern' would be a familiar frustrated refrain. Indeed, the division between the four main parties within the coalition on a range of issues was clear and related to a number of fundamental policy concerns, such as EU policy, constitutional reform and economic policy.

EU policy was an early flashpoint, with Bossi's attacks on the euro following its entry into circulation and Berlusconi's lack of support on the issue causing Ruggiero to resign as foreign minister at the beginning of 2002. Some leading members of Forza Italia (including Berlusconi himself and the finance minister, Giulio Tremonti) appeared to sympathise with the hostility of the LN towards the euro. This contrasted strongly with the Europhile stance of the UDC (following in the footsteps of the Europeanism of the DC), which was increasingly shared by the AN leadership. Berlusconi took on the role of foreign minister himself for several months, before a replacement, Franco Frattini, was chosen. Berlusconi sought to distance the Italian government from the rather unquestioning Europhile positions of the post-war Christian Democrat governments, at least in terms of the general compliance with positions emanating from the French and German capitals. Notably, the Berlusconi government sided with the US and UK governments in relation to the European divisions caused by the invasion of Iraq in 2003 (and against the positions of Germany and France and the other original EC members). This also meant committing 'peacekeeping' troops to the post-war occupation of Iraq, as well as to Afghanistan following the September 11 attacks and the consequent US-led invasion in 2001. In general, although there was some unease, Berlusconi's coalition partners backed him on these stances. The AN, in particular, was keen to laud the contribution of Italian military forces.

Divisions were apparent in a number of other key areas of policy. While the LN supported Berlusconi on the need for tax cuts, the AN and UDC were more concerned with maintaining levels of public spending, as befitting parties representing predominantly state-dependent southern constituencies (Diamanti and Lello 2005). In relation to constitutional reform, this southern orientation meant that the AN and the UDC were also rather uneasy about proposals for devolution favoured by the LN that would favour the northern regions (for example by reducing fiscal transfers to the south). Nevertheless, there was a recognition that devolution was the price paid for the LN's continued adhesion to the coalition. Berlusconi himself was personally committed to fulfilling this promise made to the LN, even if Forza Italia's position on the constitution was closer to that of the AN in terms of prioritising a strengthening of executive powers at the centre of the Italian state.

The divisions within the coalition would become particularly pronounced from the spring of 2003 onwards, when Fini began repeated public calls for a *verifica* (a verification or stock-taking) among the governing parties, in order to re-establish the objectives of the government and ensure a greater equilibrium among the governing parties and greater collegiality in government decision-making (Fella 2006). Local election losses in Rome and the south were blamed by the AN on the northern bias of the government and the extremist discourse and positions of the LN (particularly its repeated references to *Roma ladrona* – thieving Rome). In seeking to present a moderate centrist front within the government, Fini often found common cause with the UDC, and its leader Marco Follini.

Berlusconi's apparent favouritism as regards the positions of Bossi and the LN was particularly galling to the AN considering that its vote share had been three times that of the LN in 2001. While Berlusconi presented himself as an arbiter or mediator between the conflicting positions of the AN and LN in government, he and his party colleagues often took similar positions to those of LN. This was particularly the case on economic issues, although on issues such as immigration and constitutional reform, FI was closer to the AN. This was also because – despite the frequent controversial outbursts of Bossi and other LN exponents – the LN would generally support Berlusconi on key policy issues (presenting itself as a faithful and obedient ally), in order to ensure the passage of devolution.

In relation to the economy, Fini's quarrel was not only with Bossi and the LN, but also with the finance minister Tremonti who, although a FI appointee, increasingly appeared to identify with the LN, forming a close relationship within the government with Bossi (Albertazzi and McDonnell 2005). The Fini–Tremonti dispute and the related dispute between the AN and the UDC, on the one side, and FI and LN, on the other, as regards the stewardship of the economy appeared to overshadow the government's progress for much of 2003 and 2004. Fini viewed Tremonti as having too much power and an approach to the economy and expenditure plans that was biased towards the interests of the north and characterised by excessive recourse to 'creative financing'. Although both Berlusconi and Bossi vigorously defended Tremonti, Fini finally got the upper hand in June 2004 when he forced the dismissal of Tremonti, following another poor showing by the centre right (and Forza Italia in particular) in the European elections. But this came only after a year of public bickering between the party leaders, numerous threats by Fini to withdraw his party from government, various broken promises to involve Fini more closely in economic decision-making and, critically, Bossi's enforced departure from the public stage following a severe stroke in March 2004, which weakened the LN's and Tremonti's position.

Despite Tremonti's eventual replacement by a civil servant from the finance ministry, Domenico Siniscalco, disagreements among the ruling parties continued on a range of issues, notably on taxation where both the UDC and the AN sought to safeguard resources for the public sector and the south. The continued differences among the ruling coalition led to the government 'crisis' following the centre-right's disastrous performance in the 2005 regional elections (losing twelve of the fourteen contested regions). Fini's strategy appeared rather confused here: he initially responded by calling for fresh elections, but then changed his mind and appeared to be content with the cosmetic government changes offered by Berlusconi. However, Follini withdrew the UDC from government, forcing Berlusconi to resign and then re-form a new government. In the best traditions of the post-war republic, the new government appeared to be much like the old one, with the UDC returning. However, Follini, who had entered government as joint deputy prime minister following the fall of Tremonti, remained outside and, much to Fini's chagrin, Tremonti returned to government in Follini's place (Tremonti would later return as finance minister, following Siniscalco's resignation[11]) (Fella and Ruzza 2007).

While the shenanigans of the post-regional elections seemed to undo much of what Fini had sought to achieve in 2004, he had in the meantime been assuaged by his appointment as foreign minister in November 2004, replacing Franco Frattini following the latter's nomination to the European Commission. Fini had originally sought this position at the beginning of 2002, following the resignation of Ruggiero. Fini had hoped to establish an international legitimacy for himself and the AN that would be essential to the realisation of any future desires to lead the Italian government. While Fini's subsequent appointment as the Italian government representative on the European constitutional convention was initially viewed as compensation for his thwarted ambitions as regards the foreign ministry, it allowed Fini to pursue his strategy of international rehabilitation for the AN and himself through other means. Indeed, Fini took full advantage of the opportunity the convention role provided him to boost his standing on international matters and to contrast his statesman-like tone with that of some of his government colleagues. While Berlusconi's appearances on the EU stage were notable for a series of monumental gaffes (for example his comparison, during a statement to the European Parliament, of a German Socialist MEP with a Nazi concentration camp guard), Fini won plaudits from across the political spectrum for his constructive conduct, which could be contrasted sharply with the LN's explicitly anti-EU position. Thus, when the foreign minister's job became vacant again, Fini was viewed as the obvious candidate for the job across the Italian media and political spectrum (Fella and Ruzza 2006).

Fini's elevation to the foreign ministry, combined with Bossi's illness-enforced absence from the political scene, shifted the equilibrium in the ruling coalition somewhat towards the AN. This meant that Fini appeared less preoccupied about Tremonti when he returned to government in 2005. Proximity to the next general election also began to refocus minds in this period, and a spirit of compromise was demonstrated in the adoption of the constitutional reform package in 2005, designed mainly to deliver Bossi's cherished devolution. The compromise package eventually adopted also met the AN's longstanding demand for a directly elected executive with enhanced powers over parliament (albeit in the person of the prime minister rather than the president). Fini chose to emphasise the gains to be brought by the increase in executive powers, despite concerns within the party about the nature and extent of the devolution proposals.[12]

A compromise package on tax cuts was also adopted in 2005, as Berlusconi strove to meet one of the promises made in his contract with the Italian people. In January 2006, *Il Sole 24 Ore*, a respected business publication in Italy, published an assessment of the degree to which the contract had been met. The contract had promised a simplification of income tax with a tax-free amount of €11,362, and two tax rates, a standard rate of 23 per cent and a higher rate of 33 per cent, to be paid on income above €103,291. Although tax cuts were implemented, they fell short of these ambitions – the no-tax amount would be €7,500 for dependent workers and four different tax rates remained.[13] Pasquino notes that, while cuts were successfully implemented to the benefit of the wealthiest sections of the population, the promised restructuring of the fiscal system had not been achieved, and the proportion of Italians who successfully evaded tax remained 'abysmally high' (Pasquino 2007: 49). While the government failed to meet the second promise, that of significantly reducing crime and increasing the number of policemen (recorded crimes actually increased), the third promise – ensuring that those dependent on the state pension received at least €516 (a million lire) – was realised. In relation to the fourth promise – creation of 1.5 million jobs – around 80 per cent of the target (1.074 million) was reached, while in relation to the fifth promise, only around 25 per cent of the proposed investment in major public works had been funded and initiated – as opposed to the promised 40 per cent (Picchio 2006). In general, one can point to the difficulty for Berlusconi in reconciling the promise of tax cuts with others implying a large hike in public spending. These varying policy priorities were themselves a function of the need to appeal to the differing constituencies within the ruling coalition, and also the differing constituencies of Forza Italia itself, given its large pools of support in both the south (particularly Sicily) and the north. In general, while the coalition delivered on elements of its policy programme, the much vaunted economic miracle did not materialise, and the appearance was of a divided coalition with conflicting policy priorities. While Berlusconi himself espoused a neo-liberal discourse, which suggested a desire to launch a Thatcherite wave of liberalisation and deregulation, there was no coherent attempt to apply such a programme, partly due to the differing priorities within the coalition and partly due to Berlusconi's own conflict of interests.

One final legacy that the Berlusconi government left the Italian political system was the electoral reform adopted at the end of 2005 (Newell 2006: 802–5). This represented a renunciation of the majoritarian system adopted in 1993, one of the pillars of the so-called Second Republic. The reform not only cancelled the result of the popular referendum of 1993, which abrogated the proportional electoral system, but it also contradicted the previous fervent proclamations in favour of majoritarianism from the likes of Berlusconi and Fini, although the reform included a number of clauses that would continue to foster a bipolar logic (i.e. the premium of seats given to the coalition with the highest number of votes, and thresholds to prevent smaller parties not aligned with the larger coalitions gaining representation in parliament). The reform was heavily criticised by the opposition as being designed to increase the chances of a centre-right victory at the election or minimise the scope of the centre-left victory. However, the centre right's tinkering with the system for its own advantage backfired. Despite only a tiny advantage in the share of votes in the chamber of deputies, the centre left benefited from the premium of seats the reform afforded to the winning coalition. Moreover, in the senate, it benefited from another reform introduced by the centre right – the creation of constituencies for Italian citizens living abroad (a reform long championed by the AN). It was these overseas constituencies that delivered victory to the centre left in the senate.

Re-invention and resurrection: 2006–8

Following the return to opposition, Berlusconi initially refused to accept the legitimacy of the victory, alleging electoral fraud. The election of a new president of the republic, Giorgio Napolitano,[14] was the focus of wider complaints by Berlusconi that the centre left was filling all the major institutions with its representatives (as if the centre right would not have done the same itself). The centre left's control of political institutions would be associated with an alleged domination of the public TV networks and of the judiciary, as part of a broader centre-left occupation of the key institutions. Similarly, Bossi and the LN would reaffirm the populist message with hints of a need to return to the secessionist strategy of the 1990s, while its general anti-immigration message would be reiterated in the wake of the outcry over alleged Romanian criminality in 2007, and its Islamophobia colourfully demonstrated by the initiative to graze pigs on proposed sites for the construction of mosques. The AN, for its part, also returned to a more aggressive stance on immigration and the rejection of multiculturalism, with Fini seeking to make full political capital in relation to the Romanian criminality question in 2007 (Romanians were now able to enter Italy freely following Romanian entrance to the EU, and media reports were focusing on criminal incidents involving them). The populism of the alliance as a whole was also demonstrated by the united opposition to the proposals of the centre-left government to make it easier for immigrants to become Italian citizens (Bigot and Fella 2008).

The reaffirmation of previous strategies on the part of the centre right appeared to suggest a reluctance to address and analyse the causes of its electoral defeat and derive lessons from the past. The narrowness of the defeat of 2006 and the unstable nature of the centre-left government (itself riven by disputes between its centre and radical left) engendered a waiting strategy on the part of Berlusconi at least, who was confident that the centre-left government would soon collapse allowing for new elections to be held and the centre right to take its rightful place back in government. However, when Fini and Casini criticised this strategy, suggesting that a broader rethink of the centre right's platform and strategy was needed, Berlusconi's response was to attempt to outflank them by proposing the new 'party of liberty', designed to draw voters away from their parties. This resulted in bitter recriminations between Berlusconi and Fini in particular. Although Fini had previously been favourable to discussion of a new centre-right formation, it was clear that the proposal was meant to bypass him. This led to talks between Fini and Casini on developing a new centrist alliance, which would rival Berlusconi's envisaged populist creation for centre-right and moderate voters. Although Berlusconi originally talked of dissolving the FI into the new party, he then later moderated his position and suggested that the new movement would be a confederation open to all forces – and that FI would continue to exist within it.

The tiny majority that the centre left had in the Senate meant that its hold on power would always be tenuous. The collapse of the Prodi government in early 2008 perhaps vindicated Berlusconi's 'wait and see' stance. Furthermore, it provoked a reconciliation between Fini and Berlusconi and agreement on a joint PdL list. Recognising its unique nature, the LN ran in alliance with the joint list in the north of Italy, although not part of it. To give the alliance a semblance of symmetry, another autonomy movement – for the south – the Movement for Autonomy (MPA) was also tacked on. The PdL would poll 37.6 per cent of the vote for the chamber of deputies (the combined AN–FI vote in 2006 was 36 per cent), while the LN vote shot up to 8.3 per cent (from 4.6 per cent in 2006). The MPA polled 1.1 per cent. The increase in vote for these parties came despite increased competition on the right from La Destra (The Right), a new breakaway party (from the AN) formed by the disgruntled former government minister, Francesco Storace, which achieved 2.4 per cent of the vote.

The launch of the PdL project had come following the successful completion of the formal merger between the Democratic Left (DS) and Margherita (mainly former Christian Democrats), the two main parties of the centre left, to form the Democratic Party (PD) under the leadership of Walter Veltroni (who had previously succeeded Rutelli as mayor of Rome). This meant that the election was fought between two consolidated formations – the PD and PdL (the former in alliance with Antonio Di Pietro's IDV,[15] the latter with the LN and MPA). While the UDC refused the invitation from Berlusconi to submerge its identity in the PdL list, Fini blocked Berlusconi's efforts to include La Destra (though Alessandra Mussolini's group was included in the list). At the same time, the PD had decided to run separately from the radical left and Green parties – their joint list suffering a haemorrhage of support and failure to reach the thresholds required for the allocation of seats in the chamber and senate (a fate that also befell La Destra). Thus, the 2008 election also had the end-result of causing a significant decrease in the number of parties represented in parliament and a consolidation of the two main party blocks. Berlusconi and Fini also stated their intent to merge their two parties into a new PdL party. However, the period of transition towards the new party proved less harmonious than initially thought. The AN felt repeatedly compelled to reassert its identity and allay fears that their party would simply be swallowed up by the larger FI organization. Differences of political style also continued to mar the process of integration of the two parties, given the more centralistic and personalistic nature of FI and the more internally democratic but fragmented nature of AN. The cycle of re-invention of the Italian right had clearly not ended. The merger was confirmed at the founding congress of the new party at the end of March 2009, with Berlusconi becoming leader by acclamation. While the new party appeared initially to reflect the style and personality of Berlusconi, representing a high degree of continuity with FI, Fini continued to reiterate the distinctive and less populist profile of the AN element, emphasising the need for a modern conservative right based on a strong ethical sense of state.

The manoeuvres leading up to the creation of the PdL clearly demonstrated Berlusconi's capacity for opportunism and willingness to engage in further re-invention in order to restore novelty and freshness to his political project. Fini also appeared to have demonstrated a high degree of opportunism in first shifting to the right following the launch of Storace's party, and then moving back to the centre in his discussions with Casini, and then moving back into the arms of Berlusconi when the prospect of a return to power was imminent and the possibility of being Berlusconi's heir apparent in the new party became a distinct one. Fini was rewarded for his manoeuvring with his election to be president of the chamber of deputies, the third highest office of the Italian state. His party's success was also confirmed by the victory in the Rome mayoral election at the end of April of Gianni Alemanno (who had succeeded Fini as leader of the MSI's youth wing in the 1980s). The shouts of '*Duce, Duce*' and Roman salutes exhibited by some of his more unreconstructed supporters during the victory celebrations were, however, not quite the image of the reformed post-fascist right that its leaders had hoped to present.

Following a brief period of optimism that the consolidation of the centre-right and centre-left blocs might lead to a normalisation of party competition and responsible dialogue between its leaders, relations appeared to have reverted to type by the summer of 2008, with the centre left denouncing the return to *ad personam* policies on the part of the Berlusconi government. Thus, the *Lodo Alfano* was passed, again granting immunity from prosecution for the four top office-holders of the Italian state. Furthermore, the new Italian government was denounced by international bodies, including the European Parliament and the Council of Europe, for its proposal to fingerprint all Roma children, even those with Italian nationality. This came amid a climate of growing public hostility, seemingly endorsed by the government, towards the Roma communities, accused of being responsible for a range of criminal activity. The government also revived previous proposals to make clandestine immigration a criminal offence, punishable by imprisonment. The new government, shorn of the moderating influence of the UDC, with the LN more influential than before and the AN more confident in expressing a right-wing authoritarianism seemingly reflective of the public climate, appeared to have taken on a more decidedly right-wing character than the previous Berlusconi-led coalitions.

Conclusion

By the end of the 1990s, the conundrum of Italy's absent democratic right appeared to have been resolved. Indeed, three parties had emerged that could lay claim to being democratic parties of the right (or at least centre right). AN and FI appeared fairly comfortable with this allocation on the political spectrum, and their leaders ready to take things further by creating a new party of the centre right. Although the LN still claims to be neither of the left nor of the right, it can certainly be labelled as a party of the populist right. Some of its detractors might go further and point to the xenophobic aspect of its populism as reflective of its allocation on the extreme right. The chapters that follow will explore the nature of these parties in more detail, utilising an analysis of party programmes to ascertain their ideological placement. However, the brief historical overview provided here clearly demonstrates the differing ideological strategies employed by the various parties – the AN and the LN in particular – thus rendering the definition of a coherent centre-right pole rather problematic in Italy. Moreover, none of the three parties can lay claim to being conventional parties of the European centre right, and it is unlikely that the new PdL party will be either, at least while Berlusconi remains at the helm.

It is clear that the establishment of a centre-right pole in Italy would not have been possible without the convulsions that shook the Italian party system at the beginning of the 1990s and engendered a wider transformation of party formations and alignments. However, the long-term developments outlined in this chapter, such as economic change, a certain level of secularisation and the declining importance of the Catholic and Communist subcultures, also paved the way for these transformations. The role of leadership has been particularly crucial, with Berlusconi, Fini and Bossi taking a lead in shaping and reshaping their respective parties in line with the opportunities offered by the changing political climate, although some of their successes might be attributable to chance and a unique intersection of events.

3 Populism and the right

An explanatory model

This chapter proposes a model and a methodology to examine the reasons for the success of the right-wing coalition that won general elections in Italy in 1994, 2001, and 2008. It is a puzzle how a heterogeneous group of parties, which have at various times been described as fascist, populist, racist and xenophobic, could have been suddenly so successful, hold government for longer than any single government in the post-war era and retain a substantial following over time. In a country whose republican constitution was built on an anti-fascist consensus following the defeat of fascism in Italy in 1945, their initial appearance in government caused shock and surprise among external observers. This success requires an explanation, which we believe has broader implications for other European right-wing parties.

To explain this continuing success of the right, the interactions within the political system and between parties and society need to be examined in detail. We will make a connection between some key findings in the literature on the right and on populism, arguing that the success of the right in Italy lies in a unique and innovative interconnection between elements that characterise populist parties and traditional right-wing features that have however been re-interpreted and updated. We will argue that the Italian right has been successful because it has fostered and reflected an ideological isomorphism with society, and because it re-defined political space through populism and anti-politics. By thematising the interconnection between political ideology and social developments, we will propose a model for analysing the trajectory of the Italian right. In order to do this, we will show how a right-wing response as well as a populist response was facilitated by a set of changes in the Italian institutional set-up and in the responses of other political actors. We identify key areas of recent social change and trace their connections to the success of the right. We argue that a populist ideological focus based on values of anti-elitism, anti-politics and anti-state notions offered new opportunities to those political formations that could re-frame their ideological platforms in populist terms. We posit that the success of the three parties lies in their ability to interpret in a populist framework the need of individuals to re-define their territorial identities and the enlargement and re-definition of political space that recent social and institutional developments have made necessary. The following chapters will support this model with analysis of party materials. First, a broader theoretical reflection is necessary.

Defining the right

Various classifications and definitions of the right exist in the academic literature. For example, Ignazi refers to the categories of traditionalist conservatism, liberalism and neo-fascist authoritarianism deriving from post-French revolutionary currents (Ignazi 2003:11–12), and Eatwell outlines five categories: the reactionary right, the moderate right, the radical right, the extreme right and the new right (Eatwell 1989: 62–76). In distinguishing right from left, Bobbio refers to different approaches to equality, with the left stressing egalitarianism and the right taking an inegalitarian approach (Bobbio 1996). The emphasis in the recent literature on the post-materialist cleavage also has implications for the left–right divide with the right taking a more authoritarian conservative and anti-libertarian approach on such issues (Inglehart 1971, 1990). Mudde's recent work on the populist radical right sheds light on the different terminologies used in discussing the right. He brings some of these terminologies together in providing a definition of the populist radical right which refers to three core ideological features. These are: (1) nativism – 'an ideology which holds that states should be inhabited exclusively by members of the native group ("the nation") and that non-native elements (persons and ideas) are fundamentally threatening to the homogeneous nation-state' (Mudde 2007: 22); (2) authoritarianism – a belief in a strictly ordered society, in which infringements of authority are to be punished severely;[1] (3) populism – an ideology juxtaposing a 'pure people' against a 'corrupt elite', which argues that politics should be the expression of the popular or general will of the people (Mudde 2007: 22–23).

While the use of terms such as 'radical' and 'right' have been disputed in the literature on populism and the right (McDonnell 2006, 2007; Zaslove 2007), Mudde justifies the use of this terminology in the following manner: the term 'radical' is defined as opposition to fundamental values of liberal democracy – for example political pluralism and constitutional protection of minorities – while 'right' – following Bobbio's definition – is defined as the belief in a natural order with inequalities (Mudde 2007: 26). Thus, populist radical right parties, such as the French FN and Austrian FPO, while not rejecting democracy *per se*, tend to be rather dismissive of the facets of liberal democracy, such as constitutional checks and balances that might prevent a populist leader from implementing the popular will of the majority in-group to the detriment of members of the out-group. As Mudde suggests, the primary feature of such parties is their nativism. Hence, they are referred to as populist radical right parties, indicating that they are radical right parties of the populist variety (Mudde 2007: 26).

Rydgren's definition of the extreme right-wing populist (ERP) party family focuses on similar elements. Thus, ERP parties share the fundamental core of ethno-nationalist xenophobia (based on the so-called 'ethno-pluralist' doctrine) and anti-political establishment populism. The ethno-pluralist doctrine derives from French *Nouvelle Droite* thinking, which suggests that, in order to preserve the unique characters of different peoples, they should be kept separate. This ethno-pluralism usually comes embedded in a broader socio-cultural authoritarianism (Rydgren 2005a: 427).

Categorising the different political forces on the right in Italy according to the various models posited in the literature presents some problems, relating partly to the peculiarity of the Italian context. The LN has often been situated in the literature on the radical right and/or populism. In the Italian context, it can be described as regionalist populist, although it can also be grouped within the broader family of radical right-wing populist (RRP), extreme right populist or ethno-populist parties, which includes other anti-establishment, xenophobic or nativist parties such as the Austrian FPO or French FN (see McDonnell 2006; Mudde 2007; Zaslove 2007). Its leadership's demagogic use of propaganda, conspiracy and myth-making also lends itself to extreme right interpretations. Like the FN and FPO, the LN fits into both Rydgren's definition of ERPs and Mudde's definition of the populist radical right.

In its previous incarnation as the neo-fascist MSI, the National Alliance was perhaps easier to frame within the neo-fascist tradition, and was categorised in the literature as a leading European example of the old-style extreme right, usually with its roots in a neo-Nazi/neo-fascist movement of some sort. The metamorphosis of the MSI into a post-fascist party makes it more difficult to classify. In seeking to distance itself from its past, the AN has portrayed itself as a conventional moderate conservative party (akin to another European party which shook off links with its country's fascist past, the Spanish Popular Party), and has inherited part of the conservative southern electorate of the discredited Christian Democrat party that dominated Italian politics until the 1990s. It has also sometimes sought to present itself as a Gaullist party along the lines of the French moderate centre-right model (advocating a French-style semi-president republic and also an EU based on the principle of the *Europe des patries* advocated by de Gaulle). Thus, this strategy can be juxtaposed with that of the LN, which has sought to garner popular support by denouncing traditional conservative parties (and establishment parties of the left and right in general).

Forza Italia is altogether more difficult to classify in terms of the usual categorisation of right-wing parties, although it appears to have adopted some of the LN's populist and anti-establishment discourse while inheriting most of the DC's old electorate, seeking to present itself as a traditional 'catch-all' party of the centre right. Much of its political programme can be placed firmly in the mainstream of moderate European centre-right parties, with a neo-liberal discourse on the economy which reflects Berlusconi's admiration for Margaret Thatcher. Nevertheless, this new right neo-liberalism is clouded by the *ad personam* nature (i.e. reflecting Berlusconi's personal and business interests) of many of the policies advocated and laws promulgated in office by the Berlusconi governments. In addition to this, the method of foundation and type of organisation of FI (focused around the leadership of Berlusconi and a network of key personal allies placed in key party positions by him) appear to make Forza Italia rather *sui generis* in relation to other European parties, although it has been portrayed as an extreme example of the electoral professional model of political party, as explained in more detail in Chapter 5. Some comparisons can be made between Berlusconi and populist politicians in the USA, and in the Far East, who have mobilised extensive economic and financial resources to fight elections and portray themselves as representing new movements in opposition to the traditional political establishment (Ginsborg 2004: 8–10).

In approaching the Italian right, different theoretical lenses have been utilised. The most relevant in our research framework are those that examine radical right parties and those that study populism. Each of the two literatures have produced a rich array of perspectives and related approaches to naming their object of study – for instance 'far right', 'extreme right', 'radical right', but also, with reference to important differences, 'new right'. For instance, Mastropaolo (2005) identifies a common concern with migration issues as distinctive of the new right in Europe, and distinguishes this new focus from the anti-democratic authoritarianism that was typical of the previous fascist tradition.

For convenience, we will refer to this entire literature as the literature of the radical right, which we will integrate with reference to the literature on populism. Our objective in considering these theoretical traditions is to show the similarities but also the relevant differences in the Italian right.

There are several explanations of the successes of the radical right, and there are useful typologies of explanations and comparisons in the literature (Eatwell and Mudde 2004; Mudde 2000; Rydgren 2005b). Explanations are generally multi-causal, although they might stress one aspect more than others. It is now well recognised that the success of the right cannot be explained by a single variable. Rather complex configurations of variables lead to the often short-lived success of radical right parties. Norris summarises this complex causation by arguing that the success of the radical right is rooted in societal factors such as reactions to the impact of migration and a crisis of political representation and of political identification, which have freed voters previously attached to mainstream parties, some of whom have embraced the right, thanks to its successful strategies. These involve ideological adaptation to the fears and concerns of the public. Also important are changes in institutional frameworks that have made nomination, campaigning and electoral rules conducive to the success of radical right parties (Norris 2005: 18).

While it is useful to consider this literature, it should however be pointed out that studies of the radical right generally focus on small radical right parties which, despite episodic victories and the fact that they might have a diffuse agenda-shaping impact on centre-right parties (Bale 2003) generally remain small and short-lived outsiders to the political system. They might occasionally be co-opted by centre-right parties, but not in a stable and durable manner. In analysing the success of the Italian right, the explananda needs to be fairly different – we face a successful and longlasting alliance that, despite fundamental disagreements, has integrated the ideologies and policies of the extreme right in an otherwise conventional and longlasting centre-right coalition. Its component parties are no longer fringe groupings but established and legitimate political actors. Yet reference to the literature on the radical right remains more appropriate than the literature on the centre right, as the policies advocated by components of the Italian right coalition and its political style are still more similar to the former. At present, the Italian right-wing coalition cannot, however, be called a radical right. As will be argued, it still shows some thematic reference to the radical right, but its distinctive element is its populism. We will first consider its right-wing character and later in the chapter its populism. Thus, our goal is to thematise and provide a model to explain the social, institutional and political processes that have played a role in the institutionalisation of the Italian right and made it longlasting and successful. To do this, we will consider some of the hypotheses generally discussed in the literature and propose some new ones.

Dynamics related to the political system, societal factors and institutional developments

In the literature, the success of the Italian right has been explained in terms of a mix of societal factors, institutional developments and dynamics related to the political system (Bull and Newell 2005; Campus 2006; Gilbert and Pasquino 2000; Giordano 2003; Ignazi 2005b; Newell 2006; Paolucci 2006; Sassoon 1995; Tarchi 2002). In this volume, we will frame the success of the right in terms of its ability to seize emerging social and cultural opportunities – an ability that derived from the fracture that the *tangentopoli* events imposed on its structure and not to the same extent on the left, and in terms of skilful political entrepreneurs who realised the potential advantages of cultural innovation. In addition to this distinctive ability, we also need to point to a set of structural changes in Italian society that the right was in a better position to interpret.

To articulate this model, we will distinguish (1) societal factors from (2) institutional developments and from dynamics related to the consequences of a new electoral law on the party system, and (3) we will posit the emergence of new ideologies and re-definitions of the ideological space. We will frame these three factors in terms of related chains of causation that have converged, opening up growing cultural opportunities for the right. We will posit a (4) distinctive contribution of populism and anti-politics as a political style and as an ideology, and frame their contribution as a distinctive additional cultural opportunity. Finally, we will propose ways to test several significant parts of this model.

Social change and its interpreters

In terms of social changes, the post-*tangentopoli* society was already very different from the society that, despite a polarisation between the PCI and the DC, had in practice emphasised social solidarity, job security and a degree of resource re-distribution. The new society was dealing with an increased globalisation of the economy and consequent labour flexibilisation, declining levels of trade unionisation and declining social homogeneity, which made the ideological and organisational model of the mass party anachronistic. The right utilised opportunities that had suddenly opened up as a result of an epochal political crisis that was in turn possible because, in a new Europeanised and competitive environment, the continuation of the corrupt and clientelistic political system was no longer economically and socially viable (Cento Bull and Gilbert 2001; Gilbert 1995).

But the fundamental innovation of the right was also cultural and was rooted in a set of sociological changes that had affected Italian society. First, the collapse of the mass party, the emergence of a new professional class, politically more mobile and indifferent to the old rigid schematisation of left and right was realised and tapped by FI, which approached voters in new ways: as consumers and citizens and no longer as crystallised electorates. Its participation in politics was less ideological and more pragmatic, and utilised for the first time a communication style borrowed from advertising, presenting itself as a kind of value-driven temporary public service to the country – 'people only temporarily lent to politics for the good of the country'. Forza Italia was therefore able to re-define the political space and to carve out a niche that was from the beginning different from the activist niche of the other two right parties, the AN and the LN. It was different because, in emphasising an anti-political stance, it could appear as truly innovative and transversal to old political divides. In this, it expanded the space of politics.

Other right-wing parties also reacted to sociological and cultural changes. The LN provided a needed new sense of community (Ruzza and Schmidtke 1996a). The AN reacted to fears about personal security that the first waves of immigration induced.

Other political parties were less able and less agile in interpreting emerging social change. Unaffected by a systemic crisis, the left remained anchored to state-centred re-distributive ideologies that many came to see as increasingly outdated.

Institutional developments and emerging new political space

In terms of institutional changes, the most relevant was the new electoral law opening up new political space. In the literature, the increased availability of political space for political outsiders is typically stressed by *political opportunity theory*, which interprets success as resulting from new opportunities related to the breakdown of elite alliances (McAdam et al. 1996). This happened with the collapse of the old Italian party system and made possible Berlusconi's decision to recruit the LN and the MSI into coalition politics. The question remains, however, of why the heirs of fascism and new xenophobic and regionalist formations such as the League were able to fill that space.

On the one hand, this happened because of a perception of the relative blamelessness of the right. As mentioned previously, the collapse of the old political system affected to an extent all parties of the post-war republic. It directly affected governing parties – notably the DC and the PSI, around whom most of the revelations focused. But it also affected all other parties such as the communist PCI, which had on occasion externally collaborated with the governing parties through consociational practices and was a major actor at regional and city levels of government, and therefore also suspected of involvement. The right, on the other hand, had no previous involvement and could appear as clean and extraneous to these practices. However, being uninvolved was not sufficient as other marginal political groups were also uninvolved but did not profit from the collapse of the post-war system. Here institutional and sociological factors come into play.

In terms of institutional factors, political restructuring emerged from the creation of two distinct electoral blocs in the north and in the south. It sanctioned the real victor of the re-definition of the political space, Forza Italia – a new formation able to quickly produce an entirely new ruling class coming from the reservoirs of the media empire of Berlusconi, from the business world and from younger generations of professionals. The dual alliance with the LN in the north and the old extreme right in the south was an institutional solution that many observers found brilliant in that it short-circuited the obvious incompatibility between the separatist north and the state-dependent south. Moreover, parties that might otherwise have been regarded as beyond the arch of democratic acceptability, such as the LN and the MSI–AN, were regarded as necessary additional components of a centre-right coalition; their inclusion was deemed necessary because of the polarisation induced by a new predominantly majoritarian political system. The polarising effects of the new electoral system were central to the continuing success of this broad centre-right coalition.

The question remains, however, of how it was possible for the right to innovate culturally, while the left remained for several more years limited in its ability to renew its communist legacy. Here some specific consideration of ideology as a variable is necessary.

Ideologies of the right

As historical examinations show, Italy is a country of traditionally intense ideological conflict. Political conflict has historically been fought from the standpoint of contrasting ideologies that have marked the political identities of regions and social groups. One need only recall the ideological differences between the historically leftist Tuscany and Emilia Romagna, the Christian

Democratic Veneto and the conservative traditions of some southern regions. Nonetheless, the specific make-up of these ideologies has changed over time. The ideologies of the right and left have been constantly and often radically re-defined in Italian history, and this has also occurred in recent years. In this context, a brief excursus on the present ideologies of the Italian right will be useful. Then, newer on the scene and particularly relevant is the role of populism, which can be conceptualised as an ideology in its own right and related to other political ideologies.

In this context, with reference to Freeden's conception of ideology, one can characterise ideologies as having different degrees of coherence. At any point in time, there exist a few distinct ideological families to which political formations, parties and social movements refer. They reflect political theories with varying degrees of consistency and permanency. Just as a language may have several local dialects, so ideologies take distinct forms in specific local contexts, for instance within the EU and its member states. Ideologies are employed to react to specific sets of problems and are shaped by specific political contexts. Thus, the right has traditionally utilised references to the ideology of nationalism and cultural protectionism. In this framework, one can also conceptualise populism as an ideology that is still relatively weak and unorganised (Freeden 1996, 1998).

Reflecting a proportional electoral law, during the First Republic, the ideological offering of the Italian political system was very differentiated. However, the two largely dominant parties – the DC and the PCI – reflected a *de facto* ideological polarisation, which also masked several common ideological elements. They were both anti-individualist ideologies, suspicious of markets and in favour of a substantial role for the state. They were universalist ideologies that reached beyond the confines of the nation-state: one conceptualised the proletariat as a transnational subject, the other the entire religious community – the people of god. There have of course been several historical variants that re-defined this philosophical stance, but they were not the dominant ideology. With processes of secularisation and the collapse of the Soviet bloc, things changed. Both ideologies had lost some of their relevance. The political implications of their adoption by sympathetic parties also changed.

The collapse of the communist bloc had undermined the necessity of a catholic party, and the events of 1992–93 had removed the DC from the scene, freeing a large DC electorate in search of new political identities but also of new ideologies. With *tangentopoli* and the collapse of the party system, previously minor ideologies gained strength and pervaded the entire political system. The reflection of an international liberal turn, and of economic globalisation, made relevant in Italy a neo-liberal ideological framework better able to interpret processes of secularisation and the collapse of Marxist models. It re-defined views of the market in more positive terms in the minds of many Italians. The default worldview became a more pro-market approach to politics and a diminished role for the state. References to territorial identities increased. Most parties, both left and right, accepted this transition but interpreted it with substantial variations.

A framework for understanding the success of the right

We posit that a skilful re-interpretation of the new societal climate was the key to the longlasting success of the right. In other words, the right utilised and in part created a set of discursive opportunities that resonated with an emerging popular ideology (based on notions of self-reliance and entrepreneurship, as well as law and order and family values) (Koopmans and Olzak 2004). Thus, our explanation of the right will combine insights from political opportunity – as discussed above – with insights from the *theory of discursive opportunities*, conceptualised as a component of the larger political opportunity (Ferree et al. 2002). The literature has sometimes stressed that the right was more responsive to emerging ideologies than the left, and particularly of specific sectors of the population – such as the bourgeoisie (Ignazi 2005a), but we need a more specific assessment of the fit between the values of the population and the offering of the political system. In order to do this, we need a measure of what the ideologies of the different parties consisted of in their actual use. In the remainder of this chapter, we will provide a method to accomplish this.

In sum, we posit that

- there was a good fit between the ideology of the population at large as measured by surveys and some of the key values emphasised by the right, which were however in many respects self-contradictory.
- there was a specific fit between the law and order core element of ideology of the right-wing electorates as measured by surveys and the values emphasised by the right. This provided motivation for activism and lowered abstention levels.
- the values of the right as emphasised by electoral programmes were complementary at least in some respects, making the right-wing coalition credible, at least initially.
- the coalition could often effectively mask internal differences. The masking of differences was accomplished at least in significant part through a populist rhetorical style and through significant control of the media.
- that right-wing actors proposed new values that occupied a new political space, which had become relevant due to social developments but had no representative in the old political system.

The book will examine and address each of these factors though a variety of methods, which will be described later in this chapter. However, prior to this, a brief description of the emerging ideologies of the right will help to frame the issue of ideological convergence and divergence.

The coalition that Berlusconi created was from the beginning representative of old and new political values, communities of reference and visions of society. Each of these visions was recognised and acknowledged by the architects of the coalition. The AN was unified by a call for strong law and order policies and Italian nationalism, but was internally split on the ideal role of the market. It remains internally divided between a social right, which advocates a re-distributive state and particular support for the south, and more neo-liberal components. After the foundational Fiuggi meeting, it also attracted a former DC component bringing greater emphasis to its already conservative stance on family values and traditional ethics. Its ideology then evolved in relation to its electorate which expanded beyond parts of the underclass and the southern petit bourgeoisie attracting voters of the Christian Democratic right.

The ethno-regionalist Northern League emphasised cultural protectionism and localism but also welfare chauvinism, xenophobia and, gradually, anti-Europeanism. However, ambivalence emerged over conservative catholic values, with factions supporting them and others identifying the church as the carrier of a universalist project inimical to the League's cherished localism. Furthermore, the small and still self-acknowledged Christian Democratic component of the coalition contributed to a curbing of attempts to engage in the liberalising reforms that much of the electorate desired.

Forza Italia, the last group to emerge within the right, was nominally a more neo-liberal party, even as over time its critics would lament the absence of authentic liberal policies. Its emphasis on the market was connected with an approach based on consumerism and anti-communism. There was however also an emphasis on 'family values' and religion. This was in part due to the incorporation of large sectors of the former DC with its distrust of liberalism and concern for religious values. FI's strategy of merging the conservative Christian and the neo-liberal worldviews was at the root of its electoral success, but it also proved to be a very difficult goal once in power.

It is clearly apparent that, given such ideological differences, the right-wing coalition would struggle to converge on policies. Fundamental differences emerged from the onset in the early 1990s, engendering a climate of protracted conflict among the partners, which would hinder the coalition's decision-making ability during periods in government. The main axis of conflict remained the conflict between the regional and cultural protectionism of the League and the Italian nationalism of AN. Conflict also frequently emerged over the church–state relationship which, as mentioned, divided some parties internally (also a problem for the centre left), and diverging views on the relationship between the state and the economy.

Populism and anti-politics

We will argue that the right-wing parties were unified in espousing and utilising a fundamentally populist anti-political stance. It has been observed that, even when in government, the right-wing coalition and Berlusconi in particular continued to present an anti-political worldview. Berlusconi, the industrialist 'only temporarily lent to politics', continued to criticise professional politicians and define himself as an alternative. Anti-political values were natural to the heirs of the MSI who had been marginalised for decades, even if, once in government, the AN's history required it to present itself as a responsible partner and thus steer clear of the populist histrionics of its allies. As for the LN, anti-politics was a necessity for a party engaged in fighting a political class unified by a still recent process of nation-building. Thus, anti-political populism became the cementing element of the right-wing coalition. Paradoxically, it remained the dominant keynote even during periods in government. Observers noted that Berlusconi in particular ran governmental affairs as if he was in opposition. Similarly, the LN kept emphasising the temporary character of the right-wing alliance and the untrustworthy nature of its allies. In addition to an anti-political stance, other elements of the ideology of populism defined the right-wing coalition and deserve specific attention.

Different authors have expanded or narrowed definitions of populism. It would not be possible here to review the variety of uses of this concept, but a few references to its relevance in the literature are useful. When examining right-wing parties in a European context, the concept of populism is among the first that comes to mind. Although applied to both left-wing and right-wing parties, it is recently, in the European context, a concept more often utilised to characterise radical right formations and distinguish them from other centre-right parties – thus, in studies of other countries, it is rare for it to be used for the centre-right counterparts of FI. However, we posit that the right-wing coalition owes its success precisely to the adoption of a populist discourse and populist strategies that elsewhere the European counterparts of FI would refrain from using, or would possibly not have the resources and know-how to use effectively.

The concept of populism

Populists typically see society as hierarchically ordered and posit a threat to society in the form of corrupt self-serving ruling elites, who have 'betrayed' their people. Populists glorify 'common people' as honest carriers of positive moral values and seek to reflect the 'popular will' in decision-making processes. This is often accomplished through the intervention of a charismatic leader who alone expresses their concerns and values and directly represents them, thus bypassing social hierarchies. Useful recent definitions include that of Mudde: 'an ideology that considers society to be ultimately separated into two homogeneous groups and antagonistic groups, "the pure people" versus "the corrupt elite" and which argues that politics should be an expression of the *volonté générale* (general will) of the people' (Mudde 2004). Another pertinent definition of populism in relation to this volume, particularly given the tendency of a new wave of right-wing populists in western Europe to scapegoat particular 'out-groups' such as migrants, is that posited by Albertazzi and McDonnell (2008): 'an ideology which pits a virtuous and homogeneous people against a set of elites and dangerous "others" who are together depicted as depriving (or attempting to deprive) the sovereign people of their rights, values, prosperity, identity and voice'.

Populist demands may include institutional architectures which promote the inclusion of ordinary citizens in the decision processes of social and political institutions such as parts of the judiciary, and/or through citizens' participatory and deliberative input into policy-making, particularly at local level. Nevertheless, as Mudde notes, populist movements tend to be hostile to the institutions of liberal or constitutional democracy, thus placing a reliance on charismatic leaders who can instinctively interpret the will of the populist heartland (Mudde 2004: 561).

Although there are authors such as Norris and Mastropaolo (Mastropaolo 2005; Norris 2005) who see populism as merely a generic rhetorical strategy devoid of coherence or a mystifying strategy to attract votes – which is often the case – many other authors identify distinct traits. The literature points to a rejection of aspects of representative democracy as leading to chains of untrustworthy intermediaries as a principal characteristic of populism. In this sense, populism often seeks to look beyond the right–left axis, even asserting its irrelevance, as the political class is, by definition, all corrupt. Nevertheless, populism is often described not only as an ideology, but also a rhetorical political style – a form of political communication.

The concept of populism has long been utilised in historical and political analyses of democratic politics but also more broadly of transitions from authoritarian regimes and in analyses of authoritarian regimes (Conniff 1981; Drake 1978; Durden 1965; Griffiths 1992; Isser 1996; Love 1984; McMath and Foner 1993; Saloutos and Hicks 1961). In works on contemporary societies, analyses of populism have ranged from general works on the concept (Canovan 1981; Taggart 2000) to analyses of populism that have focused on specific locations, and notably Latin America where Peronism is typically seen as its prototypical example (Buckley 2005; Conniff 1999; Dornbusch and Edwards 1991; Little and Herrera 1995), the US (Adam and Gaither 2004; Holmes 1994; Kazin 1995), but also western Europe (Albertazzi and McDonnell 2008). Populism has been studied in relation to democratic and authoritarian regimes, and in relation to political theories ranging from Marxism to elitism (Bell 1992; Brock 1973; Lukacs 2005; Munro-Kua 1996; Raby 1983).

Frequently, analyses of populism have been connected to the radical right (Berlet and Lyons 2000; Betz 1994; Federici 1991; Harrison 1995; Luther 2002; Rydgren 2005b). It has also been used to examine more broadly the protest sector of European societies (Taggart 1996). Within the context of representative democracy, the concept of populism has been used to illuminate trends ranging from the growing role of the media to the introduction of elements of participatory democracy in western political systems (Zimmerman 1986). The role of the media and a political communication perspective has also been particularly connected to populism in several recent works (Mazzoleni et al. 2003; McGuigan 1992; Ociepka 2005).

Populism as a strategy can be connected to a re-definition of the political space that a new type of political communication has engendered. This consists of a weakening of party loyalty, issue-centred politics and, in the world of communication, a marginalisation of political news in favour of a politicised reporting of social issues such as crime and immigration. The changed role of the media has led to a de-mystification of political office, with more and more citizens claiming to have a good understanding of what politicians do and thinking that they can do it better (Mudde 2004). In this context, as will be discussed in detail, FI has been able to become a prominent actor for a set of reasons. First, because its ideological flexibility allows it to dodge the need to remain consistent in its public positioning. Second, media ownership on the part of the leader of FI has facilitated the systemic impact of several television channels, bolstered when in government by the political control of state television.

The adoption of populism as a strategy has been related to types of electoral laws. Norris (2005: 27) argues that a majoritarian law encourages vague populist appeals, while a proportional law encourages the emergence of parties with strong ideological identities. As mentioned, we see populism not simply as a synonym of 'generalist'. However, we support the consideration that a majoritarian law encourages catch-all discursive strategies, which can be related to the category of 'politician's populism' as defined by Canovan (1981). In the Italian case, the transition to a majoritarian law certainly made it necessary to attract a wide electorate through such vague discursive strategies.

But the ideology of the right was also based on pre-existing parties – the LN and the AN – with very distinctive identities. To them, a generalist strategy was not appropriate. Nevertheless, the new electoral law retained a proportional component, which stimulated these parties to retain their strong ideological identities, while at the same time allowing for a generalist approach from FI. However, one needs to emphasise that the indisputable vagueness of the FI ideological platform results from the internal contradictions related to its different components – the Christian Democrat and the Liberal – as much as from external discursive strategies.

Populism as an ideology

From these brief references to the literature, one can see that the concept of populism has been utilised in widely varying contexts. Its versatility depends in part on its relevance in a wide variety of contexts and probably also its excessive breadth. But the flexibility of the concept also needs to be explained. Populism is a political ideology that relates in complex ways to the other major recent political ideologies (Laclau 1977). As a concept, populism has rarely been espoused by those who identify with its prescriptions. As Meny and Surel (2002) note, populism is generally used by critical commentators of political formations rather than by their participants, and it is generally used with negative connotations. Thus, as an ideology, not having been claimed by its users, it has not undergone the process of streamlining and clarification that other political ideologies have undergone. It is also a relatively newer ideology. As a result, its conceptual features are still relatively undefined. It has, however, been recognised as increasingly relevant to explain transformations of western democracies and it is in this context that we use it.

Like other ideologies it has, as posited in Freeden's framework, a core and a conceptual periphery. The ideological core is relatively stable, while the periphery is more changing and adaptable to external contexts and to the other ideologies with which it comes into contact. As noted, as an ideology, populism has a smaller less specific core, and this makes it adaptable. Its meaning is more easily re-defined by the peripheral ideological elements that accompany it in empirical contexts. Its anti-incumbent character also contributes to its flexibility. With reference to a specific context, such as that of the Italian right, one can thus seek out the stable traits of the ideology of populism and identify its changing aspects, and one can identify the processes that over time have stimulated conceptual innovation and adaptation.

In an age of accelerated circulation of ideas through global media, and therefore of a globalisation of political ideas, the adopters of populism as an ideology and as a form of politics can draw from an increasingly wide repertoire. They can compete by outbidding each other in the adoption of ideological elements that are perceived as electorally rewarding, or appealing to their activist base. In so doing, they come to partially re-define the conceptual centre and periphery of populism. The analysis of these dynamics will be conducted in later chapters. Here, only the general central and peripheral features of populism will be discussed.

For analytical purposes, we can therefore distinguish ideological frames that are available in the broader context of the global western media, and the 'dialects' that are relevant in the Italian context (Freeden 1996, 1998). As determinants of ideological strategies, the latter might well be more relevant in local situations, but will tend to be less permanent. The emergence of populism in its globalised version and in its local variants has been documented by several authors who have also advanced explanations as to the reasons why an increased salience of the populist frame has occurred.

Betz (1994) sees the emergence of recent populism as the outcome of the crisis of the main ideologies of modernisation. These ideologies have inspired European politics on the basis of different utopias, but they have all undergone a crisis. Keynesian liberalism, moderate republicanism and social democracy have not withstood well the challenge of globalisation. Populism has therefore appeared above all as a reaction against politics, which is typically conceived by populists as marked by a set of ideologies in a state of crisis. In this perspective, populism is then mainly a differentiated reaction against different types of politics that are dominant in different places. It is for this reason that populism is an ideology with a small core of common anti-modern ideological elements (where modernity is meant as an ideological construct which of course allows for the emergence of different visions of modernity) and a large periphery which varies and is shaped by a specific reaction against different versions of political modernity. These common elements in the anti-political sentiments of populism are however important.

As the literature points out, different versions of populism share a perception of a 'crisis of politics' – western political systems perceived as corrupt, biased in favour of big corporate power, economically oppressive and insensitive to the traditional moral values of 'common people'. The dominant features of the current ideological core of populism are reflected in Canovan's (1981) ideal type of politician's populism.[2] This stresses more participatory democracy, reactionary law and order values, anti-elitism and emphasis on charismatic leadership. In particular, the anti-political component has emerged through a media-spurred distrust of elected representatives, together with distrust and professed indifference towards conventional political cleavages such as the right–left divide. The search for a charismatic figure, able to bridge these divides, characterises much recent populist politics. Anti-political values are a pervasive trait that populists express in all western democracies (Rydgren 2005b). Substantial discontent with current democratic arrangements is shared by most of the political figures who at different times have been commonly labelled populists, such as Pauline Hanson in Australia, Jörg Haider in Austria, Evo Morales in Bolivia, Jean-Marie Le Pen in France, Silvio Berlusconi and Umberto Bossi in Italy, Pim Fortuyn in the Netherlands, Ross Perot in the United States and Hugo Chávez in Venezuela.

Social analysts have connected populist sentiments to anti-political phenomena such as declining electorates due to a generalised sense of irrelevance of the political process, a crisis of legitimacy of certain levels of government such as the European level of government and, in some contexts – as per the LN – in the nation-state. A fundamental mistrust of politicians and politics has been identified in connection to widespread media-fuelled negative portraits and frequent corruption scandals. Although there are dissenting voices that deny or qualify sweeping theories of a crisis of politics (Norris 2000, 2002, 2005), the issue of a pervasive disenchantment with politics has often been related to the emergence of populism.

Populism has also been related to the changing role of the state in an age of economic globalisation and erosion of authority in favour of subnational and supranational levels of government. A weaker state allows and may even need links between citizens and decision-making processes that are complementary or even alternative to those taking place within the institutions of representative democracy. One of these links is an unmediated connection between a populist leader and its electorate. This is often marked symbolically by the use of linguistic codes that belong to the spoken and informal register of a language, as has often been noted with reference to the language of the LN. A second link, which is frequent in right-wing populism, takes place through an idealisation of the role of the market which replaces certain functions of the state, or – more frequently within the left – a strengthening and re-definition of the role of civil society – organised or unorganised. Even mythologised references to civil society can imply a re-definition and even a restriction of democratic channels of representation (Mastropaolo 2005). One can often identify populist undertones in the now recurrent approaches that seek to enhance public deliberation at local levels, and other forms of political participation of non-state actors, such as promoting referenda, incorporating the actors of protest politics in decision-making, fostering participation of social movements in decision-making, enhancing the political dimension of third-sector activities or increasing electronic forms of democracy. These approaches are more or less viable according to the context in which their adoption is attempted. They are however connected to solutions that attempt to integrate or, less frequently, to substitute representative democracy.

Italian populism has been inspired and has developed in parallel with other European populist models, borrowing both the core elements of populism and anti-politics and some peripheral ones. Although it could be argued that this is the case for both the left and the right, in the following chapters, we will only examine linkages in the right. In particular, we include anti-politics as a component of contemporary European and Italian populism rather than a substituting concept, as has sometimes been suggested (Mastropaolo 2005). Idealised references to 'the people' and derogatory references to the political class often appear together, but their connection varies and, as mentioned previously, the concept of populism as it appears in the literature also includes other traits, such as a frequent reliance on charismatic leadership.

As a weak ideology – in the sense discussed previously – populism acquires meaning in relation to other more completely formed ideologies of the right. It is connected to these ideologies through a set of peripheral elements that are also part of different right-wing ideologies. In effect, as has been noted, vague appeals to 'the people' of populists often hide more exclusionary visions typical of the right (Mastropaolo 2005). Disentangling these differences is a complex theoretical and empirical task that we will approach through a variety of methodologies.

Methodological notes

Methodologically, this volume assumes that populist, anti-political and other concerns can be identified and measured. It then assumes that dislike for an ineffective, costly and immoral political system is an attitudinal component that can be identified and measured in both political texts and the attitudes of the population. It posits that, if there is a resonance between the two and effective policy choices, the likelihood of success for parties will also increase. If the solutions prospected by specific political forces and relevant sections of the electorate coincide, then the relative success of parties will increase. To test this model, one then needs to gather and relate the following kinds of empirical data: (1) ideological contents of party discourse; (2) attitudinal data of the population at large and of the relevant electorates; (3) voting behaviour over time; (4) policy changes of selected parties over time; and also (5) contents emerging in opinion-forming agencies such as the printed and television media.

A triangulation between these sources is necessary, as certain contents will tend to emerge more prominently in some than in others. For instance, an emphasis on the role of the leader and his charismatic qualities will emerge in the party media – less in electoral manifestos. In the 2001–6 legislature, the three parties acted in coalition, and another centrist party was also involved. The unit of analysis will thus also be the coalition and its internal dynamics.

In focusing on the complex relationship between the use of anti-political and populist language and electoral outcomes, we have therefore adopted a multi-method approach. The examination of electoral outcomes was conducted with the help of data sets on voting patterns and their change over time. The examination of party strategies was supplemented by interviews with political actors and activists[3] and a contextual historical examination of policy choices over time. The identification of anti-political contents was conducted through a structured computer-supported content analysis of party texts. Texts oriented towards different audiences were identified and examined. The assessment of anti-political sentiments of the population availed itself of secondary analyses of large surveys of political attitudes.

There are several sources of data concerning attitudes towards politics in general, and towards different repertoires of political participation. Notably, we utilised the ITANES data sets collected by the Cattaneo Institute,[4] and key questions from the European Social Survey series. We identified a set of indicators of anti-political sentiments and assessed their relevance in specific electorates and groups of the population.

Examination of ideology drew from a content analysis of key party texts. As mentioned previously, ideological issues such as claims to modernity, but also more specifically to some of the parties, claims to economic freedom, or to regional self-determination or to Christian values, are an integral part of the strategies of the right that need to be specifically identified and described to ground the analysis. We do this by paying sustained attention to the issue of ideological identity and change within the right-wing coalition. Our empirical attention to ideology is part of a tradition of research that needs to be summarised briefly before explaining our methodological approach.

The role of ideology is frequently emphasised in the academic literature on the right. There are in this literature works that specifically focus on fascism as a historical phenomenon and follow its evolution after the war, and there are works that only examine recent formations, often in a comparative framework. Both stress the role of ideology as the variable that, in the mind of activists, and among the public at large, differentiates this family of parties. In the first category, as Tarchi notes, the role of ideology has come under particular examination in recent years. Among the authors who specifically underline the role of ideology, it is useful to cite as an example Juan Linz who identifies a distinctive ideological flexibility which marks right-wing formations, and is often utilised for openly instrumental reasons.

With reference to Linz, Tarchi notes:

> the ideological hetereogeneity of fascist movements was caused by their nature as latecomers, they were the last to arrive, the latecomers in the politics of their respective countries which was by then occupied by other

actors, a fact forcing them to incorporate and transform elements which were already present in other doctrines, and movements with different modalities, in order to make clear to their public the identity and the oppositional style which characterized them and allowed them to fight a few clearly defined enemies.

Tarchi (2003a: 85)

Roger Eatwell also notes the large number of texts that identify a lack of coherence in fascist ideologies but emphasise the instrumental aspects, the rationality of fascist ideological adaptation (Eatwell 1996). Cas Mudde stresses the function of ideology in his comparative study of right-wing parties (Mudde 2000: 5). All these authors point to ideological analysis as a particularly useful tool in the analysis of the right. Nonetheless, it is not unproblematic to use the concept of ideology as there are several and often contrasting definitions of the concept. In the context of this book, we will utilise a broad definition of ideology as 'a body of normative ideas on human nature and society and the organization and purpose of society' (Sainsbury cited in Mudde 2000: 19). With this broad conception of ideology, authors such as Mudde (2000) and Tarchi (2003b) have examined, utilising qualitative methodologies, the party political programmes and other relevant texts of the right. Mudde identifies, for instance, ideological contents such as various kinds of nationalisms (i.e. state nationalism, ethno-nationalism) racism, ethno-centrism, anti-semitism, pluralism and corporatism.

Different groups and parties characterise themselves through a variable mix of ideological elements such as those identified by Mudde. Clearly, some elements are more central than others and more recurrent. As mentioned previously, following Freeden, we can therefore characterise ideology as having a core that is constituted by the most frequent ideological elements and a conceptual periphery which includes a varying set of elements (Freeden 1996). The peripheral elements will emerge and disappear in different geographical and historical contexts, while the core traditionally includes central elements such as nationalism and identity politics and conservative positions on law and order and social–moral issues, which define the right-wing party family and are less prone to modifications. Strategic factors affect the conceptual periphery and respond to changes in public opinion and tactical positioning in electoral competitions.

Relations among the CdL–PdL parties in Italy are for some aspects synergetic and in many other respects competitive. They converge on some typical themes of right-wing party families – for instance their emphasis on 'law and order' policies, tough immigration control positions and the positive function of strong leaders – but, as we will see, they diverge on key issues such as economic policy, Europe and, of course, the application of nationalism to a territory of reference, which in one case is a limited area of the country and in the other the entire nation-state. Through a comparative analysis of their ideology, it will be possible to identify the salient elements of these formations and their peripheral elements, and examine their impact on Italian politics.

In this volume, we have adopted a methodology of computerised qualitative text analysis that is somewhat more formalised than methods used by other analysts of ideology (Mudde 2000; Tarchi 2003b). In order to compare the ideology of the right-wing parties, we utilised the research tradition of frame analysis as developed in the field of social movement research and discussed in Appendix B.

We have also monitored general media sources and the party press since the early 1990s. The three parties have different relations with the general media. Given its founder's ownership of a large media empire, FI views are frequently aired in different media. They are also reproduced in newspapers such as *Il Giornale*, which is owned by the Berlusconi family. The other two parties have less impact. However, the views of AN are reproduced in its newspaper *Il Secolo d'Italia*, and the views of the LN in its newspaper *La Padania*. From their own press, the positions of the parties often find an echo in the right-wing press in general. As is shown in the party chapters, there is a substantial alignment of these party newspapers with the frames emerging in electoral manifestos.[5]

Summarising, we have employed a multi-method approach that includes analysis of survey data, interviews, the media and content analyses. Through the frame analysis of documents, we aim to identify in a systematic and reliable manner the set of themes that define the concerns and policy proposals of the different parties at different points in time. We can then characterise their ideology in terms of what are the central elements and what are the peripheral features – peripheral either because they are important but only for a short period, or peripheral because they are constant but receive limited attention.

A model to study populism

In line with the relevant literature, this volume argues that there are different types of populism (Canovan 1981) but that, in the context of advanced liberal democracies, populism (particularly when connected to ideologies of the right such as nationalism) is a weak ideology (Freeden 1996, 1998) with a loosely defined core and a changeable periphery of concepts and related practices that are connected to other political ideologies. The common core constitutes the 'essence' of the populist phenomena we examine in our case studies. Beyond the core element – which is itself composite – there are a host of peripheral elements. Their presence is related to the specific political opportunities that different political formations seek to maximise. Different populist formations will tend to follow different trajectories and appeal to different strands of voters. Furthermore, it is argued that the indeterminacy of populism is a key constitutive ideological feature that responds to its need to be adaptable as an ideology. There is therefore little similarity and no convergence between populist formations beyond the core key elements.

We argue that the core features of populism consist of a distinct configuration of ideas, styles and policies. (1) The core ideas present in all populist formations are appeals to the people and anti-politics as recurrent discourse often channelled through a charismatic leadership. (2) Styles distinctive of populism are a certain type of language which indicates its anti-elitist character. (3) The policies of populism are policies intended to symbolise and justify dynamics of inclusion and exclusion – the adoption of these policies constitutes a quasi-tribal form of politics, in which a 'tribe' is symbolically identified and protected. Populism would then include the use of Edelman-style symbolic politics to show allegiance to one's 'people' (Edelman 1973, 1988).

The main peripheral elements are:

- Other ideologies of reference, the territorial area and political status of the 'people' of reference, the extent of the leader's control of his/her formation.
- The main context variables that orient the features of peripheral elements are:
    - the party system,
    - the political environment (electoral law, etc.),
    - individual party history and trajectory,
    - the features of the civil society in which political opinion is formed.

In the following chapters, we will review the role of these variables with reference to our three parties, and in the concluding chapters, we will return to this scheme and discuss contextually the variables that orient the manifestation of the peripheral elements of populism.

Conclusion

In this chapter, it has been argued that the success of the Italian right is rooted, on the one hand, in a unique conjunction of factors that have spurred and helped right-wing parties and particularly the appearance of a new political space. On the other hand, dynamics that have spurred a search for populist solutions to Italian problems have been more effectively interpreted by the right.

Among the factors that have helped the right in Italy, but are part of a general European trend, one needs to point to sociological factors such as the impact of globalisation and, in particular, fears and displacements resulting from increased migration. Also important are shifts towards bipolarism that have led to a rapprochement between the moderate and extreme right in some cases. Europe-wide regionalisation processes have also provided the political opportunity for the re-invention of ethno-nationalism in the north of Italy. The fact that this took a right turn is also connected to the new relevance of cultural protectionism in an age of globalisation.

We have posited that, as for the right specifically, populism has sociological, institutional and political facilitators. Populism cuts across the left–right divide, but the right has more resources to tap into it effectively. Material and symbolic resources have come from the self-interested communication politics of the media tycoon Berlusconi. Ideological resources have come from the greater ideological flexibility of the right. Institutional resources have come from an electoral law that favoured the cohesive coalition behaviour that charismatic leaders were in a better position to achieve. As we show, the right is and has been internally divided. Populism is an ideology that is not embedded in a specific party, but that emphasises a set of themes such as anti-politics, anti-elitism and a tendency towards charismatic leadership, which can be persuasively developed both by the right and by the left. Yet it is the right that appears to have capitalised on these themes, using them to win three major general elections in 1994, 2001 and 2008.

4   The Northern League

An effective mix of ethno-nationalism, populism and a new conservative ethos propelled the Lombard League and then the Northern League (LN) into national politics. Despite early successes in a very favourable situation, the LN has not been able to develop into a broader vehicle for conservative sentiments. Indeed, it has been the subject of a repeated co-optation of its agenda by other parties and re-definitions of it in terms that are more compatible with a broader electorate, while its localistic anchor has prevented it from similar successful re-orientations. Nevertheless, it has retained an administrative role in villages and small towns at the local level regardless of its periodic radicalisations. Its institutional activists[1] have gradually learned to operate within the state institutions of a circumscribed area, forging links with middle-class professionals and other political forces in the day-to-day administration. Moreover, the electoral system since 1993, favouring broad coalitions, has allowed the LN to continue to exercise a disproportionate influence within the Italian party system at the national level, notably through its participation within the centre-right governing coalition of 2001–6.

Because of its localised constituency, the LN could manufacture a distinctive brand of ethno-nationalism connected to the glorification of its constituency – appropriately named 'the peoples of Padania' – which indicates both a common destiny and a homeland, but also internal differentiation. Its populism is therefore a form of economically based nationalism in which images of victimhood and territorial belonging are prevalent. This chapter will demonstrate how this process of symbolic construction occurred and will show how the LN exploited existing regional cleavages, in terms of both their economic and cultural dimension, together with the political opportunities that emerged with the collapse of the Italian party system in the early 1990s. It will highlight in particular the shifting ideological positioning of the LN in accordance with changing political opportunities and how this is strongly linked to its employment of a strategy which harnesses core elements of populism such as an anti-political stance, a tribal approach to politics, a tendency towards charismatic leadership and a nativist, exclusionary discourse.

The League in a changing political environment

The political identity of the LN at the time of its inception was mainly focused on traditional ethno-regionalist claims, which characterised it from 1981 to 1989. From the beginning, the LN positioned itself ideologically so that it bridged the gap between the historical ethno-nationalism that emphasises cultural traits – the Basque movement would be an example – and minority nationalism of the economic kind emerging in affluent European regions, such as Rhone-Alps and Baden-Württemberg (Harvie 1994). Economic grievances seemed to be felt more conspicuously within the movement. While a glorification of supposedly distinctive cultural traits echoes through activists' accounts, one is often led to see economic issues – the asserted deprivation imposed by an iniquitous public finance – as the most fundamental, and it could be supposed that cultural issues were not infrequently emphasised to dignify and legitimate economic grievances.

During its formative period, the Lombard League did not have the historical patterns of national identification at its disposal that older ethno-nationalist movements had. Nor were any of the elements that normally preclude the formation of such movements available, such as a distinctive language or religion. The League advocated a new awareness of Lombard regional identity and the regeneration of Italian politics through a renewal of the political class. Northern Italian enthusiastic acceptance of the League's message puzzled traditional political forces, some of whom had stressed similar themes, such as the moralisation of political life, but without success.

The League acquired some electoral visibility in 1985, when it first competed in the electoral arena. Initially, it participated in a few local elections and obtained 2.5 per cent of the valid votes in the province of Varese. In 1987, it participated in national elections running only in Lombardy and was chosen by 2.7 per cent of registered voters. This figure grew to 6.5 per cent in the European election of 1989 and to 16.4 per cent in the regional election of 1990.

Gradually, the League learned to play a role in a world of institutions that still rejected it, but had to come to terms with its strength. The League's prospects changed dramatically in the early 1990s, as the party system collapsed. It won 20.5 per cent of the vote as the Northern League (where it competed) in the national election – 8.5 per cent of the total national vote – in the general election of 1992, obtaining fifty-five representatives in the chamber and twenty-five senators.

The events of *tangentopoli* saw the LN as the most appropriate political interpreter of a generalised disaffection with the political system. In the collapse of the old system and the emergence of a new one, the LN enjoyed both ideological advantages rooted in its populism and the credibility of being a new actor in an otherwise discredited system (Ruzza and Schmidtke 1993). The need for an institutional renewal that the LN had advocated for years became a shared belief for a majority of Italians.

In 1994, tempted by the prospect of quick success and real policy changes in a federalist direction, the LN accepted the chance to join Berlusconi's new centre-right coalition, ending its political isolation. It obtained 117 representatives and 8.4 per cent of the vote, as well as entrance to the ruling coalition. This changed the features of the party, marking a new phase. As the LN was continuing to win electoral support in a period of political uncertainty, its acceptance grew, but only marginally. However, after a few months, it left the coalition.

There were various reasons why the LN felt that the alliance with the centre-right coalition was detrimental. One is the fact that, as mainstream national parties, the LN's partners in this alliance were eroding its constituency. There were also ideological reasons, with the LN claiming that the other coalition parties ignored its insistence on federalist reforms. Of the two prongs of the LN's discourse – ethno-nationalism and political conservatism – the second came prominently to the fore in this period. However, the new FI party could present itself as a more credible interpreter of neo-liberal values. It was free from the locally protectionist policies that the LN had to advocate to retain its electorate. In addition, the LN was haemorrhaging support in parliament to the more resourceful Berlusconi at an alarming rate. It was undergoing an identity crisis in the party, which led several representatives to defect to FI, and losses of popularity in its traditional strongholds.

After leaving government, losing more than one-third of its parliamentarians who defected, and achieving rather poor electoral results, the LN returned to some of its former themes, adopting a secessionist stance. In 1996, in running separately from the centre-right pole, the LN achieved 10.1 per cent of the vote – a result that confirmed its entrenchment in its traditional strongholds but not its impact on large northern cities. Despite its good electoral performance in 1996, which saw the victory of a centre-left coalition, the LN remained politically isolated and in many ways returned to its pre-institutionalised character of protest movement.

This was a soul-searching period, which threatened the leadership and the core identity of the movement. By pleasing its activists and its populist village-based electorate, it put off its urban moderate electorate. The LN's strategy of espousing secession from the Italian state was excessive and threatening to much of the northern middle class that had previously supported it. In a set of local elections in November 1997 and afterwards, the LN maintained its support in small centres, but lost it in large cities such as Milan, Turin and Genoa.

In this period, a significant exodus took place of people who had thought that the LN would become 'respectable' and could be used for personal and social advancement. Interviews point to the defection of industrialists who thought that the newly acquired political power of the LN would result in state contracts of various sorts and real influence in industrial policy. The same thing happened with a large number of professionals who, on a smaller scale, had had similar concerns or had thought that the LN would have given them jobs in local politics.

A number of new initiatives of an accentuated symbolic character revived the LN's social movement-style activism, and the social component of activism was revamped. A greenshirt uniformed organisation of activists was funded, the 'Padanian Guards', new pilgrimages took place to the source of the Po river – the longest river in the region and a 'national' symbol. A new generation of young activists emerged for whom the sense of common belonging was as crucial as it had been in the early 1980s. Institutionally, the strategy of the LN was to abandon efforts to be accepted and attempt the creation of independent institutions. They were to create their own internal parties (formalising different approach to politics in 'currents'), their own media, schools, trade unions, etc. The LN also sought to become entrenched in local politics and to develop a cohort of local administrators who could achieve a reputation for effective local administration. Nevertheless, the continuing radical rhetoric was making the conservative electorate uneasy and increasingly attracted to FI.

In the European elections of 1999, the LN was again heavily defeated, losing about a quarter of its 1994 northern Italian electorate. Bossi decided to approach an emerging conflict between activists and administrators in a new way and instead of siding with the radical base – as he had done previously – proposed a fundamental transformation of the LN's approach. At the Pontida festival – an annual gathering with great symbolic value for the LN – after resigning his mandate and being re-confirmed as undisputed leader, he declared that the epoch of uncompromising separatism had to end. This marked the end of yet another phase in the LN's history and the beginning of a new one. According to its leader, a new more strategically adept LN had to emerge. Alliances had to be accepted, even if they were unpalatable to base militants. At the Padua administrative election, the LN formed an unprecedented alliance with FI and AN – an alliance that had not even taken place in 1994 when there were two separate alliances, one in the north between FI and the LN and one in the south between AN and FI.

A re-institutionalisation in the context of an accentuated right-wing political identity led to a long experience in government until 2006. Despite again suffering heavy losses (it achieved 3.9 per cent of the vote in the lower chamber), the LN was granted three ministries in the new Berlusconi government, as it was indispensable to the success of the coalition. The LN in government proved a relatively accommodating ally. Its big devolution goals were frustrated by the presence in the government coalition of the centralist AN. Just prior to leaving government in 2001, the centre left had approved a regionalist reform that was not supported by the LN because it was considered too tame. This law was however welcomed by regional elites across the political spectrum, undermining the LN's claim to be the only true defender of regionalism. Under the Berlusconi government, a weakened LN could not obtain any significant improvement on that reform. With some hostility and embarrassment from the AN, a moderate federalist reform of the state was approved by the coalition. The constitutional reform package approved by the centre-right government, while falling short of the LN's ambitions as regards devolution (for example through a fiscal federalism giving regions control over revenue raising), would have given more power to the regions in schools, police and health policy. However, a referendum to confirm the changes held on June 2006 resulted in rejection of the proposals, constituting a serious defeat for the LN.

Following electoral defeat, the return to opposition and the defeat of the devolution reform in 2006, a new phase of re-definition of goals and tactics began again. In retrospect, many LN activists were able to assess the value of the alliance with Berlusconi, and many realised that the fruits of collaboration were rather limited. Once again, the LN started to re-define its role – it began to publicly re-evaluate its position – a positioning by now traditionally set between an activist social movement party and a party in government, with occasional and generally limited deviations. The LN continued to support the centre-right alliance, but with degrees of doubt and ambivalence. Occasional hints at a return to secessionism were made by Bossi, but these were symbolic gestures not taken too seriously by its political allies.

This attitude implied a concerted attempt to keep and strengthen the territorial rooting of the party instead of simply relying on Berlusconi's media empire. During the 2008 electoral campaign – but also before and after – the LN, more than any other party, consolidated its strong territorial presence through petitions and other protest events. These included manifestations against projects for mosques or public housing for immigrants. This attention to real contact with its constituency paid off through a spectacular victory. The LN eroded the centre-left electorate frightened by ethnic rivalry on the job market and security concerns. It also attracted votes from other centre-right parties through a more decisively anti-political and also protectionist anti-neo-liberal image. It could also profit from skills in local administration which were now well honed and gave credibility to its northern protectionist claims. For these reasons, positive results, which for very long have been interpreted as essentially based on a protest vote, are now increasingly seen by both journalists and scholars as the outcome of superior territorial rooting (Staff Reporter 2008c).

Elections and electorates

The LN's electoral support has come mainly from the former Christian Democratic electoral heartlands, which began to decline long before the appearance of the Leagues (see table 3.1 in Diamanti 2003a: 59). As a northern Italian regionalist formation, the LN's electoral constituencies are in all northern Italian regions, but its strongholds are in Lombardy and Veneto. In general, it is important to note that both regions exhibited substantial stability during the post-war republic (up to the 1990s). Regional governments (*Giunte*) in Lombardy had always been drawn from the DC and PSI. In Veneto, governments were composed of either the DC alone or in association with the PSI (Vassallo and Baldini 2000: 545). Since the fall of the old party system, centre-right formations – particularly Forza Italia – have been pre-eminent in both regions. Within this relatively stable context, analysis of electoral trends reveals an initial rapid expansion and then a moderate reduction in support for the LN. Figure 4.1 illustrates the oscillating level of support for the LN in its two strongest regions.

As we see from Figure 4.1, the LN's electoral performance peaked in the early and mid-1990s and remained relatively constant at a lower level in the following years.[2] In 2008, however, it achieved a new and substantial success, which brought it back to the level of the earlier peak – a success that many observers related to its superior ability to retain local roots in a period when other parties appeared increasingly distant from their electorate.

It is also important to reiterate that the 2008 election was disputed in a new climate in which the LN could reassert its territorial roots against other centre-right parties engaged in a still untested process of re-invention, as reflected in the metaphor used by Berlusconi who, in November 2007, likening his coalition to a ghost (Staff Reporter 2007d). As many observers noted, the creation of the PdL also diluted the AN's distinctive ideological identity (Giannini 2008). The LN remained the only large party of the right with strong territorial roots and a distinct radical message. The merger of the two main parties of the centre left in the new PD also had the effect of freeing portions of the electorate, uncertain about the dissolution of strong Christian and leftist identities in an unproven new formation. We were thus at a turning

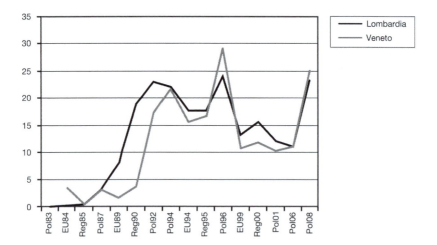

Figure 4.1 Electoral trends of LN in Lombardy and Veneto. Source: elaboration by Paolo Pasi on the basis of Biorcio (1997: 47), Diamanti (1996: 64, 81, 90), Fava (2000), Legnante and Maino (2000), Schmidtke (1996: 179) and ministerial data.

point in Italian politics, in which the innovation of FI as a party scarcely rooted in territorial identities (Diamanti 2003b) was being extended to the other parties – leaving only the LN as the proud defender of its identity and territoriality. This was reflected in an ability to assert a strong presence through small but frequent protest events, the use of local media and local government for publicity and the use of extensive political symbolism by its sympathisers in everyday life.

Throughout its history, a peculiarity of the LN has been its differing electoral results within the same regions – an indication of its strong territorial roots. While it is strong in Lombardy and Veneto, there are different levels of success in certain provinces, and there are also provinces outside these regions, such as Pordenone in Friuli–Venezia–Giulia and Cuneo in Piedmont, where the LN has achieved strong results.[3] As Cento Bull and Gilbert note (Cento Bull and Gilbert 2001: 79), the significant factor in these areas are the 'territorial political subcultures', a term utilised by Trigilia (1986: 13) in the tradition of local government studies to refer to 'some areas characterized by a specific political tradition and by a number of institutions – parties, interest groups, cultural and voluntary organizations – which are rooted in the territory and share the same political origins'. In the early republican years, these 'white areas' had a close political and religious tie to the DC. With the process of secularisation, this relationship became more and more instrumental, and the DC became the party that represented the interests of small and medium enterprises. During the 1980s, the DC became increasingly clientelistic but also, in the new harsher economic climate, increasingly unable to satisfy the needs of its clientele. It gradually lost its capacity to represent the interests of the northern industrial areas (Cento Bull and Gilbert 2001: 79–82). In opposition to it, the LN developed as the party that linked the interests of small business with the request for a serious process of regionalisation (Cento Bull and Gilbert 2001: 90–93). The distribution of votes for the LN seems to be related to the socio-economic reality of these areas, with its performance particularly strong where small and medium enterprises are diffuse.

During the emerging period of the early 1990s, the electorate of the LN appeared to reflect the social characteristics of the entire northern electorate with the exception of an over-representation of the middle classes – particularly the self-employed (Biorcio 1997: 251). From 1991 to 1996, the LN achieved an increase in support among manual workers. In terms of education, the most interesting data concerned the limited percentage of university graduates. This has remained a distinctive feature of the LN. The LN then lost much of its middle-class electorate and support in big cities, but has remained entrenched in small towns and villages.

A large portion of the LN's early electorate rapidly migrated to Forza Italia leaving it with a level of support of just over 4 per cent in the 1999 EU election (Diamanti 2003a: 72). 1999 was a turning point, after which the LN electorate characterised itself more clearly as a right-wing and no longer a mainly ethno-nationalist electorate. The profile of LN voters has since remained essentially constant: more concentrated in villages and small centres rather than in big cities, less educated than the average for the Italian population and distinctly identified with the locality and the north of Italy in terms of territorial belonging.

A low level of electoral support continued to characterise the LN and marked its failed attempt to reach the 4 per cent threshold in the national election of 2001, despite the resounding success of its coalition partners (Pasquino 2001). However, in the European election of 2004 and in the regional elections of 2005, it regained some of the lost ground (respectively 5.1 per cent and 5.6 per cent at national level). In 2006, with a new electoral law which re-introduced elements of proportional representation, and a narrow defeat for the right-wing coalition, the performance of the LN was considered just acceptable. It retained its electorate in its stronghold regions in Lombardy and Veneto, but it lost support in other northern regions, notably in Piedmont. On the national level, it achieved 4.58 per cent of the vote in the lower chamber. In 2008, this increased to 8.3 per cent giving the deciding edge to the new winning coalition.

Sociologically, in recent years, the profile of the LN has changed. In 2001, the LN was, as previously, a predominantly male party (59 per cent). It included fewer people in the age group 25–44 (20.5 per cent out of 38.1 per cent of the population) but more in the age group 45–68 (48.7 per cent out of 32.2 per cent). Artisans constituted the professional background of many voters (46.2 per cent out of 24 per cent). LN voters were less educated, with a higher rate of voters interrupting education after middle school (30.8 per cent versus 26.8 per cent of the population) and a lower rate of voters achieving college degrees.[4] In 2006, the LN electorate had a profile similar to the one identified in recent years. It was an electorate predominantly male (60.4 per cent) and older, with the age group 45–64 over-represented. It was relatively uneducated (with a proportion who interrupted education at middle-school level of 49.2 per cent against a national proportion of 29.6 per cent, and a proportion of college graduates of 2.8 per cent, which is below the national proportion of 5.1 per cent). In terms of occupation, the LN electorate tended to be more highly represented in the category of entrepreneurs (16.7 per cent against a national proportion of 10.8 per cent) and artisans (38.9 per cent versus 26.7 per cent).

In 2008, the LN's electorate broadened and increasingly included workers who had previously voted for the left, but also for other centre-right parties (Meloni 2008). It also broadened geographically, the LN significantly increasing its vote share in the Emilia-Romagna region and doubling it in the previously leftist city of Bologna (Staff Reporter 2008b).

The LN has typically been viewed as torn between appealing to middle-class voters with mainstream liberal and moderately federalist policies and coalitions with other centre-right parties, and appealing to smaller, territorially circumscribed and less affluent identity-driven constituencies of border areas. Electoral results since 1999 have seen its support generally confined to the latter.

Leadership

The LN is a political formation dominated by its leader. At any point in time, the influential and successful cadres are those currently enjoying the favours of its fickle leader. The overwhelmingly dominant position of the leader is generally well known and accepted by followers. As studies of the popularity of LN politicians show, the difference between Bossi and others is very large. Understanding its leadership is the key to understanding the LN at all territorial levels. Bossi plays the role of the charismatic leader of a populist movement, able to interpret the hearts and minds of the popular heartland and possessing a kind of political sixth sense as to the tactics that need to be employed to defend their interests. While remaining 'of the people', Bossi is perceived as possessing unique qualities, a 'man of destiny' capable of leading them to salvation (McDonnell 2006: 130).

In his youth, Bossi was a communist party sympathiser and later an admirer of ethno-nationalist and regionalist movements such as the Unione Valdotaine in the French-speaking Valle d'Aosta. His political career took off in 1987 when he became the first and only senator of the Lombard League. The nickname 'the *senatur*' in the local dialect stuck for the rest of his political career. All biographies point to Bossi's complex political personality: he has always acted as the agitator with his characteristic fiery rhetoric, fighting for the federalist or secessionist 'revolution', but he has simultaneously presented himself as the prudent statesman guiding events towards a peaceful transformation of the country's political system. Notions such as 'responsibility for the democratic order' and 'need for stability' enter his political discourse at the same time as the threat of angry villagers brandishing rifles to fight for secession from the Italian state.

Bossi has traditionally formed alliances that he would publicly explain to followers as purely instrumental – at times announcing his contempt for his allies and then soon after denying what had just been clearly stated. This was the case with his alliance with Berlusconi, who Bossi despised and had attacked for years before entering into coalition with his party. He called him Berluskaiser deriding his authoritarian personality, and accused him of dealings with the Sicilian mafia. However, Bossi did not hesitate to support Berlusconi when he could justify it to his electorate as a sensible strategic move. Suggestions of financial support from Berlusconi as a reason for engagement with Forza Italia have also been made repeatedly.

Throughout the LN's history, as a strategy, Bossi has continued to vigorously attack those forces with whom the LN has co-operated just as he attacked its political opponents. The LN has been at the same time a movement among movement activists and a party among party activists. This is because, early in the history of the LN, Bossi realised that it was crucial to maintain the LN's distinctive political identity as a social movement, to stress that any accord with old parties was only limited and tactical. On this distinction between short- and long-term goals rested the LN's claim to stand outside the logic of party competition as a qualitatively different political entity. Thus any connection to the existent political system has always been presented – at least to the activist base – as temporary, as a tactical step towards a new political system.

While detractors have accused Bossi of a confused and ever changing political vision, one can in fact identify a set of key themes that have received variable attention over the years but were never completely abandoned. These themes emerge clearly in his discourse. One important theme is the idea that in his vision the LN is more than a party. It is a movement rooted socio-culturally in local communities and, for this reason, as in the case of other ethno-nationalist movements, Bossi claims to transcend all political divisions and party identifications. On the essentialist difference of his political formation, he states: 'The Northern League is not a party, that is to say, it does not represent a political part. Rather it is a political movement for the freedom of the North and for Italian federalism' (Bossi 1996: 109).

Bossi suggests – as many similar movements do – that the real conflict is between centre and periphery and not between left and right. As leader of the Lombard League he proclaimed:

> Lombards! It doesn't matter how old you are, what job you've got, what political side you are on: what matter is that you are – and we all are – Lombards. This is the really important fact and the time has come to remember it and give it political concreteness. In fact, it is because we are Lombards that we all have a fundamental common interest and all our motives of division in parties of any colour must take second place: Italian political parties that use us instrumentally and deter us from defending our own interests and serve other people's interests (and theirs, first of all!).
>
> *Lombardia Autonomista*, March 1982 – reprinted in Bossi (1996: 7)

The attempt to present the LN as outside the logic of party competition has been increasingly contradicted over the years by the attention given to political alliances. Possibly in order to rescue some of its 'out of the system' identity, Bossi occasionally seemed to be politically irresponsible and even dangerous. Yet the further success of the LN became critically dependent upon achieving concrete results. Five years in government was then the standard that many former supporters used to judge the LN's effectiveness.

Examples of Bossi's colourful discourse over the years are numerous. For example, Bossi was convicted by a court in 2001 for defaming the Italian flag in a speech in 1997. He had said: 'When I see the tricolour, I go mad. I use the tricolour to wipe my arse' (Staff Reporter 2001). He has also offended the church, invoking the ire of his catholic centre-right allies in 2004 by stating:

> We need to withdraw the eight per thousand lire [special tax covenant] from the church, make them walk barefoot and give them the chance of acting like the Franciscans [monks]. Finally religion will be saved.
>
> Luzi (2004)

Many of Bossi's more contentious statements have come in relation to the immigration question. For example, he made the LN's welfare chauvinism clear in 2003 stating:

> There are no houses for immigrants. There can not be any. In Milan there are already 42,000 persons waiting for a house. Houses should be given first to the Lombards and not the first bingo bongo that arrives.
>
> Passalacqua (2003e)

Earlier in the same year, he had caused outrage by making the following suggestions as to how to deal with the boats bringing clandestine migrants to Italian shores:

> At the second or third warning, boom ... fire the canon. Without mincing one's words. A canon which hits whoever. Otherwise we'll never finish.
>
> Cavalera (2003)

As noted already, many of Bossi's irresponsible comments have come when in government, as if to send a signal to his party militants and hard core supporters that he is still with them, and to underline the movement's unique identity. Following the return to opposition in 2006 and the failure of the devolution referendum, he again hinted at a return to a more radical secessionist strategy:

> The Lombards have never taken out their rifles, but to do this there is always a first time.
>
> Buzzanca (2007)

These threats continued following the return to government, for example in November 2008, Bossi stated in a speech to party activists:

> The road to federalism is a difficult one, but this time we will manage to bring it home, if not everyone can begin to grease their rifles.
>
> Vecchi (2008a)

Possibly imagined conspiracies followed by ruthless expulsions have characterised the history of the party. If this has ensured continuity of leadership, it has alienated many gifted supporters, administrators and intellectuals, undermining the chances of the party developing a much needed skilled political elite. Not only did the few gifted intellectuals attracted to the LN, such as the political philosopher Gianfranco Miglio, and some others leave the party in bitter disagreement, but the lack of an intellectual elite was compounded by an electorate with generally low levels of education (Biorcio 1997b: 252), which Bossi never appeared to consider a problem, but which has generated much ridicule among Italian political elites throughout the history of the LN. For decades, Bossi has led the party decisively, confronting internal dissent, reacting to frequent factional struggles with expulsions and imparting quick and often unexpected changes of policy. He devised the original format of a political formation that at least at the beginning rejected the normal practices of Italian political parties, such as proper rules of internal bureaucracy and a clear division of labour. Particularly in the adoption of a direct and conversational linguistic style, Bossi sought to differentiate the LN from a discredited political elite which typically expressed itself in a convoluted Byzantine language (Ruzza 2000).

However, Bossi's distinctive leadership style was abruptly interrupted when he suffered a massive stroke that left him in a hospital bed for many months in 2004, and from which he has not fully recovered. This also curbed his career in public office, with Bossi eventually resigning his position as minister for institutional reform (a position to which he returned in 2008). After 2004, the party went through an extended period of uncertainty with a weakened leader, who nevertheless refused to withdraw. In-fighting, splinter group defections and disputes over the LN's direction ensued. Nevertheless, the party has retained enough electoral support to continue to play a relevant role in the politics of the Italian right, with Bossi remaining at the helm and continuing to inspire devotion among the party loyalists. Since 2005, Bossi's health has improved somewhat and his presence in daily political life has increased. To justify his continuing appeal, one could argue that his leadership image has changed from the symbolic representation of the ordinary villager of the north to the weak but dignified father figure of the movement founder. The tone of his interviews has also changed; his style has expanded to include statesmenlike utterances, such as when he declares to a newspaper (and his statement is reported on the LN website) that he is trying to moderate Berlusconi's excessively fiery rhetoric.

> Every political season requires an appropriate attitude. You cannot always stir up trouble (fare casino). We went to government with a pact with our electorate: we promised federalism and security. And it is this that we need to bring home. Quickly. For the League, all that can distort from these objectives is an obstacle that needs to be removed or resolved.
> Berizzi (2008)

Nevertheless, such utterances were balanced by occasional reversions to the demagogic discourse of old. For example, in July 2008, Bossi was criticised by the presidents of the two parliamentary chambers (Fini and Schifani) for criticising the national anthem (erroneously referring to its reference to Italy as a slave of Rome) and raising his middle finger to illustrate his point. He also appeared to have returned to the LN's historic anti-southern discourse in his call to halt the number of teachers coming from the south of Italy to teach in northern schools, as they did not understand the culture or history of the north (Luzi 2008).

The party organisation

The League emerged initially as a cultural and social movement and, soon after, it became a regionalist party but retained the organisational characteristics of both a party and a movement. The unruly protest-oriented cadres and activists of the social movement League have co-existed often with difficulty with the more institutionalised functionaries and supporters of the party. The different components have been kept united by the extremely strong influence of the founder and undisputed leader, Umberto Bossi. In this sense, the party is largely the creation of Bossi, and it is mainly a vehicle through which identities are cemented in countless political rituals, and enemies and deviants are marginalised. However, with the engagement in government roles and with Bossi's illness in 2004, the party has become more important for the co-ordination and development of institutional strategies.

The party's initial informal character was reflected in the small number of staff – just five as late as 1989 – working out of a small apartment, which grew to ten in 1992 and then to about 100 in 1993 when the party moved to a larger location in Milan (Tambini 2001: 90). In the same period, Bossi introduced a system of tiers of membership, whereby important positions in the party required extensive periods of previous membership. Gradually, an internal bureaucracy emerged,[5] but the essentially hierarchical character of this party has been kept in place by the use of informal rules in which Bossi's views remain the deciding factor in policy formation and in orienting the allocation of responsibilities within the party (Tambini 2001: 93).

The LN is organised in 'national sections' – a term that emphasises its ethno-nationalist character but also the plurality of components within it. The dominant sections are the Lombard and the Veneto sections. Other sections are those of Trentino, South Tyrol, Emilia, Romagna, Friuli–Venezia–Giulia, Liguria, Marche, Piedmont, Tuscany, Umbria and Val d'Aosta. In organisational terms, the LN's political life has been shaped by large meetings at which Bossi would deliver long charismatic speeches and indicate new priorities and sometimes strategic U-turns. Elaborately staged congresses are important occasions for the LN. Also important are meetings at Pontida – a small village near Bergamo where a large festival and LN meeting is held annually to celebrate the battle of Legnano, the historic battle where the warrior Alberto da Giussano fought for the Lombard League – the historical League of northern Italian municipalities from which the League took its name. On this occasion, LN militants come from throughout northern Italy in delegations and discuss and socialise. Slogans are reiterated and a new generation of activists is socialised. For instance, during the June 2008 Pontida festival, one could observe in the nearby LN campsite several dozen young people in the age range 16–19 singing activist songs and slogans. These included chants of 'we are not Neapolitans' and other more insulting anti-southern slogans with reference to a set of corruption scandals in which organised crime was found to control illegal landfills. These slogans marked a strong difference in tone from the official LN line as enunciated by the *Padania* newspaper the next day, which lauded the arrival of a southern Italian delegation.

Great use is made on this occasion of political symbolism. Flags, anthems and a vast array of LN souvenirs and merchandise ranging from posters to watches, Padanian 'currency' and neckties are marketed.

Over the years, the LN has sought to strengthen its relations with civil society by creating a set of organisations which could address a variety of purposes and therefore become relevant in the daily life of its members. These ranged from recreational organisations to trade unions, professional associations and mutual support groups.[6] At least in some periods – particularly during its 'secessionist' phase as Diamanti argues (Diamanti 2003a: 76) – concern with involving members in a project of creating a territorially based community has been an important electoral strategy and an ideological goal for the LN. It is in this context that 'Padanian associationism' has merited special attention.

The presence of associations supposedly testifies to the LN's roots in its territory and to its broad appeal, and reflects the desire to circumvent traditional associational resources which are typically characterised in the Italian context as connected to the catholic or ex-communist subculture. It also reflects how left–right distinctions or class divisions are subordinated to a more essential national community. Furthermore, one should bear in mind that, from its inception, the League recruited entire pre-existing social networks, reflecting awareness of the electoral advantage of keeping a presence in recreational and corporatist networks (Ruzza and Schmidtke 1992). However, several organisations created by the League have never represented a real constituency, and have been supported mainly for ideological reasons. They are given special prominence on the LN website, in the media and at the Pontida festivals.

As the fundamental cleavage within its ideology is the centre–periphery, there is a view within the party that other conflicts can and should be incorporated into the movement and resolved internally. Thus, the LN has tried to promote the image of a lively internal dialogue between left and right. This has included for instance the creation of a northern Italian parliament (which was located in Mantua), in which different factions would argue their views and take sides on a left–right divide.

In claiming to transcend left–right rivalry, the LN has occasionally hinted at the possibility of an alliance with the left, possibly of a limited nature to secure a decentralising constitutional reform (McDonnell 2006: 131), although an electoral alliance would seem very unlikely given the conflict between its increasingly right-wing xenophobia and the left's universalism and multiculturalism. Nevertheless, the centre left and the LN did collaborate to prop up the caretaker administration of Lamberto Dini in 1995–96.

In-depth interviews with activists indicate the adoption of a fairly instrumental approach to forming coalitions – the belief that the leader Bossi is able to assess what is best for Padania and act accordingly regardless of contingent left–right divides. It is in this perspective that, even with some disconcert, the activist base could accept the frequent reversals of attitudes towards allies such as Berlusconi, who was described on occasions as a corrupt mafioso and in other periods in the history of the LN was seen as an inspiring leader, a reformer, an innovator. A similarly changing attitude characterises relations with the AN, described alternatively as unacceptable fascists, unreconstructed centralists or as allies. In any event, the instrumental approach to coalition formation allows the LN to retain a fundamental undercurrent of hostility to all allies and therefore a plurality of views and expressions in different arenas with allies in the institutions often vilified at activist events.

The party in government

The LN's behaviour in government has been markedly different in its periods of office (1994, 2001–6 and 2008 onwards). In the first period, it was a strong coalition partner, assertive but also fearful of seeing its parliamentarians lured by Berlusconi's resources. In the second, it was a much weaker and essentially compliant partner. It is perhaps not a coincidence that, for the 5 years of the governing coalition, Bossi was portrayed by cartoonists as a small and irate dog at Berlusconi's leash. Nonetheless, while the LN voted for all the controversial *ad personam* laws that were viewed as protecting Berlusconi's personal and media interests, it remained in a state of constant and well-publicised tension with both the AN and the UDC.

Indeed, the LN continued throughout the period in government to play the dual role of faithful ally but also of populist social movement. It has been suggested that, in government after 2001, the LN managed – unlike populist movements in government elsewhere in Europe – to walk the tightrope of reconciling its radical constituency and its institutional character, appearing to have 'one foot in and one foot out' of government (Albertazzi and McDonnell 2005). It did this by uniting around a number of clear objectives, most obviously devolution, but also restrictive policies on immigration and a populist localist and anti-cosmopolitan stance on issues such as globalisation, immigration and European integration. Unlike in 1994, when Bossi quarrelled with Berlusconi and eventually brought down the government, in 2001, he sought to portray his party as a faithful ally to Berlusconi and FI, in the hope that this would deliver the objective of devolution, as promised by Berlusconi when the alliance with the LN had been forged once again in 2000. This therefore meant facilitating the passage of the so-called *ad personam* laws.

Bossi himself was initially appointed as minister for institutional reform, responsible for overseeing devolution and other constitutional reforms, while other LN exponents were in key ministerial roles, Roberto Maroni as minister for welfare and Roberto Castelli as justice minister piloting Berlusconi's desired reform of the judiciary. However, the LN retained an oppositional populist anti-establishment stance by constantly attacking the positions of the other coalition allies, the AN and UDC, cast as recycled professional First

Republic politicians. As already noted, this caused disgruntlement within the latter two parties, given the perception that Berlusconi was overindulgent of his fellow Lombard populist Bossi. Indeed, Bossi, Berlusconi and the finance minister, Tremonti, were depicted as an 'axis of the north' controlling the direction and priorities of the government (Albertazzi and McDonnell 2005: 956). The repeated references to *Roma ladrona* by Bossi and other LN exponents caused particular annoyance to the leaders of the UDC and AN. Despite the LN's shift towards an emphasis on Christian identity, the attack on Rome-based institutions also sometimes spilled over into attacks on the tax privileges of the Vatican, as already noted. Fini accused Bossi of having 'over-stepped the limits of decency' at the end of February 2004 for attacking the pope and 'cardinals who speak only in the name of the god of money'.[7]

In this period, the LN's growing Euro-sceptic, anti-immigration and Islamophobic stances came increasingly to the fore (McDonnell 2006: 128–30). Bossi and other exponents made a number of well-documented outbursts that could be categorised as xenophobic. As regards European policy, the hostile position taken by Bossi to the entry into circulation of the euro at the beginning of 2002 would lead to the resignation of Renato Ruggiero – dismissed by Bossi as an unelected bureaucrat – as foreign minister (Albertazzi and McDonnell 2005: 965). In March 2002, during the fourth LN congress in Milan, Bossi referred to the EU as 'a Stalinist super-state – the USSR of the West'. Brussels was frequently depicted as a den of paedophiles.

There was also a strong focus on classic 'law and order' issues, which was exemplified by the LN proposals in 2004 for a 'ministry of crime' and for rewards for apprehending criminals to be instituted. In 2005, following a number of well-publicised sexual attacks on Italian women (of which migrants were depicted as the leading perpetrators), Calderoli proposed castration as a punishment. Nevertheless, the law and order issue did provide for some common ground with the LN's erstwhile allies. For example, the AN and the LN joined forces to block attempts to secure presidential pardons for the former leaders of left-wing extra-parliamentary groups such as Adriano Sofri of Lotta Continua, who had been convicted of a politically motivated murder committed in the 1970s.

While the LN progressed in its identification as a rightist party, it retained its regionalist focus, threatening its allies – particularly the AN – with withdrawal from government if the devolution reform was not approved quickly. It also continued to insist on issues of cultural policy. For instance, in 2003, it achieved a controversial transfer of the second national television channel (RAI2) to Milan, where it could be politically controlled more easily. This was opposed by the AN and UDC, reflecting the longstanding tension between nationalist and ethno-nationalist agendas. The LN also differed from other partners in emphasising policies of local economic protectionism against neo-liberal policies. This occurred for instance in 2003 when there was a controversy within the government as to whether to support stringent controls to enforce EU milk quotas and detect evasion and fraud. It also occurred the following year when the LN insisted on state subsidies to the national airline company Alitalia, which employs a large number of personnel in the LN heartlands north of Milan. The protectionist stance was also reflected in the call for tariffs on cheap Chinese imports that were perceived as highly damaging to small businesses in the north.

The movement was plunged into confusion by the massive stroke that Bossi suffered in March 2004, forcing him to disappear from public life for a significant period. This led some exponents to seek to express themselves more forcefully in order to keep his populist flame alive. For example, at the end of the same month, the LN deputy Alessandro Cè was reprimanded in the chamber of deputies by its vice-president Publio Fiori (of the AN) for his repeated use of the *Roma ladrona* term. When asked to leave the chamber, Cè refused, and his LN colleagues formed a human barricade to prevent his ejection, amid cries of 'fascist' towards Fiore and his AN colleagues. The stand-off lasted several hours.

Following Bossi's resignation from government in 2004, his place as minister for constitutional reform was taken by Roberto Calderoli, who stepped up the populist discourse on a number of themes. This was particularly notable following the 7 July bombings in London in 2005, when he repeatedly invoked a 'clash of civilisations' between Christianity and Islam. Calderoli was eventually forced to resign from government after his inflammatory gesture in the wake of the worldwide controversy over cartoons depicting the prophet Mohamed published in a Danish newspaper in early 2006. Calderoli revealed on a TV show that he was wearing a T-shirt depicting the images.

The LN's influence in government diminished following the departure of Bossi, as reflected also in the enforced exit of his close ally, Tremonti, following the 2004 European election and Fini's elevation to the foreign ministry. Nevertheless, the eventual passage of the constitutional reform bill in 2005 was trumpeted by Bossi as vindication of the LN's participation in government, despite the package falling short of its original aspirations as regards the extent of devolution. The later rejection of the reform in the referendum of 2006 would place in question the value of the LN's participation in government. Despite the portrayal of the LN as having had a disproportionate influence in government, its policy impact was indeed rather limited in the second Berlusconi government. Aside from the ultimately failed devolution, the immigration law had also proved ineffective in terms of combating clandestine migration (its measures being undermined by judicial rulings) while also similarly providing for a mass regularisation of nearly 700,000 previously irregular immigrants (Zincone 2006). Moreover, while LN spokesmen – whether in government or not – had been free to make numerous controversial statements and proposals on core policy issues ranging from law and order to Europe (e.g. on withdrawal from the euro and rejection of Turkish accession and the EU constitution) and trade policy and protectionism, these were largely ignored in the framing of government policy.

This situation may have changed in the third Berlusconi government. The electoral victory gave the LN a newly authoritative influence on the winning coalition and appears to have constrained the Berlusconi government as never before (Verderami 2008). Notably, both Bossi and Calderoli returned to government, the former once again as minister for institutional reform, and the latter as minister for legislative simplification, while Maroni was given the important post (for a coalition emphasising law and order and strong action on immigration) of interior minister. Maroni's ministerial role proved crucial in advancing the agenda of the LN following the 2008 election. A new and strict government decree regulating security issues was passed in early 2009. Among other provisions regulating immigration, it blocks universal access to free health care for clandestine migrants and obliges doctors who treat them to report them to the police. Most importantly, clandestine immigration is newly defined as a crime. There were also attempts to legitimate vigilante groups who patrol cities at night.

Ideology

Culturally, the League project was feasible because it filled an ideological vacuum left behind by those political and social institutions that dominated the political scene in Italy until the 1980s: communism and catholicism. The concurrent processes of secularisation and crisis of the communist ideology were undermining the Italian institutional framework at the local level. Old institutions were not infrequently abandoned, and with them disappeared the socialisation and rules that they provided. A political vacuum emerged that the League came to fill by providing new forms of aggregation, but also a new way of defining interests: a new ideology. Catholic human solidarity and, to a lesser extent, communist class solidarity made way for northern Italian solidarity. Within these new parameters, the defence of the economic interests of craftsmen and small industrialists could be legitimated with reference to a larger ideal community of northern Italians. On to the central ideological features of ethno-nationalism, the League added a set of peripheral ideological contents, which changed over time and in different arenas. The shift from an ethno-nationalist party to a right-wing party significantly contributed to a re-definition of its peripheral ideological features. In later years, xenophobic sentiments became more frequently aired. However, its cultural strategy of asserting the importance of cultural and linguistic elements was not totally abandoned. It re-emerges frequently in the party newspaper *La Padania*, launched in 1997, and constitutes a different but important source of ideological content.

For this reason, in the case of the LN, it is important but not sufficient to analyse its electoral programmes. In considering the ideology of the LN, we performed two different content analyses of different sources. On the one hand, electoral programmes were analysed in order to identify political priorities. Subsequently, the LN programmatic materials were re-analysed to identify more specific views on immigration, which are increasingly central to this party. This is supplemented by analysis of *La Padania* and other statements by LN politicians. In a different analysis of views of culture and language, we examined *La Padania* again. Language, in particular, is a key element of distinction, which has received much attention from the leaders of the movement over the years. By examining the role attributed to the Lombard language, and subsequently to the entire family of northern Italian dialects, we will tap into the self-understanding of this movement.

Ideologically, the LN has been characterised by much eclecticism and frequent re-orientations, which have been motivated by changing political opportunities. Its ideological variability has been made possible by the tactical thinking and whims of its charismatic leader – Bossi – but also by his subtle political intuition and his refusal to be hindered by a desire to appear consistent. His complete control of the party, ruthless purges and absolute power have allowed for frequent and relatively effortless re-definitions of the direction of the party. However, the ideological mix has sometimes been unappealing and even confused to some part of the LN electorate. It has been, above all, unappealing to mainstream social and political institutions.

Culturally, the main ideas of the movement proved from the start unappealing to any Italian social institution. They appeared anti-capitalist in their glorification of localism and their indictment of large capitalist enterprise, even if the LN somewhat unconvincingly professed to believe in the values of the free market and enterprise. The LN's ideology appeared at times anti-Christian in its intolerance towards migrants, who are generally poor and in need of support. Yet at other times, somewhat unconvincingly, the LN used Christianity as a source of identification and mobilisation.

During its formative period, the League did not have historical regional patterns of identification at its disposal as older ethno-nationalist movements do. It could not therefore develop its ideology using pre-existing materials grounded in popular culture. The party was in a position to construct its ideology in relative freedom. This freedom was utilised to bring together in a new ideological package a heterogeneous set of traits that were appealing to the electorate. The 'manufactured' character of the LN's ideology, its use of nation-state symbolism to posit a territorial homogeneity that never existed before and to construct a notion of symbolic and political unity in the Italian north have been explored in the literature on the party (Cachafeiro 2002).

Lacking the legitimacy that nationalist movements find in their history, the LN has been able to adapt its ideological package relatively easily to suit changing electoral preferences and even appeal to different audiences at the same time. As could be expected, ideological variation relates to the radicalism of the message, with a more radical and separatist focus expressed in communications for its activists and a more moderate one for its general electorate. Also, in areas where the LN could present itself as an element of social integration at community level, it has stressed linguistic factors and its contribution to collective belonging throughout its history (Ruzza 1996). However, the amount of radicalism as well as the nature of grievances and proposed solutions has also changed over time.

At the beginning of the 1990s, the focus on Lombardy was expanded to include the entire north of the country and other regional leagues, within the Northern League. Some of the more local Lombard symbolism was abandoned. In this period, the ideology moved from a local and regional focus to a federalist one based on the proposal to split the country into three macro regions (Giordano 2001). After the 1993 local elections, the LN gained control of a set of large northern Italian cities and began to believe that, with the collapse of the traditional centre of the Italian political system, and by taming its ideology and focusing on centre-right Thatcherite policies, it could aspire to a prominent role in national politics. It also stressed law and order policies, not infrequently connected to its anti-southern ethos. However, in this period, Forza Italia also emerged to fill the vacuum left by the collapse of traditional parties. It competed in ideological terms on very similar ground, undermining the LN's claim to a prominent national role.

At this stage, a re-radicalisation and a return to ethno-nationalism appeared inevitable and, in the mid-1990s, the LN moved to embrace a strong separatist ideology. It also re-discovered ethnic identity and linguistic issues. It was not, however, a mere return to origins. New factors such as awareness of the acceleration of processes of economic globalisation and the increasing presence of immigrants offered an opportunity for the LN to update its proclaimed role as defender of the territory. In this context, one can explain the growing emphasis on anti-EU sentiment and against migration. In this context, one can also frame the specification of the territory which, in the political imagination of the LN, took a newly minted name – Padania – a name with the resonance of a nation-state and an indication of boundaries and symbolism that could reify the claim to cultural distinctiveness (Giordano 2001: 28).

Whereas initially, in the late 1980s, the League concentrated on positing an almost anthropological tension between northern and southern Italy, following electoral and coalition logics and the political opportunity that opened with the collapse of the party system, the opponent was gradually re-defined as 'Rome' as the quintessence of an unresponsive and corrupt state and, subsequently, immigrants as representative of a threat to the safety and cultural integrity of the north (Ruzza and Schmidtke 1996a). This characterisation altered the party fundamentally, re-defining it away from ethno-nationalist formations and towards parties of the extreme right, of which it has been described as a typical representative (van der Brug and Fennema 2003).

These shifts can be explained in terms of a reaction to coalition partners and even the centre-left coalition taking over in a diluted form some of the original League emphases such as those on 'clean politics' and then federalism (Ruzza 2004). In this context, and given the difficulty of pursuing nationally divisive anti-southern ideologies while in government with national-based formations, an exclusionary focus on immigrants appeared an attractive choice. The LN has continued its politics of the enemy, but has had to replace the enemy with the new negative icon of the immigrant depicted as a threat not only to northern cultures but to the security of citizens. Since 11

September 2001, in particular, this has also come with a stress on the threat presented by Muslim immigrants in terms of both security and Christian identity (McDonnell 2006: 129).

In this latest period, the anti-European character of the LN is accentuated and overlaps with the LN's anti-capitalist component – its rejection of big capitalism in favour of diffused small entrepreneurship (Ruzza 2004). Indeed, whereas the LN had been portrayed in the early 1990s as a neo-liberal party, protectionist and pro-market positions have actually sat uneasily together in the LN's platform since the early 1990s, indicating a degree of ideological uncertainty. This apparent contradiction is perhaps best explained by an enthusiasm for neo-liberal rhetoric when attacking Italian state assistance for the south and other sectors not part of the LN's constituency, but an eagerness to propose protectionist solutions when the subject being protected is the LN's northern small town constituency, a form of welfare chauvinism that is even more pronounced in relation to the immigration question (Fella and Ruzza 2006). Its anti-EU, anti-immigrant character and its territorial protectionist instincts can all be interpreted as deriving from its essential nativism.

The LN was initially supportive of the process of European integration, but later became hostile. It was for a period a member of the European Free Alliance – the umbrella group of ethno-nationalist parties in the European Parliament – but its extreme right positions proved incompatible with that group and long before its dissolution led to a number of tensions which resulted in its expulsion (De Winter and Tursan 1998). The anti-European position has acquired prominence in the party and now constitutes a consolidated position that is argued in terms of loss of sovereignty and distance from 'the people', a construct that recurs frequently in recent years and is used to place localities and regions in opposition to Europe as the levels at which impersonal and remote decisions are taken.

The new anti-European stance has been linked to the emphasis on a more general anti-globalisation stance, which has also manifested itself in anti-American statements on the part of Bossi and other leading party exponents. This also involved a pro-Serb stance in the Kosovo conflict. The development of anti-European and anti-American attitudes – combined with an increasing focus on anti-immigration rhetoric – was illustrative of attempts to pander to popular anti-cosmopolitan sentiments while finding common ground to unite the LN's radical activists with its more institutional face evident in its prominent role in local government in the north. The shift to a Eurosceptic position can also be explained in terms of the centre-left government's success in ensuring that Italy would take part in the launch of the single currency in 1999, which once adopted would be blamed for the Italian economy's problems (as would the centre-left's role in securing this). In the mid-1990s, it had been assumed that the weakness of the Italian economy would have prevented its participation in the single currency. It was thus believed by the LN leadership that only an independent Padania would be strong enough economically to join the euro, and that this would be a trump card to play in winning popular support for independence (Giordano 2003; McDonnell 2006: 128–29).

The increasingly anti-European positions of the LN have been interpreted as a reaction to the fears of economic globalisation in its constituency. The EU is now portrayed as a homogenising force threatening to destroy cherished local identities (Quaglia 2005). Connected to this, Diamanti argues that anti-Europeanism has to be seen as an indicator of a desire to control the territory (Diamanti 1993: 103). A perception of lack of control has certainly resulted from processes of European integration and the challenges that an under-developed northern Italian capitalism faces in a globalised European market. More concretely, these have been reflected in tensions over the European Union's Common Agricultural Policy (CAP) in recent years. The LN has sided with northern Italian farmers in controversies over fines for violations of milk quotas, proposing to organise cavalcades of tractors to protest in Brussels.

The LN's growing protectionist and anti-globalisation stance combines both cultural concerns and economic concerns – the need to protect small entrepreneurs in the north is reflected for example in the campaign against cheap Chinese imports (the LN called for the imposition of tariffs), which also spills over into xenophobia. Globalisation, as with the EU, is also viewed as a vehicle for an undesirable multiculturalism. Thus, immigration is vehemently opposed as threatening both security and identity. Nevertheless, there has been a certain broadening of the LN's point of reference when referring to identity, i.e. it is a broader European Christian identity that needs to be protected, not just a Padanian identity or an Italian identity. This is seen not just in the LN's anti-immigration position but also in the campaign to prevent Turkish accession to the EU. The main concern remains the challenge of multiculturalism, of which Europe is the vehicle, together with the connected impact of immigrants who remain the target of most recent LN activism. The stress on Christian identity is also useful for the coalition as a whole in showing that the LN does have something in common with the other governing parties. The emphasis on Christian identity created a conceptual bridge between the Padanian nationalism of the LN and the Italian nationalism of FI and AN, as well as the catholicism (also strong within AN and FI) of the UDC during the second Berlusconi government. This also created a differentiation from the secular internationalism of much of the left.

The main concerns of the LN were presented in schematic form in the Padania newspaper just before the 2008 election and amounted to an electoral programme for the contest. These consisted of five objectives, each commented on in only a few lines of text: federalism, taxes, immigration, security and legality, and infrastructure. Federalism referred to the proposal to create three macro regions with independent legislative, administrative and judicial powers and a federal upper chamber. The tax issue focused on retaining locally a large portion of revenues collected in the north. The immigration issue was articulated in terms of combating illegal migration. Security was articulated in strict connection with immigration. Infrastructure referred to a programme of new airport construction, railways, waterways and roads in the north.

Frame analysis – the main ideological features of the League

Analysing the programme of four general elections – until 2006 – that saw the LN as an independent participant with a separate electoral programme[8] allows a clear picture of its ideology to emerge. For the 2008 election, however, the LN presented only a very brief programme that could not be included in our analysis as it was too short to be comparable. Nevertheless, as noted above, the substantive ideological contents of the 2008 election – even in their brevity – reiterate previous contents, which the technique of frame analysis has articulated over time.

A key feature in this ideological portrait is the LN's stress on federalism and devolution: clearly there is a difference between these two concepts, but together they indicate a strong preference for a different decentralised constitutional arrangement for the Italian state. Second comes the LN's emphasis on family values. Then one finds frequent references to localism, that is the conviction that a wide set of policy issues needs to be co-ordinated at local level. In this local context, one can find frequent references to the need to support and protect local communities: a form of welfarism. Then there are a number of frames that can be broadly grouped under populism and anti-politics. These involve condemnations of political corruption and inefficient state institutions, advocacy of more popular control on decision-making, references to 'the people' as an idealised constituency and denunciations of the political establishment. Added together, these populist frames are central to the LN's discourse. Finally, in this truncated list, comes a negative focus on migration and related threats to personal security, which relate to the LN's ethno-populist character. Related to this are the frequent use of frames rejecting multiculturalism. The focus on anti-immigration also relates to a preoccupation with other right-wing themes, such as law and order frames, which are also a significant presence in the LN's discourse. Thus, to summarise, the LN can be characterised as a traditionalist localist and populist movement that is also infused with right-wing xenophobic and nativist themes. Figure 4.2 represents the most frequent ideological concerns.

If Figure 4.2 defines the ideology of the LN, variations over time contribute to clarifying it. If we consider the insistence on constitutional arrangements as an indicator of a party concerned with ethno-nationalism and the form of the state, we see from Figure 4.3 that, over time, the LN has become somewhat less concerned with this issue and has shifted its emphasis towards more right-wing issues such as immigration and law and order.

The LN's emphasis on federalism and devolution

The most frequent LN concern is with autonomy for the north of the country. As we see from Figure 4.3, while references to devolution decrease over time, references to federalism increase. The LN preferred references to 'devolution' (a non-Italian word) when the Scottish issue was topical in the European media, and federalism subsequently, as the default name for the concept in Italian. There is a demand both for greater political power for subnational levels of

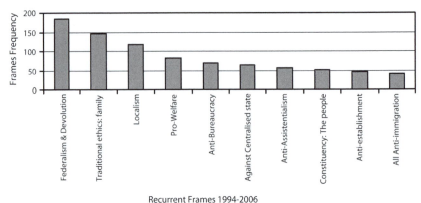

Recurrent Frames 1994-2006

Figure 4.2 The LN's main ideological frames (total n. 312).

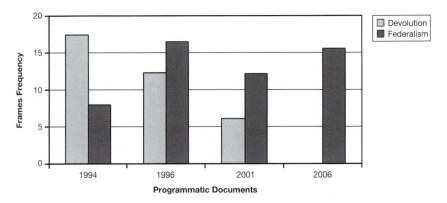

Figure 4.3 LN: proportion of frames differentiated by federalism and devolution.

government and for economic independence – a concept often expressed through the key term 'fiscal federalism', which encapsulates the demand that locally raised taxes should not be appropriated by national government.

The LN's populism, localism and family values

Central to the LN's populism is its anti-politics, which takes an anti-establishment and anti-bureaucracy focus. An anti-establishment emphasis emerges for instance in 1994 in the global indictment of the entire political class in relation to the way it dealt with the south.

> The presence of the army to guard some southern cities is the obvious evidence of the difficulty the state has in containing the Mafia, and it is the result of decades of indifference if not brazen connivance.
>
> Lega Nord (1994)

The LN posits a logical continuity between a corrupt political class and its corrupt recruiting strategy for state-run public services, where hirings have traditionally been used to acquire votes and political support. In this sense, the inefficient Italian bureaucracy is part of the political class, and its indictment reflects the LN's anti-political ethos. Thus, the 1994 programme states:

> Although it does not provide adequate services to citizens, the public administration manages, however, to block any political-institutional process of innovation due to its inefficiency, to the extent that all on-going change taking place in the country finds in the public administration – at all levels – a 'rubber wall' which halts and slows down and diverts the innovative democratic and modern forces.
>
> Public administration is made useless by large pockets of parasitism, which are distributed in a manner inversely proportional to necessity, with salaries that are totally unconnected to levels of productivity, and with norms which make it impossible to achieve the necessary flexibility of the working environment.
>
> Lega Nord (1994)

Similarly, the 1996 programme points out that:

> a quick, efficient, transparent and effective bureaucracy is the best protection against corruption, and a democratic state cannot develop if its citizens are convinced that money paid in taxes – earned with sweat and tears – is wasted by a remote, impersonal and corrupt bureaucracy.
>
> Lega Nord (1996)

In 2001, the anti-bureaucratic focus recurs in similar terms. However, whereas the earlier quotes have a neo-liberal undercurrent, by 2001, there is a broader anti-establishment message with anti-European and anti-big finance undertones such as in this passage:

> Therefore the State must be rethought, also because it is losing powers to bureaucracies and financial groups, hidden behind Europe, more space needs to be left to the people, its elected representatives, the associationism of civil society, and families, as is required by democracy.
>
> Lega Nord (2001)

Nevertheless, Figure 4.4 shows how the emphasis on anti-bureaucracy has decreased as the LN has become more institutionalised at the local and national level.

Also central to the LN's ideology is its localism, as in the following extract where localism is understood as local decision-making in fiscal matters:

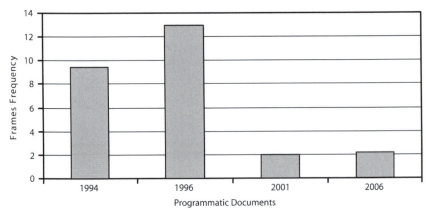

Figure 4.4 LN: anti-bureaucracy frames.

> It must be local communities that acquire the wealth produced by their own territory, and in the main they must manage them for the services that, by their nature, do not need wider aggregations at the level of coordination
>
> Lega Nord (1994).

This localism can be connected to other ideological focuses of the LN, such as its emphasis on law and order and family values. Families are presented as the primary nucleus of local communities. The LN's ideology is thus also defined by its focus on family values. This emerges in requests for a wide range of services and subsidies for families, such as in the following excerpts:

> The Northern League recognizes the family as the founding element of local communities and a privileged interlocutor as far as the management, provision and planning of social services are concerned
>
> Lega Nord (1996).

> Marriage and the family are the heart of a civilization. They are the custodian of the most intimate and deepest nucleus of the culture and tradition which are at one with our collective identity. It is this ultimate value that we must defend if we do not want to die, or witness the disappearance of our western traditions
>
> Lega Nord (2001).

While some issues exhibit a linear trend, reflecting a steady evolution of the LN's thinking, such as the growing emphasis on immigration, others seem more variable over time but remain central in the absolute number of references. This is the case with family values, as can be inferred from Figure 4.5, which shows a high number of references to family in 2001, when the LN was

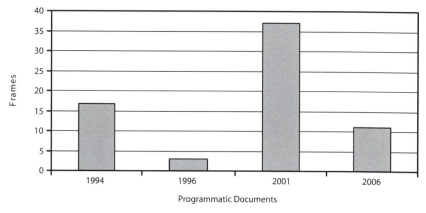

Figure 4.5 LN: frames on family values (n=147).

trying to play down its previous ethno-nationalism as part of the centre-right coalition, instead placing a stronger emphasis on a traditional conservative theme.

The politics of the enemy, immigration and ethno-populism

Throughout the history of the LN and reflecting its nativist character, various social groups have been vilified or idealised, which, as in other extreme right groups, has helped in defining the specificity of the movement. Creating social boundaries builds identity. Entire groups are seen as carriers of particular conceptions of life. Attributing worldviews to groups symbolically clarifies despised and idealised moral traits. However, the subjects of vilification might change over time in relation to the changing political opportunities that might be involved.

In its initial phase, the casting of the '*meridionale*' (southern Italian) as the 'other' was central to the LN's strategy of emphasising a distinct northern identity around which it could base its appeal. This bore fruit given the negative perception of migrants from the south who were widespread in northern Italy (Biorcio 1997b: 45). In the 1990s, however, southern Italians became less central to the LN's discourse. Indeed, its focus switched to the perceived problem of immigration and the alleged threat posed by the presence of non-EU nationals in the territory. In many respects, as Figure 4.6 shows, immigrants have remained the main source of negative connotations in recent years. The LN's anti-immigration discourse can be categorised as ethno-populist, and this is a form of populism that has become increasingly central to its character.

We conducted a specialised analysis to document changing views on immigration and its relevance over time. Ten documents expressing the key LN concerns were selected to cover the period from the late 1980s to 2006.

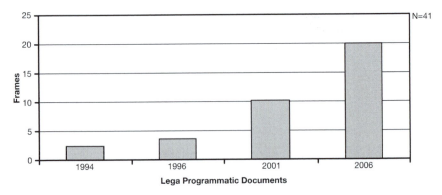

Figure 4.6 LN: percentage frames on migration (n=41).

Analysis was also undertaken of samples of articles on immigration in *La Padania* (as well as the newspaper of the Lombard League, *Lombardia Autonomista*) and of interventions by LN speakers in key parliamentary debates on immigration and other statements. Our findings indicate that the immigration issue has become progressively more important. In the five documents collected for the period of the late 1980s and the 1990s, concerns about immigration occur ninety-seven times. After the turn of the century, they occur 243 times, indicating the increasing definition of the LN away from cultural and political ethno-nationalism and towards a radical right ethno-populist identity.

In this study, one can distinguish views that have always been an integral part of the ideology of the LN from more recent acquisitions. The general views include a principled rejection of multiculturalism and the idea that immigration is not necessary for the economy (contrary to the position of the other main parties and business leaders). Moreover, immigrants are depicted as a drain on economic resources and as being unfairly prioritised in welfare policies. Thus a welfare chauvinism is posited, whereby it is argued that natives (northern Italians or Italians in general) should have priority access to welfare resources, ahead of migrants. This relates to the general economic and social localism of the LN.

There had been references to non-EU immigration in the documents of the Lombard League in the 1980s, although it was presented as the result of the developed countries' imperialism (Lega Lombarda 1983b). In the 1980s, southern migrants to the north were discussed using the same kind of frames that would later be used to discuss non-EU immigrants:

> In fact today Lombardy does not belong to the Lombard any longer, Pada-nia does not belong to the Padanian people. It is a geographic expression with no political value, a territory without rights towards invaders.
>
> Lega Lombarda (1982)

The focus on non-EU migration grew gradually and accelerated strongly during the 1990s (as indeed the presence of non-EU immigrants in the territory accelerated in the same period). The emergence of non-EU immigration as a salient issue coincided with the formation and consolidation of the unified Northern League at the beginning of the 1990s. Again, discourse on immigration was often linked with the anti-establishment theme, with the establishment parties (and particularly the centre-left parties which governed Italy from 1996 to 2001) being depicted as incompetent and weak in dealing with the immigration 'problem'. Hence, the LN presented the tightening of the law on immigration as a priority in the run-up to the 2001 election.

References to immigration and the use of ethno-populist frames – directed at non-EU migrants (generally referred to in Italian public discourse as *extracomunitari*) – are prevalent in all the LN's documents and in speeches by its leader Bossi and other party exponents. Such references are also rife in the party newspaper *La Padania*. From its launch in 1997, the immigration issue was central to the editorial line of *La Padania*. Immigration was generally treated as a front page issue, with lead articles. In the local sections, incidents of crime committed by immigrants are covered on a daily basis. In a sample of fifty-one articles that were analysed, the association of immigration and crime was central (seventeen citations), as was that between illegal immigrants and crime (thirteen). There was also a strong criticism towards inefficient governments (twenty-five) and towards a weak left (twenty) as regards the issue. Quite often, identity aspects were underlined with a strong opposition to multiculturalism (twelve) and nationalistic appeals (eleven). On the positive side, the importance of helping migrants in their country of origin (five) and the need for more law and order (five) were mentioned.

Often LN documents invoke the metaphor of invasion, an invasion by a foreign population that could lead to the replacement of the local population – a loss of control over the territory for the people who originally lived there. The laceration of the social structure caused by immigration is also emphasised. Immigrants have also often been presented as bringing disease and therefore representing a health risk, as exemplified by the intervention in the parliamentary debate on the 1998 centre-left Turco-Napolitano immigration law by Mario Borghezio (a former deputy and now MEP, notorious for his extremist positions on immigration), who referred to 'the presence of millions of immigrants' reintroducing previously overcome diseases to the country 'for example typhoid, cholera, TB' and even cases of the Ebola virus (Borghezio 1997).

As shown in the following subsections, the discourse of the LN on immigration can be grouped into a number of themes that ethno-populists seek to exploit: crime and security fears, economics and welfare chauvinism, identity protection and blaming the political establishment for immigration.

Crime and security themes

The link between immigration and crime is made very frequently in the LN's discourse. It is the most frequent frame found when discussing immigration in

La Padania and the second most frequent in party documents (after identity themes). In particular, the tendency for immigrants to fall into criminal activities is stressed. The problem of illegal–clandestine immigration is focused on as a major problem to be resolved. However, it also notable that many of the LN's statements do not exempt legal immigrants from the blame for crime. Indeed, some statements make no distinction. For example, a 2002 document on the issue referred to immigration and the rise of crime in Italy as 'a true equation' (Lega Nord 2002: 9) and that:

> Only bad faith or obtuseness without limits can deny the correlation between non-EU immigration and the rise in crime. This dramatic link, besides being easily demonstrable through any local press review, is shown by figures, statistics and university studies.
>
> Lega Nord (2002)

The way in which news stories are reported in *La Padania* also stands out. In the reporting of crime incidents, the involvement of immigrants is always emphasised. Crimes committed by foreigners appear to be highlighted over those committed by locals, with the nationality of the perpetrators always mentioned.

Again, there are echoes in the way the law and order frame was employed in the documents and newspapers of the earlier regional Leagues, the 'immigrant' referred to being the southern Italian. For example, in the newspaper of the Lombard League, *Lombardia Autonomista*, in 1983, there was a call for 'the repatriation of immigrants who commit crimes or are involved in kidnappings, extortions or drugs trafficking' (Lega Lombarda 1983a). Southern Italians were often accused of bringing mafia practices to the north. For example, in the very first programme of the Liga Veneta, this statement appeared: 'We want that justice in the Veneto region goes back to the old Venetian principles, and fight vigorously and with adequate tools, mafia and racketeering' (Biorcio 1997b: 41).

Sometimes, traces of the earlier anti-southern rhetoric can be found in statements linking newer migrants to crime, as exemplified by this intervention in the parliamentary debate on the 1998 Turco-Napolitano law passed by the centre left:

> In the name of the citizens I represent, I say that we are fed up of being invaded first by the Italian mafia and now by the Albanian one and also the Russian one. (...) Now the Albanian mafia is transforming our cities with far West scenes and it almost seems like living at the frontier.
>
> Fongaro (28 October 1997)

More recent documents, particularly since 9/11 (although examples can also be found prior to 2001), focus on the threat posed by terrorism, linking Muslim immigrants with an increased terrorist threat within Italy and the EU in general. Thus, for example, in the electoral programme for the 2004 European Parliament elections, this statement is found:

> Thanks to the far-sightedness of false do-gooder politicians, who opened the door to hundreds of thousands of non-EU workers, it was possible for Islamic terrorists to create an invisible (or almost) network of cells ready to bring death and destruction into the Western countries.
>
> Lega Nord (2004)

Economic themes

While the centre left, the other centre-right parties and employers' associations have generally accepted that the Italian labour market requires immigrant workers, this need tends to be rejected in LN statements. Indeed, immigrants are generally portrayed as taking jobs from local workers. This was notable in the debate on the Turco-Napolitano law adopted in 1998, which the LN went as far as to label 'racist' against Italian workers:

> The act is also racist against our own people and workers ... Our workers, or at least some of them, will be expelled from the productive world, from the job market in favour of these non-EU workers. ... it is obvious that for every place taken by a non-EU worker there will be one less for our workers. And this, in due course, will provoke huge social conflicts and public order problems. And in this war among the poors, in this conflict of the weakest, it will certainly be our people who will lose out.
>
> Fontan (19 November 1997)

Generally, there is a complaint in the LN's recent documents that discrimination exists in favour of immigrants, e.g. in housing policy, it is claimed that 'any immigrant has higher points than one of our families' (Lega Nord 2001). The LN has thus called for a welfare system that puts Italian citizens first: 'Social policies should favour Italians, not illegal immigrants' (Lega Nord 2001). It is notable here that this example of welfare chauvinism emphasises the need for preferential treatment of Italians and not just Padanians. A more notorious example of the LN using the welfare chauvinist frame was Bossi's complaint about the 'bingo, bongo' getting priority access to housing over the Milanese in Milan.

Again, there is a continuity here between the LN's present rhetoric and that used by the Lombard League in its earlier phases against southern migrants. The immigrants referred to in the following excerpt are migrants from the south of Italy:

> Certainly the wrong political class which has not yet realised that the economic development model based on immigration is finished, and that

laws which assigned council homes to immigrants, discriminating local residents, must be changed.

Lega Lombarda (1986)

Identity themes

The dominant theme in the LN's discourse on immigration is the identity one. The need to protect 'national' identity and culture in opposition to non-EU immigration is generally emphasised. However, in emphasising local or national identity, there is often an ambiguity in the LN's documents and speeches as to what the reference point for this national identity is: Italy or Padania. References to Padanian nationalism are present mainly in the phase of the earlier regional Leagues and in the early phase of the LN. In general, however, the identity to be defended is not always clearly defined and can refer to Lombard, Padanian, Italian, European, western or Christian identity. The LN appears to be moving increasingly to an emphasis on a general European or western Christian identity, in the face of Islamic immigration. Its anti-Islamic stance has become particularly pronounced since 2001 and the 9/11 attacks, and is also linked to its campaign to prevent Turkish accession to the EU launched in 2004–5.

The emphasis on defence of identity (be it Padanian, Italian or Christian) is connected to the specific theme of ethno-pluralism, and the correlation made between the ethnic homogeneity of the community and the integrity of the nation. The immigrant therefore represents a threat to this ethnic homogeneity and potentially damages the national fabric, perceived as dependent on the homogeneity of culture that derives from the single ethnic unit. Thus, for example, Bossi, in his speech to the 1991 party conference, suggested that immigration leads to the destruction of ethnic identity and that by 'destroying the process of ethnic identity, the multiracial society provokes the decline of morality and therefore of solidarity' (Bossi 1991a). These themes are repeated in party documents and speeches from the 1990s and 2000s. For instance, the electoral programme of 1994 stated:

No to pseudo cultural interventions aimed at the diffusion of a multi-racial mentality from which is derived the Italian population's loss of its sense of belonging to its own ethnic, cultural and religious entity.

Lega Nord (1994)

Thus, there is a strong rejection of notions of multiculturalism and a multi-racial society, disdained as 'an imported heterogeneity' (Bossi 1998). Multi-culturalism is also rejected within the context of globalisation: the two are presented as a twin threat to local identities and cultures. The LN's 2002 document on immigration referred disdainfully to 'the sanctified multiracial society of the various multinationals such as Benetton, McDonald's, Nike, Nestlé, Del Monte or Adidas' (Lega Nord 2002: 19).

The LN's growing Islamophobia was particular prominent in its European election programme of 2004. This was underlined in relation to both the link with terrorism and the need to resist Turkish accession to the EU. Nevertheless, the Islamophobia theme was also present prior to 2001, particularly in the parliamentary debate on the Turco-Napolitano law.

> In another article, it is permitted to issue residence permits also for 'religious tourism'. The striking effect of this norm will be to allow millions of Islam fundamentalists to enter our territory and then become clandestines.
>
> Dussin (23 October 1997)

In *La Padania*, the greatest attention to the Islamic theme can be found in articles published in September 2001. However, this theme had also cropped up previously, with LN spokesmen stressing the need to protect Christian culture and give preference to Christian immigrants:

> The Lega, on the contrary, has always stated that immigration is a phenomenon that can and must be governed: firstly, by avoiding an Islamic invasion, which is a great threat to the cultural and religious identity of a country with deep roots in Christianity.
>
> Borghezio (2000)

Following the terrorist attacks on London of July 2005, LN exponents (notably Roberto Calderoli) stepped up the anti-Islamic rhetoric, endorsing the clash of civilisations' thesis and claiming that there is no moderate side to Islam: all Muslims are potential terrorists.[9] As already noted, Calderoli was forced to resign from government after his inflammatory gesture in the wake of the worldwide controversy over cartoons depicting the prophet Mohamed published in a Danish newspaper in early 2006. In 2007, Calderoli proposed that farmers graze their pigs on land designated for the construction of mosques, thus desecrating the land in the eyes of Muslims.

Blaming the establishment

The LN's anti-immigration rhetoric is often combined with an attack on the failings of political elites as regards the regulation of the immigration issue, combining two classical populist themes: anti-immigrant and anti-establishment. This was particularly the case at the time of the centre-left government from 1996 to 2001, when the LN made frequent attacks against its perceived soft and inefficient stance, allowing clandestine immigrants to enter the country uncontrolled and thus allowing crime to increase and terrorist bases to be established. In addition to the accusations that the centre-left government had been too soft, the judicial system was also attacked as an 'accomplice' in facilitating immigration. In more recent documents (e.g. the 2004

European election manifesto), the same accusations are also directed at the European Commission.

But these accusations against other political leaders go beyond inefficiency and *buonismo* (do-goodism). The LN has alleged that immigration policies derive from a specific socio-economic and political plan on the part of the ruling capitalist elite. Accusations regarding the global capitalist system were present in the very early statements of the Lombard League and could still be found in LN statements in the early 1990s, when an unlikely alliance comprising capital, the left and the catholic church was theorised. Thus, the left sought immigrants as potential electoral supporters, the church sought immigrants as potential priests and to boost flagging congregations, and capitalists sought immigrants as a reservoir of cheap labour:

> It is so true that behind immigration of coloured people is not only the disbanded left which is looking for a new proletarian under-class to gain votes; it is not only the Catholic Church, closed in the palaces of greed, which has lost all credibility and tries to fill its empty seminaries with religious people that can only be found in the Third World; but there is also the capitalist interest, that through migrations, lets its citizens pay the cost of its development.
>
> Bossi (1991b)

This theory of conspiracy and alliance has also cropped up in recent statements:

> Non-EU immigration is favoured and supported by different forces that represent it as a spontaneous and irreversible phenomenon which you cannot oppose; the multiracial society is mainly supported by an alliance of financial globalization forces and the international left and is based on economic and ideological reasons.
>
> Lega Nord (2002: 19)

General racism and xenophobia

The anti-immigration policy of the LN appears to be more closely related to specific populist themes stressing security or economic insecurities or cultural difference rather than to biological racism. In the documents analysed, the only statement that could be interpreted as deriving from biological racism was found in Bossi's speech at the first conference of the LN in 1991, where he underlined the impossibility of integration of 'coloured' people:

> This is not possible for coloured immigrants, whose integration is not foreseeable even after centuries. The usual integration mechanisms, such as marriage and children, do not work with them and therefore it would

be impossible to realise ethnic links without creating strong racial tensions in society.

Bossi (1991b)

However, such statements do not appear in later documents and speeches by Bossi. *La Padania* also follows the trend: in the editions analysed, no biological racism appears. Distinctly xenophobic views have been expressed *vis-à-vis* Albanians and Romanians (viewed as delinquent), and xenophobic positions are notable in relation to the Chinese and Turks. In terms of generalised xenophobia, it is worth pointing out the recent campaigns launched by the LN against China (due to the perceived flooding of EU markets with cheap Chinese goods) and against the entrance of Turkey in the EU. The campaign against China relates strongly to the LN's anti-globalisation message. It has called for the imposition of tariffs in order to protect locally produced goods. However, this sometimes spills over into xenophobia. For example, a poster in the local election campaign of 2005 mocked the difficulty Chinese people have in pronouncing the letter 'r'. Thus, it used the slogan 'no glazie' (instead of the correct Italian: 'no grazie' – no thank you).

There are numerous examples of inflammatory statements, such as Bossi's proposal to fire canons at clandestines, or Borghezio's suggestion that the Bossi–Fini law would 'give the clandestine bastards a thousand per thousand kicks up the arse' (Staff Reporter 2002), or indeed Calderoli's various utterances on Islam. Calderoli also suggested, when opposing the right of immigrants to vote in local elections, that if they didn't like it, they could 'get back on their camel and go back to their tent' (Cremonesi 2002).

Some LN exponents sometime stray much further into overtly racist territory. For example, one of its more extremist parliamentarians, Enzo Erminio Boso, stated in 1995:

> The Italian white race is disappearing and the black race is taking its place. And if we die out the black man will be rampant. (...) non-EU immigrants should also give their foot prints, and this is because of the risk of tampering with the finger prints, only from feet can you trace particular tribe's features (...) Me, a racist? Balls, I've had women of all colours, even a yellow one. And a black one. Those I do not like are the criminals, the transvestites, the thieves. I can't even stand the white ones of these, can you image, the black ones. (...) The immigrants, priests and nuns should take them home, and all those moralists who preach (...) If Hercules planes are not enough, we put them on ships and we take them home. We can even put bunk beds (...) The immigrants on regular flights could rape the hostesses. Well, it's true that some women are pigs and enjoy it, but (...) The airline captains refuse to embark illegal immigrants because they stink. But on military planes, with a nice pump we can water them without any problem.

Cited in Staff Reporter (1995)

Calderoli has also strayed into overtly racist territory: following the 2006 football world cup final, in which Italy emerged victorious over France, his comment that France in 'fielding negroes, Muslims and communists, had sacrificed its own identity to get a result' provoked an official protest from the French ambassador (Staff Reporter 2006).

On the TV programme *Matrix* (a political discussion programme on the Mediaset Canale 5 network) on 4 June 2008, Calderoli commented: 'Can I make a racist point, but a racist point in inverted commas? ... There are ethnic groups with a greater propensity to work and others that have less. There are some with a greater propensity to be delinquent'. He sought to clarify this racist remark by adding that this amounted to 'a predisposition, rather than a reference to DNA'.

Language in the League's political culture and communication strategy

The programmatic documents analysed tend to speak to an audience of political actors. As a social movement, the LN also speaks to its activists and does it in a language that is sometimes different from the language used in political arenas. This is notable in some of the more inflammatory statements by individuals cited above, which can be interpreted as signals to activists rather than genuine proposals for action. While declarations on immigration speak to a national (Italian) audience, other statements and activities by activists reflect a continuing ethno-nationalism, a never abandoned culturally essentialist belief in the special character of the northern Italian people. For a movement and a party that aims at broadening its electorate and appeal at national level, this theme cannot be aired too frequently outside its activist base. But as several in-depth interviews reveal, themes of ethnic difference remain central. These crystallise around a set of values that the linguistic issues capture well – that is, the right to use a separate local language as a medium for conveying the different values of the northern people and differentiating them from southern Italians.

Language issues feature centrally in all the LN media – radio, television channels, newspapers and magazines. Padanian radio frequently broadcasts songs in local northern dialects. Phone-in programmes host dialect speakers. There are talk shows in which participants talk in a local dialect. The website reserves a special permanent space for 'specials' on 'local and regional languages' that is separate from 'northern culture' and 'Padanian history'.

It is not, however, only the ideological use of local dialect that characterises the LN's linguistic strategy. The LN has traditionally oscillated between its attempts to claim the status of repressed minority, and therefore dignifying local dialects to the status of interconnected and repressed languages, and its self-definition as a populist movement struggling against all elites, and therefore inventing a language use that symbolises populist allegiance. The socio-linguistic evolution of Italian has clearly differentiated a spoken language from a literary written language, which is now used in both a written and an oral form by the contemporary Italian political establishment. The spoken language is therefore different from dialects but also from the language one finds among cultured elites, and can be used to express symbolic allegiance to an idealised conception of 'the people' – a strategy that is the linguistic equivalent of populism in politics.

This populist strategy holds particular potency in Italy against the background of the extremely convoluted and baroque political jargon developed by the former mainstream political parties over the years, which sounds obscure to most Italians. The pre-*tangentopoli* language of politics assumed an insider's knowledge of political affairs, and the ability to 'read between the lines'. Presenting itself as an anti-system movement, the LN was the first party that chose a language which, as an activist said, 'seeks to bring politics down to the level of common people', and thus de-sanctifies politics. Vulgarity was and still is sometimes raised to the status of a virtue because it possesses a simplicity and directness that is felt to be lacking elsewhere.

Over recent years, several other parties have attempted linguistic innovation and to an extent have imitated aspects of the League's linguistic codes. For instance, much has now been written on the language of Berlusconi, which is more than a moderate version of the LN's, but which reflects the strategies of a politician who has learned from the LN that language can be a powerful channel to express an outsider status from a system that is still distant to many Italians (Amadori 2002). Other political actors have also modified their language in recent years, sometimes infusing it with populism. But the LN remains well known for its simple and even rough use of language, which amounts to a cultural code that expresses an anti-elitist ethos.

Using this language variant is now the default linguistic strategy of the LN. While in an earlier period, the use of dialect constituted an exclusionary device to deny access to the movement to anyone other than indigenous northern Italians, in recent years this exclusionary strategy has been replaced by the adoption of a popular variant of Italian. This linguistic strategy served the purpose of re-defining 'the enemy' by including first- and second-generation southern migrants as potential movement supporters and excluding a political class perceived as corrupt and Byzantine, a class which, in the LN's mythology, has its base in Rome, a city that symbolises 'otherness' from the LN 'homeland' (Ruzza and Schmidtke 1996a). The first approach exemplifies a relationship with language typical of other minority nationalisms; the second is distinctive and is more closely related to populism. In both cases, the territorial claim to self-determination could be sustained and grounded linguistically.

To investigate the role of language, a content analysis of the LN's media was conducted for the period 1998–2004, based on sampling and examination of *La Padania*, which is available for the entire period online, and an examination of the LN's television and radio programming in order to formulate a typology of language uses.

Certain linguistic features contribute to a distinctive form of 'identity politics' that is utilised to sustain ethno-nationalist sentiments. First, Italian dialects are mutually intelligible only in territorially circumscribed areas, creating the possibility of local identities over broad areas encompassing 'families of dialects'. To exploit this possibility, Radio Padania's frequent broadcasts of songs in a variety of dialects is intended as an inclusionary device – evidence that throughout northern Italy the native population will be able to understand all dialects and therefore feel and be part of a common ideal family – a nation. It is also possibly exclusionary to the extent that speakers know that central and southern Italians would not be able to understand the songs broadcast. In any event, knowledge of the local language can be used as a filter. For instance, in October 2003, Bossi stated that immigrants who want to obtain Italian citizenship should show proof of some knowledge of the local languages of the areas in which they want to live. Calderoli observed that such an approach would encourage real integration (Messina 2003).

This exclusionary intent is exemplified in the following sentence, which also demonstrates the strategy of symbolic creation of a territorial homeland in which state officials are seen as intruders.

> Do they [the traffic police] stop you and want to give you a fine? Taking a courteous attitude, you can talk to the authorities of the Italian State in your local language. The language is yours; the State is their business! Do they not understand you? But you are in your homeland! Remember that any occasion is a good chance to re-assert your language: political and cultural posters, press releases, public speeches. (...) Try then to organize at all territorial levels (even in your neighbourhood) local language courses – even self-organized – and circulate (even as photocopies) materials of any kind in your language.
>
> Incerti and Polli (1999)

A frequent use of local languages occurs in the context of re-discovering traditional songs, poems and sayings. They are intentionally utilised as a political statement: social history is re-visited, popular literature re-discovered and their presumed noble origins are ideologically asserted. In its activist materials, the LN emphasises a connection to Celtic roots and therefore an otherness from standard Italian, the 'language of Rome'. In this respect, one could cite the frequent articles on the historical and linguistic aspects of northern Italy. A similar concern occurs in reflections on language policy – attempts to promote courses in local dialect that are emphatically defined as languages. An emphasis on the historical importance of local languages also emerges in the following sentence, but its connection to a distinctive culture and set of values is emphasised:

> Milanese language and civilization should not die. It should not be killed by the nearly always neglectful lack of attention, and by conformist

mono-lingualism. It constitutes a treasure to be newly valued and passed on to the younger generations.

Polli (2000)

For an almost 'just-minted' ethno-nationalist movement (Rognoni 2004), sharing pride in a distinctive language can be a way of acquiring legitimacy. If movements based in truly distinctive and historical languages such as the Sardinian movement meet with LN activists, a sort of legitimacy by contact can ensue. Thus, language is sometimes discussed in the context of ethnic linguistic events, such as in a poetry recital that brings together Lombards and Sardinians and that *La Padania* publicises with emphasis in an article entitled 'Poetic handshake between Sardinians and Lombards', thereby implying that the distinctive and universally recognised Sardinian language is similar to what are currently regarded as northern Italian dialects (Rognoni 2004).

Frequently, in phone-in radio programmes, listeners to Radio Padania complain that their intentional directness in language use is misunderstood by political elites as stupidity and is derided. This typically elicits feelings of victimisation, which are then the basis for identity-building.

The word 'the end' is about to be spoken with reference to the hopes of – at least – the Piedmontese, Venetians and Milanese who the Italian state considers carriers of a culture and an identity deserving to be erased for ever. Last Wednesday the Senate's select committee on Constitutional Affairs passed the draft bill for law 169, which was previously approved by the lower chamber and which concerns the supposed 'norms for the protection of language minorities'. This protection becomes in effect a real and hateful discrimination as the state has established a fixed list of languages that deserve protection.

Polli (1999)

With respect to language use, one needs to clearly differentiate the populist use of the Italian language from the use of the dialect. The populist use of the Italian language is an interesting linguistic creation that stands apart from the typology. A new linguistic invention – a language code taken directly from the street and imported into the political arena – has increasingly replaced the dialect. The public speeches of the LN rely heavily on metaphors, catchphrases and other elements of everyday language, and re-interpret these elements in political terms. For instance, a LN billboard poster reads 'the League cleans the engine (of politics)'. It is a simple message, taken directly from advertising and expressed in ordinary language. In this view, 'the people' that matter are the 'ordinary folk' who, with their roots in common sense and their attachment to local communities, oppose all elites, particularly elites in the capital – Rome – who are intrinsically corrupt and untrustworthy. This simplified and essential language use expresses the essence of populism, with its glorification of localities and clear-cut truths against the swindling attempts of all elites (Mény and Surel 2001).

Conclusion

Since its inception, the impact of the LN on Italian politics has been critical: its emphasis on clean politics, then its emphasis on federalism and latterly on anti-immigrant sentiments have been incorporated across much of the political spectrum, albeit with different nuances. The LN has certainly contributed to revolutionising several important aspects of Italian politics. It accompanied and initially spurred the crisis in the system that led to fundamental changes and the profound re-definition of the party system. It has espoused political ideas that have had a fundamental impact. Its emphasis on federalism has been accepted by allies and competitors. Moreover, its emphasis on the threat of immigration has contributed to more restrictive policy-making in this area.

However, despite its delayed and diluted impact on agenda setting, the LN has only partly been able to profit politically. Its electoral support has oscillated over the years, making it often dependent on its flamboyant attempts to grab media headlines through xenophobic and populist statements such as the comments of Bossi and others on issues of immigration and asylum, the countless references to the 'Padanian people' and the derogatory remarks about politicians in Rome. During its periods of isolation from other political forces, observers and possibly its disaffected electorate have considered the policy impact of this party to be modest. During its periods as a coalition partner, the LN has been considered as too small and subordinate to achieve a real impact.

Nonetheless, two decades after its foundation, it is clear that the LN has acquired a stable and committed body of supporters who will remain faithful and persuaded by the original mix of ethno-nationalism and right-wing extremism regardless of policy impact. It is also clear that its chances of expansion are now limited. However, it retains a king-making role in coalition politics – without its participation, electoral success remains difficult for the centre right (as was the case in 1996) in a bipolar system, and it thus has the capacity to have a decisive say over electoral outcomes as well as to affect public debates on policy issues.

The LN has oscillated between a socio-cultural ethnic movement and a right-wing party. The frame analysis identified a recurrent set of contents that can be grouped into a number of ideological categories. One concerns expressions of dissent with the workings of the institutions of representative democracy. These concerns often occur in parallel with calls for a stronger input from the people and with implicit or explicit references to the people, and an exclusionary approach towards migrants, which can be grouped under the overarching label of 'populism'. The LN thus reflects the core characteristics of populism: evocative rhetorical language and symbolic policies emphasising belonging and drawing boundaries – particularly in the field of migration, and anti-politics, combined with a reliance on charismatic leadership for success.

More specifically, with reference to what we defined previously as peripheral ideological elements, the populism of the LN manifests itself in a rejection of the institutional procedures of the Italian state and its actors. One aspect of this can be labelled 'anti-bureaucracy', but it is related to a broader 'anti-establishment' ethos, which also involves rejection of national political parties and stress on the importance of a direct relationship with 'the people'. There is also an ethno-populism, which pits a homogeneous northern Italian people against the migrant outsider (and, most insidiously, the Muslim migrant), who poses a threat to the identity and cohesion of the community, and also a threat in terms of security and access to economic wealth and resources. The LN's specific brand of exclusionary ethno-populism is thus a peripheral ideological element that links its populism to its right-wing cultural essentialist nativism. While nativism is peripheral, in that it is not an essential element of all populist movements, it can be described as a core element of the LN's ideology, alongside it populism. Hence, we can describe it as a populist radical right party, using Mudde's definition (Mudde 2007: 22–23).

If these factors define the LN's populism in terms that are often identified by the literature on populism, an aspect that is more often stressed in studies of ethno-nationalism emphasises a preference for the local level of action, which amounts to a localist view of politics, defining in populist terms the confines of its political frame of reference.

This local political identity has revealed itself viable but limited and declining in the long term – confined to small social niches and not attractive to new generations of voters. It is also unattractive and will remain so in the south of the country, despite attempts to create sister organisations there. The second identity – the right-wing anti-immigrant and 'law and order' profile – which seeks to appeal to Italians beyond the LN's northern heartlands and has become more prominent since 1999 – has also had a limited impact, although it provides some common ground with the other centre-right parties and reaches beyond the LN's traditional constituencies. Nevertheless, the alliance with the nationalist right has not yet delivered the federalist revolution that the LN seeks. This is partly because it is a demand too incompatible with the values of the right, but also because Italians are not ready to abandon in such a fundamental way the constitutional architecture that emerged from the Second World War, as shown in the rejection of the LN's vision in the referendum of June 2006. Its recent electoral successes have given it a strong influence over the PdL and a strong parliamentary base from which some of its targets of reform of the institutional architecture of the Italian state might finally be in sight. Nevertheless, its strong presence in a territorially limited area of the country is also a weakness and can reduce its influence at the national level. It remains vulnerable to changes to the electoral system which punish parties without a significant nationwide vote. Hence, the LN was strongly opposed to changes in the electoral law - such as that proposed in the June 2009 referendum - which would reward the larger parties, e.g. through giving a bonus of seats to the party or party list with the highest proportion of votes (rather than the coalition as a whole, as was the case in the existing law) and establishing much higher electoral thresholds for parties to gain parliamentary representation. This would have the effect of allowing the PdL to fight elections without the need to gain the support of the LN. Any further consolidation of this bipolar trend in the Italian political system would put the future influence of the LN in jeopardy.

5 Forza Italia

Following its sudden emergence, Forza Italia was described as a 'virtual' party (McCarthy 1996). However, it would become more institutionalised over time, and following electoral setbacks, notably in 1996, it would develop deeper organisational roots. The invention of a political party, almost from scratch, by Silvio Berlusconi at the beginning of 1994 transformed the political landscape in Italy, offering political scientists an ideal example of the electoral–professional model of party organisation, and providing a whole new ball game for Italian voters when it came to the manipulation of mass communications and leadership style. The importation into Italian politics of modern techniques of marketing and consumer polling was central to the success of the new party. This chapter will explore the development of Forza Italia, drawing particular attention to the way in which Berlusconi was able to draw on the organisational strengths, personnel and finances of his Fininvest business empire to construct a new party. Such were the interconnections between Fininvest and Forza Italia that the term 'business-firm' party would become particularly apt to define the model of party organisation that Berlusconi pioneered. Discussion of Forza Italia is impossible without highlighting the unique role played by its leader and founder. Hence, particular attention will be paid to Berlusconi's personalised and charismatic leadership of the party, and of the centre-right coalition as a whole. Examination of Berlusconi's leadership and his style and form of political communication is also central to understanding the nature of the party's populism and the way in which it utilises core aspects of populism, combining them with more peripheral facets of populism that depend on the particular context of political competition in Italy. This also needs to be put in the context of a broader examination of Forza Italia's ideological nature, requiring an analysis of key programmatic documents. However, the dominant role played by Forza Italia in the centre-right coalition, and Berlusconi's leadership position within it, make it difficult to separate an analysis of Forza Italia's political platform from that of the coalition as a whole. Thus joint documents adopted by the coalition will also be analysed.

The foundation of Forza Italia

The rapid success of Forza Italia in 1994 could be attributed to the mobilisation by Berlusconi of the economic, organisational and intellectual resources of his Fininvest business empire and of his own personal network of friends and associates. As Poli describes in great detail in her analysis of the genesis, organisation and development of Forza Italia, Berlusconi manoeuvred on a number of fronts simultaneously from the summer of 1993 onwards to create a viable political force that would appeal to the catholic vote and represent liberal values (Poli 2001: 29–30). This involved the development of a network of intellectual and business elites around a political manifesto developed by Giuliano Urbani, a liberal political scientist who founded the political association *Alla Ricerca di Buongoverno* (in search of good government) in November 1993; the launch at the beginning of December 1993 of the 'Forza Italia clubs' – with the objective of promoting liberal ideas and mobilising grassroots activism – and the creation of a public opinion monitoring institute Diakron in October 1993, which served to identify the potential electoral base of the new party.

McCarthy portrays Forza Italia as a continuation of the clan politics of the post-war republic. Politicians had treated industry and finance as part of their territory. The expansion of state involvement in the economy had served the need to satisfy their expanding clienteles. Clans had been formed to fight over the spoils, and Berlusconi himself had been a prominent member of the Craxi clan. When Craxi fell in 1993, Berlusconi – fearing the implications of a centre-left government – put himself at the head of a new clan, using his own company, Fininvest, as its chief resource and instrument (McCarthy 1996: 45–46). Following the string of centre-left victories in local elections in the summer of 1993, Berlusconi had begun touring various cities in order to talk to businessmen, interest group representatives, academics and journalists and whoever shared 'liberal democratic values' and 'believed in free enterprise'. Although at this point Berlusconi was publicly proclaiming the need for a new political class detached from the corrupt political processes of the past, it was not clear whether he intended to take to the political field personally. Rather, he was seeking to convince his interlocutors of the urgent need to select a new class of political leaders. Berlusconi and Urbani were working in tandem, with the latter's association also aimed at selecting a new political class and platform. *Alla Ricerca di Buongoverno* involved many academics and businessmen who had previously collaborated with Berlusconi. The initial idea thus appeared to be to bring together a team of fresh clean candidates, of a neo-liberal persuasion, who would be offered as a 'package' to those DC and allied politicians who had survived the *mani pulite* investigations. This package would be sold 'much as any other financial or advertising package would be offered to Fininvest clients' (Hopkin and Paolucci 1999: 324–25). Berlusconi initially seemed to want to persuade Segni or Martinazzoli (who had emerged as secretary of the ever diminishing DC) to lead a new centrist movement. Berlusconi would give backing and propose candidates but would not become personally involved in leading. However, talks with Segni and Martinazzoli were not successful. Both were reluctant to get involved with Berlusconi, suspecting his conflict of interests and not wanting to play second fiddle to him. This led to Berlusconi's decision to enter the field at the head of his own new party in January 1994.

As Poli suggests, the launch of Forza Italia followed the classic sequence of the launch of a new product: analysis of demand, the identification of the target and the definition of the product characteristic, followed by publicity and advertising (Poli 2001: 50). Key to this process was the establishment of the polling organisation Diakron, staffed mainly by employees of Fininvest's marketing arm. It organised continuous surveys of the electoral market for Berlusconi. These polls indicated the favourable public image of Berlusconi and the potential for a new political movement led by him. According to these polls, 78 per cent of the electorate 'favoured a new liberal-democratic electoral movement composed of candidates new to politics'. Moreover, these polls demonstrated the extent to which the electorate had lost faith with old politics – with antagonism being displayed towards both the DC and the left. Respondents wanted a new technically competent politically elite who used 'simple language' (Poli 2001: 50–51). Like Bossi, Berlusconi was aware of the importance of language, as the following excerpt from one of Berlusconi's early speeches shows. Explaining why Forza Italia had been successfully received by electors, he noted that, as well as revulsion for Communism, there was,

> ... also a desire for change, for moral renewal, a desire to change the language of politics. Not any longer the use of the language of the initiated few that no one would be able to understand: there was a need to use simple, concrete and understandable language.
>
> Berlusconi (2000: 22)

Extensive use of focus groups was made in order to fine tune political strategy and programme and to provide Diakron with samples of the language and the way of thinking of ordinary people, which were used to shape Berlusconi's communication strategy (Hopkin and Paolucci 1999: 327).

Berlusconi launched a strategy based on these findings. The launch of the Forza Italia clubs was a deliberately different style of organisation from that of the old-style mass parties (being more flexible and less formal and hierarchical). The specific role of the clubs would be rather vague, amounting to little more than 'supporters' clubs' for the nascent movement. The clubs were heavily promoted by Berlusconi's Mediaset TV channels. According to February 1994 data, 6,840 clubs had been formed. Rather dubious estimates from the party on the eve of the election suggested a total of around a million adherents (Poli 2001: 47–48). This enabled Berlusconi to present Forza Italia as a ready-made mass movement, with the clubs providing important support for candidates and the staging of local meetings, while giving the new party a degree of physical visibility at the local level.

The Forza Italia political platform focused on tackling unemployment and public debt (the polls showed that these were the issues of most concern to the electorate). Polls indicating the affinity of the potential electorate with the MSI, LN and PLI meant that their electors were targeted and alliances with these forces sought. The level of popularity of Mario Segni demonstrated by these polls had also led to the unsuccessful attempt by Berlusconi to involve him in the project. Given the political context, there was little attempt by Berlusconi to win over moderate left-wing voters. 'Rather than a strictly catch-all, non-ideological strategy, FI started by fostering the formation of a moderate coalition of liberal personalities from the world of business, journalism, and the liberal professions in order to attract centre-right voters, and put a halt to the dissolution process affecting the right' (Hopkin and Paolucci 1999: 324).

In terms of finance, logistical support and personnel, the establishment of Forza Italia was entirely dependent on Berlusconi's Fininvest business empire: Forza Italia clubs were encouraged and supported by 'Programma Italia' – a financial subsidiary of Fininvest; Diakron was formed by communication experts from the Fininvest marketing network; the selection of candidates at the end of 1993 was undertaken by the twenty-six area managers of the advertising arm of Berlusconi's TV network (Publitalia). Berlusconi had massive resources at his disposal: Fininvest had a turnover of 21,800 billion lire (€11 billion) with a diversity of activities that touched Italians in every walk of their lives, from supermarkets, TV, sport and cinema to financial services and advertising. FI represented an unprecedented political experiment: a large political party put in place by a large private commercial enterprise. As Poli notes, it initially appeared almost as 'a mere diversification of Fininvest in the political market' (Poli 2001: 41).

The 1994 election

Despite the wealth of resources at the new party's disposal, Berlusconi realised that there was a need for electoral allies under the new electoral system. Forza Italia would act as a glue binding the otherwise incompatible, disparate forces of the centre right together. For those centrist and conservative voters concerned about the great leap into the unknown that the existing alternatives on the right offered, and unwilling to vote for a centre-left coalition led by former communists, FI provided a balance between continuity and reform. It was 'a new but basically conservative political party untainted by involvement in the *pentapartito* system, which could offer political change and renewal with reassurances that existing privileges would be protected' (Hopkin and Paolucci 1999: 321). McCarthy suggests that, although the LN and FI may have appeared similar in their espousal of a neo-liberal programme, they differed in that Bossi's role had been to destroy the old regime, whereas

Berlusconi sought to unite the nation around a new set of values (McCarthy 1996: 41). Nevertheless, the coalition he sought to build focused mainly on the former supporters of the *pentapartito*.

Berlusconi's communications skills and resources were utilised to the full to ensure victory in the 1994 election. In particular, Berlusconi's ownership of the three private TV channels was exploited to ensure maximum coverage on both news and general entertainment programmes, with popular TV personalities openly endorsing Berlusconi on their shows. Given the lack of regulation of the provision of airtime[1] to candidates and parties during election campaigns and the general absence of rules on political bias, the role that the Mediaset channels played in facilitating the centre-right victory was exceptional. The use of TV obviated the need for Forza Italia to have a mass membership to canvass supporters with traditional labour-intensive methods, allowing the charismatic leadership of Berlusconi to be projected directly into peoples' homes. 'In FI the search for support was almost entirely carried out on televisions either owned by Berlusconi, or linked to Fininvest through business contracts' (Hopkin and Paolucci 1999: 327). As Hopkin and Paolucci explain, around 100 local TV stations already connected to Fininvest were offered free programmes in exchange for free time for political advertising. The leader of the centre-left coalition, Achille Occhetto, received only 25 per cent of the airtime given to Berlusconi on the Mediaset channels (Hopkin and Paolucci 1999: 327–28).

Forza Italia's election campaign in 1994 was run by Publitalia with a key role being played by its head, Marcello dell'Utri (Poli 2001: 57). The selection of candidates for the election was also conditioned by the impact such candidates could have on the nascent party's media communications. The preferred candidates were young up-and-coming professionals and political outsiders. They received candidate kits with useful hints on how to handle the media and how to present themselves to both the media and the public at large and were obliged to attend courses run by Publitalia on how to communicate on TV. Publitalia was responsible for the headhunting and selection of candidates, and for providing them with training in campaigning skills. Training involved TV and public relations (PR) skills as well as advice on what to wear. During the election campaign, Publitalia managers continued to work as regional co-ordinators. Some became part of the national structure (eight were elected as deputies), although most returned to work normally for Fininvest/Publitalia after the election.

The resources at the coalition's disposal contributed to the centre-right's success at the 1994 election, in winning 46.4 per cent of the vote – an absolute majority of seats in the chamber of deputies and three seats short of a majority in the Senate. FI itself was the biggest single party, winning 21 per cent of the vote in the proportional part of the count (amounting to over 8 million voters). In relation to the 1992 election, FI inherited 50 per cent of the vote of the PLI, 31 per cent of the LN, 27 per cent of the PSI, 24 per cent of the DC and 18 per cent of the MSI. It did best in the north (Lombardy, Piedmont,

Veneto and Friuli-Venezia-Giulia) and in Sicily. It did worst in the central red belt of Italy. It became the strongest party in the north (followed by the LN), the second party of the centre (after the PDS) and the third party of the south (after the AN and the PDS). For technical reasons tied to the number of signatures required for presentation of the list, it did not compete in Puglia. If this region is excluded from the calculations, then FI actually got 22.4 per cent of the vote (Diamanti 1994: 665–67; Mannheimer 1994: 30–35).

FI in opposition (1995–2001) – consolidation and re-organisation

The euphoria of the 1994 election victory was soon punctured by the squabbles and the eventual collapse of the government in December 1994. While FI had been constructed rapidly in late 1993–94 for a 'lightning war' as a lean and successful election-winning machine, its model of development was less appropriate for a protracted period of opposition. Indeed, the assumption of Berlusconi and his lieutenants was that new elections would take place quickly, thus there was no time or need to address any possible defects in the party's organisation. However, discontent and frustration within the party at its top-down and undemocratic nature, which had already begun to ferment in 1994, became more evident in opposition. Nevertheless, Berlusconi continued to make a virtue out of the party's light model of organisation, contrasting it with the bureaucratic and heavy structures of the traditional parties. In May 1995, he declared: 'We want to remain a movement. We cannot make ourselves into a party, also because we are a movement of opinion and then because we don't want the necessary costs of becoming a heavy structure ... We cannot think about becoming what one would define as a political party, with vast structures and apparatus and fees' (Poli 2001: 97).

In this phase, as suggested, Forza Italia could be described as 'the business firm masquerading as a party' with the territorial structure of representatives of Publitalia substituting that usually in place for the traditional parties (Hopkin and Paolucci 1999: 329). Berlusconi's confidence in the superiority of FI's mode of organisation was severely damaged by the defeat of FI and the centre right when elections were finally held in the spring of 1996. FI lost 38 per cent of its electors from 1994, losing votes in the north to the LN – which ran against it – in particular. Nevertheless, FI still grew in the south, overtaking the AN and the PDS to become the largest party there.

Following this defeat, Berlusconi appeared to realise that the weak local organisation of FI was a problem that had contributed to the electoral loss (Poli 2001: 114). The new statute of 1998 ended the uncertain organisational form of Forza Italia, giving it a level of internal democracy and turning it into a membership party. This appeared to herald a process of institutionalisation. Nevertheless, there was some resistance from within Berlusconi's entourage – from Fininvest and some parliamentarians – in relation to the new statute. Many were wary of losing power and privilege to the new membership base. This also reflected a tension between some of those involved in the original founding of the party – many of whom came from Fininvest and had no previous background in politics – and those who had jumped on the Forza Italia bandwagon when it had demonstrated its success as the most viable conservative centre-right force. Thus, FI found itself housing a number of recycled politicians from the DC, PSI and the other smaller parties of the *pentapartito*. Notable among the former DC politicians within the FI hierarchy was Claudio Scajola, the former DC mayor of Imperia (in Liguria). He took the lead in the committee that drew up the new FI statute, later being made party co-ordinator by Berlusconi, and became increasingly influential in the revamping of the FI organisation, utilising his experience in the DC.

1996–97 had been a difficult political period for FI, still reeling from the defeat of 1996 and having difficulty in local elections. Tensions within FI concerning the political and organisational direction of the party had led to a number of parliamentarians leaving the party. There was also the threat of a new centre-right party in this period – the UDR of Cossiga founded in February 1998 – which aimed to erode the electoral and parliamentary strength of both the centre-right and the centre-left poles.

The re-organisation of the party cemented by the first party congress in April 1998 signalled the launch of a fightback for Berlusconi, previously under the cosh given the judicial proceedings against him, the schism with the LN, wrangling with the AN and internal criticisms of the party organisation. His rehabilitation was of course greatly aided by D'Alema's close involvement with him in discussions on constitutional reform. Berlusconi's attempts to have FI taken seriously as a party were also aided on the international front by the FI's admittance into the predominantly Christian Democratic European Peoples' Party (PPE) group in the European Parliament (EP) in 1998 (the group was also home to the various Italian delegations that had emerged out of the DC). The decision of the PPE to admit FI was aided by the latter's internal reforms, which allowed it to present itself as a real popular democratic party.

The 1999 European elections re-established Berlusconi as the leader of the centre-right pole. The election was a great success for FI, winning 25.2 per cent of the vote. In the months leading up to the election, FI had organised various manifestations against the policies of the D'Alema government (which had replaced that of Prodi in October 1998). The main manifestation was 'Tax Day', a day of protest against the taxes of the centre-left government – held in Verona and beamed via satellite to 100 other cities. There was also a massive media campaign prior to the election: 1,781 publicity spots were put on air at a cost of 6 billion lire (Poli 2001: 142). The election was also a personal success for Berlusconi. He was a candidate in all five EP constituencies and got the highest in each – getting over 3 million personal votes. With the vote of both the LN and the AN falling, the result re-established FI as the indispensable cement of the centre-right pole.

The campaign for the regional elections the following year proved an excellent example of Berlusconi's showmanship and the capacity that his charismatic presence, combined with his wealth of communication resources, had to woo a substantial sector of the Italian electorate. At a convention held on 9 March 2000, Berlusconi declared that the electoral campaign would be conducted 'from the sky, land and sea' (Poli 2001: 149). Most notably, the campaign would be marked by the use of a cruise ship by Berlusconi – 'Azzurra, the ship of liberty' – from which he would base his campaign, sailing around the peninsular and stopping off at various ports in the disputed regions. Candidates were again equipped with a 'candidates' kit' which, alongside the tips on dental hygiene, included a collection of Berlusconi's speeches '*L'Italia che ho in mente*' (the Italy I have in mind), which would be heavily publicised in this period.

Crucially, the election also saw the reconstitution of a centre-right pole, the CdL, also including the LN. The campaign bore fruit with FI confirmed as the leading party in Italy, winning 25.6 per cent of the vote. The CdL won eight regions (including six for FI, meaning it held seven in total after winning Friuli-Venezia-Giulia in 1998). In Piedmont, Lombardy and Veneto, FI won more than 30 per cent of the vote. The result definitely confirmed the candidacy of Berlusconi for the 2001 general election. It also led to the resignation of D'Alema as prime minister and his replacement by Giuliano Amato. While reaffirming Berlusconi's supremacy on the centre right, the effect of the inclusion of the LN in the CdL made clear the benefits of ending the damaging effect of electoral competition within the centre right. It also appeared to reflect a new organisational capacity on the part of FI, with a greater rooting at the local level, allowing it to mobilise support more effectively.

The 2001 general election and the return to government

The communication strategy of the CdL for the 2001 general election was focused almost entirely on the image of Berlusconi. FI candidates were requested not to produce posters and campaign literature bearing their own image, so as not to conflict with the unitary image of the official party communications (Poli 2001: 159). A new collection of Berlusconi's parliamentary interventions, '*Discorsi per la democrazia*' (speeches for democracy) was published in January 2001 to go on the bookshelf with his previously published collection of speeches '*L'Italia che ho in mente*'. Several hundred local events were organised by FI's local leaders to publicise the new collection. A glossy photo history of Berlusconi's life '*Una storia italiana*' (an Italian story) was also produced and sent to around 15 million Italian households (Poli 2001: 160).

In personalising the campaign around the controversial figure of Berlusconi, the centre right forced their centre-left opponents on to the same terrain. Thus, the centre-left's campaign was also focused on the qualities (or defects) of Berlusconi. Coverage of the rival campaigns in the media also reflected this personalisation. The campaign was constructed as a plebiscite on the figure of Berlusconi. Did the electorate want him to lead the country or not? The electoral campaign was characterised by reciprocal accusations of delegitimation and attacks on Berlusconi that came not just from his Italian political opponents, but from journalists in Italy and abroad. The most notable example was the denunciation of Berlusconi by *The Economist*, which questioned on its front page whether this man was fit to govern a leading capitalist democracy. This allowed Berlusconi to play the victim under attack from politicians and the media and subject to anti-Italian prejudice from international journalists (Poli 2001: 161).

The campaign was of course a great success, particularly in relation to the strategy pursued by Berlusconi. Forza Italia won 29.4 per cent of the votes in the proportional lists for the chamber of deputies (this was an increase of over 3 million from 1996). FI was reaffirmed as the most voted for party in Italy (as in the EP and regional elections of 1999 and 2000). It finished 13 per cent ahead of the second party (the DS). It got more than 30 per cent of the vote in Piedmont, Lombardy, Veneto, Campania, Puglia, Sicily and Sardinia. Even within the central red belt, it achieved between 20 and 25 per cent of vote. It became the leading party in fifteen regions.

Electorates

Given that Forza Italia emerged out of nowhere at the beginning of 1994, its electoral record has been astonishing, never falling below 20 per cent of the national vote in subsequent general elections. Unlike its coalition allies, it has enjoyed strong support throughout the Italian territory, although it is particularly strong in the more highly developed northern regions, notably Lombardy, Piedmont and the Veneto, as well as in parts of the south, especially Sicily. Thus, it has proved highly successful in occupying the political space vacated by the DC and its coalition allies in 1993 (Pasquino 2003b: 209).

Mannheimer's study of the FI electorate in 1994 showed that it reflected all types of persons, ages and social groups. In general, its electorate was younger (40 per cent of FI voters were under 35), housewives and women were over-represented (55 per cent of FI electors), as were businessmen and the self-employed and those with a low level of education (Diamanti 1994: 665; Mannheimer 1994: 35–36). Forza Italia's anti-political stance was also important. As Diamanti notes, FI's electorate showed deep distrust towards traditional political institutions (even more so than the LN electorate). In a sense, it reflected 'average' Italian society 'anchored in traditional values and institutions – the family, the market, the Church – characterised by a demand for order and stability' and recently left orphaned by the collapse of the traditional parties. Many of these voters had flirted with the idea of voting with the LN or the MSI prior to the formation of the FI but were put off by the extremist language and ethno-territorialism of the former and the fascist past of the latter (Diamanti 1994: 666). While FI represented median Italian values, there were exceptions to this: (1) a demand for greater territorial autonomy and a greater faith in regions of the north of the country; (2) a strong faith in private enterprise; (3) a strong identification with the Mediaset

TV channels and a concomitant lack of faith in the public RAI channels. Despite coming from different social groups, there was a consensus among voters regarding this 'cultural model' which, Mannheimer suggests, explains the success of FI. FI represented a cultural model diffused for years by Berlusconi's TV channels (Mannheimer 1994: 38–40).

While in 1994, Forza Italia's vote had an impressive close-class appeal, in 1996, while its overall share of the vote remained relatively stable, its social composition underwent a number of changes, most significantly the loss of support among manual workers. Biorcio explains this as a result of the controversy surrounding Berlusconi's attempts to reform pensions in 1994, and the break with the LN which was able to attract the votes of employed workers away from FI (Biorcio 2002: 97). Overall, while support among the sectors of voters who had most keenly supported Berlusconi in 1994 grew, it struggled to retain support among dependent workers. However, in 2001, FI was able to recover support from the categories in which it was weak, and increase it further among the social groups in which it was already strong. This was especially the case in relation to shopkeepers, artisans and housewives. Notably, FI's support among manual workers shifted from being under-represented to being above average. Biorcio attributes this to Berlusconi's extravagant promises on pensions and on major public works projects, which would increase employment. The high level of support among the working class also relates to the high proportion of FI's electorate with less than the minimum school-leaving qualification (while its support is under-represented among graduates) (Biorcio 2002: 97–98).

Gender-related patterns of voting have often been highlighted in studies of the Forza Italia electorate. Ginsborg notes how an extraordinarily high 48.8 per cent of housewives voted for Forza Italia in 2001, a particularly significant figure given the low levels of female occupation in Italy. Moreover, the more television women watched, the more they demonstrated a propensity to vote Forza Italia: 42.3 per cent of those who watched three hours a day voted for the party, compared with 31.6 per cent who watched between one or two hours daily. Ginsborg remarks: 'The connexions between housework and the advertisement of commodities, between the consumption of goods and the formation of subjectivities, between female viewing and the packaged messages of the charismatic male political figure, are here to be found in striking form' (Ginsborg 2003: 6).

In the 2006 election, FI was the biggest loser within the CdL. Its share of the vote fell from 29.4 per cent to 23.7 per cent, a drop of 5.8 per cent, while the vote of the AN and the LN increased marginally, and the UDC vote doubled. The FI vote fell by around 6 per cent in both the northwest and northeast and in the south and islands, and by around 5 per cent in the centre-north and centre-south. However, the votes lost by the FI in the northwest and northeast went mainly to its coalition partners. Indeed, the biggest gainers in these areas were the AN and the UDC (the UDC gained an additional 4 per cent of the vote in these areas, winning back some of the former DC heartlands).

In the south, however, the biggest gainers were the centre-left parties. Southern voters were likely to have been disillusioned by the failure of FI and the CdL as a whole to deliver on its promises on public works and employment, and also likely to have been put off by FI's apparently northern bias in government. While increasing its share of the vote among its core electorate of the self-employed, the CdL in general, and FI in particular, lost a significant share of the vote among manual workers. However, high-income employees voted in ever greater numbers for the CdL. This group was more susceptible to Berlusconi's warnings about the higher taxes a centre-left government would bring (Diamanti and Vassallo 2007).

Berlusconi's populist leadership

Observers of Italian politics and political parties have found it difficult to discuss the nature of Forza Italia without discussing Berlusconi himself. The nature of the party and its political appeal is intrinsically linked to the figure of Berlusconi himself. Berlusconi's charismatic appeal has been key to Forza Italia's success. As Paolucci comments: 'Charisma played a legitimising function which diverted attention and criticisms away from the centralised management of the party and its atypical business firm nature' (Paolucci 2006: 169). FI enjoyed the typical attributes of charismatic movements, 'in which the leader and founder alone selects the aims and the social basis of the party and is the only true source and legitimate interpreter of the party's doctrine' (Paolucci 2006: 169). The identity of the party and that of its leader would be completely integrated. As such parties tend to rise and fall with their leaders, it was questionable as to whether or not Forza Italia could continue to exist without the presence of Berlusconi.

Berlusconi's political style in many ways reflects a classic populist approach, casting himself as a political outsider, speaking the language and thinking the thoughts of the common man and representing the interests of the latter against a self-serving political elite made up of 'professional politicians'. When Berlusconi entered the political field in 1994, he presented his party and himself as a 'non-political' response to the political crisis, extraneous to the old system and using the language of the 'man on the street', directed at an electorate that was sick of years of 'politicking' (Poli 2001: 28). He obviously benefited from the unique political opportunities of the circumstances of Italy from 1993 to 1994, the discrediting of an entire political class by *tangentopoli* and the collapse of the old parties which opened up a political space for a new party and a new class of political leaders. After initially appearing to want to play the role of 'king-maker' to this new political class, he then decided to play at being king himself, placing himself at the head of the new political class, as a new and unblemished political leader.

Berlusconi's success related to the circumstances of the political crisis, his ability to seize on discontent with the existing political alternatives and to offer a new style of political leadership. However, his success was based not only on 'novelty' and on 'non-party' characteristics, but the ability to understand changes in Italian society, culture and politics and respond to the new market demand (a demand his TV channels had helped to create). Berlusconi utilised his credentials as a highly successful entrepreneur to play up his portrayal as a political outsider. 'Not only was Berlusconi predominantly a businessman, but he also decided to emphasise this quality and structure the party very much like the firm he owned' (Paolucci 2006: 168). Berlusconi was 'narrating a myth about the ingenuity of the Italian entrepreneur', proclaiming that his entrepreneurial success meant that no other man was better placed to revive the Italian economy (McCarthy 1996: 41–42). In the Berlusconi vision, his business empire was built on the story of 'the pioneers of commercial television', the 'passionate builders of utopias', the men with 'the sun in their pockets' who challenged the monopolies of RAI and Sipra (the public advertising regulator), fighting against the 'anti-Fininvest lobby' directed by the RAI, 'composed of politicians, newspaper editors and intellectuals of the left who shared an "anti-modern prejudice" against commercial TV', 'spreading the philosophy of a healthy market economy, of the freedom of the individual, of meritocracy' (Poli 2001: 34). This same interpretation was also projected by Forza Italia in 1994 to persuade the country that these entrepreneurial values that had brought such great success in business could also bring success to the country. Of course, Berlusconi has been rather disingenuous in casting the rise of his TV channels as some kind of titanic popular struggle against an elite-backed public media monopoly, given that the success of this battle depended on his close friendship with the PSI leader, Bettino Craxi – one of Italy's most powerful politicians in the 1980s and early 1990s (and prime minister from 1983 to 1988) – who smoothed the regulatory pathway to ensure Berlusconi's dominance of Italy's private network. Berlusconi's links with the pre-*tangentopoli* political establishment involved a close relationship with Craxi and the PSI in general, together with broader connections with the conservative establishment, which was also reflected in his membership of the shadowy P2 masonic lodge.[2]

Despite this background, Berlusconi successfully presented himself as the 'outsider from politics, the anti-establishment candidate in combat against the old and corrupt political-party order, conquering the electorate with the entrepreneurial and managerial myth of success, able to create riches' (Poli 2001: 65). Berlusconi's discourse involved references to 'dreams' and 'miracles' – images, symbols and metaphors that were not conventionally political, sometimes derived from sport or religion (see also Cheles 2006).

His populism involves a belief that he speaks for the Italian silent majority, the popular 'heartlands' – as per Taggart's (2000) description of the populist constituency – that is the average hard-working Italian, who is not very political but anti-communist and holding traditional catholic and conservative values, who dreams of achieving the kind of material success that would allow him/her to live the kind of lifestyles portrayed on the Berlusconi-owned TV channels that are watched religiously by a large swathe of the Italian population. As with other populist leaders, Berlusconi plays the role of the 'man of destiny', uniquely able to channel the thoughts and aspirations of the Italian people. Berlusconi has sometimes even gone as far as to compare himself with Christ, a reluctant leader, forced to bear the cross or accept the bitter chalice of leading his people. When his government was hanging by a thread at the end of 1994, he suggested that he was 'anointed by the Lord' as the people had chosen him to lead them (McCarthy 1996: 41–42).

Unlike other western political leaders, Berlusconi has made great play of the anti-communist theme, and with remarkable success (despite the abandonment of communism by much of the ex-PCI and the rather mild form of social democracy championed by the centre-left leadership). The following excerpt is among the countless examples of Berlusconi's anti-communism and explains the reasons for his decision to create Forza Italia:

> Then we took a decision, we looked at what the feeling of the country was, what was the feeling of the voters, most of all of the voters who had chosen to vote for the democratic parties, and who, suddenly, didn't feel represented any longer. In the air there was great fear, worry that the future of Italy could be an illiberal and suffocating one if old and new communists were to govern the country.
>
> Berlusconi (2000: 22)

Obviously, this emphasis on anti-communism has a historical context, given that the PCI was the largest communist party in the western world up until the 1980s (notwithstanding the Italian Euro-communist interpretation, which was rather distinct from the Marxist–Leninist democratic centralism of other communist parties). Moreover, the leadership of the DS remained dominated by figures who grew up in the PCI, and are thus – as Berlusconi would readily argue – likely to have been imbued with a communist political culture. Berlusconi's political speeches are thus littered with references to the 'communist' opposition, and this often comes as part of a general demonisation of both communism and the opposition in general. This chimes with Mudde's characterisation of populism as presenting 'a Manichean outlook, in which there are only friends and foes' (Mudde 2004: 544). Examples of this Manichean approach include Berlusconi's message to a FI meeting in January 2005, when he warned that, if the centre left returned to government there would be 'misery, terror and death' (Jerkov 2005). Another speech in which he referred to how the Chinese communists in the Mao era boiled babies to fertilise their fields (and somehow equating the Italian 'communists' with this abomination) did not go down too well with the Chinese regime.

While anti-communism has been a constant in Berlusconi's populist portrayal of his – and 'the people's' –enemies, the focus of some of his attacks has evolved over time. As with many other populists, Berlusconi has a deft ability to switch positions according to changed political contexts, and to switch the focus of his populist ire. When initially launching himself into the political field, Berlusconi emphasised that he was a new man untainted by the corruption and inefficiency of the First Republic. In this, there was an implicit endorsement of the work of the prosecuting magistrates who had investigated and brought down many of the political leaders of the old order. However, after investigations into Berlusconi's affairs were launched by some of the same magistrates (precipitating the downfall of his first government in 1994), he began to denounce politically motivated communist-inspired judges. Indeed, the attack on left-wing judges would be broadened during Berlusconi's second term of office, when he would repeatedly refer to a left-wing elite that dominated key institutions such as the (non-Berlusconi-owned) media and the judiciary (even at times citing the theory of hegemony of the Italian communist thinker Gramsci, and suggesting that the communists had successfully implemented his ideas by establishing such a hegemony in certain institutions). Again, the demonisation of a left-liberal or politically correct metropolitan elite dominating public life is a key plank in the discourse of the modern populist of the right (Mudde 2004), also borrowing this conceptualisation from the *Nouvelle droite* school. Berlusconi argued that such elites were hampering his ability to govern, and that criticisms of his 'man in the street' style of political language simply reflected this elitism.

Similarly, Berlusconi has rebutted criticisms of his political style as belonging to the 'old ways of doing politics'. His anti-elitism in this sense continues to go beyond a supposed left-wing elite and refers to an elite of professional politicians, a hangover from the First Republic. Indeed, during his second government's term of office, his attacks on recycled First Republic politicians referred not only to the recycled communists of the DS and RC, but also the recycled Christian Democrats and *missini* within his own coalition, i.e. the UDC and the AN, from whom a great deal of criticism of his political style had emerged. As in the past, 'the evident differences in style between the dynamic if unsophisticated entrepreneur and the Machiavellian manoeuvrings of the existing political class were constantly emphasised' (Hopkin and Paolucci 1999: 325–26). Thus, Berlusconi found he was closer in political style and spirit to his fellow Lombard, Bossi, a man with similar disdain for old-style politicking and the convoluted language of the old political elite. This was reflected in his closer relations with the latter during his second term.

Nevertheless, the return to government in 2001 made it more difficult for Berlusconi to set himself apart from the recycled political class of the post-*tangentopoli* republic. Not only was his party in alliance with recycled political parties, but his own party also contained a number of recycled politicians, notably from the DC and PSI. Furthermore, his *ad personam* laws involved granting political immunity to certain office-holders, sending out the message that incorrect, and indeed corrupt, behaviour by certain politicians could go unpunished. Moreover, his attacks on the judiciary also included criticism of the way magistrates conducted the *mani pulite* investigations in the early 1990s. Berlusconi appeared to be on a mission to rehabilitate the political leaders brought down by these investigations, notably his political patron, Bettino Craxi. He also defended the reputation of the former prime minister, Giulio Andreotti, who faced lengthy judicial investigations into alleged links with the Sicilian mafia (his eventual acquittal on appeal came in 2003, and Berlusconi would later back his candidature for president of the senate in 2006). Similarly, Berlusconi would denounce the proceedings against his friend and right-hand man, Marcello Dell'Utri (former head of Publitalia), which resulted in his conviction for mafia association in 2004. Berlusconi claimed that Dell'Utri was guilty only of helping to construct Forza Italia (and that there was thus a judicial plot against the party's founders, which had also led to a corruption conviction against another close collaborator, Cesare Previti).

The following extract from a speech made by Berlusconi in November 2008 is instructive in terms of his attitude to both the *mani pulite* judges and his 'communist' opponents:

> In 1992 the magistrates began an action against the five democratic parties which, though with many errors, had managed to guarantee 50 years of progress and wellbeing … It was here that we began our freedom adventure. We found ourselves in a situation in which we citizens who never thought about entering politics were faced with a situation in which the elections of 1994 could have resulted in the PCI and its allies with 34% of the vote occupying 82% of parliamentary seats. This was the result of accurate surveys which were presented to me in June 1993. From there, thinking that the country could not deliver itself to those who had, in their creed and symbol, the hammer and sickle, which history had taught us was the symbol of fear, terror, a police state and death.
>
> Staff Reporter (2008f)

At different times, Berlusconi has claimed that the judges were part of a communist plot, were 'mad' and in need of psychiatric help, and that the pool of magistrates conducting the *mani pulite* investigations had been worse than fascism. During the 2008 election campaign, he suggested that the judiciary be subject to regular mental health checks. These were examples of his tendency to demonise his political opponents, as well as his contempt for constitutional checks on popularly elected leaders. Moreover, the comparison with fascism was also a reflection of his rather flippant attitude towards Italy's post-war anti-fascist consensus, upon which the constitutional principles of the First Republic were constructed. Other examples of this were when he stated in an interview for *The Spectator* that the fascist regime in Italy was rather a mild affair, in which nobody had been killed and in which political opponents had been sent to holiday camps, and when he likened a German Socialist MEP, who asked a critical question following his address to the European Parliament in 2003, to a German concentration camp guard. This approach is also reflected in the nature of his political alliances. Of course, he played a key role in rehabilitating Gianfranco Fini and the then MSI in 1993 (when Fini and his party were still regarded as neo-fascists by many observers). While in retrospect, the latter may seem more justifiable given Fini's subsequent moves to the centre ground, Berlusconi's more recent political dealings have involved unashamed attempts to bring unreconstructed fascists into his political coalition. For example, the centre-right alliance for the 2006 general election included Alessandra Mussolini's new political formation, Alternativa Sociale, which is fairly unrepentant about Italy's fascist legacy and contains unreconstructed neo-fascists from other extremist groupings as well. For the 2005 regional elections, Berlusconi brought the latest political grouping of the great fascist survivor, Pino Rauti (Movimento Idea Sociale), into the CdL. This group had broken away from MS-Fiamma Tricolore – with which the CdL formed an electoral pact in 2001 (when Rauti was still leader).

These dealings reflect a general political pragmatism or indeed amoralism in Berlusconi's willingness to engage in political alliances with a range of actors, including not only the extreme right, but extreme libertarians such as the Radical party (despite the evident incompatibility between their positions and the catholic conservatism shared by the other coalition partners). This promiscuity in political alliance-building reflects a lack of interest in ideological coherence and sometimes a lack of knowledge of who he is dealing with. For example, when confronted with the fact that Ms Mussolini's formation included notorious fascist extremists such as Roberto Fiore (leader of Forza Nuova) and Adrian Tilgher (formerly of Avanguardia Nazionale), he claimed not to know who these people were (Bei 2006).

In 2007, Berlusconi was involved in further controversy about his political alliances when he attended the launch meeting of the new breakaway group from the AN, Francesco Storace's La Destra, where fascist songs were played and a number of activists openly stiffened their arms in the Roman salute. Berlusconi was present while Storace attacked Fini for his trip to Israel in which he apologised for the crimes of fascism (Staff Reporter 2007e). Berlusconi was later condemned by the president of the Jewish community in Rome for his failure to distance himself from Storace (Staff Reporter 2007c). Berlusconi was also alleged to be financing Storace's party in order to cause discomfort for Fini.[3] In 2008, Berlusconi's attempts to bring La Destra into the PdL were blocked by Fini, although Mussolini was brought in. Another controversial candidate brought in by Berlusconi was Giuseppe Ciarrapico, a businessman, newspaper publisher and former president of the AS Roma football club, and also a self-declared fascist. While the inclusion of the latter brought criticism from the Jewish community, and also caused Fini some unease, Berlusconi maintained that Ciarrapico's inclusion was necessary given the support that his local newspapers could offer.

Berlusconi's political pragmatism can be characterised as a vital ingredient of his populism. While his coalition includes ethno-populists such as the LN, and his discourse is often classically populist in his demonisation of his opponents and his anti-political attacks on professional politicians, the political programmes that he has pursued have been more pragmatic, representing an attempt to appeal to a wide variety of constituencies (even where his appeals are openly contradictory). This brings him more into the category of politician's populism elucidated by Canovan (1981). Thus, Berlusconi tries to be all things to all people, simultaneously appealing to the northern petite bourgeoisie who want less government and lower taxes (rivalling the LN for this electorate) and state-dependent voters in the south to whom he promises major public works – such as the proposed bridge linking the toe of Italy with Sicily (here playing to a similar constituency to that of the AN and UDC).

Berlusconi's pragmatism and need to appeal to a wider constituency mean he nevertheless generally steers clear of the ethno-populist rhetoric that characterises the LN. However, while he sometimes registers embarrassment and seeks to distance himself from such positions, this generally falls short of outright condemnation, and there is sometimes a tacit understanding that he actually agrees with the sentiments of the statements made by Bossi and other LN exponents. In this sense, Bossi and other LN figures have acted as rottweilers for Berlusconi, saying the things that he would like to say, but falls short of staying because of his and his party's political location and need to appeal to more moderate voters and gain the respect of his international peers.

Despite this, Berlusconi's many gaffes and public indiscretions are legion, and have often been the cause of embarrassment on the international stage. For example, his comment following the victory of Barack Obama in the US Presidential election in November 2008 that the president-elect was 'young, handsome and also suntanned' hit the headlines throughout the world. His comment likening the German Socialist MEP Martin Schulz to a concentration camp guard in 2003 was also widely reported. Following a dispute with Finland over the selection of the seat of the European Food Safety Authority, he commented that he had had to use all his old playboy skills to persuade the Finnish female president, Tarja Halonen. He also further annoyed the Finns by making derogatory comments about the food he had had to 'endure' in Finland. Berlusconi has made great play of his friendship with Russian president/prime minister Putin. At a joint press conference with Putin in 2008, Berlusconi came to his friend's aid when asked an awkward question by a female Russian journalist, by imitating a gunman shooting at her, reducing her to tears. More seriously, at a previous joint press conference with Putin in 2003, he had stridently defended Russian actions in Chechnya, irritating his EU partners, given that this went against their joint policy (and Italy held the EU presidency at the time).

Other moments of international embarrassment included Berlusconi's behaviour at an EU summit in 2002. During a group photo, he made the Italian hand gesture for a 'cuckold' behind the head of the Spanish foreign minister. At a meeting with Danish prime minister Anders Fogh Rasmussen in the same year, Berlusconi complimented him with the words: 'He's so good looking, I'm even thinking of introducing him to my wife', adding that 'he's much better looking than Cacciari' – the reference being to Massimo

Cacciari, the centre-left mayor of Venice, with whom Berlusconi's wife Veronica Lario is rumoured to have had an affair. Berlusconi has caused his wife public embarrassment on a number of occasions. At an awards dinner in January 2007, Berlusconi was quoted as saying to Mara Carfagna, a former TV presenter and model who had been elected to parliament with FI, 'if I wasn't already married, I would marry you right away ... with you, I'd go anywhere'. This prompted Ms Lario to demand an apology from her husband in a front-page letter to the Italian newspaper, *La Repubblica*, forcing Berlusconi into a public apology. Carfagna was named as minister for equal opportunities in the new Berlusconi government in 2008 leading to comments about the appropriateness of her appointment and innuendo about her relationship with Berlusconi.[4]

Berlusconi's numerous gaffes and departures from international protocol make many Italians cringe with embarrassment. Nevertheless, they also serve to reinforce his popularity with many centre-right voters, apparently confirming his outsider status and image as a man of the people with a mischievous twinkle in his eye who refuses to bow to the stuffy protocols of the political establishment.

The business-firm party model

The nature of Forza Italia's construction would lead to it being labelled a plastic or virtual party, lacking any real roots in the Italian territory and being entirely dependent on the charismatic personality and resources of its leader Silvio Berlusconi. Forza Italia could also be described as an extreme example of the electoral–professional model of party organisation, or more aptly as a pioneer of the business-firm party model (Hopkin and Paolucci 1999). The electoral–professional model was elucidated by Angelo Panebianco in 1988 (Panebianco 1988). This developed further the 'catch-all' party model previously elaborated by Otto Kirkheimer (1966) building on its features of 'de-ideologisation, weak electoral links, and centralisation of power around the party-leadership' (Hopkin and Paolucci 1999: 307). But Panebianco's model went further in referring to the 'professionalisation' of party organisations, i.e. the increasing dependence of party politicians on outsiders with particular technical expertise.

In Italy, and in other advanced democracies, the emergence of these party models was a function of the decline of subcultures and electorates of belonging, which meant that, in seeking to win office, parties needed to go beyond traditional appeals based on class, identity and subculture, as ties with the core electoral constituencies became weakened, and electorates become more heterogeneous and sophisticated. As the traditional 'mass party' waned, there was a decline in the importance of grassroot activists, and often a greater centralisation of power around party leaders. Thus, parties developed 'catch-all' strategies, reducing their ideological package and developing programmes and campaign strategies designed to appeal to a variety of social groups and maximise their vote-winning potential. Such parties have also capitalised on the development of mass communications, and television in particular, which allows campaign messages to be beamed directly into the homes of voters. This has particular pertinence in Italy, given Berlusconi's ownership of the three main private TV networks. As Hopkin and Paolucci note, and especially relevant for Italy, in such parties, support is mobilised 'around party and leadership images carefully prepared by public relations consultants and media experts', and policy positions are 'elaborated by reference to opinion polling which sounds out the electorate's views on contentious issues and provides information on those policy proposals most likely to attract the target electorate'. Moreover, standard marketing and advertising procedures are used in order to 'sell a product' (political representatives arguing for public policies) much as an enterprise would use them to sell private consumer goods (Hopkin and Paolucci 1999: 310–11).

Electoral–professional parties have had more room for development in new democracies (e.g. the new southern European democracies of Greece, Portugal and Spain in the 1970s and, more recently, the former communist countries of central and eastern Europe) where new party systems have been established. In a sense, in these countries, a fresh slate is available on which to construct new parties, whereas in more longstanding democracies, traditional party models have survived, with party systems having stagnated or 'frozen' in time from the earlier period of establishment (Lipset and Stein Rokkan 1967). In Italy, while democracy had been longer established, the collapse of the old party system in the early 1990s had created a similar effect, in that it allowed a new party system to develop and thus new party forms to flourish. Hence, the success of Forza Italia in exploiting the potential of the electoral–professional model to the full in the new political conditions of Italy post-*tangentopoli*:

> The case of Forza Italia is probably the most extreme example to date of a new political party organising as a business firm. In Forza Italia the distinctions between analogy and reality are blurred: the 'political entrepreneur' in question is in fact a businessman, and the organisation of the party is largely conditioned by the prior existence of a business firm.
>
> Hopkin and Paolucci (1999: 320)

In a more recent work, Paolucci outlines three key characteristics of Forza Italia: patrimonial organisation, the business-firm character and charismatic leadership (Paolucci 2006: 166). As a patrimonial organisation, Forza Italia was 'owned, controlled, and directed autocratically by its founder and leader'. The business-firm character involved 'the transfer of people, but also structures, ideology, styles and procedures from Berlusconi's firms into the party', while the charismatic leadership of Berlusconi 'played an important legitimising function, by justifying patrimonialism internally and the business model externally, thereby guaranteeing the loyalty of the activists and the support of the voters'. The charismatic leadership of Berlusconi was particularly important given the importance of the media to modern political campaigning. His TV skills and ownership of the main private TV networks in Italy were crucial here. The new party was tailored around Berlusconi's personality and interests and became his personal instrument. Thus, Berlusconi personally oversaw the party's organisational design, staffed it with people from his business and dominated media images of the party as its sole figurehead (Paolucci 2006: 166–67). The patrimonial imprint of the party was reflected in the personalisation of the party's relationships.

> The modalities of candidate and party leadership recruitment and selection were such that appointment to the party's highest posts was a fully discretionary choice by the leader who, in his quality of owner, chose mainly people who were either employees of his firm or close friends or associates of his as a businessman. In any case, they were people he personally decided he could trust. The privilege of being chosen rested therefore entirely on the personal relationship with the party's owner. All power positions became a direct emanation of a purely personal relationship with him.
>
> Paolucci (2006: 167)

The business-firm style also meant the adoption of the discourse of efficient management found in business firms. Poli suggests that Fininvest '(o)ffered an organisational model and a managerial culture which demonstrated itself to be a winning one in many sectors'. It was a lean non-hierarchical structure (unlike the traditional Italian model), with a strong concentration of power at the top. It was a quasi chaotic model that was Berlusconi centred. This would also largely condition the initial organisational model of Forza Italia (Poli 2001: 40).

It was a deliberate strategy of Berlusconi to avoid the bureaucratic, hierarchical and 'heavy' structures that characterised the traditional 'mass' parties. The discrediting of the 'partyocracy' meant that even the term 'party' was eschewed. The name of the new political force was rather removed from the type usually associated with political parties. Rather, the term Forza Italia was appropriated from the chant usually used by followers of the Italian football team. This also enhanced Berlusconi's popular credentials, and reminded voters of the unprecedented success he had a brought as owner and president of the AC Milan football team. Moreover, the term Forza Italia (come on Italy!) had nationalist connotations, contributing to the image of the new force as one bringing renewal to the whole nation.

The light structure of the new party was reflected in its founding statutes, consisting of just nineteen articles. These set out a very simplified structure centred around the members' assembly, which would formulate policies and elect the council of the presidency. But as Hopkin and Paolucci note:

The Assembly never gathered, and the Council of the Presidency [or president's council], instead of being elected, was initially entirely co-opted by Berlusconi, who filled it with people from his entourage (lawyers and managers from Fininvest), adding a couple of external academics or otherwise well known personalities, mainly to convey the impression that the party was not totally dominated by Berlusconi's 'clan'.

Hopkin and Paolucci (1999: 323)

However, even the presidential council met only occasionally. Rather, key decisions and strategy formulation appeared to be developed in *ad hoc* fashion in informal meetings held by Berlusconi and his close confidantes. Meetings regarding party business and strategy would be barely distinguishable from those he would call as president of Fininvest.

This top-down structure meant that there was no room for democratic structures and grassroots accountability. This was reflected in the anomalous position of the Forza Italia clubs, which had no role whatsoever in the formal party organisation. The National Association of Forza Italia clubs (ANFI) was set up to co-ordinate the clubs, and the ANFI national co-ordinator was a member of the executive committee of the party. However, given that this figure was appointed by Berlusconi rather than elected by the clubs themselves, this did not represent a democratic link between the clubs and the party leadership. ANFI co-ordinators' loyalties were to Berlusconi (who appointed them) rather than to the club members. Moreover, the clubs had no power over their territorial co-ordinators who were mostly Programma Italia agents nominated by Berlusconi. Given the lack of input of the clubs into the party's organisation and decision-making, their membership figures declined following the 1994 elections as they became more and more irrelevant to the life of the new political movement (Hopkin and Paolucci 1999: 323).

A party with institutional and territorial roots?

The new statute adopted at the 1998 party congress was an attempt to give Forza Italia a real organisational form and set down territorial roots. The statute provided for a national congress, with the power to define the political line of the party, modify the statute and elect the president, elect fifty members of the national council and six members of the 'comitato di presidenza' (presidential committee). The congress was supposed to meet every three years. Both national congress and national council members were partly nominated by party leaders (e.g. leaders of different sectors plus regional co-ordinators), partly elected by members and partly made up of holders of elected office at the various territorial levels. The FI clubs remained a structure outside of the party, although they could affiliate to the party. The 1998 congress had been preceded in 1997 by a membership recruitment campaign and a series of local congresses. The official membership figure given at the end of this process was 140,000, a figure seen as unreliable, and deliberately inflated by some observers, although it was still low for a major nationwide party (Hopkin and Paolucci 1999: 331).

Poli argued in 2001 that FI appeared 'now to have re-entered into the more conventional models of party organisation' (Poli 2001: 41). Similarly, Pasquino has referred to Poli's analysis in arguing that FI is no longer an anomaly within the Italian party system, but has instead become an organised party, entrenched throughout Italy, relying on hundreds of thousands of members and several thousand ambitious office-holders (Pasquino 2003b). Indeed, a significant party membership base has developed. FI claims a membership of 250,000. By virtue of its participation in electoral politics at all levels, FI has built a base of thousands of party office-holders and aspiring candidates. In 2004, FI had 9,000 local councillors (including 1,033 mayors), 563 provincial councillors, twenty-one provincial presidents and 195 regional councillors (and seven regional presidents) (Hopkin 2005: 87–88).

Nevertheless, Paolucci argues that Forza Italia has still not been institutionalised: 'At the central level the organisation, although it formally exists, is irrelevant in terms of decision-making powers, which still rest entirely with the party leader and his close circle. The central party bodies, therefore, cannot attract loyalties'. Forza Italia remains a patrimonial party in which party recruitment is still personalised 'aimed at consolidating or confirming a personal relationship with Berlusconi specific party offices'. 'Those who are chosen are legitimised exclusively by this infusion of personal trust. Hence, their power is not linked to covering specific party offices, but to the oscillations of their personal relationship with Berlusconi. Loyalty converges on the leader, rather than on the organisation. The perpetuation of the genetic characteristics of the party makes its status extremely precarious, potentially leading to its disintegration, whenever the circumstances change' (Paolucci 2006: 170).

A second FI national party congress was held in 2004. Hopkin has noted the similarity between the 1998 and 2004 party congresses in reflecting the weakness of internal party democracy and leadership domination of the party (although the statute provided for a congress every three years, six years had elapsed between the first and second congresses). The congress lasted two days, with only one evening being set aside for conference delegates to speak. The rest of the congress was devoted to speeches by Berlusconi and other leading party figures appointed by him. The final morning saw additional speeches by FI leaders, followed by elections to the party presidency, the presidential council and national council. 'The congress program confidently scheduled a final address by Silvio Berlusconi immediately after the votes, prejudging the outcome of the party's internal elections. Fortunately, for want of an alternative candidate, the presidential election itself did not need to take place, and Berlusconi could close the proceedings with another rousing speech, less than two days after the first' (Hopkin 2005: 86). Hopkin notes that, although parties in parliamentary democracies generally tend to 'maintain the formal trappings of the "bottom-up" mass party, while stage-managing procedures to annul dissent and exalt party leaders', FI remains exceptional in that 'no genuine channel for contesting the distribution of power within the party has ever existed ... a unique state of affairs among major parties in Western democracies' (Hopkin 2005: 86). Hopkin and Paolucci (1999) had previously made very similar observations about the 1998 congress.

While some elements within FI, notably former Christian Democrats such as Claudio Scajola, sought to move the party in the direction of a more conventional and autonomous (from the leader) organisational model based on democratic internal procedures, there was a persistent lobby within the party associated with former Fininvest elements to retain the light party structure. Thus, figures such as Marcello Dell'Utri argued against the party drifting towards a bureaucratic 'mass party' model. The domination of the Fininvest lobby within the party following the 2001 election victory appeared to be reflected in the key party personnel. Thus Sandro Bondi, a protégé of Dell'Utri (although a former communist), was party co-ordinator, and his vice co-ordinator was Fabrizio Cicchitto, a former Socialist. They were viewed as favouring the 'lightweight' party model, at the expense of the Christian Democrat faction represented by Scajola. Although the latter's successful party re-organisation helped to pave the way for the electoral successes of 1999–2001, his own background in the DC and close relations with the UDC caused suspicion within the party (Hopkin 2005: 92).

Forza Italia in government

Analysis of Forza Italia's performance in the first Berlusconi government is difficult on account of its short-lived nature. Much of the parliamentary party in 1994 was new to politics with little or no experience of governing, with many key figures in the new government coming from the ranks of Fininvest. Some 80 per cent of FI senators and deputies claimed never to have been involved in party or electoral politics prior to 1994 (Katz and Ignazi 1996: 23). McCarthy notes that many FI parliamentarians were unskilled in the battle for spoils (unlike the AN and former Christian Democrats) (McCarthy 1996: 49). The party was also caught between the *ad personam* policies of its leader, the need to appear moderate to the electorate and the pull to the right exerted by its coalition partners. Its programme emphasised the need to cut back the welfare state and entrust economic growth to the unleashing of an entrepreneurial spirit brought about through tax cuts for business and individuals. This did not go down well in international financial markets, given the perceived need for austerity measures. Pension reform was envisaged as the main instrument for controlling public finances, but the government was forced to back down on its proposal following mass protest and a general strike by the main trade union confederations (Katz and Ignazi 1996: 30–31). As already noted, the government was also dogged by controversy over

Berlusconi's conflicts of interests, particularly in relation to the re-organisation of RAI and the ill-fated attempt to curb the investigative power of the magistrates.

A deeper analysis of Forza Italia's record in office after 2001 is made easier by the longer lasting nature of the second Berlusconi government. However, analysis remains complicated by the difficulty in distinguishing between Forza Italia as a governing party and the positions taken by Berlusconi as its leader and prime minister. Clear party positions are also made difficult to discern by the role of mediation often played by Berlusconi between the LN on one side and the AN and UDC on the other. Its position on economic matters (and on the linked question of the impact of the euro on the Italian economy) led to talk of an axis of the north with the LN (at least on the part of Berlusconi and Tremonti). However, Berlusconi and FI did not endorse the proposals made by the LN for withdrawal from the euro and the unilateral (without EU agreement) imposition of tariffs on Chinese imports. The economic outlook of Berlusconi and FI again emphasised tax cuts, economic liberalisation and labour market regulation, although in practice, the results were rather patchy, in part because of opposition within the coalition (with the LN, AN and UCD all seeking to protect their own constituencies), but also because of contradictions within Berlusconi's own position. For example, his championing of tax cuts and liberalisation sat uneasily with his promises of major public works projects for the south. Moreover, the neo-liberal emphasis on free competition did not always sit easily with the defence of his own particular business interests (for example in media regulation laws) and the numerous *ad personam* laws that his government promoted.

Aside from economic policy, FI adopted a more conventional conservative approach on matters relating to the nature of the Italian state. Berlusconi sought to play the role of honest broker between the regionalism of the LN and the nationalism of the AN. Nevertheless, Berlusconi's instincts seemed to be closer to the AN on the national question and on matters relating to the state's constitutional make-up. Forza Italia, as the name suggests, is a national party, and Berlusconi's discourse emphasises the need to restore pride, honour and success to the Italian nation. On the constitutional question, his desire to see executive power strengthened in particular mirrored that of the AN leadership. This was reinforced in government by complaints about the weak nature of the powers bestowed on the prime minister by the Italian constitution, and in relation to parliament. Hence, Berlusconi's frequent complaints that he was not allowed to govern properly (failure to deliver on campaign promises was blamed both on his weak executive powers and the need to agree matters with his coalition partners).

On the related question of Italy's relationship with the EU, Forza Italia's mild nationalism and its neo-liberal approach to the economy have led to some modification of the traditional Italian position. The positions of both FI and the LN on the European question have been unprecedented for governing parties in the post-war republic. Until the 1990s, the governing parties were engaged in a Europhile consensus, generally allying themselves with Franco-German initiatives for deepening integration and placing themselves in a federalist vanguard alongside the Benelux countries. The election of the first Berlusconi government in 1994 signalled a change in this approach, and was reflected in the positions taken by its foreign minister, Antonio Martino, a founding member of Forza Italia, who presented himself as a Thatcherite Eurosceptic. Given the short life of the first Berlusconi government, the effects of this brief change of approach were minimal, and the centre-left governments of 1996–2001 returned to a more conventional Europhile approach. However, FI's more questioning approach to the European integration process remained evident, and had a more lasting impact following its return to government in 2001.While Martino was this time appointed to the defence ministry, a new and more powerful Eurosceptic voice in the government was the finance minister, Giulio Tremonti. Although this related partly to political pragmatism (a stick with which to beat the government's centre-left opponents), Tremonti made frequent references to 'Prodi's euro'.

Tremonti, Bossi and Berlusconi, to varying degrees, openly blamed euro membership (or at least the entry terms arranged by their centre-left predecessors) for Italy's poor economic performance. Berlusconi would also ally himself with the British prime minister, Tony Blair, and the Spanish Conservative leader, Jose-Maria Aznar, in pressing for greater economic reform and labour market flexibility, opposing the stress on social guarantees of Italy's traditional Franco-German allies. Berlusconi also followed Blair and Aznar in allying with US President George W. Bush over the war in Iraq, causing another – and more damaging – split with France, Germany and other traditional European allies.

Ideology

It is difficult to avoid reducing discussion of FI's ideology to one focusing on the politics of Berlusconi. Berlusconi himself is clearly not a 'mainstream' political actor. Nevertheless, the neo-liberal conservative platform of FI could be located somewhere within the mainstream European centre right, as illustrated by Berlusconi's success in securing the entrance of FI into the European EPP confederation. As a leading member of Italy's entrepreneurial elite, Berlusconi could be described as having been representative of Italy's conservative establishment (despite his anti-establishment rhetoric) and reflecting their economic interests. Berlusconi sees himself as the Italian incarnation of the Reaganite–Thatcherite wave of neo-liberalism that hit the industrialised capitalist economies in the 1980s. Nevertheless, the emphasis in his discourse on a neo-liberal de-regulatory economic programme does signal a departure from the conservative consensus of the post-war republic, which favoured a decidedly more statist approach to the economy. Yet while presenting FI as a modern capitalist party, key positions and priorities often reflect the clan nature of the party – relating to the personal and business interests of

Berlusconi and his acolytes (McCarthy 1996: 51–52). While Berlusconi would see no conflict in following both his own interests and those of Italy as a capitalist nation as a whole, in practice the two are not always compatible.

Ginsborg notes the predominance in Berlusconi's speeches of the theme of liberty. However, this is a 'negative liberty' in which the economy and society need to be liberated 'from oppressive chains, from the weight of bureaucracy and suffocating procedures, from fiscal pressure'. The state is to be regarded with suspicion. A minimalist state is thus emphasised, and high taxes regarded as a moral imposition (Ginsborg 2003). Indeed, Berlusconi has gone on record as stating that it is moral behaviour to seek to evade high taxes (Luzi 2004).

Freedom from state intervention in the economy is coupled with a populist view of democracy in which the popular will is reflected in a personalised form, i.e. the election of a strong leader who reflects the wishes of the people and should thus be allowed to govern without the burden of the constitutional checks usually found in liberal democracies, such as an independent judiciary (Ginsborg 2003).

Frame analysis

Our frame analysis of FI was limited by the fact that, being the largest and most influential party in the coalition, in some instances no individual programmatic documents were produced. While an individual FI programme was available for 1994, in 1996 the programme was a joint one for the Polo with AN. In 2001 and 2006, there was a joint CdL programme for all the parties of the centre right. Nevertheless, it is fair to assume that FI politicians took a lead role in shaping the contents of the documents. To check for ideological consistency between coalition electoral manifestos and Forza Italia priorities, we examined a key FI document, the *Carta dei Valori* (charter of values), and found essentially similar priorities. This was also the case for the FI programme for the 2004 European election, which we also analysed. Given the central and binding role of FI in the coalition, we therefore decided to examine the various programmatic documents as artefacts mainly reflecting Forza Italia priorities. This is reasonable, as other parties presented their own separate documents, which appear quite different in terms of priorities. However, this limitation has to be borne in mind in assessing the results of the frame analysis. The main themes recurring throughout FI documents are summarised in Figure 5.1.

As Figure 5.1 indicates, the general ideological profile of FI, as reflected in all its programmatic documents, is mainly one of a typical centre-right party, but there are significant departures. All frames identified in the period 1994–2006 are considered. There are recurrent references to free-market policies, as the number of frames categorised as 'pro-free market' indicates. There are frequent references to a conservative social ethos, as shown by the large number of references to 'traditional family ethics', to 'law and order' issues and concerns with crime and security. Then one finds frequent references to concerns

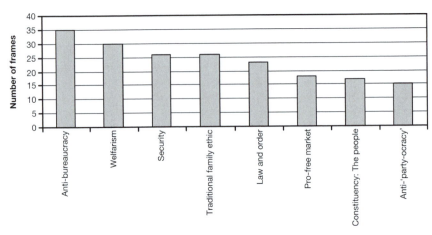

Figure 5.1 Most recurrent FI frames 1994–2006 (n. 312; first eight frames n. 190).

that are typically Italian. This is the case with the anti-bureaucracy focus – a complaint widely shared by Italian business and more broadly by all Italians. This focus is often connected to the neo-liberal cluster of concerns, as it is frequently argued that inefficient Italian bureaucracy is one of the main obstacles to economic development. Also somewhat unusual for the centre-right party family is the emphasis against the domination of the Italian state by parties and references to 'the people' – the need to reflect their common sense wisdom and free them from the stranglehold of the arrogant and inefficient Italian political class. These themes embody the spirit of populism that pervades FI in various ways.

As mentioned previously, FI's populism has several components that have varied over time. In its early years, references to the fight against the inefficiencies of the Italian state went together with the assertion of FI's almost 'essentialised' difference from other parties, which were seen as responsible for and profiting from a general failure of the Italian state. As the party of entrepreneurs, it could fix the inefficient and bureaucratic dysfunctions of the state that were seen as a great contributor to the malaise of Italy. Thus, because of its connection with FI's anti-politics, the theme of anti-bureaucracy has achieved a special consideration in FI documents and is the most mentioned frame in absolute terms.

Anti-bureaucracy, anti-partyocracy and anti-politics

Anti-bureaucracy frames are part of a complex ideological construct in which excessive bureaucracy is seen as connected to the party stranglehold on the Italian state, to excessive reliance on the state and the lack of liberal policies, to the excessive cost of the state and therefore to high taxes, political corruption and negative personality traits such as an absence of entrepreneurship, to old-fashioned attitudes, to a lack of transparency and of citizens' involvement in decision-making and to the use of a mystifying language. It is to issues such as these that Italians have reacted positively – issues that other parties had barely touched upon, often mistakenly considering them unimportant in political terms.

Some examples of anti-bureaucracy frames will clarify the concept.

> We do not want that, in the name of solidarity, the abhorrent practice continues of redistributing on a large scale power and income to the advantage of a parasitical, political and bureaucratic class (1994).
>
> Our conception of democracy rests furthermore on the simplification of the relationship between the citizen and the public administration through overcoming the Byzantine bureaucracy which in the historical period of nation states and in particular in the Italian tradition have compromised our productive life and social initiative, and even the efficiency of government action, tying it to suffocating procedures (*Carta dei Valori* 2004).

The use of anti-bureaucracy frames has often also gone hand in hand with anti-partyocracy frames and can be grouped more widely under anti-politics frames, as the following example shows.

> 57.6% of what we produce ends up being requisitioned and put at the disposition of an immense army of politicians and bureaucrats who have occupied Italy for a number of decades (1994).

Nevertheless, as Figure 5.2 shows, the use of both frames has declined in frequency over the years, as FI has become more established as a party of government, and the years of partyocracy have become more distant.

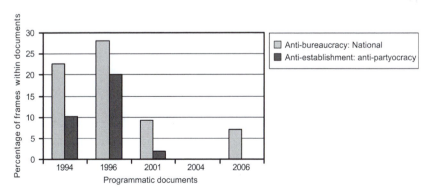

Figure 5.2 Anti-bureaucracy and anti-partyocracy frames in FI 1994–2006 (n. 35+15)

Welfarism, liberalism and protectionism

In FI discourse, there are frequent promises of assistance to disadvantaged groups in the population. This might seem somewhat incompatible with the right's focus on neo-liberalism and the free market. However, this reflects the tension between innovation and the continuation of the Christian Democratic policies of social solidarity organised by the state, often in exchange for electoral support from the weaker groups in the population, but also from uncompetitive industries large and small, and professional orders who have traditionally been DC and then FI voters. It is therefore instructive to look at these two issues – welfarism and neo-liberalism – in conjunction. Welfarism, as the second most frequently identified frame across FI documents, and neo-liberalism as the sixth are both very recurrent frames.

The tension between economic liberalisation and social protectionism has characterised the Italian right coalition throughout its history. FI, as nominally its most liberal party, has not been able to achieve even a modest liberalisation of the economy during its time in government, despite a strong parliamentary majority. However, while surveys demonstrate strong public support for a sweeping liberalisation of state monopolies of utilities and of the professions, they also suggest a high demand for social protection and public intervention. Reflecting this awareness, references to liberalism fell during the 2006 campaign while references to welfare measures continued to increase. These measures were often justified with reference to other key FI issues such as its frequently stated support for the institution of the family, which requires financial and social assistance, increased public housing and measures to support birth rates, the low level of which is often lamented (Figure 5.3).

Some examples from documents will clarify FI's use of these concepts. For welfarism, one can identify references to a wide set of population groups, and

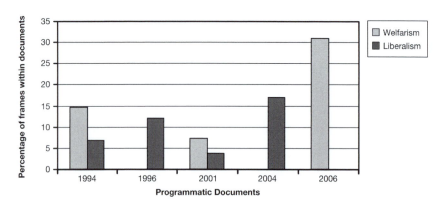

Figure 5.3 Welfarism and liberalism frames (n. 30+18). In this figure and in the following figures reporting on multiple frames, the n. is listed in the order presented in the figure. Thus, the n. of 'welfarism' is 30 and the n. of 'liberalism' is 18.

several ways of combining increased social spending with neo-liberal policies. For instance, in the 1994 programme, one reads:

> The astronomical sums that are wasted, in the name of misunderstood solidarity, in costly, inefficient and corrupted state bureaucracy, must be directed to authentic solidarity objectives for our less fortunate fellow citizens in need of assistance, through market competition mechanisms (1994).

In terms of redistribution, the groups singled out range from the entire population to the young, unemployed, women, elderly and sick and disabled.

With reference to liberalism, as mentioned, FI has promoted economic liberalisation measures but sought to blame some of the problems caused by market reforms on the way they were implemented by the centre-left governments of 1996–2001. The following quote is instructive on this issue, employing some rather creative logic:

> In the 1990s, all had been done by shock, in effect through a political choice inspired by the left, anxious to excuse its communism with this very improvised, so insane 'marketism'. Now we see – seeing and hearing the people – the effect of this folly (2006).

Security, traditional family, law and order

The cluster of socially conservative values and concerns that characterise the right in several EU countries has also been reflected in Forza Italia documents from its inception (Figure 5.4).

The following excerpt connects issues of security with the legitimacy of the state.

> The safety of the people, the safeguard of their physical safety and the protection of their properties is at the basis of the pact between citizens

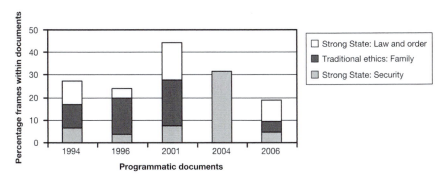

Figure 5.4 FI: socially conservative frames 1994–2006 (n. 26+26+23).

and institutions, without it the State loses its historical and moral legitimacy (2001).

The strong emphasis on family values that emerges in all documents is also present in the FI *Carta dei Valori*, as is an emphasis on entrepreneurship and patriotism.

> Our liberalism seeks to promote values which are diametrically opposed to those which are statalist and trade-unionist: we believe in the primacy of individual initiative and ethical responsibility, in recognising families as the foundation of society, in the sense of tradition and a predisposition to confront with courage all problems of life, and in patriotism (*Carta dei Valori* 2004).

Europe and the nation

Forza Italia places the themes of economic liberalisation and defence of the national interest at the core of its discourse on the EU. As Conti notes, it 'inserts the process of European integration into a broader process of economic liberalisation at the global level, and therefore it opposes any measure which creates a "European fortress" characterised by strict external boundaries to global trade' (Conti 2006). While the LN's position on Europe reflects its ethno-populism, one could argue that Forza Italia's approach (or at least that of the likes of Martino, Tremonti and Berlusconi), while influenced by populist impulses, also reflects a 'hyperglobalist' stance (at least until the more protectionist turn signalled by Tremonti since 2006). This is a stance generally associated with the British Conservative party, whereby there is a conceptualisation of a free-trading liberal national economy benefiting from a liberalised, globalised, unregulated economy. EU integration is thus increasingly opposed because it is seen as disruptive to liberalised globalisation. Rather than immersion in a European economic fortress, the most suitable solution to ensure the success and growth of the economy is to become a low-tax, free-trading paradise, attracting trade and investment from across the world (Baker et al. 2002). Nevertheless, Britain's geographical position, its historic links with the USA and other parts of the world and its general liberalised and global trading tradition make it a more suitable candidate for such a solution than Italy.

Berlusconi's and Forza Italia's positions on the EU came to the fore in particular during Italy's rather accident-prone presidency of the EU Council of Ministers in 2003. Aside from a number of well-publicised gaffes made by Berlusconi at European meetings, a number of more serious proposals caused consternation. For example, he proposed EU enlargement to Russia and to Israel, positions voiced by Forza Italia since the 1990s. While this may partly reflect Berlusconi's emphasis on his personal friendship with president/prime minister Putin in the case of Russia, and attempts to re-balance a previously pro-Arab Italian stance in the case of Israel, Conti suggests that this also relates to a broader interest in creating an 'ever-larger free-market area, rather than a federal and politically integrated entity' (Conti 2006: 221), and to orient the EU both to the east and to the countries of the Mediterranean. As Conti suggests, Forza Italia's rejection of the federal idea of European integration is evidence of a stronger emphasis on maximising domestic gains within Europe, involving a better representation of Italy in the European institutions and greater access to EU resources:

> The dimension of the domestic impact of the EU is definitely one of great relevance in the discourse of FI. It is one that is not oriented by an aprioristic evaluation but, rather by a cruder cost–benefit analysis. In particular, the idea of mobilisation to defend Italian national interests in the EU has been promoted by this party throughout.
>
> Conti (2006: 222)

This more assertive stance is reflected in international policy in general, with FI – similar to the AN – advocating a more active Italian foreign policy role, particularly in relation to the Mediterranean, and involvement in peace-keeping missions in the Middle East.

Immigration

On another issue linked to the national question, that is immigration and related questions such as identity and multiculturalism, FI's tone is generally softer than that of both the LN and the AN. Notwithstanding the occasional indiscretion by Berlusconi (for example when he stated in the light of the 11 September attacks that western civilisation was superior to Islam), Forza Italia has generally not indulged in the kind of ethno-populist discourse that characterises the LN. Furthermore, the identity-related frames that are present in both the LN's and the AN's discourse are not really present in that of FI. One could argue that FI has generally been content to sit back and let the AN and the LN make the running in formulating the immigration policies of the centre-right coalition, endorsing the policies formulated in the name of the latter two party leaders and adopted by the government as the Bossi–Fini law in 2002. The positions of FI on immigration are probably closer to the official positions of the AN than to those of the LN. The need to be firm in controlling regular immigration is emphasised as is the fight against clandes-tine immigration. However, the need to help immigrants and respect their human rights is also referred to. For example, the 2001 plan for government described its goals in immigration policy thus:

> promoting a dignified welcome for men and women fleeing poverty and misery, sometimes war and persecution, in search of a better future for themselves and for their children, who want to live in Italy and work

legally and insert themselves fully into our society, respecting the law and our culture.

Forza Italia – CdL Piano di governo (2001)

In discussing the positions adopted by Forza Italia on immigration, and indeed other issues, the heterogeneous political provenance of its political exponents needs to be emphasised. Many are ex-members of the PSI and DC (the latter in particular), while others are non-professional politicians (i.e. no previous political experience prior to 1994). Opinions range from the more populist to the more traditionally conservative. Among the former members of the DC is Giuseppe Pisanu, the interior minister from 2002 to 2006 and therefore responsible for the government's immigration policy. His positions were fairly moderate when compared with other components of the ruling coalition. For example, in the spring of 2005, a number of cases of rape, allegedly by immigrants, in Italian cities got widespread media coverage. The LN used this as an opportunity to step up its anti-immigrant rhetoric and particularly the link between immigration and crime (it focused particularly on the need to expel clandestine immigrants – it was assumed that the rapists were clandestines). In the face of this, Pisanu publicly rejected the causal link between immigration and crime made by the LN and some exponents of the AN (Staff Reporter 2005b).

Nevertheless, on the question of Italy's cultural and national identity, there have been statements from a number of Forza Italia exponents, including Berlusconi himself, the former president of the senate, Marcello Pera, and the governor of Lombardy (and former head of the conservative catholic group, Communion and Liberation) Roberto Formigoni, opposing themselves to multiculturalism (i.e. the co-existence of a variety of cultures within Italy). This related mainly to non-Christian and non-European immigration to Italy, with particular concerns evident about the large Muslim immigrant population in Italy and its impact on religious identity and cultural relations (not to mention security concerns, although direct correlations between a Muslim presence and threats of internal terrorism were generally left for LN exponents to make).

FI's rejection of multiculturalism becomes clearer in its *Carta dei Valori*:

The fact that a great part of European culture has come to believe in 'multiculturalism' as the inevitable fate of our lands, has to represent a kind of abdication of our identity (*Carta dei Valori* 2004).

Populism and the people

With respect to populism, FI's *Carta dei Valori* on the one hand frequently makes references to 'the people' as a source of democratic legitimacy but, on the other hand, defends the party from accusations of 'populism'. Thus, as an example of references to the people, but also as an example of the FI emphasis on anti-bureaucracy and its connection with anti-political sentiments, one reads:

> For Forza Italia the concept of power is based on two key words: consensus and responsibility. The first to evoke the necessity of a continuous reference to the true sovereignty of the public realm, which is the people. The second to render transparent the programmatic alternatives that each political force proposes to the country, preventing that an opaque and consociational system confuses the deserving and undeserving in an indistinct oligarchical theatre (*Carta dei Valori* 2004).

It is interesting to note that FI anti-state stances lead it to glorify civil society as free from the corruption of politics and even as the natural birthplace of the 'good citizen'.

> These are the virtues which are born of civil society and which are the basis of any moral and economic growth. If these might sound 'antiquated' this is only because the power of the state, compressing society, has repressed and forced them into oblivion (*Carta dei Valori* 2004).

But despite numerous references to 'the people', one is then reminded that:

> Our vision of politics is distant from populist conceptions of the right and the left, which seek to defend a presumed purity of the people even through an expulsion from the system of its enemies, making recourse to a demagogic use of public protest (*Carta dei Valori* 2004).

The rejection of accusations of populism is distinctive of this document. Nevertheless, examination of the range of party and coalition documents and communications is a rather better indication of the FI's populism than the denials found here. Moreover, one must add that, while the analysed documents reflect the in many ways conventional centre-right programme that FI proposes, the populism of the party is captured more clearly in the discourse of Berlusconi himself, in speeches and TV and public appearances – unfiltered by the influences of the party officials and communications professionals involved in the drafting of the more circumspect programmatic statements.

Conclusion

In founding and leading Forza Italia, Berlusconi has employed a number of core elements of populism. In particular, the anti-politics quotient in Berlusconi's political message is high. Berlusconi continues to portray himself as a political outsider, in opposition to the career politicians of the centre and left. Furthermore, Berlusconi's charismatic leadership is central to the appeal of Forza Italia and to the centre-right coalition as a whole. Berlusconi uses all the resources at his disposal, and his undoubted abilities in communications, to transmit this appeal directly to the Italian people. Indeed, reflecting a central core aspect of populism, direct appeals to the common sense and wisdom of the Italian people – unmediated by the checks and balances of liberal constitutional norms (such as judicial independence) – are frequently made. The political language used by Berlusconi also reflects a core populist trait – speaking the language of the ordinary man on the Milan metro, rather than the *politichese* for which the politicians of the post-war republic were notorious. Unlike the regionalist populism of the LN, however, the populism of FI is not territorially or ethnically circumscribed. As Tarchi notes, while the LN has based its appeal on a notion of the people 'as both ethnos and demos', FI has concentrated solely on the latter, giving voice to a popular mass, supposedly neglected by distant self-serving elites, concentrating on an 'anti-political, anti-party message' (Tarchi 2008: 85–86).

Berlusconi's message is designed to appeal to the Italian television-watching public of all classes, and across the Italian territory. Nevertheless, the nature of political communications used – particularly the use of television – means that certain sectors of Italian society are more exposed to this message. Moreover, whereas the LN can be characterised as a populist movement, FI has in some ways been more like a conventional political party, within which 'anti-political populism is entirely delegated to the leader, who has made it a trademark of his political style, but not a source of ideological inspiration' (Tarchi 2008: 86). While the LN's populism is clear in the analysis of its programmes and across all its activities, that of FI was confined more to the statements and communication style of its leader and founder, and did not always come across that clearly in its documents which sought to present the party as a mainstream centre-right force.

This brings us on to more peripheral aspects of populism. When it comes to the relationship between the state and the economy, populist movements can be protectionist or neo-liberal (or somewhere in between). While Berlusconi's populism reflects the catch-all 'politician's populism' elucidated by Canovan, his entrepreneurial background, and his own personal and business interests, mean that his populism is heavily coloured by neo-liberal *laissez-faire* ideology, and thus has a greater intrinsic appeal to certain sectors of Italian society: the self-employed, small and large business and those sections of the middle class employed in these sectors. Political opportunities and political space are also highly relevant here in determining the form that Forza Italia's populism has taken. Berlusconi's decision to enter the political field in 1994 with his new party was determined by the collapse of the DC, the ignominious downfall of his political patron, Bettino Craxi, and arguably by a concern to protect his own private interests from a possible centre-left government. This required the creation of a party that could play a leading role in the mainstream of Italian politics, occupying the position once held by the DC and attracting its voters. Thus, its appeal needed to be broad. Berlusconi would not have wanted to waste his time, and the financial and organisational resources of his business empire, on creating a fringe populist party to snap on the heels of the mainstream political establishment while being unlikely to hold governmental power. It thus needed to appeal to the former voters of the *pentapartito*, who together constituted the majority of Italian voters up until 1992. A catch-all strategy was needed to win over these voters, although the 25–30 per cent of voters who had regularly voted for the PCI–PDS could be disregarded in this sense (although some former communist voters would make the switch to FI and the parties of the centre right). The construction of a liberal conservative political force was thus required, appealing to church-going catholics, while also representing the secular, consumerist and materialist instincts of modern Italian society. At the same time, the need to appeal across the Italian territory meant making different kinds of promises to different parts of Italy – reflecting the different models of economic development of different regions. Notably, this meant promising tax cuts, which would appeal to the northern middle class, and major infrastructural projects to conservative and state-dependent voters in the south.

What is particularly unique about FI is its relationship to the vision of society to which it seeks to appeal, in that its leader and founder previously played (and continues to play) a highly influential role in shaping the value systems and popular culture of Italian society (or parts of it), through ownership of Italy's private TV networks. As Ginsborg explains: 'The advertisements, variety shows, and soap operas of Italian television transmit a bland but unceasing vision of what Italian family values should be'. While tolerantly catholic, this model Italian family is 'also [an] ambitious and even voracious entity, the site of enterprise and saving as well as consumption … surrounded by a multiplicity of commodities: cars, cell phones, televisions, computers'. This a model of a 'familist' type, in which families put their own 'acquisitive instincts and interests first', rarely willing to sacrifice part of these 'for the good of civil society, let alone the state' (Ginsborg 2003: 9). In short, without wishing to overplay the power of television in shaping culture, these are value systems that Berlusconi's TV channels have at least conditioned, and these are value systems around which his political project is based. Thus, he promises to get the state off the people's backs and reduce taxes in order to satisfy their consumerist instincts, while also playing on a traditional Italian diffidence to the role of the state and to social organisation.

When Berlusconi first entered politics in 1994, he was able to make great play of his newcomer status, extraneous to the corrupt practices of the *partitocrazia*, despite his own close relationship with Craxi. Berlusconi's anti-political stance had great resonance then. While this remains central to Berlusconi's populist repertoire, Ginsborg notes the apparent contradiction between the patrimonial nature of Berlusconi's project and his populism (Ginsborg 2003). How can Berlusconi's direct appeals to the people and claims to embody their wishes and aspirations be reconciled with a political approach that has prioritised *ad personam* laws and privileges the interests of members of his own clan? Is Berlusconi's clan itself not just an example of the kind of self-serving elite that populist movements claim to despise? This apparent contradiction perhaps helped to explain the fall in FI's vote at the 2006 election, although roughly half of Italian voters were still prepared to vote for a coalition committed to returning him as prime minister, and the popularity of Forza Italia and the centre right as a whole rose again once the centre left was returned to government. In particular, Berlusconi was able to divert attention away from the apparent pursuit of *ad personam* laws by portraying himself as a victim of a politically inspired judicial plot, dominated by left-wing magistrates, and by portraying the left and their friends in the judiciary and the (non-Berlusconi-owned) media as the true establishment.

Aside from the role of Berlusconi himself, divergences between populist and catholic currents, between secular and catholic politicians (with many conservative DC elements having re-emerged within the party), between 'recycled', 'First Republic' politicians and political 'outsiders' (or even between recycled DC and PSI politicians) have also resulted in contradictions within FI. This has not been helped by the contradictory nature of its alliances with other forces. The personalised leadership-focused nature of the party have made its ideological make-up rather dependent on the personal whim of the leader, in which a pro-market outlook and belief in the virtue of entrepreneurialism are often outweighed by narrow political calculation and personal interest. Berlusconi's PdL project indicates a personal acknowledgement that the way in which Forza Italia was constructed and developed meant that it was unlikely to outlast him. It was too associated with him as his personal vehicle, and too dependent on him for leadership, popularity and resources.

Moves towards a new party, often hinted at by Berlusconi, appeared to be becoming more concrete in 2007 with Berlusconi's sponsoring of the new '*Circoli di liberta*' (Circles of freedom/liberty) that were springing up around Italy. Although the initial figurehead was Michela Brambilla (a former beauty queen and Mediaset journalist turned successful businesswoman), it soon became apparent that Berlusconi was behind the project. Parallels could be drawn with the Forza Italia clubs that began to spring up in late 1993 with Berlusconi's backing. By the end of 2007, Berlusconi had proposed dissolving FI into a new political formation, 'Popolo della liberta' ('the people of freedom') or 'Partito della liberta' ('Freedom party') – a proposal criticised by observers as a mere recycling of FI, and by his erstwhile allies in the UDC and the AN as a populist move that ignored the need for a broader consultation involving all the various components of the centre right. Indeed, the proposal appeared to be aimed at bypassing the UDC and the AN (Berlusconi was irritated by criticisms of his leadership of the coalition by Fini in particular[5]). However, the need to refocus attention on unity in the face of new elections in 2008 led to agreement by Fini to unite the AN with FI under the common Popolo della libertà electoral list. Berlusconi's role in the re-invention of the right had clearly not run its course. In November 2008, Berlusconi confirmed the dissolution of FI into the new PdL party. The founding PDL congress in 2009 marked the end of FI, but certainly not of Berlosconi's dominance of the Italian right.

6   The MSI–AN

The turnaround in the fortunes of the MSI–AN since the beginning of the 1990s has been a remarkable one. It has emerged from the neo-fascist ghetto in which it floundered since its foundation in the aftermath of the Second World War, and is now viewed within Italy as a legitimate participant in the new party system that has emerged out of the ashes of *tangentopoli*. While its initial entrance into government in 1994 caused some consternation in international political circles and was viewed by some Italian observers as marking an end to the post-war anti-fascist consensus, ten years later its participation in government was viewed as fairly non-controversial. The period of democratic consolidation of the party under Fini's leadership in the late 1990s and its performance in government from 2001 onwards appeared to have assuaged concerns about its democratic credentials. On the international front, whereas the MSI had previously allied itself with the Front National of Jean-Marie Le Pen, the AN was now part of a mainstream centre-right political grouping in the European Parliament. The party's international rehabilitation was confirmed by Fini's selection as representative on the convention to draft the ill-fated EU constitution, and then his appointment as foreign minister and later as president of the lower house. Yet fifteen years earlier, Fini was still proclaiming the need for a return to the values of fascism and Mussolini. How was this transformation possible and is it a real and convincing one?

This chapter will assess the development of the AN's post-fascist project under Fini's leadership and explore the nature of the AN, drawing on analysis of the positions taken by the party, and by Fini personally, and of attitudes held within the party. Assessment of the party's ideology will draw in particular from the frame analysis conducted of the key party programmatic documents. This will facilitate a fuller understanding of the party's identity and its relationship to academic categorisations of right-wing parties. On this last point, academic observers appear still to be coming to grips with the AN's apparent transformation, with some studies continuing to place the AN in the broader categorisation of extreme right or radical right parties in Europe (Griffin 1996; Norris 2005). Moreover, while certain studies have focused on the way in which formerly extreme right parties with a fascist heritage have re-invented themselves and enjoyed greater electoral success by adopting new populist strategies (Ignazi and Ysmal 1992a), the AN's trajectory appears to have gone beyond this, projecting it into the centre-right mainstream in certain regards. This chapter will assess the extent to which the AN's success can also be attributed to the populism which appears more obviously present in the plat- forms of is coalition allies. Does the AN's core ideology reflect populist prin- ciples or is its relationship to populism more peripheral? As the discussion below will show, elements of anti-political and exclusionist discourse remain important to the AN as does a strong personalised leadership, despite the apparent adoption of a quite conventional conservative and state welfare interventionist programme.

Historical background

Until its submersion within the AN in 1995, the MSI remained the largest neo-fascist party in Europe. Indeed, the Italian party system had been alone in Europe in retaining a continual and sizeable neo-fascist presence since the end of the Second World War. The MSI polled 2 per cent in the historic 1948 election and generally polled around 5–6 per cent of the national vote there- after. The MSI nevertheless appeared to be an outdated and declining force at the end of the 1980s. Gianfranco Fini – the then head of the MSI youth wing – had taken over the leadership from the ailing Almirante in 1987 at only 35 years of age. He defeated Pino Rauti, the veteran of Salò and founder of ON, in the leadership contest. Fini had the clear advantage over Rauti in that he was the anointed successor of Almirante and was favoured by the party old guard. It was envisaged that Almirante would retain a guiding role over Fini's leadership. However, he died in May 1988, leaving Fini without his protector from the continual and increasing sniping from the Rautian and leftist factions. Fini was initially viewed as a weak leader, unable to reverse the MSI's decline and continuing isolation. He was briefly deposed as leader in 1990 and replaced by Rauti. To Rauti, the MSI was not a party of the right, because the right was 'conservative and capitalistic' while fascism was 'revolutionary'. Rauti believed that the MSI could attract support from the left, because only the MSI remained opposed to the capitalist system. How- ever, this appeared to confuse and alienate part of the MSI's traditional con- servative electorate, and its vote continued to decline further in local elections. The party thus turned back to Fini, who regained the leadership in 1991. The appearance at this stage was that Fini's hold on the party remained tenuous, although Rauti's failure had undermined the alternatives to Fini. Within a few years, the MSI's position had been transformed dramatically and Fini was viewed as a masterful political operator.

Between the two national elections of 1992 and 1994, the MSI leapt from a situation where it appeared to be going nowhere to being part of the govern- ing coalition. It appears that, while long-term factors such as the de-radicali- sation of the political climate and the cumulative effect of the MSI's historical strategy of insertion laid the foundations for the historical entrance into government, it would never have occurred had it not been for the more circumstantial factors emanating from the political crisis which decimated the political class and completely transformed the political climate. As explained in Chapter 2 and also stressed by Ignazi, the MSI benefited in particular from its extraneousness from the *tangentopoli* investigations, the implosion of the DC, the momentum created by the autumn 1993 administrative election results, the legitimisation provided by the endorsement of, and alliance with, Berlusconi and FI, the excellent public image of Fini and the polarisation of the political contest in the context of the new electoral system (Ignazi 1994a: 106).

The creation of the Alleanza Nazionale drew comparisons in particular with the *Destra nazionale* strategy formulated by Almirante in the 1970s. However, Fini then went much further than his mentor by presiding over the formal dissolution of the MSI within the AN in 1995, bestowing upon the AN the status of a formal party organisation which proclaimed itself to be a democratic conservative force committed to liberal values, breaking from the anti-system rhetoric of the past. Although Fini was still continuing to laud Mussolini's statesmanship, the successes of 1993–94 appeared to convince him that a more formal break with the party's past was required. Moreover, most MSI militants were persuaded that Fini's post-fascist strategy could bear greater fruits in the future. Hence, Rauti's group aside, the majority supported Fini's project to dissolve the MSI into the new AN party at Fiuggi in 1995.

The political thesis of the new AN approved at Fiuggi proclaimed the AN's repudiation of 'all forms of dictatorship and totalitarianism', commitment to democracy and liberty and 'absolute aversion to racism' (Alleanza Nazionale 1995a). Nevertheless, the transition appeared to take place without a real attempt by Fini to engage the party in a discussion of its past and its key historical reference, i.e. fascism. Indeed, the fact that it had entered government in 1994 without having had to confront its past served to encourage the belief that no real discussion was needed, as did the apparent collapse of a 'First Republic' originally established on the basis of an anti-fascist consensus (Ignazi 1998). Rauti's group aside, the majority of the party seemed content to allow Fini to proceed with the post-fascist design of the AN, given the success that he had so far delivered. Fini was aided in this respect by the highly centralised leadership structure of the AN, which allowed him to tighten his grip over the direction of the party (Ignazi 2003: 50).

In moving the MSI–AN away from its neo-fascist ghetto, Fini recognised that to continue to base the MSI's appeal on fascism would be to appeal to a declining historical residue. Therefore, it was essential that its electoral base was broadened through adopting a more moderate stance. Nevertheless, the old MSI still managed to retain the support of 5 per cent of the Italian electorate, who were not put off by its continual attachment to fascism. This traditional base remained a substantial proportion of the AN's electoral strength, requiring Fini to make occasional noises to appease them.

Since 1994, attempts to consolidate the legitimacy of the AN have been combined with experimentation in terms of the tactics the party has pursued.

Positions taken have been shaped by both external factors, notably the need to adapt to developments within the Italian political system, particularly the changing fortunes of the other centre-right parties, and internal factors, i.e. the need to maintain an equilibrium as regards the competing factions within the party.

Shifts in position could be interpreted as the result of a changing equilibrium within the party, with the 'liberal' current (favouring a more neo-liberal economic perspective) having been in the ascendancy at the Verona congress of 1998, and the *destra sociale* ('social right') current (favouring a more solidaristic approach) becoming more influential after 2000.[1] The changing equilibrium itself could be attributed to the decisions by Fini to move towards one or other current, decisions which themselves related to his perceived need to locate the AN according to developments external to the party.

The recasting of the MSI–AN as a modern conservative force had already illustrated Fini's agility in responding to the opportunities offered by changing external circumstances. The shift towards the free-market right was an attempt to exploit FI's apparent weakness (in terms of both organisation and Berlusconi's apparently weakened leadership). Following the setback of 1999, Fini was not embarrassed to change tack again. The perhaps unexpected resilience of both Berlusconi and FI forced a rethink of notions of challenging FI on its own electoral ground. Instead, more traditional values such as identity, security and law and order were emphasised as well as a social market economy approach (Tarchi 2003b: 163). Throughout this period, the AN's traditional exaltation of national identity was juxtaposed with the regionalist (and sometimes secessionist) approach of the LN. Support for a directly elected head of state encapsulating the nation, generally envisaged in terms of a French-style model, also continued to be emphasised (Fini 1999).

The central role of the AN to the reconstituted centre-right coalition which returned to government in 2001 and its status as the second party of the CdL (at least in terms of electoral support) was reflected by Fini's appointment as vice-president of the council of ministers. In government, the AN pursued these traditional themes. Fini sought to distinguish the AN from the populism and neo-liberalism of the LN and FI (and the divisive regionalist identity of the former), presenting it as the social conscience of the right and (paradoxically given previous perceptions of the MSI–AN) as the moderate component of a right-wing populist government.

Fini's tenure as deputy prime minister was marked by a number of major about-turns (*svolte*) on issues central to the AN's political identity, often setting him against sections of his party, as well as strenuous efforts to rein in the influence of the LN and assert the AN's and his own personal role in the policy direction of the Berlusconi government (see section below, AN in government). A particularly symbolic *svolta* made by Fini was his denunciation of the absolute evils of the fascist regime's racial laws of 1938 and the collaboration in the holocaust on the part of the RSI of 1943–45. This led to the decision by *Il Duce*'s grand-daughter, Alessandra Mussolini, to leave the party and form a new political movement. Attacks on Fini's dilution of the party's identity also came from Francesco Storace – governor of the Lazio region until 2005, and then minister for health in the last year of the second Berlusconi government. Following the return to opposition in 2006, Storace also left the party to form a new political party, named simply La Destra (the right). A small number of defections followed, although the vast majority of leading members of the party remained loyal.

Elections and electorates

The MSI traditionally won the lion's share of its vote in the south of Italy, particularly in deprived urban areas such as those in Rome, Naples, Bari, Reggio and Palermo. It exploited discontent at southern under-development, winning support from the unemployed and marginalised elements who felt that the political class had failed them. Its strongest regions were Lazio, Campania, Puglia and Sicily. It polled comparatively badly in the north, where the collective memory of the RSI, resistance and civil war remained (although following the transformation into the AN, it began to poll more respectably in the north). As with far right parties elsewhere in Europe, the MSI appeared to do well by exploiting a feeling of social dislocation among certain social groups in the face of socio-economic change, appealing to a general desire to restore old certainties and return authority to a changing world. Its performance in the north in the 1990s would be hit by competition from the LN for the right-wing protest vote. An exception was Bolzano and the Alto Adige, where the MSI–AN did well by exploiting Italian resentment *vis-à-vis* the majority German-speaking community – perceived as highly protected (the MSI–AN polled over 30 per cent in Bolzano in 1994).

The MSI–AN won 13.5 per cent of the vote in the 1994 general election. This was a huge improvement on the 5.4 per cent return achieved in 1992. The breakdown of the AN vote was similar to that of the MSI previously, being markedly southern, urban and young, although in much larger proportions than before (the MSI–AN vote tripled in the south and centre). A survey in 1994 indicated the youthful nature of the vote for the MSI–AN: 23 per cent of 18- to 24-year-olds voted for the AN (the AN did well among the same social groups as the old MSI, only on a larger scale). The distribution of the vote for the AN decreased with each age group, apart from among the over 65-year-olds with whom it increased. This latter group were old enough to have a fond nostalgia for the fascist regime. Some 62.7 per cent of the AN vote came from the centre and south (Ignazi 1994b: 48).

While the 1994 election had seen the AN build on the MSI vote across Italy, although remaining particularly skewed towards the south, Tarchi notes that, in 1996 (where the AN recorded its highest ever national share of the vote at 15.7 per cent), the increase in the AN vote was particularly marked in the centre-north, while it actually receded in the south (where votes were lost to Fiamma-Tricolore). There was a particularly notable increase in the AN vote in Umbria, where it reached almost 20 per cent. This regional share was surpassed only in Lazio, Calabria and Abruzzo (Tarchi 1997: 214–16).

The 2001 election, although marking a return to government for the AN, actually saw a decline in its vote share to 12 per cent. The result reinforced the AN's dependence on its political alliance with Forza Italia. Irrespective of smaller gains or losses by the AN, it seemed that the success of the centre-right coalition as a whole was dependent on FI winning a substantial share of the vote. While the 1996 result had signalled progress in making inroads into the northern electorate, the 2001 vote reconfirmed the AN as a predominantly central-southern-based party, with strongholds in Lazio and parts of Campania, Abruzzo, Calabria and Puglia. As Diamanti and Lello note, the AN vote (similar to the UDC vote) was rooted in areas of particularly high levels of unemployment, and where the public sector played a key role in the local economy. Thus, voters for both the AN and UDC were strongly identified with support for social protection and state intervention, and rather sceptical of proposals for decentralisation or devolution which might reduce the role of the Rome-based central state in providing such protection (Diamanti and Lello 2005: 16).

The 2006 election result, in which the AN vote slightly increased to 12.3 per cent, appeared to demonstrate some success on the part of the AN in shoring up these constituencies through the stances adopted in government and in the election campaign. However, analysis of the electoral data for 2006 shows that the AN share of the vote actually decreased slightly in the south (where the main gainers were the UDC and the centre left) and increased in the north, seemingly at the expense of the big losers, FI. The AN vote went up by 2.2 per cent in the northeast and 1.9 per cent in the northwest, while dropping 1.6 per cent in the centre-south and 1 per cent in the south and islands (Diamanti and Vassallo 2007). Nevertheless, the sharp decline in FI's vote share and the increased unity on the centre left meant that the increases in the vote for the AN were not enough to prevent electoral defeat and a return to opposition. The AN's individual electoral performance in 2008 is difficult to assess, given that it was part of a joint PDL list with FI. However, a decline may have been expected due to the departure of Storace's La Destra grouping.

Fini's changing leadership

The agency role played by Fini in the early 1990s was crucial to the AN's success. Fini had been exploring other options prior to the political crisis – for example the idea of moving the MSI in the direction of the French FN and radical right-wing populism, ground that the LN was already beginning to occupy. A move in a radical populist direction would have allowed the MSI to maintain a niche in the developing party system. However, it would have precluded it from garnering more moderate voters and exploiting the rich pickings offered by the collapse of the DC. The latter factor (together with the move to a majoritarian electoral system) offered more interesting political opportunities, allowing the AN to move to the centre ground. The uncertainty over the long-term durability of FI, given the way it was founded and created by Berlusconi and its consequent unconventional nature when compared with other European centre-right parties, encouraged Fini to pursue this centrist strategy in preparation for Berlusconi's exit from the political scene (Fini being fifteen years younger).

Fini's command of his party has been aided by his own personal popularity and the general shift in emphasis towards strong political leadership that has marked the evolution of the new bipolar party system. Indeed, Fini's embodiment of firm leadership would appear to have gone down particularly well with an Italian public tired of the weak and bargained leadership of the post-war republic. Nevertheless, Fini's leadership has not been of the same charismatic style as that of the other main leaders of the centre right, Berlusconi and Bossi. Indeed, his calm, rational and measured presence could be described as the very antithesis of the populist and sometimes demagogic styles of the latter two. He thus provides a reassuring alternative to those Italian centre-right voters put off by Berlusconi and Bossi.

Opinion polls have regularly indicated that Fini is Italy's most popular politician. Democracy is seen as safe in his hands. Nevertheless, Fini is very much the product of the MSI's political culture, embedded in a fascist subculture. He was leader of the MSI (anointed by Almirante) for most of the period since 1987, and leader of its youth wing, the FdG, for ten years before that. He joined the MSI at the height of the street battles of the 1970s. From his own recollections, he appears to have joined the MSI more out of a distaste for the leftist protesters of the post-1968 generation than from any great sense of ideological purpose. This pragmatic reasoning may reflect the motivations for many right-wingers who adopted the fascist label. Fini is ambiguous over the extent to which he took part in the street battles of the 1970s. He claims he was neither aggressive nor passive (Fini and Francia 1994: 20), admitting that 'On various occasions, unfortunately, I had to use my fists to defend myself' (Hooper 1995).

Nevertheless, until the early 1990s, Fini still embraced the nostalgia for the fascist regime and the anti-system discourse that were the common terms of reference for MSI militants. Thus, when acceding to the MSI leadership in 1987, he spoke of a 'fascism of the year 2000' (Ignazi 1994a: 118). In 1990, he claimed to reject the liberal views of the enlightenment inheritance (Ignazi 1994a: 76). As late as 1992, Fini declared himself 'faithful to the roots of the MSI ... to preserve the period of Mussolini' (Locatelli and Martini 1994: 215).

Despite the differences with Rauti's faction, fascism had remained the common fundamental reference across the leadership of the MSI. At the 1990 MSI congress, which led to Fini's temporary replacement by Rauti, Fini fought a rearguard action by stepping up the fascist rhetoric. In rejecting the view that, because of the collapse of communism, the MSI was obsolete, he claimed that the MSI's anti-communism was only the consequence of its fascist ideology, which opposed 'the principles of 1789, consolidated after 1945, from which originated liberalism and capitalism, and also communism'. It would thus resist the dominant western values and principles: 'liberal democratic in the political sphere, capitalistic in economics, and secular and materialistic in the spiritual sphere, in which Americanism represents the maximum expression'. Indeed, now the fight against communism was won, the MSI could reconcentrate the effort on the fight against Americanism and capitalism (Ignazi 1994a: 76).

Although this radical rhetoric could not prevent Fini's removal as leader in 1990, he was able to quickly regain ground as the party floundered under Rauti's leadership. For example, he began to emphasise the immigration question, promoting opposition to the new Martelli law, which gave an amnesty to illegal immigrants while limiting the scope for further immigration (Cheles 1995: 170). Fini also raised his profile during the Gulf War (travelling to Baghdad to secure the release of Italian hostages) and sought to utilise widespread anti-Arab feeling by raising the western standard in order to turn the MSI majority away from its anti-American, Third World-ism.

The return to the leadership would signal a turnaround in fortunes for Fini. With his authority fortified by the successes of 1993–94, Fini moved the MSI–AN fully behind liberal democratic principles, declaring democracy and liberty irrevocable in the debate of confidence in the Berlusconi government in 1994. Nevertheless, Fini still remained ambiguous about the past. In March 1994, Fini declared that 'Mussolini was the unique Italian statesman of the century. Outside of Italy, there were De Gaulle and Adenauer. Hitler? A criminal' (Ignazi 1994a: 217). Similar sentiments were expressed after the AN's election success to much consternation. In an exposition of Fini's views later published in interview form, he claimed that he was taken out of context. Thus, what he meant was that 'Mussolini, like Churchill, De Gaulle and even Hitler and Stalin (these last two in all their negatives) have made the history of Europe in this century' (Fini and Francia 1994: 123).

One of Fini's avowed intentions has been to rehabilitate the term right wing, given the previous fascist or undemocratic connotations of the term. It could be argued that such has been the identification of the right with fascism that all those who considered themselves on the right have automatically considered themselves fascist. Moreover, the MSI was the only political home for self-declared right-wingers in the post-war republic. Fini alludes to this himself when justifying his fascist past: 'Of course, everyone changes. I was a fascist at the time when all right wingers were called fascists. Today things are not like that any longer. I claimed the label because what others considered an insult to me meant belonging to my political family, the MSI' (Batista 1994). This leaves one wondering whether Fini was ever really a fascist, although he had no compunction in adopting the MSI's anti-system discourse as he rose to the top of the MSI.

The party

Organisation

After the defeat of fascism in 1945, a stubborn minority subculture remained in Italy, faithful to the tenets propagated by the fallen fascist regime. The MSI was therefore able to construct within this fascist subculture an organisational complexity akin to those of the mass parties. It engaged in mass recruitment, and it developed a centralised hierarchal structure, a strong territorial network of sections and a large network of flanking organisations that gave it the appearance of being enmeshed in a broader civil society. Its network of collateral organisations served as a fertile recruitment ground. Among these were its university front, FUAN, and its youth front, FdG, elements of which played a prominent part in clashes with the extra-parliamentary left in the 1960s and 1970s. Fini himself was leader of the FdG from 1977 to 1987, and he was later followed by Gianni Alemanno. There was also the National Union of RSI veterans and the organisation for Italians abroad (CTIM), together with social and sporting clubs and a women's organisation, as well as cultural associations and study centres. The MSI also had its own sister union, the CISNAL, founded in 1950, which had 300,000 members in the 1970s. It was strongly represented among state employees and white collar workers. The MSI also had a network of journals and a daily newspaper, *Il Secolo d'Italia*, which had a circulation of around 10,000, rising to around 30,000 with the creation of the AN (Tarchi 1997: 364).

In his comprehensive study of the MSI–AN party organisation, Tarchi cites official party sources which suggest that the number of party members oscillated around 200,000 during the long years of exclusion from the party system in the 1960s and 1970s. Membership had fallen to around 140,000 by 1990, before rising significantly to 324,344 in 1994 and to 467,539 in 1995 following the transformation into the AN (Tarchi 1997: 40). However, Tarchi treats these data suspiciously, suggesting that party records wildly inflated membership figures. Nevertheless, the MSI was strongly rooted territorially, with around 3,000 local sections in 1990, rising to 8,451 in 1994 and 10,284 with the advent of the AN in 1995 (Tarchi 1997: 46–47). Membership of the MSI had been at its highest in Lazio and the southern regions of Campania, Puglia and Sicily. Membership in these regions increased significantly following the transition to the AN, although the transition also saw a diminution in the predominantly southern character of its membership, with notable increases in membership also in the central regions of Tuscany, Umbria, Marche and Emilia-Romagna (Tarchi 1997: 180–82).

The organisational apparatus of the MSI, including various collateral organisations and the party newspaper, was inherited by the AN following the dissolution of the former in 1995. However, the FdG and FUAN would be amalgamated into the new party youth organisation – Azione Giovani – in 1996. In the same year, CISNAL formed part of the new autonomous trade union confederation, UGL, reflecting the abandonment of corporatism by the new AN and its interest in reaching out to a wider range of economic actors (particularly the self-employed and small businesses) in a more flexible fashion.

According to official party data, the transformation into the AN has led to a substantial increased in party membership, standing at over 600,000 in 2006. This placed the AN second only to the DS in terms of political party membership in Italy. However, despite the increase in numbers, the transition from the MSI to the AN involved a change from a mass party organisational model to a highly personalised and centralised leadership structure, giving Fini considerable power over the party (Ignazi 2003: 50). Thus, for example, the provincial level acquired more power over the municipal branches and the regional level accrued more power over the provincial one. Regional co-ordinators were no longer elected within the region but nominated by the national leadership. Ignazi suggests that the AN statute implemented 'Caesarist-centrist traits' that had been increasingly emerging in the later years of the MSI (Ignazi 1998: 173; 2005b: 337–38). Tarchi refers to a plebiscitary centralism, in which the leadership was less constrained by party militants and given a number of discretionary powers. For example, the new statute gave the leadership the power to control the selection of the vast majority of delegates to the party national assembly. This body was charged with appointing the party's national executive. However, this would be on the basis of the leader's indications (Ignazi 1998: 173; Tarchi 1997: 145–46). Writing in 1998, Ignazi noted that the new organisational apparatus of the party in giving Fini power over the regional co-ordinators, the party national assembly, the national executive and the new enlarged body of elected representatives in parliament, combined with the 'uncontested dominance and charismatic-like aura of the leadership', introduced traits of 'fuhrer-prinzip' into the AN (Ignazi 1998: 174).

Fini was able to use the new party apparatus to put his own people in key positions, although these remained, in the main, people socialised within the old MSI. Despite the attempts to portray the AN as a break from the past, Ignazi noted in 1998 that only 10 per cent of the national executive had no previous MSI affiliation (Ignazi 1998: 174). The AN party statute accelerated ongoing changes in the MSI's organisational structure. It was the genetic imprint of the party, i.e. the importance given to strong leadership within the political culture of the MSI, that allowed Fini, bolstered significantly by the successes of 1993–94, to engineer these changes. The new apparatus meant that Fini was able to innovate by instituting new *ad hoc* bodies within the party hierarchy. For example, the flexibility and power that the party statute gave Fini was demonstrated in late 2004 when he created an inner party directorate of three vice-presidents reflecting the major factions within the party, comprising Gianni Alemanno of the *destra sociale* faction, Ignazio La Russa of the *destra protagonista* ('active right') faction and Altero Matteoli of the 'liberal' *nuova alleanza* ('new alliance') faction (Fella 2006). However, such was Fini's irritation with sniping from the various factions that months later he decided to abolish these and various other national offices.

A new statute adopted at the end of 2006 nevertheless reflected pressure within the party to make the leadership more accountable – in the wake of disquiet aroused by Fini's tendency to take initiatives without warning or consultation. The new statute appeared to reverse the Caesaristic shift. Thus, it provided for local circles (organised territorially or sectorally) that elect their own presidents, and provincial congresses made up of all party members at the provincial level and responsible for electing their provincial presidents. Regional co-ordinators were to be elected by regional assemblies, composed of various office-holders from within the region. The national leader and national assembly are to be elected by the national congress, which is composed of the provincial presidents and delegates elected by the provincial congresses, as well as members of the national assembly and various other office-holders. The national president retains a number of discretionary powers, including the power to stage extraordinary congresses, to appoint various officials to the party's internal organisation and establish various party offices (Alleanza Nazionale 2006a). The new statute could be interpreted as both a response to internal pressures and a further step towards normalisation of the party.

Party attitudes

Analysis of the attitudes of MSI–AN party members has tended to demonstrate a persistence of nostalgia for the fascist regime and a number of conservative–authoritarian positions. However, at the same time, on a number of policy issues – even prior to the transformation into the AN (Ignazi and Ysmal 1992b) – majority attitudes have appeared to be fairly moderate on some issues, or at least rather different from what one would expect from a party of the extreme right The continuing fascist nostalgia is combined with a conservative position on social–family morality that can be associated with the conservative right as well as the extreme right, together with a predilection for state intervention or protectionism that one would not normally associate with the modern European right at all (extreme or conservative). This might help to explain the relative ease with which the MSI–AN was able to make the leap from the ghetto to government and why other 'mainstream' parties in Italy did not appear to regard the MSI–AN as too grave a threat. A party's ideology and traditions may have less relevance for its policies and actions than for cohesion among the party's members, reflecting a need to establish a collective party identity but posing no actual threat to system. Thus, MSI–AN militants have had a different view of Italy's history but did not necessarily wish to overthrow the democratic system. Fini's leadership has sought to present interpretations of history as immaterial to the present political debate. Fascism should be consigned to the judgement of history.

A favourable interpretation of the Fascist regime remained a constant among party militants surveyed in the 1990s. In a 1995 survey data of middle-level party cadres cited by Ignazi, a large majority (62 per cent) agreed with the statement that 'notwithstanding some questionable choices, fascism was a good regime'. A further 7 per cent agreed that it was the best regime possible. Of the rest, 13 per cent described it as the 'inevitable response to the communist threat', while only 18 per cent referred to it as an 'authoritarian regime' (Ignazi 2005b: 339–40). The same questions were asked at the 1998 Verona congress, soliciting similar responses despite attempts by the leadership to consolidate the party as a democratic force with liberal leanings. Some 61 per cent agreed with the statement that fascism was a good regime notwithstanding questionable choices, while 3 per cent referred to it as the best regime possible. Particularly notable were the opinions of newcomers to the party, i.e. those joining the party since the transformation into the AN of 1995: 55 per cent agreed with the first statement and 1.7 per cent with the second (Vignati 2001). Moreover, asked to rank a number of statesmen and theorists (including the likes of Croce, Tocqueville and Popper) in terms of the importance of their writings in the political education of a young person, a number of iconic figures of the fascist movement came out on top, 88.6 per cent plumped for Gentile (86.3 per cent of the post-1994 intake), 76.2 per cent for Mussolini (65.6 per cent for the post-1994 intake) and 66 per cent for Evola (66 per cent for the post-1994 intake). In terms of one of the more contentious aspect of the fascist heritage (and significant particularly given Fini's later condemnation), respondents were also asked whether they agreed that condemning the experience of the RSI regime of 1943–45 would signal a dissolution of ideological identity: 61 per cent were in agreement while 26.1 per cent disagreed. Disagreement with this interpretation of the RSI was higher among the post-1994 intake: 45.2 per cent disagreed while 36.8 per cent remained in agreement.

Unfortunately, the 1998 survey was the most recent comprehensive survey of the attitudes of AN party militants. Nevertheless, it was notable that, in a broader survey of Italian voters in 2001, 13 per cent agreed with the statement on fascism as a good regime despite questionable decisions, while 1.7 per cent stated it was the best regime possible (Ignazi 2005b: 339–40). The first figure roughly equates to the national-level vote for the AN.

The AN in government

The initial period following the CdL's victory at the 2001 general election witnessed the AN finding common ground with its coalition allies on issues where its identity was particularly strong, notably law and order, and the related and controversial issue of immigration. The Bossi–Fini law on immigration, passed in 2001, was notable not only for the key role played by Fini in its development, but for the collaboration between the AN and the LN that took place on it, symbolised by the co-sponsorship of the law by the two party leaders. While the Bossi–Fini law was criticised for its harshness by immigrant associations and the left, it helped to cement the appearance on the part of Fini and the AN of a tough, hard-line position as regards the immigration issue – which was, despite their sharply differing political identities, an area of common cause between the AN and the LN. Nevertheless, this collaboration disguised a difference in tone towards immigrants in which Fini's measured discourse could be contrasted with Bossi's inflammatory rhetoric. These differences would become notable with Fini's *svolta* of October 2003.

The svolta *on immigration*

In October, Fini's suggestion that it was time to consider giving immigrants resident in Italy for a sizeable continuous period (e.g. six years[2]) the right to vote in local elections caused considerable controversy, given the AN's previous association with a tough restrictive position on immigration.[3] While this opened up divisions within the government, with the LN predictably denouncing the idea, and much of FI also against, the proposal also encountered opposition within the AN, notably within the government from Maurizio Gasparri (the minister for communications) and from the then president of the Lazio region, Francesco Storace. Gasparri declared that, within the AN, 'everyone was opposed, even those that say they are not'. Nevertheless, Fini pressed on regardless, instructing party colleagues to table a parliamentary bill to change the constitutional law on electoral rights.[4]

Fini's move on immigrant voting rights can be interpreted in a number of ways, all of which encapsulate his political strategy within the Berlusconi government. In particular, the move seemed calculated to simultaneously distance the AN in the public mind from the extremism of the LN, and to antagonise the LN into revealing this extremism even more, with the possible welcome consequent effect of straining the close relationship between Berlusconi and Bossi, and enhancing Fini's weight within the government. At the same time, the move was central to Fini's attempts to present the AN as a moderate force within the government (again in contrast to the LN), appealing to the moderate and catholic centre-right voters that the AN was targeting to broaden its electoral base. Indeed, as Ilvo Diamanti has suggested, in focusing on the voting rights issue, Fini managed to deliberately choose a marginal aspect of an issue that is central to the political sensibilities of the LN, thereby provoking it when, in effect, the proposed change (while of symbolic appeal) would make very little change to the daily lives of immigrants, which would continue to be conditioned by the harsh constraints imposed by the Bossi–Fini law (Diamanti 2003c). The move also served to enhance the international standing of Fini and the AN. Indeed, in relation to this, two months later, AN MEPs followed Fini's line by voting with the Socialist group in the European Parliament for a motion in support of giving third country nationals the right to vote in administrative elections throughout the EU, while the EPP group (which notably contained not only FI, but also the UDC and former DC elements of the centre left) voted against (Staff Reporter 2004b). There was, nevertheless, a great deal of internal opposition to Fini's move within his own party. As well as the opposition from the likes of Gasparri and Storace, Fini was also heckled by party militants regarding the issue.[5] While Fini claimed not to be bothered about this, it was notable that the proposal appeared to be quietly shelved as Fini turned his attention to other issues in the months that followed (Fella 2006).

The svolta *on fascism*

Fini's 'opening' on immigrant voting rights could be interpreted as integral to his strategy of positioning the AN as a moderate centre-right force and carving out a political identity distinct from the populism of the LN and of FI. Shortly after this controversy, Fini made further strides in his re-moulding of the AN's identity through his denunciation of the fascist 'racial laws' and the RSI (Ignazi 2005b: 338–39). Although Fini and other AN exponents had denounced the holocaust several times previously, the denunciation of Italian fascist complicity took things further and too far for Alessandra Mussolini who quit the party in disgust, later forming a new political movement Alternativa Sociale. However, Mussolini's defection aside (probably viewed as a blessing in disguise by Fini), there was no mass exodus from the AN, despite the shock caused within the party by Fini's statement (many veterans of the RSI and their descendents continued to be involved in the AN). The slight ambiguity as to whether, in speaking of absolute evil, Fini was referring to the RSI itself or more specifically to the act of complicity in the holocaust helped to square Fini's statement with the continuing 'nostalgia' of much of the party's membership. Indeed, it could be argued that the specific criticism of the racial laws of 1938 introduced by the pre-RSI regime is no real contradiction of the view expressed by over 60 per cent of militants surveyed at the 1998 Verona congress that 'apart from a few questionable decisions', the fascist regime was a good one (Vignati 2001). Polls suggested that around three-quarters of AN voters supported Fini's strategy of denouncing the crimes of fascism. Nevertheless, the statement, together with the proposal on immigrant voting rights, did stir rebellious voices within the party who had no intention of taking part in the Mussolini sideshow. Storace, a leading light in the party's *destra sociale* faction, was particularly vocal in mobilising opposition to the direction in which Fini was taking the party. He criticised Fini for feeling the need to apologise for the past and for his readiness to offer up AN support for unpalatable laws designed to serve Berlusconi's interests, when such collegiality brought no return in terms of satisfying the AN's political priorities.

Indeed, while it seemed clear that the reason for Fini and the AN's participation in government was not to engineer some kind of fascist takeover, the question remained as to what purpose its presence in government actually served other than to prop up a ruling coalition whose political priorities seemed to be dominated by the personal interests of Berlusconi and the political priorities of the LN. This was a problem that also appeared to vex Fini, and helps to explain his more assertive stance in government in 2003 and

2004 and his calls for a *verifica*. The pursuit of a more social market inter-ventionist approach, the concern for public sector workers and the emphasis on the problems of the south were all designed to appeal to the AN's core constituency (Fella 2006).

While Fini's strategy seemed to be a centrist one – moving his party to the middle ground in order to win over more moderate voters, even if this came at the expense of losing voters on the extreme right disillusioned with his stance on immigration and/or fascism – some of the positions taken by Fini retained a symbolic nature, in that they were likely to appeal to the more longstanding MSI–AN supporters and activists and rein in any possible dis-illusionment towards his more headline-grabbing *svolte*. These positions reflected the political culture in which the AN leadership was schooled, while also appealing to broader conservative opinion. These included a traditional conservative–authoritarian position on issues relating to law and order and security. Thus, Fini continued to project an image of the AN as tough on law and order. For example, he defended the rather brutal tactics of the police in handling protesters at the G8 summit in July 2001, and complained that the behaviour of the police 'who defended the city against the rioters' had been more investigated than the rioters themselves (Staff Reporter 2003b). More-over, Fini sponsored a new law on drugs, eliminating the distinction between soft and hard drugs and introducing tougher punishments for the use of both (De Luca 2004). The latter came within the frame of attacks on the moral degeneracy of aspects of Italian popular culture.

This authoritarian approach was also combined with a continuing exulta-tion of the role of the Italian military (although the stress was on the impor-tant role it undertakes in peacekeeping and delivering aid) and scathing attacks on the peace movement. In relation to the war in Iraq, and the Italian participation in the post-war occupation (both of which Fini and the AN had strongly supported), Fini suggested that elements of the left-wing parties (all of whom had taken part in the massive peace manifestations in Italy) con-tinued to have nostalgia for Saddam Hussein (Staff Reporter 2004d). On the day of the large pacifist demonstration in Rome on 20 March 2003, the AN organised a counter-meeting to pay homage to the positive role of Italian military forces employed in various peace missions around the world. Fini denounced the peace demonstrators as being against the 'western world' (Staff Reporter 2003c).

Two examples of the more symbolic positions taken – with particular appeal to party militants – were those relating to the AN's campaign for a national day of commemoration of the *foibe* (when ethnic Italians living in the former Italian territories ceded to Yugoslavia at the end of the Second World War were massacred by anti-fascist partisans) and its behaviour in relation to the proposed Boato law to clarify the president's right to issue pardons. In relation to the former, the AN proposal (reflecting the MSI–AN's traditional championing of the Italians left dispossessed following the ceding of these territories), won approval across the political spectrum in a parliamentary vote in February 2004 (only the unreformed communists voted against). Regarding the latter, the AN blocked an attempt to clarify the president's right to issue pardons to those convicted under the judicial system, independently of a plea being made. The law had been proposed in light of the case of Adriano Sofri, the former leader of the left-wing extra-parliamentary grouping *Lotta Continua*, who had been convicted and finally imprisoned, 17 years after the event, for the killing of the police chief he allegedly directed. The dubious circumstances surrounding the case together with Sofri's apparently exemplary behaviour and emergence as a public intellectual in the intervening years had made his case a *cause célèbre* and the focus of a campaign for a presidential pardon, backed across the political spectrum. However, confusion over the president's right to issue the pardon (with the LN justice minister, Roberto Castelli, claiming that he had to give his authorisation first) had led to the Boato law proposal being blocked. Although sponsored by a Green party deputy, the law was also apparently supported by Berlusconi. Nevertheless, most FI deputies voted with the AN and the LN to amend the proposal, giving the justice minister the final say. This position needs to be understood in the context of the close involvement of MSI militants and groups sympathetic to the MSI in political violence against the extra-parliamentary left of which Sofri was very much a part during the 'years of lead' of the 1970s. Indeed, some within the AN argued that a pardon for Sofri should only come if those from the extra-parliamentary right convicted for terrorist violence in this period were treated in the same way.[6] A perhaps more extreme viewpoint came in the words of Maurizio Gasparri, who suggested that Sofri should be treated in the same way as the Nazi war criminal, Erich Priebke, whose request for a pardon was refused shortly before by President Ciampi (Luzi 2004).

The various positions taken by the AN in government must also be understood as a balancing act between appealing to traditional party militants and potentially new centrist voters. Moreover, positions also reflected the ascendancy or not of the various factions of the party and the identity of the responsible party spokesman in the area concerned. This sometimes meant contradictory positions being taken by different party spokesmen in different ministries, for example, Gianni Alemanno, a leader of the *destra sociale* faction, as minister for agriculture proposed strong regulation of genetically modified organisms (GMOs) (finding common cause with green activists), while such regulation was opposed by the vice-minister for productive activities, Adolfo Urso, an exponent of the liberal *nuova alleanza* current, which favoured a de-regulatory free-market approach. Maurizio Gasparri, on the other hand, a leading member of the *destra protagonista* faction, tended to favour a more populist position, and a closer position to Berlusconi, as reflected in his marshalling of the so-called Gasparri law on media regulation, seen as very favourable to Berlusconi's media interests. The leaders of the *destra sociale* faction, Alemanno and Storace, were critical of the subordinate role played to FI and Berlusconi's interests. Appointments to key party posts and ministerial positions generally had to reflect an equilibrium between these factions. This balance was disturbed when Fini proposed the appointment of Storace as health minister in April 2005 (following his loss of the Lazio region). Gasparri's attempt to prevent this led to his dismissal from government.

Catholicism or secularism – another svolta?

Fini's enhanced status within the ruling coalition following his appointment to the foreign ministry appeared to make him willing to take more risks in the direction of his party. Thanks partly to the vastly changed circumstances of Italian politics following the collapse of the old party system, Fini had been able to execute the transformation of the AN without requiring a serious discussion of the party's historical references. After returning to government in 2001, his attempts finally to address the party's past and set out a more moderate and modern image reflected the goal of broadening the party's electoral constituency further and preparing his possible leadership of a post-Berlusconi right. This however began to encounter increased resistance within a party no longer willing to support Fini simply for what he had delivered in the past, with discontent increasing as regards his tendency to take controversial initiatives without consulting his party. Indeed, this was illustrated by the controversy following his decision to vote for a relaxation of the law on fertility treatment in the unsuccessful referendum of June 2005, which set him at odds not only with the UDC (relations with whom had already suffered as a result of the different strategies pursued after the regional elections) but also the vast majority of his own party's parliamentarians, some of whom pointed to Fini's contradiction of the founding Fiuggi document as regards its endorsement of catholic doctrine. Indeed, Alemanno was moved to resign as party vice-president in the midst of the dispute. As mentioned, the vice-presidency posts would later be abolished by Fini in exasperation at the insubordination and bickering of the leading party 'colonels' (Fella 2006). Fini's new liberalism on family ethics would also later be demonstrated with the conciliatory tone he adopted towards civil recognition of gay co-habitations in early 2006. In 1998, he had stated that declared homosexuals should not be employed as school teachers (Meli 2008).

Fini's shift to a more libertarian and secular position on these issues could be interpreted as stemming from an acknowledgement of the limitations of his previous strategy of aligning himself and his party with the catholic right, and was possibly related to the failure of the AN to benefit electorally despite the personal strides made by Fini since 2003, the emergence of the UDC as a serious competitor for the moderate catholic vote in the same period and a desire to present himself as a modern and secular alternative to his chief rival as regards the future leadership of the centre right (until the UDC split from the PdL): Pier Ferdinando Casini, president of the UDC and of the chamber of deputies from 2001 to 2006.

Fini can be said to have been for a long time playing two distinct games. On the one hand, he had focused on retaining a leadership role within his party and on interpreting public opinion worries about immigration, and he has occasionally displayed an intransigent hard-line stance. On the other hand, Fini has also been playing an individual game, competing as the potential heir of Berlusconi for the entire PdL, and even as a potential future president of the republic and, in this respect, he has attempted to show moderation and independence of judgement. His ability to do this was possibly enhanced in 2008 following his selection as president of the chamber of deputies. He has on several occasions utilised this role to show impartiality, good judgement and commitment to his institutional role. Thus, for instance, he complained when parliamentary procedures were violated by the right, as in the protracted election of the president of the RAI – the Italian broadcasting corporation – when centre-right representatives failed to attend meetings in protest at an opposition candidate considered unacceptable.

Ideology

New right and old right

Ignazi and Ysmal argued in 1992 that the electoral success of extreme right parties seemed to be inversely related to their relationship with fascism: 'Where they are ideologically linked to the fascist experience they fail to grow, where they do not claim any heritage from fascism their growth displays a positive trend' (Ignazi and Ysmal 1992a: 1). The continuing success of the FN and the growth of similar parties, such as the REP in Germany, while the MSI continued to decline seemed to bear this out. Right-wing populist parties such as the FN in France had capitalised on a number of changes in western society such as the general impact of neo-conservatism, the general crisis of legitimacy that befell traditional political systems and parties and the emergence of new salient political issues such as immigration and law and order that were not being addressed by traditional parties. The MSI, on the other hand, seemed to be attached to unfashionable solutions based on its fascist past.

The MSI was also hampered in this period by the persistence of various competing currents within the party. Reflecting the distinction made by the historian of fascism, Renzo De Felice, the main division appeared to be between the Rautian group, which reflected the radical quasi socialistic 'fascism in movement' tradition, and the majority grouping, which while sharing a nostalgia for fascism was more conservative–authoritarian in character, reflecting the 'fascism in power' tradition (De Felice 1975: 43–60; Ignazi 1993: 78–79). In the late 1980s, Fini was hampered in his attempts to manoeuvre the MSI behind the new tide of right-wing populism by the radical and leftist currents, notably the followers of Rauti. Nevertheless, there was evident collaboration between the MSI under Fini (and previously under Almirante) and the leading party of the new populist right, the French FN. Fini travelled to Baghdad during the first Gulf War with Le Pen in order to secure the release of Italian and French hostages. More significantly, the MSI and the French FN sat in the same European Parliamentary grouping until 1989. The FN had taken the initiative in forming the Group of the European Right following its success in the 1984 European elections. Le Pen became chairman of the group, and Almirante deputy chair. MSI MEPs tended to echo Le Pen's views on race and xenophobia. Pino Rauti remained an outspoken opponent of this MSI flirtation with the FN (Harris 1994: 143). The MSI had originally been closer to the PFN (Parti des Forces Nouvelle), which had been formed by former *Ordre nouveau* elements (a group similar in position to Rauti's ON), disillusioned by Le Pen's populist leadership of the FN. Indeed, the MSI had instigated the European Right Alliance in 1979, with the PFN and the Spanish Fuerza Nuova. But neither of the latter parties made any impact, and the MSI was drawn closer to Le Pen's more successful party model. However, there was a rupture in 1989 following the accession of the German REP to the European Right group. The REP had polled 7.1 per cent of the vote. This success, together with a brand of xenophobic populism and sociological make-up more akin to the FN, seemed to suggest that it made a more suitable partner for the FN than the apparently declining and outdated MSI.[7] Moreover, the MSI refused to sit in the same group as the REP, because of a row over the status of the South Tyrol–Alto Adige German-speaking region of Italy. The REP argued that the area should have the right to choose a 'Germanic destiny'. Its leader, Schonhüber denounced the MSI as 'fascists'. Fini replied that 'Mr Schonhüber is more extreme than Hitler … Hitler had never demanded Alto Adige from Mussolini' (Husbands 1992: 277).

Although the collaboration with the FN was a cause of controversy within the MSI, the influence of the French right on thinking within the party was notable. In the late 1970s and early 1980s, new cultural interpretations based on the thinking of the French *Nouvelle droite* school – associated with the thought of the French political theorist Alain de Benoist – became influential within the party (see Bar-On 2007). This school of thought involved rejection of the Judaeo-Christian tradition, as well as Marxism, given the stress of both on universal truths that could be used to pave the way for totalitarianism. It also rejects consumerist materialism and stresses European cultural identity and the need to maintain this cultural specificity. In general, it has an anti-egalitarian worldview, and stresses the need for a metapolitical struggle, a 'cultural war with the aim of taking power through the domination of political culture' (Harris 1994: 90). Thus, Antonio Gramsci's Marxist theory of hegemony is utilised and reversed, in that a Gramscian cultural 'war of position' is advocated by the *Nouvelle droite* in order to reverse a perceived left-liberal hegemony.

The Italian application of this thinking was not as strongly hostile to religion. However, the importance of a cultural strategy was emphasised more strongly. There was a rejection of violence and authoritarianism in favour of a cultural 'war of position', entrenching values through a process of cultural renewal and hegemonisation (Ignazi 1993: 77). Although some of the leading adherents of this strategy would leave the party, *Nouvelle droite* thinking nevertheless strongly influenced many MSI militants, and found its way into the thinking of the party leadership surviving the transition to the AN. There were strong echoes of it in Fini's later denunciations of the anti-fascist, centre-left consensus in Italian culture. Thus, in a book published as an interview with Fini in 1994, he suggested that 'the left has substantially managed to hege-monise the entertainment world' (Fini and Francia 1994: 69) and that 'we have to, above all, regenerate the cultural values of the nation and defeat defini-tively the conformism of the left, which is still deeply rooted in society' (Fini and Francia 1994: 89). In his book, *Un'Italia civile* published in 1999, Fini claimed that Italian culture had been 'prostituted' by a Gramscian strategy pursued by the left, which was evident in the prominence of the revolutionary post-1968 generation and had 'threatened the roots of the family brought by the diffusion of drugs, and the legalisation of divorce and abortion', as well as an extreme process of secularisation, which brought a 'nihilistic' approach to the family. This culture had focused on the wrongs of fascism while being indulgent of the crimes pursued by the communists (Fini 1999: 16).

Initial political principles of the AN – the Fiuggi congress

The Fiuggi congress of January 1995 approved the formal dissolution of the MSI and the submersion of its organisation into the new AN party. A state-ment of the aims and values of the AN was presented and approved by the congress. It declared: 'National Alliance repudiates all forms of dictatorship and totalitarianism and believes democracy and liberty to be irrepressible values … '. It also proclaims 'our faith in Christian values, our absolute aversion to racism, our spiritual vision of life, our identification in national tradition' (Alleanza Nazionale 1995a: 4).

The new statute for the AN declared:

> National Alliance is a political movement which has as its objective, the guarantee of the spiritual dignity and the social and economic aspirations of the Italian people, in respect of their civil traditions and national unity, and in coherence with the values of personal liberty and of general solidarity, in the continuous adhesion to democratic principles and to the rules of representative institutions. National Alliance locates itself within western and European culture, and develops its political obligation promoting the peaceful coexistence of peoples, states, ethnic groups, races and religions.
> Alleanza Nazionale (1995b: 1)

Aside from some debatable attempts to account for its neo-fascist past and sudden recasting as a conventional democratic party (for example suggesting that the fall of the First Republic meant that it could now abandon its pre-vious anti-systemic stance) and to present itself as the guardian of a national cultural heritage which embraced the likes of Croce and Gramsci, as well as the more traditional fascist icons such as Gentile and Evola, the Fiuggi document for the most part reads as a policy document in the mainstream of the European centre right, mixing Gaullism, elements of neo-liberalism, catholicism and authoritarian conservatism. In relation to the latter, the policy thesis referred to the need to reconcile the necessity of liberty with the primary need for authority, itself essential for social cohesion (Alleanza Nazionale 1995a: 5). Both the section on foreign affairs and that on institutional reform had strong Gaullist overtones. The former invoked the notion of a *Europe des patries*, while the latter (pursuing a familiar MSI theme) called for a presidential system modelled on that of the French Fifth Republic. However, the MSI's previous statist centralism was reversed. In recognition of the prevailing political wind, and the outdatedness of its previous positions, local autonomy and fiscal decentralisation were now referred to approvingly. The statement acknowledged that rampant corruption had 'been made possible by the strong concentration of riches in the hands of the state' (Alleanza Nazionale 1995a: 14). But federalism or strong decentralisation were only favoured within the context of a wider constitutional reform that would also encompass presidentialism. Previous state centralism in relation to the running of the economy was also reversed, with privatisation of much of Italy's huge public sector favoured. Nevertheless, blanket, ideological de-regulation was strongly opposed, with the document stressing that the state was 'not an enterprise' (Alleanza Nazionale 1995a: 16). Only in the preface of the document, and in the second chapter on 'values and principles', was the MSI's fascist heritage alluded to. The preface, presented in Fini's name, lauded the role of the MSI in the post-war history of Italy and the role of leaders such as Almirante. The chapter on 'values and principles' stated that 'the values of the right pre-exist fascism, they traversed it and outlived it' (Alleanza Nazionale 1995a: 8).

The Fiuggi document suggested that, after the fall of the 'First Republic', the MSI–AN could now abandon its opposition to the system and participate in the re-foundation of the Italian state (Alleanza Nazionale 1995a: 5), thus implying that the MSI's previous anti-system rhetoric was being directed at the particular political institutions and parties of the First Republic, rather than as a product of opposition to liberal democracy itself. Repeated references in the Fiuggi document to the preservation of the national culture were strongly tied to an emphasis on catholic values. It was emphasised that the national community should be based on the twin pillars of family and church. The policy thesis stressed opposition to abortion, euthanasia, genetic manipulation and drug de-criminalisation, and spoke gravely of the decline of the family and the rise in divorces. It called for 'responsible procreation' and monetary assistance to families who contributed to an increase in Italy's low birth rate (Alleanza Nazionale 1995a: 18). Consequently, it referred to the promotion of marriage, the dignity of women, the need for responsible procreation, the 'plague' of abortion and the need for stronger parental authority over children (Alleanza Nazionale 1995a: 18)[8]

In foreign policy, the document favoured an affirmation of Italy's international role, and took a familiar position, with echoes of past irredentism, in relation to the former Yugoslavia. There was a call for the return of assets appropriated from the Italian minority by Tito's communist regime in Slovenia and Croatia. The AN favoured a stronger Italian influence in the Balkans, and proposed that the entrance of Slovenia and Croatia into the EU be considered on the basis of a more strenuous defence of the interests of the Italian communities in these countries. It is interesting to note that, as a direct result of the AN's position on Slovenia and Croatia, the first Berlusconi government, acting within the council of ministers of the EU, blocked the negotiation of an association agreement between the EU and Slovenia (Traynor 1994). Fini's biographers, Locatelli and Martini, give another striking example of a lingering irredentism: in 1991 after the outbreak of war in the former Yugoslavia, Fini apparently travelled to Belgrade to discuss with Serb leaders the possible Italian re-annexation of Istria and Dalmatia (Locatelli and Martini 1994: 231). The MSI had always championed the rights of the Italian communities in former Yugoslavia while simultaneously attacking the special status afforded the German majority in Alto Adige, Slovenes in the Friuli-Venezia-Giulia region and other minorities in Italy.

A liberal right or a social right?

Marco Tarchi has identified three distinct phases in the evolution of the AN from its foundation in 1995 to its return to government in 2001. In the initial foundation period, the AN sought to become 'a radical force of renewal in the Italian political system' (Tarchi 2003b: 177). Thus, a populist emphasis was placed on the AN's distinctiveness from the discredited *partitocrazia*, representing a new political force that would replace the disgraced political class of the first republic, proposing a new model of direct democracy, which would include (in addition to presidentialism) increased recourse to propositional referenda.

In a second period following its return to opposition and after the Fiuggi congress, the AN sought to rival the FI for the (economically) liberal centre-right vote. This was notable particularly at the Verona programmatic conference held in early 1998, where it presented itself as a party of modernisation, making further enthusiastic strides in its embrace of the free market and attempting to shake off its reputation for having an old-fashioned statist approach to the management of the economy. The document produced for the Verona conference called for more flexibility in the labour market, further privatisation and a general liberalisation of the economic system and criticised the distorting interference of the state in the economic sphere (Tarchi 2003b: 163). Traditional themes such as law and order and the need for strong executive rule and a strong Italian state were infrequently mentioned in this document. Rather, the emphasis was on economic issues and presenting the AN as a modern liberal force in this respect. Nevertheless, Fini's book published in 1999 reaffirmed the spiritual nature of the AN, which did not believe in the 'savage' primacy of economics, reflected in both neo-liberalism and also the materialist interpretations of Marxism (Fini 1999: 15).

As noted above, the 1999 European elections represented a significant defeat for the liberalising strategy. From 2000 onwards, a third phase is identifiable, with the AN seeking to present itself as a responsible party of government. Tarchi suggests that in this period the AN has recycled some of the central ideas of the old MSI, although adapting them to the new national and international context. Accordingly, it has focused on 'the cult of law and order, the guiding role of the state in the economy, and the exaltation of social bonds in the national community'. Tarchi suggests that official party documents produced just prior to and following the return to government in 2001 sought to establish a new ideological synthesis combining modernising and conservative elements. These documents emphasise the 'desire for the right' (*voglia di destra*) based on the need for both identity and security (Tarchi 2003b: 163). The AN turned to attacking the excesses of economic deregulation in threatening the weakest elements of society with exclusion and poverty and the 'super-class of technocrats and finance managers' who sought to concentrate power in their own hands. At the international economic level, while not rejecting globalisation, there was a concern to ameliorate its effects, to find an equilibrium to 'sustain global competition without renouncing the values of social and community solidarity, of the dignity of work and of national identity' (Tarchi 2003b).

Following its return to government in 2001, the AN continued to emphasise this social market approach. Thus, the document produced at the 2002 national congress in Bologna maintained that 'the state must not withdraw from economic processes, but must exercise functions of direction, define rules, correct the distortions of the market, and mediate between interests and conflicts, all in the national interest' (Tarchi 2003b: 164–65). Nevertheless, although its discourse on markets became more critical, the number of approving references to markets and competition remained high (Fella and Ruzza 2006).

Frame analysis: continuity and change in the ideology of the AN

Analysis of the key programmatic documents emerging from the congresses of 1995, 1998, 2001 and 2006 sheds light on the shifts in policy and discourse on the part of the AN, often reflecting reactions to the external environment as well as addressing internal equilibriums. Thus, for example, we see the AN cautiously embracing markets in 1995 as it seeks to entrench its new-found status as a legitimate centre-right party, and then moving to a more pronounced neo-liberal position in 1998 as it sought to capitalise on Berlusconi's problems with the judiciary, before shifting back to a more mixed social market position in 2001 when its leader realised the political market for a neo-liberal centre-right party was too crowded. 2006 saw a continuation of the 2001 emphasis on traditional themes: the importance of national identity and the family, tough policies on law and order and security and rigorous immigration controls. Considering this analysis more generally, one has to stress that it would be incorrect to see party ideology as always being a coherent construct. In effect, one often finds glaring contradictions. This is seen on economic issues in the AN's documents where one finds both an emphasis on the need to assist weak social groups and suggestions that the state must withdraw from a socially interventionist approach. This perhaps reflects tensions among the different internal factions in AN.

The most frequently recurrent frames in the four key AN documents analysed are presented in Figure 6.1. The preponderance of traditional themes, such as the emphasis on the family, the need for strong executive leadership and strong law and order and immigrant control policies, is notable. Certain frames that could be characterised as populist are also common: the anti-*partitocrazia* emphasis, which came through particularly in the early documents, vilifications of enemies (usually the left) and the emphasis on the 'people'. Also notable is the emphasis on liberty (ranking second). This is perhaps related to the need for the AN to distance itself from its past and emphasise its commitment to modern liberal democratic practice, while shifting the focus on to the apparent state dirigisme of the left.

When examining the AN programmatic documents as a whole, its ideology emerges as a distinctive mix that situates this party in the tradition of European centre-right parties rather than within the extreme right. The AN has generally shared with other centre-right parties an emphasis on traditional ethics and the role of family values. Like other similar parties, it stresses the necessity for a strong executive and a powerful figure in government with strong leadership qualities. However, there are also some elements that markedly differentiate the AN from other centre-right parties. These relate in part to its

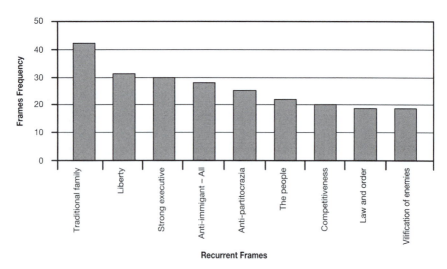

Figure 6.1 Recurrent AN frames (total n. 530)

neo-fascist heritage. For example the anti-party ethos it displayed in its foundation period can be traced back to its previous anti-system stance, and its attempt to recast the latter in terms of strident opposition to the *partitocrazia*, rather than to liberal democratic norms in general. Thus, in this initial period, it sought to define itself in opposition to the political system of the so-called First Republic, characterised by *partitocrazia*, and capitalise on its extraneousness from the corruption revealed by the *mani pulite* investigations.

As is clear from examination of the period 1993–94, the MSI–AN found that its political credibility was substantially enhanced by having been the component of the old party system untouched by the *tangentopoli* scandal. Of course, this related greatly to the fact that, because of its still substantially fascist ideology, the party had been marginalised by the entire political system and therefore deprived of even the opportunity to engage in substantial corrupted exchanges. Nonetheless, in the political vacuum that marked the early 1990s, much political capital could be gained by reiterating criticism of the old system. There was thus frequent recourse to this in the AN's founding documents. A few excerpts will suffice in conveying the ethos of the period. The following excerpt from the Fiuggi document points to the double exclusion that the MSI experienced: excluded from government because it was seen as constitutionally illegitimate, and also excluded from the legitimate opposition – which was monopolised by the PCI.

> The First Republic from this point of view has failed. Within it, a rather questionable double distinction was applied among the political forces – on the one hand – between the areas of legitimacy and representation – and on the other hand – between the majority and the opposition areas. In terms of the first distinction, only the parties within the area of legitimacy and organically allied to the DC (leaving outside the ex-PCI and the MSI–DN), were allowed to exercise a concrete and effective power of coalition, also formally taking part in government. In terms of the second distinction, the monopoly of government was left substantially in the hands of the DC while that of opposition was in the hands of the PCI.
>
> Alleanza Nazionale (1995b)

Figure 6.2 shows the declining emphasis given by AN in its programmatic documents to anti-partyocracy frames. While frequent mention was made of *partitocrazia* in the first document, its recurrence diminished substantially in later documents, as the AN needed to adjust itself to competition within a new party system in which the main players in the previous system were no longer present. Thus attacks on the *partitocrazia* were no longer relevant.

The extent to which the role of the *mani pulite* investigators in bringing down the old system was initially welcomed and referred to approvingly by the AN is particularly notable, as demonstrated by the following extract from the Fiuggi document:

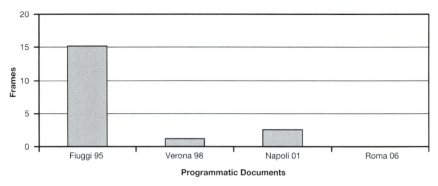

Figure 6.2 AN anti-partyocracy frames (n. 25).

The sincere appreciation and support that our political area has reserved for the actions of the Milan magistrates, from the beginning of the investigations known as *mani pulite*, should above all be restated ... after several years without significant results in pursuing positively the grave illegalities connected to the consociational system and to the climate of corruption which characterised the First Republic, just as we had denounced it for years in the political institutions.

Alleanza Nazionale (1995b)

However, the position here would change, mainly because of the AN's continuing alliance with FI. Once corruption investigations were launched against Berlusconi also, he (and his political allies) would begin to denounce the investigating magistrates as politically motivated (allied with the left). Thus, the attacks on the corrupt *partitocrazia* would also no longer be appropriate in this context. Nevertheless, in its foundation period, the AN saw a stronger role for the judiciary as connected to its strategy of overcoming the marginalisation created by an elitist and undemocratic Italian political system. There was thus a call for 'a renewal of the world of justice which has, as is inevitable and necessary, above all the recovery of the prestige and credibility of the judicial order as its first founding element' (Alleanza Nazionale 1995b). This institutional renewal also involved a new emphasis on enhancing political participation through forms of direct democracy:

direct democracy which escapes from the mafia-like intermediation of the partitocracy and bureaucraticism.

Alleanza Nazionale (1995b)

This emphasis on renewal through direct forms of democracy and replacement of the corrupt First Republic with a new political order had a populist flavour, in which the 'people' were repeatedly idealised as the party's core constituency and the reference point for political renewal. However, as with the general anti-political ethos found in the early documents, this emphasis on the people would diminish over time, becoming less frequent in later programmatic documents, as demonstrated in Figure 6.3.

Traditional ethics

Unlike reactions to political corruption, which only marked the initial period of the formation of the AN, an emphasis on traditional ethics occurs throughout the period and increases substantially over time. Emphasising family values was a way of defining the AN within the ideological parameters of much of the conventional European right. However, in doing so, some implicit references to its fascist past still occur. For instance, in the following excerpt, family values are rooted in the biological instinct of the species – a concept possibly vaguely reminiscent of that of race, but certainly not widely utilised by other political forces (Figure 6.4).

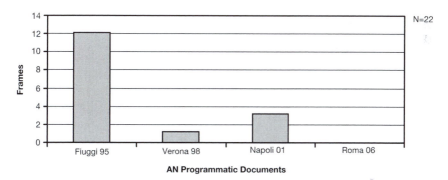

Figure 6.3 AN frames on 'the people'.

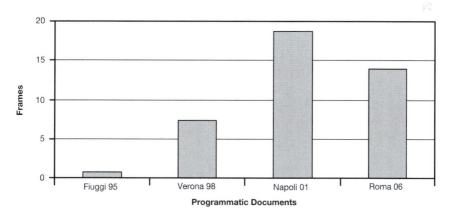

Figure 6.4 AN frames on traditional family values (n. 42).

And to limit ourselves to those that are among the qualifying aspects of our system of values which touch more directly the functioning of the economic system, we refer in the first place to the prevalence of the egoism of the species over that of the individual, which is fruit of our conception of the family and our obligations towards it, and which manifests itself in the effort to transmit to future generations more than that which has been received from previous ones.

Alleanza Nazionale (1998)

In a similar vein, but more in accord with the political discourse of other forces, AN expresses preoccupation with declining demographic trends and connects them with a need to emphasise pro-family policies. The family comes to be seen as the crucial unit in society.

The freedom to form a family. The rights of the person, in addition to having an individual importance, possess a social dimension, which finds in the family its first expression, in logical order and chronological order. There is a singular link between the family and the political order: the experience of history, in diverse epochs and in different parts of the worlds, requires that society, and more specifically, the state, and community and international organisations, recognise and safeguard the institution of the family, with measures of a political, economic, social and juridical character, shaped to consolidate the unity and the stability of the family, in order to permit it to exercise its specific functions.

Alleanza Nazionale (2001)

The centrality of the family is connected to a broader view of political participation in which families are part of civil society and are relevant political actors in an expanded set of participatory forums. The exaltation of the family also leads to a strong pro-life positioning:

The Italian right reaffirms that life must be protected beginning at the point of conception.

Alleanza Nazionale (2001)

As already noted, Fini began to take a more liberal approach on some issues of family morality towards the end of the second Berlusconi government's period of office – a more libertarian stance which caused enormous controversy within the party – given the continued adherence to traditional morality on the part of other senior party figures and its grassroots militants and supporters. However, it was notable that the 2006 document signalled a return to an emphasis on traditional family values and rejection of the idea of affording same-sex couples equal recognition with 'traditional' families:

We reiterate, not only for a religious choice, but also in consideration of the secular norms of the Constitution, that the priority and attention should go to natural families based on marriage.

Alleanza Nazionale (2006a)

Strong state: strong law and order

Law and order policies go together with an emphasis on the family in creating a cluster of concerns in the broad category of traditional ethics. The AN consistently expresses concerns over crime and the need to address it through harsher laws. There are numerous examples of the latter. For instance, the AN has consistently pursued a policy of criminalising and punishing drug consumption, and this was reflected in Fini's sponsoring of a new law stiffening criminal procedures for drug use:

Very severe penalties, rigidly determined with respect to deviant behaviour, up to providing for life sentences for the most grave cases, need to be established for whoever introduces drugs onto the national territory, and for whoever sells them to minors.

Alleanza Nazionale (1995b)

Thus, in general, the AN advocates a stronger repressive action by all state institutions:

The aggression of criminality of every type – thus not only criminality of the street – requires urgent and committed measures to combat it on the legislative level, but also first of all on the administrative level.

Alleanza Nazionale (2001)

Figure 6.5 demonstrates the continuing emphasis placed in AN documents on the need for strong law and order policies. It is notable that the 2006 document put a level of emphasis on this not seen since the founding Fiuggi document.

Liberty

The AN has combined a familiar authoritarian approach to law and order and traditional ethics with an emphasis on liberty, referring to the twin pillars of authority and liberty. The concept of liberty can be regarded as a classic core concept of the right, which it typically opposes to the concept of equality. AN has continually focused on it and its importance has grown over time. Liberty acquires both a general philosophical status of ultimate value to be advocated and pursued politically, and also a detailed neo-liberal interpretation as freedom from the state and notably freedom from excessive taxation and regulation, which came to the fore as the AN moved to a more strident free-market

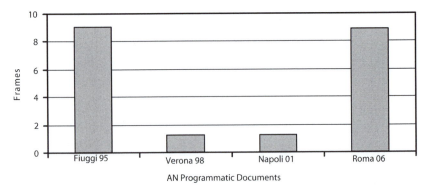

Figure 6.5 AN frames on 'law and order' (n=19).

position in 1998, where as Figure 6.6 shows, references to liberty reached a high point. The first category is well encapsulated in the following excerpt:

> If there is a constant which one can easily grasp and enunciate even within the variety and multiplicity of elements which necessarily run together to constitute the objects and tissue of the undoubtedly complex contemporary social and civil reality, then this constant should be identified in the wasting away and in the weakening of the range of concrete and real liberties, of the citizens and social groups, further to the rhetoric which in this way often revolves around the magnificent fate of a Liberty as acclaimed as it remains abstract.
>
> Alleanza Nazionale (1998)

In this second excerpt, one sees an illustration of the value of freedom in relation to the economic role of the state:

> Equally, an aggressive and voracious fiscal system, an inefficient and heavy public administration, an economic market choked by political interventions or monopolistic conglomerates (in law or de facto), a health system tending towards a lack of care, are all situations which restrict the space for the concrete liberties of citizens, preventing them from benefiting from a condition of equity in the distribution of costs (which are excessive) and benefits (which are modest).
>
> Alleanza Nazionale (1998)

Thus, in the AN conceptualisation, liberty comes to represent the essence of a partnership between political actors and their voters. In the following excerpt from the 2001 document, it appears that liberty is conceived as something to be exercised on behalf of not only the individual, but also the wider community and the people as a whole:

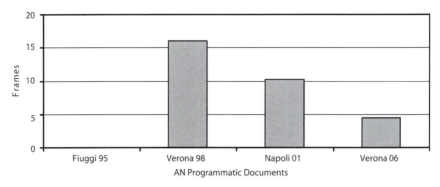

Figure 6.6 AN frames on liberty (n=29).

The pact which we propose to the Italians is intended to respond to these necessities, with incisive and structural reforms in every field, to render each one more free, stronger and placed within a more just context. The freer a person is in his/her life as a citizen, the more free the family is in exercising its primary function, the freer the community is to act, the freer firms are to create and produce, the freer the Nation is to carry out its natural objectives. Free from and, above all, free for, not only free to. Liberty as a condition to create something stable and coherent. Liberty in the plural and not only in the singular. Liberties, connected to concrete objectives, and not mere liberty, which appears as a concrete abstract, too distant from reality, moreover referable only to the individual, and not also to the community and to the people.

Alleanza Nazionale (2001)

To summarise, there is a distinctive conception of liberty that AN views as differentiating the right from the left:

It is the identitarian and communitarian culture which represents the true cleavage between the politics of the left, universalistic, homogenising, caught between the liberal temptations of the Clintonian 'third way'; and the old style social democratic dirigisme, and the politics of the right, communitarian because it is founded on values, liberal because it respects the responsibilities of the individual, inspired by the social doctrine of the church, carrier of an active national identity in international relations.

Alleanza Nazionale (2001)

The state and the economy

As already noted, AN documents have reflected a shift in emphasis on matters pertaining to the relationship between the state and the economy. Following on from the neo-liberal approach of the 1998 document, those since 2001 have emphasised the social market approach and the state's role as a regulator:

> We do not want to overcome the laws of the markets. However, we think that the task of the state and the public institutions of the territory is that of promoting development and to actuate solidaristic policies.
>
> Alleanza Nazionale (2006b)

As Figure 6.7 shows, the emphasis on competitiveness, very high in 1998, had disappeared by 2006.

Recent documents have also stressed the need to govern globalisation in order to protect social cohesion and the identity of communities.

> But it is not possible to accept the disaggregating effects that globalisation would produce if it was left free to condition, to subordinate to its indefinite expansion, any sense of sociality and identity.
>
> Alleanza Nazionale (2001)

The immigration issue

Despite its prior location on the extreme right, neither the MSI nor the AN has taken a clearly racist or xenophobic position. Although its historic leader, Giorgio Almirante (leader from 1947 to 1950 and again from 1969 to 1987), had been a journalist with the main fascist racist organ, *La Difesa della Razza*, during the fascist period, and had been chief of cabinet to the minister of popular culture in the RSI (Eatwell 1995: 198; Ginsborg 1990: 144), racist or xenophobic discourse did not appear to feature in the MSI's platform. This could be partly attributed to the need to erase the memory of the darkest and most notorious period of the fascist regime in Italy and the MSI strategy of

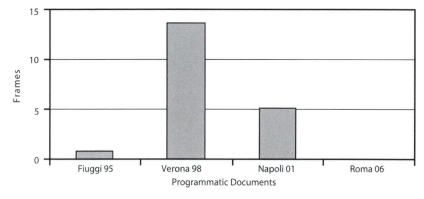

Figure 6.7 AN frames on competitiveness (n=20).

presenting itself as a conservative parliamentary force, but could also be attributed to the low numbers of foreigners, immigrants and ethnic minorities in Italy prior to the 1980s, which meant that issues of race and ethnicity were not particularly salient. Incidents of racism and xenophobia saw the immigration question enter the Italian political agenda for the first time in the 1980s. However, any move towards an explicitly xenophobic anti-immigrant platform modelled on the FN position in France was firmly rejected by the Rautian faction. It may seem paradoxical that the more radical faction opposed playing the race card. To Rauti, immigrants were 'not stigmatised per se because they are the last link in the chain of exploitation'. Rather, immigration was portrayed as the result of capitalist domination over the Third World. In order to stop immigration, the north–south relationship thus needed to be modified (Ignazi 1993: 90).

The MSI thus did not really take up the opportunity to garner votes by jumping on the crude xenophobic bandwagon of the FN, despite growing anti-foreigner sentiment among the Italian people. The official line was not shared or understood by grassroots *missini* militants and supporters, who were much more likely to hold openly xenophobic views (Ignazi 1994a: 75). It was notable, however, that the MSI did not vote with the majority of parties in support of the 1986 and 1990 laws, which went some way to regularising the new immigration phenomenon. Moreover, during his brief period as leader, Rauti himself called for the government to 'close the borders to any type of immigration and for any reason' and rather to favour the return to Italy of its own emigrants.[9]

It was only at the beginning of the 1990s, just prior to the party's transformation into the AN, that discussion of the immigration issue began to appear in the MSI's official documents, as demonstrated by analysis of its 1990 congressional policy thesis. The position taken towards the new immigration was fairly negative, although explicitly xenophobic frames were avoided. Upon returning to the leadership in 1991, Fini adopted an adapted version of the Rautian position, pressing for the deportation of illegal immigrants, stressing the threat to national identity posed by an influx of immigrants, while also emphasising the need for economic co-operation with the Third World to reduce the causes of immigration (Cheles 1995: 171).

Despite the apparent break from the past represented by the dissolution of the MSI into the AN, the broad thrust of the positions initially adopted by the AN on immigration appear to follow on from those adopted by the MSI at the beginning of the 1990s, that is the need to regulate immigration flows, vigorous confrontation of clandestine immigration coupled with the concern about clandestine immigrants falling into criminality and the general concern about the threat to national and cultural homogeneity. There has nevertheless been an acceptance in the AN's documents – particularly since the late 1990s – of the necessity for immigration to meet the needs of the Italian economy and to address its labour market shortages in particular (as opposed to the concern expressed by the MSI in the early 1990s that the labour market would not be able to absorb immigrants). This also sometimes goes hand in hand with laments about Italy's declining birth rate and proposals to address it through incentives for families, thus reducing the future reliance on immigrants caused by demographic decline and an ageing population.

While there are continuities, care has been taken since the foundation of the AN in the use of language, particularly in the party's official documents. For example, frames related to the party's traditional nationalism have remained prominent. Nevertheless, this is also balanced by some positive references to multiculturalism and the need to respect cultural diversity in the AN's documents. The document approved by the party at its national programmatic conference in Verona in 1998, where it sought to present itself as a more liberal moderate political force, provides an example of this mixed message. On the one hand, there is a recognition of other cultural identities:

> Just as it claims the cultural identity of the Italian nation and the broadest European identity, National Alliance recognises the specificity and diversity of other identities, which reflects their constitutive origins, and with which they aspire to promote and research with available spirit appropriate and reciprocally acceptable forms and methods of peaceful coexistence.
>
> Alleanza Nazionale (1998)

However, this is used as a reason to ensure that the Italian national identity is protected, even if other cultural identities are to be afforded due respect:

> The understanding that there are other identities, meriting of respect, presupposes therefore the maintenance and defence of one's own prime identity.
>
> Alleanza Nazionale (1998)

Nevertheless, this comes with a warning that mass migration movements risk bringing a destabilising clash of cultures:

> The quantitative weakening of certain peoples, the incremental explosion of others, the territorial transfers which tend to assume mass character, further to the intense risk of becoming overwhelming and destabilising ...
>
> Alleanza Nazionale (1998)

One point worth emphasising is the attention that the AN (and the MSI before it) has paid to the experience of Italians (and those of Italian origin) living outside Italy. The MSI–AN has traditionally portrayed itself as a champion of those Italians forced to emigrate in search of employment and a decent standard of living. There have thus been a number of suggestions from MSI–AN exponents that Italians and their descendents living abroad should be encouraged to return in order to address the problem of Italy's demographic decline and labour shortages. Indeed, the provisions of the Bossi–Fini law adopted in 2002 provided for privileged access for workers of Italian origin resident abroad in the determination of entry quotas.

Concern for Italians who migrated within Italy has also been a strong issue for the MSI–AN. This usually means southern Italians who have moved north. Given its predominantly southern character and electorate, this has meant that the party's position has run counter to the initially hostile (although now rather diluted) anti-southern position of the LN. For example, whereas the LN originally complained about the drain on northern resources imposed by 'parasitical' Italian southerners, AN exponents have stressed the need to increase opportunities and resources for southerners moving to the north of Italy. The statement made by Maurizio Gasparri (then deputy leader of the AN parliamentary group) in 2000 is particularly interesting in this respect.

> Before giving homes to immigrants ... you need to think about Italians and, in particular, the southerners who would move to the North if accommodation was offered them

As well as representing a strong defence of the rights of Italian southerners to move north, this is also a rare example of outright welfare chauvinism on the part of the AN (at least as far as examples uncovered by the frame analysis is concerned). One should point out here that, within the AN leadership, Gasparri appears to be one of the individuals with the strongest anti-immigration stance, sometimes employing a discourse closer to that of the LN than that of his own party leader. It should be reiterated that Fini's more moderate positions on immigration and other issues are often not shared by other leading AN exponents who sometimes put forward more unreconstructed and extremist positions. A case in point was Fini's proposal on voting rights for immigrants in 2003, which Gasparri (then communications minister) opposed. The documents of the AN analysed here generally reflect positions imposed by Fini and are thus more 'moderate'. However, more extreme positions adopted by other AN exponents can be found in the pages of *Il Secolo* or in analysis of parliamentary debates. A good example of the more strident language used by Gasparri was this intervention made in the parliamentary debate prior to the adoption of the Turco-Napolitano law:

> I was saying that we are not ashamed to say that Italians come first; of course, rights must be guaranteed for everyone, but the Italian government and the Parliament must guarantee the rights of all Italians, of the Italian unemployed and the citizens who want safety, of the people who see their freedom threatened by autochthonous Italian illegality fed also by the labour coming from abroad.
>
> Gasparri (1997)

Although many of the ethno-populist frames that characterise the LN are absent from the AN's discourse, and its rhetoric on immigration has generally been less strident (even in its previous MSI incarnation), one could never-theless argue that the new attention paid to the immigration issue, first by the MSI in the early 1990s and then by the AN, was motivated not only by the recent emergence of this issue as one of central salience to the Italian polity but also by observing the success that the LN had in exploiting an issue seen as the traditional preserve of the European far right, of which the MSI had previously been a leading light. However, any move to adopt the discourse of ethno-populism contradicted the post-fascist strategy launched by Fini in 1994, in which he sought to steer the AN into the political space vacated following the collapse of the DC. Thus, official party documents since the foundation of the AN party in 1995 have used measured language, while at the same time advocating tough immigration controls. In seeking to place itself within the European centre-right mainstream, the AN has sought to justify the stances it has adopted as regards immigration in terms of EU-level agreements. Thus, for example, it was argued that the stringent measures introduced by the Bossi–Fini law of 2002 were in line with Italy's obligations under Schengen and other EU-level agreements. In relation to this, the centre-left government of 1996–2001 was attacked for not having done enough (by means of stringent immigration controls) to ensure that Italy respected the Schengen agreement. The AN attacked the inability of the centre-left gov-ernment to protect Italy's borders from clandestine immigration.

The AN's tough position towards clandestine immigration is in line with its general emphasis on law and order questions. Clandestine immigrants, by their very 'illegality', are depicted as threatening the maintenance of law and order in Italy. AN discourse here can be distinguished from that of the LN, where little distinction is made between illegal and legal immigrants, as regards the threat to security and law and order that they are depicted as bringing to Italy. Even on clandestine immigration, the tone of the AN is less strident than that of the LN.

> The consequence of this interpenetration is that clandestines already stopped and sent to temporary holding centres are being put back in cir-culation without being identified, expanding the line of illegals, easy prey to delinquency, often adopted as labourers for criminals.
>
> Alleanza Nazionale (2001)

The AN has proposed strong law and order measures to fight clandestinity. For example, the Verona document of 1998 called for 'severity against human traffickers'. The documents analysed throughout the period 1995 to 2006 emphasised the need to expel clandestine immigrants and treat those who defied orders to leave the Italian territory as criminals. The situation whereby clandestine immigrants were served expulsion papers but were not then sub-ject to measures to ensure they left the country was severely criticised. It was notable that, in the elaboration of the Bossi–Fini law, Fini sought to intro-duce measures criminalising clandestine immigrants, although the compromise adopted (after pressure from the UDC) was that only recidivist offenders would be punished in this way. The AN sought to re-introduce this measure following the return to government in 2008.

The AN also strongly opposed the proposals by the centre-left government of 1996–2001 to grant the right to vote in local elections to long-term immigrant residents. Thus, Fini's about-turn on this in 2003 came as quite a shock within the Italian political world. Fini argued that this proposal, in promoting social integration of legal immigrants, went hand in hand with the previous emphasis on eliminating clandestine immigration and strictly regulating further legal immigration (Casadio 2003, Polidori 2003). In this sense, the stress on the need to promote social integration of immigrants was not such a fundamental break from the past. References to the desirability of social integration are found in the AN's programmatic documents, although they are very occasional and not particularly detailed. For example, the Fiuggi document in 1995 suggested that immigrants could eventually have rights of citizenship:

> those with a definite employment relationship should be granted residence permits, in stable form, up to the concession of formal residence status and even citizenship.
>
> Alleanza Nazionale (1995b)

In justifying his apparent softening on the immigration issue in 2003, Fini adopted frames previously employed by the left, i.e. the importance of social integration, and the responsibilities of Italy as a former country of emigration. At a party meeting in November 2003, Fini reiterated the need to integrate immigrants, in the face of some heckling by hard-line party militants:[10] 'We are a people who for centuries exported bodies ... If immigrants send their children to schools with our children, respect our laws, then they cannot be discriminated against. We cannot turn back' (Staff Reporter 2003b). Indeed, Fini has used the Italian collective experience of once being a nation of emigrants itself as a means to justify his new position. Italians would accordingly understand the experience of immigrants and their desire to be treated with dignity, and would agree that the discrimination suffered by Italians who went to live abroad in the past should not now be revisited on immigrants to Italy.[11] He challenged Bossi on this theme at an AN party meeting in January 2004, calling on the LN to renounce their extremism on immigrants, as 'until 40 years ago, it was us (the Italians) who were the bingo bongo' – bingo bongo being the derogatory term used by Bossi to describe immigrants in Milan (Passalacqua 2003).

Despite the apparently more open stance on immigration developed by Fini in government, the document discussed at the 2006 programmatic conference in Rome appeared to signal a return to a tough positioning on immigration control. This could be attributed to a refocusing of attention on fighting the centre left in the run-up to the general election, highlighting the latter's alleged weakness on the issue and playing up the centre-right's populist credentials on the question. This contrasted with the strategy pursued by Fini in government, which involved signalling his moderation in contrast to the populism of the LN. Thus, the document stated:

> On the clandestine immigration front and that of the integration of foreigners who arrive in our country, there is still space for the assumption of initiatives which, without falling into any form of intolerance, avoids leaving to others the role which we have undertaken to defend the security of our cities and our coasts, and also the identity of our nation. ... We wanted a law, the Fini–Bossi, which others sought to sabotage, we need to make it even more stringent and severe. And we have to call on Europe to work with us to guard the Mediterranean frontiers.
>
> Alleanza Nazionale (2006b)

The changing emphasis on the anti-immigration theme, and the notable return to this in 2006, is shown in Figure 6.8.

Discussion of immigration in recent years has increasingly focused on the need to resolve the question of the social integration and citizenship status of foreign immigrants. As already noted, Fini's positions in government appeared to indicate a greater openness on this issue. However, prior to and following the 2006 election, the position appeared to have hardened somewhat, with scepticism expressed towards the proposal launched by the new centre-left government in 2006 to make it easier for long-term resident immigrants to acquire Italian citizenship. The 2006 document had stressed the need for checks on the willingness of would-be citizens to belong to and respect Italian culture. Warnings were also made about the experience of Great Britain, where British-born citizens of the Muslim faith had launched terrorist attacks against their country of birth.

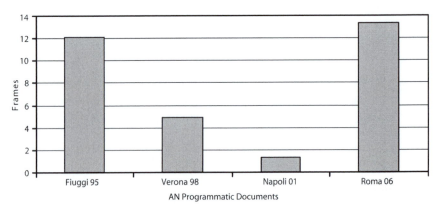

Figure 6.8 AN anti-immigration frames (n=28).

In late 2007, Fini's discourse on immigration appeared to take a harsher turn, in the wake of the controversy over alleged Romanian criminality (with Romanians now able to enter Italy more freely as a result of Romanian accession to the EU). In particular, a great deal of media coverage was afforded the case of an Italian woman who was savagely murdered in Rome by a Romanian of Romany origin. Referring to the Roma community in an interview with the *Corriere della Sera*, Fini stated:

> I ask how is it possible to integrate those who consider it just about normal, and not immoral, to thieve, to not work because it should be the women who do so, maybe through prostitution, and who have no scruples in kidnapping children or producing children for the purpose of begging. To talk of integration for those who have a 'culture' of this type does not have sense.
>
> Di Caro (2007)

Fini's intervention here could be interpreted as deriving from a belief – given the success he had had in establishing himself as a mainstream politician – that he could perhaps now get away with such statements, without being accused of being a fascist. This was particularly so given that he knew he was reflecting widespread public sentiments towards the community in question. Moreover, it was also an opportunity to shore up his credentials with his party hardcore, in order to dissuade further defections to Storace's new formation.

Europe and the nation

The theme of protecting national identity pops up often in the AN's statements on immigration, even if outright intolerance of foreigners is avoided. In general, the national question remains of great importance to the AN, and is reflected in its position on constitutional reform, where it seeks to preserve the integrity of the nation-state against the assaults launched by the LN, and also in foreign policy, where it continues to exalt the role of the military – with the Italian role in peacekeeping missions often pointed to as a source of national pride and honour. As already noted, a hangover from the past can also be noted in positions relating to the treatment of the Italian community in the former Yugoslavia. Fini has been careful, however, to stress that the emphasis on the nation should not be mistaken for an aggressive nationalism, but rather should manifest itself in a love of the homeland (*patria*) and respect for its culture, history and traditions, as well as the Italian state itself. These were themes stressed in his book *Un'Italia civile* published in 1999 (Fini 1999). The AN leadership has sought to model this approach on that of the French Gaullists, and this comes through clearly in the echoes of De Gaulle found in the invocation of a *Europe des patries* made in the AN's founding Fiuggi document. Although Fini appeared to pursue a Europhile line akin to that of the post-war DC as government representative on the European

Convention in 2002–3, party documents have also continued to emphasise the need to pursue the national interest within the EU, and to ensure that the European architecture reflects the Gaullist approach in guaranteeing the leading role of the nation-states within it. This approach was re-emphasised in the 2006 document, which sounded a note of greater scepticism (or realism) in the wake of the rejection of the European constitution in the French and Dutch referendums:

> We have been inspired in many of our documents and positions taken by the Gaullist model. And even Chirac has said with realism to his European colleagues that the result of the French referendum should lead to a rethinking of European policy. … We also have to put ourselves in play in this phase, focusing our action on national interests and reviewing our European course, not to exclude it, but to rethink it and relaunch it.
>
> Alleanza Nazionale (2006b)

As Figure 6.9 shows, the AN's position on Europe also involves recurrent references to the need to re-emphasise common identity, culture and history. This is generally related to a stress on Europe's common Christian roots. Fini was a strong supporter of the inclusion of a clause referring to Europe's common religious roots in the European constitutional text. The AN's position was reiterated in the 2006 document where it lamented the victory of a 'technical–secular post-Europe':

> Europe is not just a reality defined in geographical terms, but it is rather a cultural and historical concept … Europe seems to have been emptied inside, resigned to a loss of identity … We need to repropose values to a Europe which no longer loves itself, which flees from its own history and lives, like a shadow, its own identity.
>
> Alleanza Nazionale (2006b)

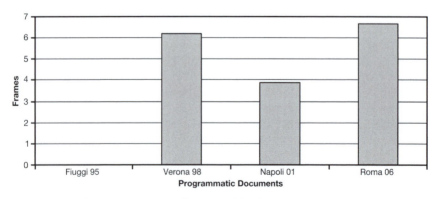

Figure 6.9 AN frames on common European identity.

Conclusion

The AN has come a long way since the early 1990s, emerging from the ghetto in which it had wallowed – in its previous guise of the MSI – for much of the post-war republic, and becoming a leading player in the Italian party system by the mid-1990s, with five years' experience of government behind it by 2006. Nevertheless, the party remained troubled by an identity torn between a desire to exploit the opportunities provided by the ongoing transition of the Italian party system and an attachment to traditional certainties. Examination of its documents reveals a set of positions that in many senses can be located within the European centre-right mainstream. However, the emphasis on traditional ethics and identity politics is stronger than most, and a style of language is used that could be interpreted as a hangover from the past. One more obvious hangover from the past is the AN's official logo, in which the old logo of the MSI – the tricolour flame (burning over the coffin of Mussolini) – remains in the centre (Mastropaolo 2008: 30), and approving interpretations of the role of Mussolini's fascist regime remain the norm within the party. This still extended to leading figures in the party such as La Russa and Alemanno, despite Fini's denunciations of aspects of the regime. In September 2008, La Russa (AN national co-ordinator and defence minister in the third Berlusconi government) referred to the patriotism of military forces of the RSI that had fought against the invading allied forces during the Second World War (Buzzanca 2008). Alemanno stated he did not and never had regarded fascism as an 'absolute evil'. Although he agreed that this description could be used for the racial laws of 1938, he argued that fascism was a complex phenomenon to which many had signed up in good faith (Bei 2008).

Nevertheless, given the positions taken on a range of issues and its behaviour in government, the AN can no longer be placed in the category of old-style neo-fascist or extreme right parties. Furthermore, while elements of populism have been utilised by the party to great effect and it has benefited to a great degree from its membership of a political alliance greatly reliant on populism, the party in 2008 did not quite fit into the general categorisations of right-wing or radical right populism. The AN's earlier employment of an anti-politics stance, from which it benefited in the wake of *tangentopoli*, can be described as a core element of populism. However, this waned in later years and the AN sometimes found itself on the receiving end of populist attacks on 'recycled First Republic politicians'. At the same time, a virulence in attacking its enemies remained, as did an emphasis on national identity often found in the repertoire of populists. This was linked to a strong stance on immigration control and against multiculturalism, which appeared to resurface both prior to and after the 2006 general election. This reflected a tendency towards exclusionism which, notwithstanding Fini's attempt at a more moderate positioning in government, remained strong within the party and is the staple of right-wing populism. While perhaps being more peripheral to populist ideology and indeed not being populist *per se*, the emphasis on family values and tough law and order policies (more broadly its stance on traditional ethics) also lent itself to populist appeals and, together with the tough stance on immigration, a common ground with the other populist parties of the centre right. However, Fini's leadership of the party, while being strong and personalised – reflecting the traditions of the Italian right – was not quite of the charismatic type usually found in populist movements, and the organisation of the party was of a more conventional form. In sum, conservative authoritarian tendencies remained strong, despite Fini's attempts to present the party as a modern secular and liberal force. This was a reflection of the political culture of a party whose leaders in the main spent their formative political years in the MSI's youth wing, and whose followers generally shared a strong belief in the values of nation, family and church and a belief that the state has a strong role to play in safeguarding their security and economic well-being.

The controversy surrounding Fini's various *svolte* brought into the open the difficulties Fini had in reconciling his modernising efforts with the preferences of his party cadres and militants, despite his popularity among centre-right voters. Indeed, while one interpretation was that some of Fini's statements were intended as a challenge to his party to follow his lead and modernise (or else fail to prosper), it could also be argued that his tactics really related to his own personal goals – to promote himself as a future leader of the Italian centre right, irrespective of the impact on the cohesion of the AN, and with or without the AN behind him. Indeed, doubts continued as regards the beliefs and intentions of Fini's colleagues in the AN party leadership – most of whom came through the ranks of the MSI youth movement – and the party as a whole. It was notable that the AN's share of the vote still lagged considerably behind the personal popularity of Fini himself. Indeed, despite the strides made by Fini to reposition the party, the AN still appeared to be perceived by Italian voters as a far right party. A poll published in *Corriere della Sera* in November 2005 in which voters were asked to position parties of the CdL on a scale of 1 to 10 (with 10 representing extreme right, 5 centre, and 1 extreme left) gave the AN an average score of 8.5, FI 8.1, the LN 7.9 and the UDC 5.6 (that the LN was viewed as to the left of both the AN and FI was also particularly striking).

Thus, although Fini originally rejected the proposal of a new formation made by Berlusconi in November 2007, partly because it seemed clear that the proposal was aimed at marginalising the AN (and Fini in particular), and was not based on consultation among the centre-right parties, the imminence of a new election in 2008, and the hope that he could position himself as Berlusconi's heir apparent, led him to reverse this original position and pledge to dissolve the AN into the new PdL formation. He had previously responded to the Berlusconi initiative with a shift back to the centre, engaging in talks with Casini about a possible centrist formation or alliance with the UDC. These shifts demonstrated once again the importance of political opportunities and political space in shaping Fini's thinking. The AN was dissolved amongst much emotion at its final congress in March 2009. However, attempts to keep its identity alive would continue within the new formation.

7 Sources of success of the Italian right

This book began with a general question concerning the determinants of the electoral performance of right-wing parties in Italy. This question led to the examination of why the right and not the left profited electorally following the remarkable collapse of the DC – the party that had represented the centrist sensibility of the Italian electorate for several decades. Our response was that the right made better use of populism by connecting it to other ideological elements that resonated with Italian society and by using specific political and extra-political resources to optimise electoral appeal. In this chapter, we will frame the performance of the right in a comparative context, summarise the main and the peripheral elements of populism identified in the party chapters, explain their contribution to the success of the right through an analysis of the values of the electorate and draw some general conclusions on the fit between the right-wing voting bloc and the institutional framework. In the following chapter, we will review the findings more broadly from a theoretical perspective and examine what lessons can be learnt for Europe more generally.

Throughout the book we have emphasised the contribution of a populist ideological framework to the success of the right, a way to use politically the category of 'the people' as a metaphor for a collective identity – of an emotionally loaded belonging to a social category. It is a way to thematise and politicise the *demos* beyond the boundaries of formal citizenship as defined by the nation-state. It is a reactive response to multiculturalism. We shifted our explanation of the success of the right away from other approaches that mainly focus on the electoral space left available by the collapse of the DC. The first point that has to be recalled from the introductory chapters is that the success of the right was not due to a simple continuation of the success of the DC during the First Republic. After all, the DC – while a moderate party – generally did not encourage views such as the xenophobia of the LN or the consumerist views of Forza Italia or the sympathetic interpretations of fascism found within the MSI–AN. And its patriotism was moderated by its allegiance to universalist Christian values. Thus, the rapid affirmation of a right-wing coalition and its survival over the years – even if with alternate fortunes – requires an explanation, which we have provided by pointing to the innovative aspects of each of the parties of the right, and which we will now consider contextually as a coalition. We have argued that the answer provided by some analysts – that the Italian electorate is fundamentally socially conservative and would not have preferred a coalition of secular leftist parties – is not fully satisfactory. One should note that the ex-DC currents flowed into both coalitions. Moreover, not only did the left not succeed, but neither did the forces that tried to re-package in more modern terms the moderate Christian views of the discredited DC. The various catholic political formations that emerged within the centre left and centre right did not win a substantial proportion of the vote. Rather, completely different formations such as FI and the AN emerged successfully in the aftermath of *tangentopoli*, and small regionalist formations such as the LN came to play an important role in Italian politics.

Much emphasis has been attached to the advantage that these forces possessed in emerging at a time when they could fill an empty political space: the space within the right left free by the collapsed DC and also the space freed within the left in the aftermath of the collapse of the Soviet bloc. But even a 'displacement' theory based on a static conception of political space and the resulting advantages of political opportunities coming from timing and positioning strategies is not fully satisfactory. The emergent Italian right of the early 1990s did more than just fill an empty space. In Italy, as in other EU countries, right-wing parties re-invented themselves and in the process re-defined the concept of the right, whose conceptual domain expanded from the socially libertarian message of the likes of Pim Fortuyn to the social interventionist intents of the Italian social right. Thus, the right did more than just inherit a victory – it created the conditions for it. In this chapter, we will bring together the lesson of ideological innovation that the Italian right learned in the context of an evolving European right, but also a consideration of the impact of institutional changes on the success of the right – such as changes in the electoral law. Thus, as suggested by Pasquino, on the one hand, we investigate the success of populism in Italy with reference to some key social and cultural features of Italian society and, on the other hand, we will discuss the specifically political–institutional factors that have facilitated populist formations (Pasquino 2008).

As mentioned the Italian institutional framework has altered in radical ways in recent years. In explaining the evolution of the right, one must emphasise the impact of the Italian institutional architecture and of the political debates that have accompanied the many attempts at reforming it.

The collapse of the party system that ensued from the corruption scandals of the early 1990s sparked a wide-ranging debate on the institutional architecture of the Italian system at all levels of government. These included debates pertaining to the institutional framework that organises political competition and decision-making, and to the institutional framework that organises relations between the state and the economy, and the state and civil society. As mentioned previously, the initial success of the right was dependent upon a change in the Italian electoral law from proportional representation to a predominantly majoritarian system that forced coalition behaviour among the parties. The right was more able to form effective coalitions due mainly, but not exclusively, to the strength of Berlusconi's control of his coalition. The stimulus to form cohesive coalitions resulted from the polarisation of the party system, which emerged as a consequence of the new electoral law, but the right was more able to respond to this need. Even with the frequent recurrent squabbles we have documented, the multiple sources of power of a leader such as Berlusconi enabled the coalition to be kept together after elections much more effectively than the centre left has managed.

Electorally, the right profited from the innovative institutional solution that Berlusconi devised: two different coalitions, one in the north with the LN and one in the south with AN. The change in electoral law was made possible by a 1993 referendum that reflected the political entrepreneurship of a small group of liberal politicians, but above all it reflected an ideological change in the Italian population that reacted against what it identified as one of the main causes of *tangentopoli*: the proportional electoral law that contributed to the perpetuation of an unaccountable political class that had gone unpunished for its misdemeanours for decades. The Italian clientelistic system was increasingly unaffordable and spurred rebellion in business and professional elites, which the magistrates interpreted. Thus, while stressing the importance of institutional developments, it is also important to emphasise the ideological changes that had set Italian political values at loggerheads with the Italian political offering.

The factors that brought the right to power were to a substantial extent connected to expectations of economic policy, to worries about the dilapidation of state resources and to concern about the inefficiencies of state services. In this sense, the success of the right was rooted in both its ability to produce a discourse that could chime with the culture of a changing country, but also specific expectations about economic performance and system innovation. However, the right in government would encounter insurmountable problems when it came to matching expectations and promises with actual policy action and results – for instance in delivering liberal policies that would benefit consumers, improve the workings of the service sector and de-regulate the overly regulated professions.

At the end of the first decade of the new century, a new wave of disaffection with politics is clearly manifest and relates to the widespread realisation that politics has found new ways of persisting with the old practices of misappropriating and wasting societal resources. In the opinion of many observers, the transition from the First Republic was never accomplished. Necessary institutional reforms, such as the correction of the system of perfect bicameralism, which slows the legislative process, or the strengthening of the role of a prime minister hostage to squabbling coalitions, have not been undertaken. The second Prodi government paid a high price for these unaccomplished reforms. It was a fractious coalition which could not take decisions, had a constant low rating in public opinion and a short duration. However, throughout the history of the Second Republic, the right has also remained torn by internal conflicts and, given the precedent of protracted personality conflicts, even new developments such as the PdL party project do not necessarily guarantee additional stability.

Given this renewed bout of re-invention, now is a good time to review the right's performance throughout the entire 1993–2008 period and to assess prospects for the future.

Reviewing the findings: core and peripheral elements in Italian populism

As posited in the Chapter 2, our model for the study of populism included a set of general elements, developed on the basis of the relevant literature and as such verified to be present in other European populist movements and parties, and a set of peripheral elements that we posited to be context related and characteristic of the particular empirical trajectories of the Italian populist formations we examined. The presence of the first set of variables constituted a hypothesis to be verified in the Italian test case. The second set was identified empirically through structured readings of party documents and leaders' speeches. The extent to which this latter set of variables can be generalised more broadly needs to be investigated in future comparative studies. Here, we can discuss their relevance in recent years and differentiate their role in different parties and in the entire right-wing coalition.

We posited that the *core features of populism* consist of a distinct configuration of ideas, styles and policies, and we stressed the *tendency towards charismatic leadership, appeals to the people and anti-politics.* In terms of styles, we emphasised the use of rituals and of symbolism in the *choice of language which indicates anti-elitism, vilification of enemies and homogeneity of the constituency.* In terms of policies, we pointed to *symbolic policies* that thematise inclusion and exclusion. All these elements have been discussed in the party chapters and summarised in the discussion above, therefore justifying their inclusion as key elements in our model.

The main *peripheral elements* we emphasised were tenets of other ideologies of reference that were emphasised through the populist devices of symbolic policy proposals, theatrical politics and the use of protest repertoires (even while in government and occasionally even by one party against the other). As variables for the choice of peripheral framings, we also posited a specific role for the territorial area and political status of the 'people' of reference, and the extent of the leader's control of his formation. The main *context variables* that orient the features of peripheral elements in our hypotheses are *the party system, the political environment, individual party history and trajectory, and the features of the civil society in which political opinion is formed.* Here, we will need to distinguish between elements that relate to the entire coalition and elements that differentiate the behaviour of the three parties.

Core elements in the Italian populist right

The powerful role of the parties' leadership emerged clearly in all three parties. This role was asserted and justified in documents and interviews with activists. In fact, it can be argued that one of the reasons why renewal in the Italian right has been slow and difficult is precisely because the leadership of the three parties is so strong that it hinders change.[1] The same leaders had been at the helm of their parties for a long period, steering them but also stifling internal dissent and proposals for change. *Appeals to the people* also emerged consistently in all documentary sources, although as pointed out, the 'people' was differently conceptualised across the parties. The frame 'the people' as an ideal constituency appears among the first eight frames for all three parties. *Anti-politics*, defined as the need to transcend some of the confines of representative democracy (or even also anti-establishment in the case of the LN), appeared as a recurrent theme in all three parties. The means to be employed to do so were somewhat different in different parties, but included the use of protest repertoires even while in government, and other forms of symbolic politics, which we posited as central to populism. A populist style embedded in anti-political linguistic and symbolic usage was recurrent in all the parties, even if the specific *linguistic style* was different among them. Scholars of political communication have often emphasised this aspect, particularly in the case of Bossi and Berlusconi (Amadori 2002). However, populist signals are not simply conveyed through a particular use of language in political communication. They are also conveyed through an effective use of visual media. The leader appears 'larger than life', he dominates his audience, jokes and threatens his adversaries. In addition, signals are conveyed by the *symbolic use of policies* and policy proposals. This aspect needs some additional analysis.

Here, even if only briefly, the complex relationship between rhetoric and policy change needs to be addressed. Political discourse consists of a set of framing exercises in which political entrepreneurs compete in a set of discursive arenas, which include parliaments, the media, workplaces and civil society arenas, such as churches and social movements. Their competition concerns, among other issues, the definition of problems to be tackled by politics, preferred solutions, the identification of obstacles and of opportunities and relations with allies and opponents. The specification of the final goals of policy change are context dependent, often fuzzily enunciated, poorly implemented and prone to hyperbolic statements. This has of course traditionally been facilitated by Italian electoral laws in which individual parties have very weak accountability.

These rhetorical elements are an important constitutive part of political discourse. They come to constitute a signal of the desired direction of change which, for instance, a potential electorate can interpret and evaluate as such – as a signal rather than actual intentions. Thus, for instance, when Bossi states that the boats bringing clandestine immigrants to Italian shores should be sunk with cannonballs or that rifles should be used to implement federalism, he is not actually suggesting a specific policy change, and his electorate knows that. They vote for him because they agree with the signal, not with the proposed policy. Nonetheless, signals are there to indicate the intention of policy changes, which could be more moderate. In this respect, some feared that the signals were too strong and potential harbingers of unacceptable policies, but others felt that the signals remained empty promises. The use of this language of signals which strain the boundaries of representative democracy characterises Italian populism. Nonetheless, one needs to emphasise that strong signals do over time lead to some radical changes, though not necessarily at the extremes conveyed by the signal.

In particular, a populist style has characterised Bossi and Berlusconi and cemented a kind of populist axis based on hyperboles, defiant posturing and accentuation of signature personality traits – such as the frequent jokes of Berlusconi or the manifestly absurd threats of Bossi. These two leaders have thus marked the style of the entire coalition and in their different populisms cemented their alliance – an alliance that many observers have considered closer than the relationship between other parties. In their alliance, observers have identified a 'northern axis'. However, while Berlusconi might well have needed to be particularly mindful of Bossi's desires, given the disastrous experience of 1994, and while they reflected a similar geographical background and representation goals, there has also been a similarity in their personalistic conception of politics (On the relevance of the geographical aspect and the northern axis, see Shin and Agnew (2008: 132).

In the same populist vein is the use of protest repertoires of marches and rallies by all parties – both in government and not. One should note that the electorate might respond to signals not only in terms of trust regarding the likely adoption of future policies, but also in terms of reassessments of the current situation. For instance, after a 2008 election marked by widespread and media-fuelled fears about security, social alarm markedly decreased as noted by a Demos survey analysis (see Diamanti 2003b; Polchi 2008). This took place after the new right-wing government implemented highly symbolic but limited action to control crime. For instance, a limited number of soldiers were deployed in full combat gear in some city centres, steps were taken to make legal the deployment of citizens' vigilante groups and harsher penalties were discussed for street crime.

The three rights have manifested a different relationship between the signals they have launched through rhetorical devices and the policy change they have pursued. While all have utilised a bombastic approach to political discourse with proclaimed emphases on cultural protectionism, anti-communism, demands for law and order and for Christian and family values, they have done so differently.

At least in part, FI has been supported by its moderate electorate because its policies have not been perceived as extreme. Nonetheless, it can also be argued that it lost electoral support in 2006 because the actual outcomes of its actions in government were perceived as too modest. The LN, on the other hand, chose to use a rhetoric that, while pleasing its activists, was in many ways not completely comforting for its potential electorate, which was not convinced that the gap between extremist rhetoric and policy would remain reassuringly large. Nonetheless, the LN has tried to reassure its local electorate with reasonable local-level policies and good administration, and has tried to develop a class of competent local administrators, and partly succeeded (Ruzza 2004). This was also possible because of the institutional changes that reformed local-level politics, giving mayors real decision-making power (Catanzaro et al. 2002). The failure of the LN lies in its inability to develop a credible national political class and an intellectual profile that would offer guarantees to concerned middle-class voters. As for the AN, its fascist background has meant that the use of excessive rhetoric would have aroused great suspicion. Thus, the AN is the party which, in terms of populism, has proceeded more cautiously. Opponents have argued that, beyond the façade of a respectable leader such as Fini, a political class of nostalgics longing for the fascist past still characterises the party. The AN has participated in all the colourful street protests that Berlusconi has organised over the years and which have certainly exhibited populist features, but it could be argued that it was not a protagonist in them.

As the relationship between rhetoric and political outcomes is difficult to assess and there are several distinct political arenas, the smaller parties have often found themselves in the position of having to use bombastic rhetoric to please their activists and to attract media attention, while also trying to use moderate discourse in institutional settings. This strategy has paid off to an extent, but has also created suspicion and disenchantment at least in the most educated part of the electorate. Thus, the gap between rhetoric, intentions of institutional and policy change and actual outcomes has remained at the core of the success and failure of the Italian right and has even coloured the internal competition within the coalition. In this sense, it can be argued that the continuing success of the right also lies in the failure of the left to provide a convincing blueprint for the institutional changes that would appeal to the majority of Italian voters. A consensus has emerged in public opinion on the need for changes to make the country more economically competitive, to improve the working of the political system and to improve state services. But neither the left nor in many ways the right has provided a clear blueprint for change. However, if the left has typically appeared internally divided and marked by a radical leftist component, the right has appeared more able to provide at least guarantees of continuity – the 2001–6 legislature was the first to last to the end. Beyond their populist rhetoric, their economic policies have, to a large extent, ensured the support of the business and professional elites that have controlled the country for decades. At the same time, much of their law and order emphasis and moderate discourse has ensured the support of important social institutions such as the church and the acquiescence of the moderate electorate. We can thus argue that the right in power has utilised populist discourse to implement – even if rather ineffectively – mainstream conservative policies.

In the Italian case, the presence of distinctive populist traits is verified by our findings. In addition to core elements, we also posited that there was a set of peripheral elements that were part of other ideologies – notably conflicting right-wing ideologies – but which were used in connection with populist features. In other words, elements of right-wing ideologies lent themselves to the populists' emphasis on the use of symbolic politics, protest repertoires, calls to the 'good sense' of the people and so on, enacted by a strong charismatic leadership.

Peripheral elements in the Italian populist right

Table 7.1 summarises in order of priority the first ten elements that our frame analysis identified out of a total of sixty frames. After the tenth, the number of instances declines rapidly and they can no longer be considered very representative of the discourse of these parties.

The ideological elements listed are all solidly part of the family of right-wing concepts as they also appear in other EU countries. Some of them are shared by all the parties and constitute the grounds on which a thematic unity could be constructed or at least represented to public opinion over the years. Some of them are more conducive to a 'populist' interpretation than others.

Among the elements where a populist interpretation has proved most advantageous for the right, apart from the mythology of 'the people' as an undifferentiated entity, which we defined as also part of the core elements of populism, is the thematic cluster on migration and the related connections to security. With reference to migration, one could identify a populist interpretation that stresses issues such as the use of the symbolic language of the 'state of siege' and related suggestive metaphors, the skyrocketing crime rate, the positing of essentialist cultural or racial boundaries. This is familiar to

Table 7.1 Dominant frames in the Italian right

	AN	LN	FI
1	Traditional family	Federalism and devolution	Anti-bureaucracy
2	Liberty	Traditional family	Welfarism
3	Strong executive	Localism	Security
4	Anti-immigration	Pro-welfare	Traditional family
5	Anti-partyocracy	Anti-bureaucracy	Law and order
6	The people	Against centralisation	Pro-free market
7	Competitiveness	Anti-assistentialism	The people
8	Law and order	The people	Anti-partitocracy
9	Vilification of enemies	Anti-partitocracy	Economic competitiveness
10	Nationalism	Anti-immigration	Italian military role

students of the extreme right – the Italian parties have, however, adopted a more moderate version of the same theme. The issue is clearly treated through the core features of populism by all the parties: it comes framed in suggestive language. Migration is considered unmanageable and the blame is put on politics and opposition politicians. Populists also produce policies, the main effect of which is to signal allegiance to one's 'people', against the 'people' of other 'tribes'. One can interpret the 'Bossi–Fini' law on immigration, or at least the way it was presented to public opinion in Italy, in this context. The anti-immigrant ethos increasingly became a rallying issue after the 2006 defeat, with the usually restrained Fini taking more radical stands, possibly to fend off dissent within his party. In late 2007, following an episode of sexual violence by a migrant, a set of angry protests was organised by the right against a perceived invasion of Romanian immigrants.[2] On that occasion, calls for mass expulsions of immigrants were made by the right, despite the fact that blanket expulsions of EU citizens would be illegal in the European Union. The immigration issue has been regularly discursively connected to security issues, and a number of prominent initiatives, including mass rallies and a 'security day' organised by the right, have taken place.

All parties have utilised broader anti-political frames that encapsulate the core of populism. In the case of the AN and FI, this is illustrated by the prominence of anti-partyocracy frames. In the case of the LN, this is part of a broader anti-establishment discourse, which involves virulent attacks on the entire apparatus of the central state. The broad anti-political ideological cluster has been much used by all parties and has been re-interpreted in a variety of ways in the language of the right, from a glorification of markets against the state to an anti-elitist localism and advocacy of pro-civil society involvement. In its former meaning, it is connected to the frame of anti-bureaucracy, which also has a pro-market undertone, particularly for FI. Conversely, for the LN, the anti-bureaucracy frame is used as a byword for its anti-central state ethos, which is encapsulated by an old and now characteristic slogan '*Roma ladrona*'. It also has anti-southern connotations. In this respect, the AN stands out in not pursuing an explicitly anti-bureaucratic discourse, probably because its largely southern electorate with a high representation of public employees would militate against explicit attacks on bureaucrats *per se*.

The anti-political stance has emerged in conjunction with an action repertoire of theatrical protests by all the parties of the right. As mentioned previously, the right has borrowed heavily from a social movement-style protest repertoire to express its anti-political nature. Ideologically, the actual specific identification of the causes of and remedies for the degeneration of the party system has varied among the three parties, but the differences could, on occasions, be glossed over through unclear and evocative populist language. The parties differ in the reasons why they see politics as corrupt and inefficient. For FI, it is because it is conducted by professional politicians instead of entrepreneurs. Professional politicians are viewed as ineffective because they are not selected or promoted through meritocratic criteria (notwith-standing Berlusconi's own patrimonial practices in the political arena) and have never had 'real jobs', having worked for parties all their professional lives – a point often made particularly with reference to 'the communists'. Thus, the neo-liberal solution he has traditionally advocated over the years – at least until the international financial crisis of 2008 – has been to inject more 'market' into the conduct of public affairs.

The situation changed radically after a more interventionist mood swept Europe as a result of the necessity to rescue a set of financial institutions in late 2008. The widely approved rescue of ailing British banks spurred a rethinking of the role of the state and was instrumentally utilised by the right in government to reclaim a more prominent steering role for the state in the economy. A more protectionist mood was best exemplified and celebrated in a widely debated and applauded book by the figure who became the symbol of this ideological rethink: the finance minister Giulio Tremonti. His *La Paura e la Speranza* (the fear and the hope) laments an excessively hasty compliance with the imperatives of economic globalisation and proposes a more cautious approach (Tremonti 2008). Tremonti summarises his recipe for overcoming the crisis in seven keywords, which are listed on the back cover of his book and read like a manifesto to homogenise and reform the right. They are: values, the family, identity, authority, order, responsibility and federalism.

Thus, the classic neo-liberal recipe, which was in fact only modestly applied – considering the minor scale of privatisations of parts of the bloated public sector – became even less attractive over time. A new protectionist and statist ethos had already emerged during the 2008 electoral campaign, during which the promise to keep the national airline company Alitalia 'in Italian hands' probably contributed significantly to the electoral victory of the right. But after the collapse of the stock markets, Berlusconi sensed the opportunity for a re-interpretation of his leadership role as a state-controlling popular leader, not only above politics but possibly above the economy as well.

Nonetheless, the anti-political ethos has continued to define the right, par-ticularly in its public rituals – especially the anti-communist political rituals that have marked the political style of the right, often populist in character, the features of which have sometimes been borrowed and re-interpreted from leftist groups such as the '*girotondi*'.[3] Thus, FI activists hold hands, jump and sing 'those who do not jump are communists'.

Anti-political rituals, however, did not remain confined to national events. From a localist viewpoint, for the LN, bad politics is the result of a lack of federalism and devolution, and corrupt Rome-based politicians. Politics is conducted in Rome and not near 'the people' who can monitor and shape it. The populist range of LN public statements, protest actions and symbolic politics is probably the most flamboyant. Protest against Italian unification, Rome and centralist politics continue to this day, notwithstanding years of participation in national government. For instance, in late 2007, a set of actions was organised to abolish the celebration of the birth of Garibaldi, a national hero who fostered Italian unification by conquering and annexing the Italian south, but whom the LN considers a 'war criminal'.[4] As mentioned previously, the AN has utilised anti-partitocracy images in different ways. It proudly proclaimed its independence and outsider status from national politics during the *tangentopoli* years. It softened these claims in recent years while in government, but it returned to virulent attacks on the left-wing establishment following its return to opposition in 2006.

Other peripheral elements, such as the emphasis on competitiveness and traditional values, were less conducive to populist interpretations – they did not result in anti-elitist rallying cries or in emotional but vague populist language. They did, however, function to keep the coalition together. There were, for instance, several widely publicised and well-attended initiatives connected to these themes, such as a 'family day', which brought a large number of participants out on to the streets of Rome in 2007.[5]

As argued in the party chapters, the reasons why a populist approach was effective in strengthening the right in Italy are manifold, and it is precisely the vagueness of the populist language that can have an integrating function. A list of the contextual features that influence the adoption of peripheral elements of populism would be long and variable over time – within Europe, they could be expected to vary in national contexts as they respond to different political opportunities. Here, we can focus on some elements, summarising in a comparative framework the impact of the structure of the party system, territorial divides and the changing political environment.

First, in terms of party systems, the unfreezing of the organisational structures and ideological traditions of the previous party system meant that a new system could be constructed that was more attuned to the 'spirit of the time'. In an epoch and a country of television viewing where, in the opinion of many observers, a progressive lowering of the cultural standards of broadcasts has taken place, and in a country with a comparatively low level of education and very low newspaper readership,[6] vague populist appeals are more likely not to be perceived as such. Thus, one can posit a connection between general levels of education, media quality and populism. Assuming a generalised impact of the popular press and television, one can then also posit a connection between the unfreezing of the party system and emerging populism. Second, territorial divides and migration issues can also be exploited politically to the extent that there are perceptions of economic injustice and ethnic rivalry that can be highlighted and politicised. They can also benefit from populist framings, as shown previously for instance with relation to the LN's framing of language issues and re-definition of the meaning of territorial identities. In Italy, on the one hand, pre-existing territorial divides rooted in historical dynamics – notably the north–south divide – offered ideal cultural material for a process of nation-building and boundary construction in an ethno-nationalist framework of ethnicisation of regional traits. This helped the LN in formulating and diffusing a 'politics of the enemy' (Ruzza and Schmidtke 1996a). On the other hand, mounting job insecurity in a country not used to immigrants also created a space for another type of 'politics of the enemy', in which all right-wing parties could unite. Third, several variables pertaining to the changing political environment played a role. As suggested by Norris (2005: 27), our case studies confirmed that a transition to a majoritarian law encouraged vague populist appeals. However, the retention of a proportional element in the electoral law utilised before the 2006 election also stimulated the retention of strong ideological identities and needs for differentiation in the coalition parties. Both in the left and in the right coalition, parties had to show commitment to the coalition and unity while at the same time having to keep a distinct profile. Thus, ironically, the Italian electoral law engendered the negative aspects of both proportional and majoritarian arrangements: vague populist appeals and over-emphasised signature policies and rivalry even among allied parties. This was a rivalry that marked the entire 2001–6 legislature, hindered policy formulation and implementation and would in time result in the electoral defeat of the coalition.

Fourth, a key role was played by the features of the civil society in which political opinion is formed. We would emphasise the re-definition of political space that comes from the association of anti-politics and appeals to 'the people'. It causes a general relocation of politics away from representative institutions and a preference of populists for other non-representative forums, but also the emergence of styles, issues and decisions that would not emerge if political debate remained confined to agonistic institutions. The concept of political space has frequently been utilised to explain party strategies. It has for instance been used to examine shifting self-positioning along the left–right axis, to explain typologies of parties and their evolution over time. A theory of political space has also been utilised both in the literature on parties and in the social movement literature to examine various dimensions of what comes to constitute the terrain of political conflict (Maier 1987). Of all the different issues that contribute to forming and changing the 'boundaries of the political', processes promoting the politicisation of particularistic identities are the most frequently studied (Benhabib 1996). However, the enlargement or reduction of political space has a dimension that exceeds the social–psychological and cultural issue of identity. It also has a relevance in terms of how the choice of themes to be processed by politics activates different social constituencies, and re-defines conceptions of interest and the borders of potential alliances. It is on these terms that the ideological innovations of the right have been rewarded electorally through the politicisation of territorial but also other identities, and the de-politicisation of former identities. While re-distributive issues have often been de-politicised – for instance by recasting them as technical or managerial problems – moral issues such as issues pertaining to the theme of 'family values' have been over-politicised, stemming a wider process of secularisation that was taking place until the 1980s.

In terms of de-politicisation of a set of policy issues, we would stress the consequences of the emerging mythologies of 'policy by experts', which is often emphasised at the EU level (Majone 1989). If de-politicising and technicalising issues is functional to a system such as the EU that has severe decision-making blockages and benefits from removing controversial issues and confining them to agencies and other non-agonistic forums, doing the same at member state level opens up political space for various forms of moralised politics, which selectively benefits the right in a catholic country such as Italy. At the same time, de-politicising and technicalising policy-making gives legitimacy to a politics inspired by successful business leaders such as Berlusconi, and, on the left, to representatives of the ethos of 'civil society' and its involvement in policy-making through participatory forums. Also important is the political role of the media. Political talk shows are very popular and very influential in Italy. Shows such as *Porta a Porta*, *Matrix*, *Ballarò*, *Annozero* and *L' infedele* have come to replace political institutions – they shape the political agenda and are often organised in ways which, as recent surveys show, many Italians find very partisan (Bordignon and Ceccarini 2007: 34–35). We would stress the consequences of these trends in terms of a re-definition of political space and the new rules that this re-definition implies.

Finally, one would have to conclude a discussion of the success of the right and the political opportunities achieved by merging a populist and a right-wing ideology with a note of caution and a mention of other variables that are difficult to explore in detail. One such variable is what has sometimes been euphemistically referred to as the 'extra-political' means at the disposal of the CdL/PdL and its leader Berlusconi. There have been accusations over the years regarding Berlusconi's use of financial resources to facilitate his desired political outcomes, although ascertaining the facts here is not feasible. For instance, in mid-November 2007, an Australian senator, elected in an Italians-abroad constituency, reported the offer of a substantial monetary sum by Berlusconi should he change side (reported in Fusani 2007). The charge was, however, later dropped.

Similarly, there were claims that Berlusconi was funding Storace's new right-wing movement to cause difficulties for Fini and the AN. Clearly, such accusations are impossible to examine, but they should at least be mentioned. This issue is also connected to the interpretation of differences between the southern and the northern vote. If public opinion in the north, and therefore populist and right-wing framing of issues, is crucial, several observers have pointed out that the southern vote appears more often oriented by clientelistic exchanges (Piattoni 2003), and that FI has benefited in particular in inheriting the old DC clienteles (although parties within the centre-left coalition have also benefited from these). For example, an advertising spot for the PdL in the regional election in Abruzzo in November 2008 caused a furore and provoked opposition attacks for offering a job interview for all young people presenting their CVs at the PdL local election committees and gazebos (Caporale 2008).

Recent media investigations[7] and academic studies (DellaPorta and Vannucci 1999) have shown that corruption is still widespread across the political spectrum. Thus, its relevance in parts of the country should be seen as important, but this represents a class of variables that are additional to the ideological and institutional ones we have identified for examination.[8] Hence, we will now proceed with an examination of why the populist ideological positioning of the three parties was successful through a comparative examination of the concerns of the electorate and the fit of the parties' discourse.

Mythologies of the right and their fit with the electorate

As noted earlier, this volume does not conceptualise the success of the Italian right as an expression of marked intolerance and xenophobia – an approach that would be more appropriately used to explain the occasional and often limited successes of the extreme right, such as the localised successes of Storace's La Destra. The Italian right-wing coalition has represented the vote of the majority of Italians. In Italy, as elsewhere, there is an element of insecurity that affects many social institutions – insecurity in the workplace, insecurity with reference to key state services as a consequence of the retrenchment of the welfare state, insecurity related to fundamental demographic changes and migratory phenomena. While these elements are present in the mind of most Italians, and are in fact widespread throughout the electorate, the appeal of the right in recent years should be framed in terms of its better ability to propose acceptable policies to face these insecurities within the confines of a political discourse judged acceptable by the majority of the population.

Fundamental changes in social and political values have occurred that are also shared by the great majority of Italian citizens – including young people – but are better interpreted by the right. There has been increased attention to the private sphere which, as several authors have pointed out, has produced a devaluation of social and political commitment in the entire western world (Mastropaolo 2005). One might also refer to the loss of credible alternative models that, according to several observers, has characterised the left in recent years. As with the left elsewhere, the Italian left has responded to the undermining of the state as a credible set of regulatory institutions by re-defining its values away from equality – and therefore re-distribution – and towards inclusion as its specific focus. But in a context of a perceived weakened *demos*, on the back of migration flows and a re-definition of territorial identities, any attempt at inclusion also appears problematic and often unappealing to the electorate – as the debate on granting administrative voting rights to immigrants documents. As territorial belonging is increasingly problematic, the various and even incompatible recipes of the right appear more attractive than what is sometimes perceived as the worthy but ineffective cosmopolitanism of the left. It is in this broad context that Italian sentiments towards left and right have first to be explained. This said, however, we argue that the specific success of the right in recent years has also been connected to an effective use of both the general traits of populist discourse, of an effective connection of this discourse with the ideologies of the right and, therefore, with a set of peripheral values that connect populism, anti-politics and the right. It is also in this broad context that a connection between the right and populism should be established. As noted previously, and as argued by Betz, a general weakening of the ideologies of modernisation has opened up new political spaces and made right-wing populist solutions relevant as a search for new idealised communities (Betz 1994).

Finally, and still in broad terms, political communication is changing in Italy (Novelli 2006). The fragmentation of audiences and increased reliance on soundbite news, the personalisation of politics and reliance on political leaders as a source of news, info-entertainment and the emergence of some politicians as television personalities have given new power to both the right – which can more easily justify reliance on leaders – and to all populist framings, the simplistic discourses of which are more attuned to recent media formats. Of course, in Italy, this is compounded by Berlusconi's control of important sectors of the media, but it could be argued that the general trend in political communication is not unlike that taking place in other countries. Even within this generally favourable context, however, the Italian centre right has been very successful – more successful than elsewhere in Europe.

An explanation of this success must consider in more detail the mix of ideologies deployed and the features of the Italian electorate, its values and composition. In the party chapters, we have stressed the role of anti-politics, populism and exclusionism as ideological markers of the right and the competitive advantage that derived from the fact that they resonated with the Italian population. These concerns, however, could have been, and in part were, addressed by other parties as well. Over recent years, various forms of left-wing anti-political movements have emerged, such as the previously mentioned *girotondi* movements in 2002 or the V-day initiatives of Beppe Grillo in 2006–7.[9] In both these cases, a principled rejection of corrupt politics was stressed, and references to 'the people' abounded. But, while these initiatives remained at the margins of representative politics, anti-political sentiments were central in the centre right, and echoed clearly with their electorate.

To explain this success, we will discuss the fit between the values and political discourse of the right and the views of the electorate on key crucial issues that our frame analysis has identified: migration issues and traditional values. Then we will discuss the functions and structure of populist discourse, and the advantages held by the right in producing and exploiting it.

Anti-politics, populism and xenophobia

As already discussed, the long-term legacy of *tangentopoli* was to further undermine trust in the political system, a level of trust that was already endemically low because of the legacy of the processes of formation of the Italian state. Anti-political sentiments were thus widely distributed across the electorate. However, as the right was more able to claim that its leaders were not part of the political class, a resonance and even a self-reinforcing cycle of mutual influence between the media sphere, the political sphere and public opinion could be created that connected the anti-political sentiments of the electorate and the discourse of the parties of the right. We have created an index of 'anti-politics' based on answers to three questions related to attitudes towards professional politicians.[10] The results are illustrated in Figure 7.1.

As one can see, anti-political sentiments are generally high and relatively evenly distributed in the entire population, and are particularly well represented in the parties of the right. These findings correlate with our analysis of the discourse of the parties, which also classified the LN as the most anti-political party, followed by FI and the AN. This finding indicates that the party discourse was well tailored to the expectations of electorates. In this context, it could be noted that survey data also show a widespread perception of complexity in the political system and an absence of political efficacy (Diamanti 2007; Porcellato 2008).

As discussed earlier, concerns about race and ethnic identity are also crucial in explaining the success of the right, and have gained new prominence in Italy on the back of increased immigration flows since the beginning of the 1990s. We have constructed an index of xenophobic sentiments in the Italian population and examined its relevance for the 2001 electorate. From Figure 7.2, we see that concerns about race are generally relevant in the Italian population, and are particularly high in the parties of the right.[11] Once again, the discourse of the parties on these issues follows closely the perceived relevance for their electorate.

From Figure 7.2, we see the close fit between the xenophobic values of part of the right and its electorate. To interpret this fit, a broader discussion is necessary.

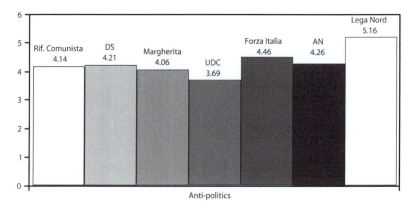

Figure 7.1 Relevance of anti-political sentiments in selected electorates (index, range 1–9, ITANES 2006, n. 702).

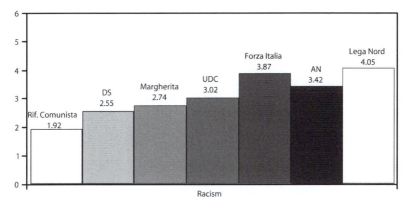

Figure 7.2 Index of xenophobia on a scale 1–6 (ITANES 2006, n. 730, range 0–6).

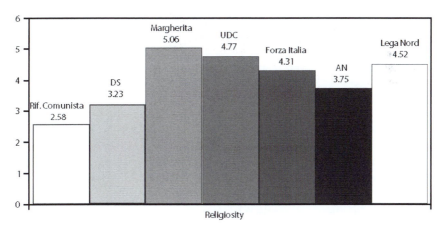

Figure 7.3 Index of religiosity on a scale 0–7 (ITANES 2006, n. 1,058, range 0–7).

The success of the right is often explained with reference to a complex set of sociological factors pertaining to the social profile of its electorate, its feelings of insecurity, increased ethnic rivalry, disaffection with politics and social displacement connected to various aspects of globalisation. It has been observed that, in Europe as a whole, changes in previously dominant industrial work patterns (for example through the shift towards a system of spread-out workplaces) and successful economic innovation and technological change have undermined the existence and identity of the industrial working class, increasing perceptions of rivalry in the labour market and competition for resources of the welfare state and engendering feelings of displacement. The process of secularisation reduced the socialising role played by the church, and the collapse of mass parties contributed to a sense of social isolation. The substantial migration flows of the early and mid-1990s had a particularly relevant spatial and cultural impact in many European cities. This engendered fears well documented in the literature, with ethnic separation seen as connected to the rise of the extreme right. If we now consider the relationship between the groups of the population that are most likely to experience these fears and the profile of the right-wing vote, some correlation seems to emerge. But there are also distinctive aspects that require a different explanation.

In Italy, the right-wing electorate shows a profile that is not too different from the profile that has been identified in other countries. As with the European populist right in general, the electorate of the Italian right is generally rather old and uneducated and, for these reasons, less able to face some of the challenges of globalisation (Norris 2005). But it also shows several distinctive features. A very important variable is generation. In the key election of 2001, two generations contributed heavily to the success of the right: the 25–34 generation and voters over 65 (Baldini et al. 2001: 31). However, the youngest generation exhibited a different orientation in 2001 and regressed to the mean in 2006, reducing the role of generational variables (Barisione et al. 2006: 84). Clearly, generational variables are related to other variables, as older voters are less educated. But there are other features that stand out prominently in the Italian case.

There is a strong connection between certain occupational sectors – particularly the status of housewives and the vote for right-wing parties – especially Forza Italia and notably for housewives with low levels of education (Barisione et al. 2006: 81). The condition of housewife is distinctive in that it is often an indicator of a condition of relative social isolation, low interest in politics, low political information and higher levels of television viewing, which were also strongly correlated with the right-wing vote in the 2001 Italian election (Baldini et al. 2001: 47–58). Other variables are also associated with the right-wing vote, albeit less markedly. In professional terms, the self-employed were more likely to vote for the centre right in both 2001 and 2006. In territorial terms, the right-wing vote was prominent in the northeast and the south (Baldini et al. 2001: 61–66).

The traditional bedrock of regions in the centre of Italy where support for the left was at its strongest appeared to be weakening in 2001, while a clear reservoir for right-wing votes was emerging in the north and in the south – a trend confirmed for the north in 2006. But what emerges clearly and more powerfully from attitudinal studies is a connection between cultural traits and voting. The Italian right-wing electorate is diffident towards others in general, has low levels of social capital and is strongly materialist in Inglehart's terms (Baldini et al. 2001). It is an electorate strongly exposed to the television channels of Berlusconi and therefore to the 'personalisation' of politics that has marked the political offering of several countries in recent years. In Italy, this phenomenon, which is possibly media related, was enhanced by the shift to a predominantly majoritarian electoral system. The electoral reform of 1993 provoked a bipolar tendency and focus on coalition leadership that, together with the expanding television offering of non-state channels, promoted a political competition based on personality previously unknown in Italy. It created a strongly fractious climate that many observers have lamented in recent years. This climate has persisted despite the partial retrenchment from majority voting of the electoral law of 2006 (Barisione et al. 2006). It is a polarised climate that is not necessarily strongly connected to socio-demographic indicators. Evaluations of rival candidates to lead the government did not appear strongly related to socio-demographic variables, at least in 2001 (Baldini et al. 2001: 129) and 2006 (Barisione et al. 2006: 67).

Thus, the relevance of cultural variables and of political communication and the weakening of territorial cleavages provide indicators to explain the successes of the right in 2001 and 2008 and the near success in 2006 despite a declining economy and a poor record of delivering electoral promises such as lower taxes and more economically liberal policies. Occupational and economic explanations, or socio-demographic ones, are unconvincing – at least alone. A cultural–ideological explanation appears necessary – an explanation that better accounts for the widespread support for the right even beyond demographic categories. Such an explanation would highlight the role played by insecurity and fear in the period leading up to the 2008 election, diminishing subsequently in conjunction with a lesser emphasis in the media and symbolic policies aimed at reassuring citizens (Diamanti 2003b; Polchi 2008). Among the several insecurity-related factors, immigration plays an important role.

Since the 1980s, Italy has become a country of immigration reversing a long trend of outward migration. Rapidly increasing immigration flows deeply shocked a country with inadequate social policies to cope with social emergencies and no significant imperial past, and therefore little adaptation to cultural and ethnic diversity. Coming largely from poor countries and often entering illegally, immigrants were frequently perceived as the cause of new social problems, and encountered suspicion and fear. The weakness of the Italian state in its ability to control its territory, the prevalence of organised gangs of human traffickers and the objective difficulty of controlling a very long coastline meant that illegal immigration escalated rapidly in the late 1980s and 1990s, spurring fear of crime but also engendering feelings of cultural displacement in the population. The LN and the AN certainly profited from these fears.

However, one has to note that a similar situation in other Mediterranean countries did not result in the emergence of a comparable right-wing response. This suggests that other factors have also played a relevant role. We argue that one such factor is ideology, and the role of the media in diffusing it – the importance of which we seek to emphasise, reflecting our underlying belief that politics is not only the outcome of institutional mechanisms, but that ideology matters and that its adoptions and re-definitions are limited by the available repertoire of ideological frames which are politically available at any point in time in society, and the opportunities that key political actors have to innovate (Talshir et al. 2006).

Even beyond the role of the media, an understanding is required as to the reasons why the ideologies proposed by the Italian right to respond to the challenge of migration had a stronger echo in the Italian population than elsewhere. This, we would argue, was in part because of the need for cultural protectionism, which was not addressed by other parties, and as we will see, in part because the right appeared to respond more than the left to other problems – particularly the perception of a growing gap between politics and society, which the populist discourse of the right addressed directly.

Traditional values, religion and post-materialism

The right's emphasis on traditional family values amounts to an attempt to transfer into the political arena views and demands that have characterised the catholic church in recent years. To fully understand the advantages that come to the right in performing this task, some general reflection on the influence of the church and the role of religion in Italy is necessary. Religion constitutes a complex, self-contradictory but extremely relevant social identity for the Italian population. Surveys in recent years[12] show that a quarter of the population goes to mass every week, and almost half the population goes to mass at least a few times every month. Over 80 per cent of the population, which is almost entirely Roman catholic, considers religion to be very important or rather important in their lives. The catholic vote is over-represented in the right but, even within the left electorate, there is a significant proportion of voters for whom religion is considered 'very important in their lives'.[13] In this context, the church has been perceived as very vocal in the past few years on issues of traditional family morality, and a public discussion has ensued. This has been connected to the new necessity for it to act directly as a pressure group in the new climate of a dispersed catholic vote (Bull and Newell 2005: 96–97). It is therefore not surprising that much political capital can be derived by aligning parties with church views. The right has attempted to do this, possibly also confident in the fact that the minority of people who never go to church are mostly voting for the left. Of the respondents who stated in 2001 that 'religion is very important in their lives', 43.6 per cent voted for the left coalition and 54 per cent for the right. Of those for whom religion was 'rather important', 52.7 per cent voted for the left and 44.7 per cent for the right. But among those for whom religion is absolutely not important, 81.8 per cent voted for the left. Thus, religion is clearly a more divisive issue for the left than it is for the right. It is therefore a concern that the right has been able to address more effectively. In Figure 7.3, the relevance of religion for different parties is represented visually.[14] Religiosity is naturally higher among the heirs of the DC – the UDC in the centre right and the Margherita in the centre left (now a wing of the PD). However, it is rather high overall, albeit unevenly distributed.

There are relevant differences in the proportion of church-goers who vote for the right. This appears to correlate with the frame 'traditional family values' that emerged from our analysis. Figure 7.4 illustrates the frequency of church attendance among the electorate of the right in 1996–2006.

Again, if one refers back to the frame analysis presented in the party chapters, we see a connection between the relevance of religious themes for electorates and their relevance in party discourse. Religion emerges with higher frequency in the discourse of FI and the LN than in that of the AN. Nonetheless, the LN has traditionally endorsed Christian identities merely as a marker of differential belonging against non-Christian migrants, while its discourse has traditionally been rather ambivalent on Christian themes. On the one hand, it has espoused a traditionalist version of Christianity and for instance symbolically affirmed it through the choice of Irene Pivetti[15] as president of the lower chamber in 1994. On the other hand, Bossi has used his anti-elitist and populist rhetoric against the church and its hierarchy on several occasions. Generally, however, on religion, there is evidence of a good fit between the electorate and the parties' discourse, whereas the left has been split by internal controversies on a set of morally loaded issues on which the church has taken firm stands.

It should also be stressed that, according to several observers, after the election of Pope Benedict XVI, the church has become not only increasingly more conservative but also more interested in Italian affairs, and militant, and this has therefore provided, at least symbolically, a relevant help to the right.

Statements from the church have also coloured the debate on immigration and Italy's cultural identity, although the message here has been mixed. While elements of the church hierarchy – including Pope John Paul II – have emphasised the need for a humanitarian and Christian reception of immigrants, and catholic politicians from the former DC and its offshoots have generally followed this approach (seen also in the primary role played by catholic associations in giving support to immigrants on the ground), there have also been concerns expressed as regards the need to maintain Italy's catholic culture and identity. This is particularly relevant in the light of the large number of Muslim migrants to Italy. For example, in 2000, Cardinal

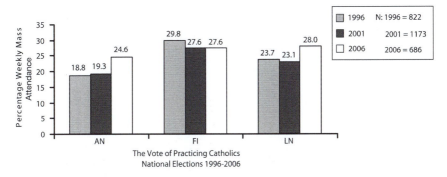

Figure 7.4 Practising Catholics (ITANES, n. 2006 = 686; 2001 = 1,173; 1996 = 822, %).

Biffi of Bologna controversially called for the restriction of Muslim immigration and the need to give preference to Christian immigrants. This call won support in the catholic world, for example from Gianni Baget Bozzo (a clergyman close to Berlusconi and Forza Italia) and Rocco Buttiglione (formerly president of the UDC).[16] While references to the threat to Italy's cultural identity posed by Muslim immigration are infrequent in the statements of the catholic parties, the frame analysis has revealed the greater tendency of the centre right, the AN and the LN in particular, to cultivate such fears, reflecting also the concerns of their electorates.

One could argue that traditional values are not just measured in terms of attitudes towards religious issues, but more generally address the divide between a traditional and a modern set of values on relevant social issues. To address this issue, in this comparative examination of the concerns of the electorate and the fit of the parties' discourse, it is worth concluding with a discussion of the nature of the Italian right in terms of the post-materialist dimension. Much has been written on the thematic expansion of the right in Europe. Themes such as gay rights were claimed by the Pim Fortuyn List in the Netherlands, and similar post-materialist themes have been incorporated by the French *Nouvelle droite* thinkers. In Italy, however, the expansion of politicised issues by the right – to the extent that it has occurred – has taken place in a socially moderate direction, and has not concerned a re-interpretation of post-materialist themes. As an illustration, one can look at environmental issues, where right-wing parties show evidence of retaining the traditional scepticism of the old right. This attitude is represented in Figure 7.5, which shows the electorate of the Italian right holding the lowest level of concern for environmental protection.

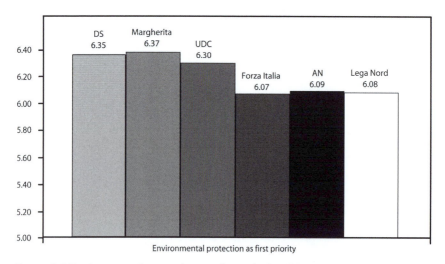

Figure 7.5 Environmental protection as first priority (ITANES 2006, n. 881, mean

Taken together, Figure 7.1–7.5 give an indication of the way in which the right has addressed issues that are central to the Italian population and, with some exceptions, they show that, despite differences of emphasis, the right, at least on some issues such as 'law and order' and a restrictive approach to immigration, has produced a relatively convergent ideology that resonates with its electorate. Of course, the differences are as large as the similarities in many respects – and, as noted in the case of the AN, they are also internal to the party.[17]Considering the entire period of existence of the opposing coalitions, internal tensions certainly played a detrimental role and made governing less effective. To an extent, the differences of emphasis also had the role of broadening their electoral appeal. Irreconcilable differences were only seldom presented to the electorate and appeared balanced by tensions within the left, which has been torn by strong tensions between its radical and reformist wing, particularly in recent years.

On the basis of these comparisons, we are now in a position to address broader theoretical and institutional issues, such as the role of populism and the crisis of politics in Italy. We will argue that through them the right has been in a position to posit new and acceptable solutions to old Italian problems.

The opening of a political space is not sufficient to explain the success of the Italian right parties if one does not consider the incentives that they had in forming coalitions, which despite internal tensions, lasted longer than any post-war government. This stability resulted from changes in the electoral laws and other institutional changes, and from the symbolic and material means at the disposal of Berlusconi, which in turn were made possible by the dynamics that had occurred during the process of collapse of the previous system. But the success of the right was also made possible by the differentiations of the ideological offering that the right achieved, even through its sometimes bitter divisions. We posit that each of the three rights operated a successful conjunction of distinctive right-wing themes and populist ideological elements.

Convergence and divergence in populist frames: three types of right

The right-wing coalition that governed Italy from 2001 to 2006 can be regarded as a paradigmatic example of different populisms that have found a difficult compromise on some issues and have clashed, often in bombastic terms, on other issues. They have followed as examples models of populism that appeared on the European political scene in recent years and developed them in distinctive ways, on the basis of the idiosyncratic traits of the leaders of their parties. The 'people' idealised by Forza Italia is a people made up of modern consumers. The inspiration was, however, not parties of the classic right-wing populist family, but moderate conservative parties of the centre right. Only the somewhat eccentric personal style of its leader – Berlusconi – and its use of the ownership of the mass media turned it into populism. The 'people' of the LN is made up of local communities – villagers and small town inhabitants who want to preserve their way of life against all intrusion of foreign elements. The inspiration was the many regionalist movements, some of which had very influential leaders such as the Catalan Pujol, and operated with degrees of populism. The 'people' of the AN is formed by self-professed Italian patriots. Thus, their idealised community is the nation of classic nationalism. But important innovations have taken place with respect to the old fascist conceptions of the MSI.

Borrowing elements from democratic conservative parties and from the French new right (Taguieff 1994), the old MSI could over the years re-define itself in terms that made it look distinctly modern – modern in the sense of making modernity into an ideological feature to be promoted as a distinctive trait – a marketing strategy. In doing this, it continued the effort of revision and updating that several far right parties have undertaken in recent years (Minkenberg 2000). The AN could promote modern policies that expressed tolerance, respect for minorities and marked a clear difference from its fascist past. Thus, for instance, Fini was the first right-wing leader in Italy to advocate the vote for immigrants at local elections and openness towards homosexuals, and he also embarked on a process of improving relations with Israel and the Jewish community. However, this has taken place at the same time as he advocated an explicit reference to Christian values in the European constitutional treaty. Here, as pointed out previously, a gap has developed between the party's socially conservative electorate and the leadership, and even between Fini and the party's cadres, as shown by the defection of Storace and others in 2007. But these tensions have been surprisingly well tolerated by the electorate and by the activists of the AN, whose acknowledgement of the successes brought by Fini is combined with a party culture that has bred deference to its leader.

Fini's vision is and has been for many years emphatically a vision of a modern right, trying to distance itself from the legacy of the past (Ruzza and Schmidtke 1996b). A similar emphasis on modernity has characterised the social utopia of Berlusconi – a world of affluent consumers who could shed the legacy of poverty and the backwardness of traditional Italy, while still retaining solid moral values. An emphasis on a distinctive vision of modernity is also a characteristic trait of the LN, but again it expresses a dissent against the enlightenment-modelled one-dimensional secular and cosmopolitan version of modernity. It is a conception of modernity based on the myth of a 'Europe of a federation of peoples', where local identities and languages are re-discovered and co-exist with economic success and affluence, rather than one based on multiculturalism or cosmopolitanism. The Italian right has attempted to present itself as distinctly modern in juxtaposition to a left which they accuse of continuing to idealise an industrial world of factories and manual work.

All these idealised constituencies have in common a rejection of the traditional Italian political class, which is perceived as 'a caste', with no real concept or even interest in any idealised 'people', but merely as a self-serving elite. They are in this sense populist and specifically anti-political. Nonetheless, even after several legislatures, the right failed to converge on even a minimalist understanding of its idealised community – and its components continue to view each other with suspicion. Thus, the AN has often been derided (by LN and sometimes FN) as recycled fascists, FI as a party of self-interested individuals, and the LN as rough uneducated villagers proposing risible extremist policies. However, these forces successfully play down this reciprocal rejection by emphasising different factors and a strong connection to their own charismatic leaders who bypass – or transcend – the political process of representative democracy in an idealised direct connection with the 'people' – people whom each leader is seen as understanding and representing. In this process, confrontation and competition with other parties and particularly with the left takes an almost tribal connotation, and many observers have pointed to an exaggerated political climate in which insults are frequent.

Despite the previously mentioned violation of democratic norms, none of the three parties openly rejects representative democracy – which would be unfeasible in the context of any contemporary European political culture – rather, they integrate it with novel elements. These are elements which, as posited previously, enlarge and re-define the political space in distinctive ways. Thus, Berlusconi is the dynamic and successful entrepreneur whom his supporters would like to become, or would have liked to be. Bossi is someone whom his electorate instantly recognises as one of them – one who speaks their dialect and shares their thoughts about inefficient public services and excessive taxation, but also shares their lifestyle and their values. Fini is likewise a source of personal identification for the conservative southern bourgeoisie. They all speak a political language that is easily understood – different from the convoluted language of professional politicians. The language of Bossi is sometimes barely grammatical, but is clear and incisive. The language of Berlusconi is less radical but equally accessible – its style expresses moderation and fear of radicalism, but also common sense and irony that many Italians see missing in professional politicians. Fini presents a traditional mindset that embodies the thinking of many conservative voters, the voice of the 'silent majority' perhaps. In addition, one should point out that, while the language of Bossi has for years been stylistically marked by excess and therefore 'discounted' by its audience, a linguistic radicalism also occurs in Berlusconi's speeches. As the leader of a very large and moderate party, his deviations from the cautious language previously used for instance by the Christian Democratic party can be interpreted as a sort of 'functional equivalent' meant to express a unique brand of centre-right radicalism. Thus, for instance, Berlusconi's calls for tax evasion as a form of political protest carry a relevance well beyond the LN's occasional threat of armed insurrection. Fini's language is equally accessible and, somewhat incongruously given his 'post-fascist' past, is particularly reassuring. Hence, the anti-elitist character, the search for charismatic leadership and the anti-political sentiments of populists mark and join all the parties of the Italian right.

As mentioned previously, this does not of course imply that all or even most of the policies actually pursued are necessarily populist or radical: not in the sense of any of the right-wing partners being necessarily ready to actually violate constitutional arrangements, not in violating the mechanisms, and the checks and balances of representative democracy, and especially not in the sense of violating the expectations of powerful social or economic elites on the basis of direct allegiance to popular opinion. Elitist policies could in fact be pursued despite, and sometimes even through, populist discourse. For instance, the large consensus for privatisation of state services has remained largely unheeded both when the right was in government but also, to an extent, when the left replaced it after 2006. Many observers explained this in terms of the historically strong influence of professional elites within Italian politics with a protectionist inclination.

The PdL and the 2008 election

Following the return to government in 2008, the narrow defeat of 2006 could be regarded as a temporary blip, spurring the realignments that took place in 2007 and 2008. In a sense, the 2006 elections could in any case be regarded as a vindication of Berlusconi's centre-right coalition, particularly as, in the year or so before the election, opinion polls suggested it was heading for a significant defeat. This was especially so following the severe blow of the regional election losses of 2005. Nevertheless, in reality, analysis of electoral data shows that the proportion of the electorate voting for the centre-right coalition only decreased by a small margin in 2006 before increasing again in 2008, by a small margin for the PdL parties and by a large margin for the LN. Although the CdL's share of the vote went down from 49.9 per cent in 2001 to 49.4 per cent in 2006 (and the centre-left's share increased from 46.1 per cent to 49.9 per cent), the LN and the AN actually marginally increased their vote share in 2006. The biggest loser within the CdL in 2006 was FI. Its share of the vote fell from 29.4 per cent to 23.7 per cent, a drop of 5.8 per cent. The biggest gainer within the coalition was the UDC. Its vote share more than doubled from 3.2 per cent to 6.8 per cent, while other minor forces within the coalition also gained. The increase for the UDC was particularly interesting, given its refusal to don the right-wing label and its emphasis on centrist policies and remaining aloof from the coalition's populist instincts. This suggested that a significant number of voters for the coalition, while refusing to vote for the centre left, still wanted to send a message of disapproval to Berlusconi and his brand of populism. The UDC's positioning would lead it later to refuse to take part in the PdL project, despite collaborating with Berlusconi in forcing early elections in 2008.

The decline in the vote for FI in 2006 could be attributed to a number of factors relating to the nature of Berlusconi's populism. As discussed in the chapter on FI, there is an evident contradiction between Berlusconi's populism and his patrimonialism. The rejection of self-serving political elites and promises to reflect the will of the sovereign people sat uneasily with a prioritising of *ad personam* policies, which reflected the interests of Berlusconi and his clan. More generally, there was dissatisfaction with the failure to fulfil the grand promises of Berlusconi's contract with the people. Berlusconi may have been a victim of his previous success in raising the expectations of the Italian people as to what a centre-right government could deliver. It was notable that FI did not perform as well as it had previously in the south, where his promised major infrastructural projects, which would have generated employment as well as delivered the much needed improvements in roads and bridges, etc., did not materialise. The apparent northern bias of the coalition (and fears about the implication of devolution for the southern regions) may also have taken their toll in the south. In general, the ITANES pre-election survey showed a high level of dissatisfaction as to the performance of the Italian economy and the effect of government policies in relation to it. Moreover, on a range of issues asking voters to evaluate the ability of the centre-right and centre-left poles to deal with certain issues, the centre right trailed the centre left. While it performed better than the centre left on the signature issues of immigration and combating criminality, it trailed as regards management of the health system, schools, fighting unemployment, improving the justice system and the public administration, making the taxation system fairer, managing relations with Europe and general ruling competence (Belucci 2007).

Despite this apparent dissatisfaction with the centre-right's performance in 2006, the centre right was able to quickly re-conquer popular consensus and return to power in 2008. This can be attributed in part to the failure of the centre-left government. The Prodi government had quickly become unpopular because of increases in taxes (deemed necessary to address the hole in public finances left by the Berlusconi government) and by its attempted liberalisation reforms which angered various professional lobbies. Moreover, it was unable to deliver governing stability, with contradictory signals being given by its centre-left core and its radical left on a number of issues, and with rebellions also coming from centrist parties. This was largely the consequence of the new electoral law which fragmented political representation and engendered instability.

It was the withdrawal of the centrist UDEUR from the coalition that precipitated the collapse of the Prodi government. The centre right was once again able to capitalise on popular fears related to security. As noted above, its positions on crime and immigration had resonated better with public opinion even in 2006. In the intervening years, it was able to better reflect concerns on issues such as the alleged influx of criminals from Romania and the delinquency emanating from Roma camps. At the same time, fears about economic security were also exploited. Worries about restricted and reduced employment opportunities were associated with an apparent concern by the left to protect the employment rights and pension privileges of those already in jobs rather than a concern with increasing employment opportunities for the large number of young people without a fixed job. These themes were reflected in the electoral programme of the PdL, and also its new *Carta dei Valori* (charter of values) published in early 2008.

A frame analysis conducted by the authors, using the same methodology utilised previously, found a preponderance of a small number of themes in the *Carta dei Valori*. Two key themes emerged: freedom and traditional family values. In the short document, out of forty-seven codes identified, there are sixteen references to freedom, six to family values and five to Christian values. The electoral programme, on the other hand, made a number of vague policy statements without making particularly bold ideological statements, to the extent that only a very few of our codes applied.

The *Carta dei Valori* began with the following statement:

> The 'People of Freedom' was born from freedom, in freedom and for freedom, so that Italy can be ever more modern, free, just, prosperous, and authentically solid.

The repeated emphasis on freedom was sometimes complemented by a refer-ence to the need to maintain social protection and safeguard the European social model, perhaps reflecting the influence of the AN, and the need to help the poorest in society. In a departure from FI's usual emphasis on economic liberalism, the document also had a rather protectionist slant (also reflecting the increasing prominence of a protectionist faction around Giulio Tremonti). The 'not always positive changes' wrought by globalisation were referred to for example. The emphasis on identity themes and the protection of Italy and Europe's Christian roots was however pronounced:

> We believe that there is a need to add to freedom another value, com-plementary to it: the security of identity in the face of immigration.
> We have to and we can be open to the new, but without renouncing ourselves, reinforcing our traditions, our identity, our freedom.
> The Judaeo-Christian roots of Europe and its common classical and humanist cultural heritage, together with the best part of the enlight-enment, are the fundamentals of our vision of society.

Christian and family values were stressed together and the left attacked for destroying them. Moreover, there was a clear rejection of same-sex unions and an emphasis on 'natural' families only:

> We propose a society based on liberal and Christian values, on natural families based on marriage, based on the union of a man and a woman, within which children are born, brought up and educated.
> The left's politics destroy the family, and do not respect the moral values of the Italian people, the values of our tradition.

The PdL programme for the 2008 election was generally a mainstream con-servative document – referring to the need for liberalisation and de-regulation, reduction of taxes (including the abolition of local property tax and inheritance tax), the building of more prisons and tougher sentencing and reaffirmation of the Bossi–Fini principle linking immigration visas to work permits and vigorous combating of clandestinity. A pledge was also made to tackle abusive camps of nomads and to remove from the territory people without regular residence and unable to support themselves. On the question of immigration, while reaffirming the principles of the Bossi–Fini law, the programme – rather ironically, given the regularisation of nearly 700,000 clandestines by the second Berlusconi government – pledged an initiative by the Italian government within the EU to prevent any further indiscriminate amnesties. It also repeated the stress in the *Carta dei Valori* on 'natural families' founded on marriage between a man and a woman. While the *Carta dei Valori* of the PdL had stressed the need for constitutional reforms bringing a stronger executive, the electoral programme – reflecting the alliance with the LN – placed the stress on plans to introduce fiscal federalism.

Passages on law and order made references to the threat of Islamic fundamentalism and also leftist groups promoting civil disobedience.

> the fight against internal and international terrorism, also through the close control of centres linked to fundamentalist preaching; protection of public order from the attacks of various 'disobedients' and also through the increase in penalties for crimes of violence against the forces of law and order.

The programme also made a number of pledges implying increased spending and state interventionism, for example the relaunch of public works projects such as the bridge from Sicily to the mainland and the re-introduction of a baby bonus to promote childbirth, together with promises of housing for all, improved access to higher education and reduction in hospital waiting lists. References to economic liberalism were again balanced by some rather protectionist messages. For example, there was a call for:

> Interventions within the EU to reduce Community regulations, to defend our production, against the asymmetric competition that comes from Asia.

Whether or not the creation of the PdL made a huge difference to the result is not totally clear. Accurate calculations for 2008 as regards the AN and FI are impossible given that they ran a joint list of candidates. Nevertheless, the vote for the PdL in 2008 was 37.6 per cent, compared with a combined AN–FI vote in 2006 of 36 per cent. The increased PdL vote could be partly explained by the influx of a number of smaller groups, ranging from Mussolini's unrepentant neo-fascists to Gianfranco Rotondi's new DC and defectors from the UDC such as Giovanardi. One should also take into account here that the AN in particular would have lost votes to Storace's La Destra. In any case, the PdL performance in 2008 is much less impressive when one considers that the combined AN–FI vote in 2001 was 41.4 per cent. Clearly, votes had been lost since then to the centre and to La Destra. However, in 2008, the biggest gainer was the LN, which stormed back to levels not seen since the mid-1990s, polling 8.3 per cent of the vote (rising from 4.6 per cent in 2006 and more than double its vote of 3.9 per cent in 2001). Despite the consolidation of the two party blocs witnessed in the election, the LN's role remained indispensable to the centre right, and its increased vote was decisive in ensuring victory in 2008. Early data on electoral flows from the Piepoli polling institute show that a large majority of the increased vote for the LN in 2008 had come from those who voted FI and AN in 2006. In particular, the LN had succeeded in winning back voters in its northern heartlands lost to FI in the mid-1990s, as well as new generations of voters. However, while the PdL lost votes in the north, it gained them in the south – winning back voters lost in 2006 to the UDC and the centre left. The PdL did particularly well in the urban peripheries and provincial towns and countryside of the south (less so in the urban centres), winning support among all types of workers, many attracted by Berlusconi's promise to abolish local property tax for owners of one home. It also garnered support from voters dissatisfied with local centre-left administrations. For example, the PdL won 49.1 per cent of the vote in Campania (the AN–FI combined score was 39.1 per cent in 2006), where dissatisfaction was high with the centre-left's handling of the refuse crisis, which had seen piles of rubbish blighting the streets of Naples (Salvia, Zuccolini 2008).

One other notable feature of the 2008 election was the collapse in the vote of the Greens and radical left. Their joint list collapsed from 8.1 per cent to 3.8 per cent. Most of their former voters appear to have switched to the PD (which in turn lost votes, mainly from its catholic element, to the UDC, but also to the PdL). Some Green voters, however, also appear to have switched to the LN (Staff Reporter 2008d). The LN thus appeared to have benefited both from dissatisfaction with the centre left and a diffidence among some northern voters towards both Berlusconi and the predominantly southern AN. More positively, it benefited from its rooted presence on the ground and experience of local administration in the northern regions and an appearance of being more in touch with local concerns to many voters.

Despite the gap between what the centre right had promised and what it had delivered between 2001 and 2006, it was able to capitalise successfully on the failure of the centre left to provide a convincing or united alternative between 2006 and 2008. At the same time, its general alignment with conservative tendencies within the electorate, particularly on issues such as tax, family values and immigration, and its appeal to anti-political sentiments continued to bear fruit. Its use of populist signals and symbolic discourse, which even many centre-right voters knew would not result in actual concrete policies, continued to find favour among a significant proportion of the electorate, cutting across socio-economic groups and appealing to a cultural model diffused through the media, to which those sections of the Italian population who spent a large number of hours in front of their televisions were particularly susceptible.

Conclusions

This chapter has compared the parties of the Italian right in terms of their overall performance, electorates, political discourse and prospects. Over the long 'incomplete transition' of the Second Republic, much has changed, but the discourse of the right in its differentiated identities has accompanied and interpreted many institutional and social changes. Despite numerous fractious disputes, personal animosity, unexpected defections and realignments, the right has formed a successful voting bloc that has shaped the history of Italy in recent decades. The 'Berlusconi years' have been years of accelerated economic and social change, which the right has interpreted with a thematically and territorially differentiated offering, and with the continuing ability to re-invent itself to interpret in novel ways the fears and opportunities of a country that in the intervening period has had to come to terms with epochal changes, such as the impact of economic globalisation, large-scale immigration and the economic and social consequences of European integration. In the eyes of many observers, the country has never been so politically divided. The right has fostered and profited from these divisions. Electoral contests have been bitterly fought with the language of 'anti-Berlusconismo' on one side and with the somewhat anachronistic but effective threat of communism on the other. In the meantime, the trajectory of the right has been one of gradual convergence. Leaving aside the fascist background and delimiting territorially ethno-nationalist claims of certain parts of the coalition, a new right is now once again re-inventing itself.

8 Conclusion
Populism and the right

Introduction

In this chapter, we will review our findings and contextualise them in a broader European perspective, examining the extent to which general lessons can be learned from the Italian case. We will conclude with a discussion of implications for democracy in general as well as more specifically for Italy.

In previous chapters, we have argued that the success of the Italian right is related to a set of concurrent factors that can be summarised as a set of favourable political opportunities – such as the collapse of the previous party system and the growing relevance of migration issues – agency factors related to the strategies of parties and the charismatic leadership of Silvio Berlusconi and, to a lesser extent, of other centre-right leaders and particular public communication dynamics rooted in Berlusconi's ownership of a large swathe of the Italian generalist media. Clearly, many of these factors are only relevant to Italy but, in this chapter, we would argue that there are findings that can be usefully considered in a broader context as they appear to manifest themselves in other European countries. With reference to the literature, we will first locate the Italian right in the European context.

Reassessing the literature on the right

In seeking to locate the Italian right in a broader European and global context, we need to reiterate the specificity of the Italian case. We are not analysing a single party, or comparing a set of parties cross-nationally, as is generally the case in the literature on the right. We are examining a coalition in which a centre-right liberal populist party has acquired some of the themes and style of extreme right parties and has incorporated and legitimated to an unusual extent a populist radical right party – the LN – and a formerly extreme right neo-fascist party – the AN. Thus, while many insights from the literature are still relevant, and some generalisations to the European context are warranted, major distinctions need to be made.

The literature presents a set of explanations for the success of the right, which, as noted, are often untenable if presented as mutually excluding alternatives. A model that combines different kinds of explanations is necessary, while the exclusive reliance on a single explanation needs to be excluded. Eatwell reviews the main theories of the extreme right and shows the problems that each has in explaining its success (Eatwell 2003). His review is useful as it demonstrates that, while several explanations have been identified that are applicable to a range of cases, they often fail to stand up if a broader set of comparisons is considered. As we are dealing with a diverse coalition of parties, his criticisms are valid, as dominant explanations do typically apply generally, but with exceptions. We will mention briefly some of his criticisms and take up some of these theories later in the chapter.

In terms of demand-side theories, as Eatwell suggests, one cannot identify immigration as the only relevant issue responsible for the success of the right. As for other countries, one can also rule out the anti-politics thesis as the only explanation. In Italy, a substantial amount of leftist anti-politics exists. But, as we have sought to explain, one needs rather to understand why the right has been effective in attracting a large share of anti-political votes for such a long period. The 'anomie–social breakdown' thesis also needs to be contextualised. As we have shown, the voting profile of each of the parties is sufficiently differentiated to require more detailed explanations than a blanket social breakdown theory. The same consideration applies to an explanation exclusively focused on a reaction to post-materialism and its values of personal freedoms and cultural innovation, seen as irrelevant by many low-skilled and less educated voters. Such an explanation is generally applicable, but as noted there is, for instance, a liberal wing in FI which would not fall into this category in social and cultural terms. An exclusive focus on economic interest would be equally unwarranted as, within the right-wing coalition and each of its major components, a range of professional and social groups cohabit with differentiated interests, although as mentioned there are common features such as a lower education level.

Turning to Eatwell's list of supply-side theories, the Italian case is highly illustrative of the importance of electoral space in political opportunity theory, particularly in relation to FI strategic identification and maintenance of a distinctive electoral positioning. Noting with Eatwell that, in some countries where space was available, no successful radical right developed, we believe that it is necessary to emphasise the strategic cultural adjustments that all parties undertook in order to retain control of political space (Eatwell 2003). For this reason, we will explore the trajectory of the Italian right with reference to Eatwell's framework, but we will strive to integrate it with a culturally dynamic explanation that emerges in the literature on discursive opportunities or cultural opportunities. Into our emphasis on cultural adjustments, we will subsume Eatwell's 'mediatisation thesis', which emphasises the role of the media, and also his 'national tradition thesis', which in Italy relates to the residual historical acceptance of authoritarian rule, and his 'charismatic leadership' thesis. The concept of 'discursive opportunity', as formulated by social movement theorists, can usefully be utilised in this context to complement the political opportunity approach rather than replace it (Koopmans and Olzak 2004; Koopmans and Statham 1999). We would point, on the one hand, to the stable cultural features of a society that can be utilised instrumentally by tailoring political messages to them and, on the other hand, to the dynamic aspect of culture and to processes of cultural change as enabling ideological re-framings that can result in variations in electoral support. We also refer to attempts to manipulate culture, such as when security themes are highlighted in the media and a specific political offering on those themes is then proposed to the electorate.

As we have shown, each of these theses is to a large extent appropriate, but needs qualifying as they have different relevance for each party and for the coalition as a whole. With reference to the social movement literature (Gamson 1988, 1998; Gamson and Meyer 1996), we would not therefore collapse the discursive opportunity approach into the national tradition approach, but employ it with reference to a broader set of explanatory cultural elements. Finally, we have emphasised a need to accept but better qualify Eatwell's 'programmatic thesis', which emphasises populism and *ad hoc*, inconsistent but effective electoral strategies. The parties we studied displayed very different preoccupations with consistency and clearly enunciated ideologies. We would therefore accept, but seek to articulate in more detail, Eatwell's framework, which focuses on a multi-factor explanation and which he summarises as 'growing extremist legitimacy + rising personal efficacy + declining system trust'.

On the basis of this multi-causal approach, we will now identify some approaches in the literature that are particularly useful in interpreting the behaviour of specific components of the Italian coalition. Then we will propose a reading of political opportunity theory that comprehensively organises our findings.

Mudde's recent work on the populist radical right is also useful – particularly for his discussion of nativism (Mudde 2007). In the Italian context, his definition for this family of parties – which share three core ideological features: nativism, authoritarianism and populism – can only be applied to the LN. Similarly, Rydgren's definition of the extreme right-wing populist (ERP) party family, sharing the fundamental core of ethno-nationalist xenophobia, derived from ethno-pluralism, combined with anti-political establishment populism, can also be applied to the LN.

While the LN may project itself as beyond left and right, an authoritarian conception of social order and a rejection of the kind of state intervention to re-distribute power and wealth that one associates with the left places it on the right of the political spectrum. At the same time, it can be characterised as radical in its disdain for the institutional niceties of liberal democracy and, indeed, its rejection of certain tenets of the Italian constitutional order, while not being anti-system *per se*. Its nativism, understood as a doctrine encompassing a rejection of all alien peoples, characteristics, cultures and ideas, is clear. According to Mudde, nativism is 'an ideology, which holds that states should be inhabited exclusively by members of the native group ("the nation") and that non-native elements (persons and ideas) are fundamentally threatening to the homogeneous nation-state' (Mudde 2007: 19). The alien can be defined as an outsider group such as immigrants – as is common among the populist radical right in western Europe – or more longstanding historical minorities such as gypsies or Jews, as is often the case among nativist parties in eastern Europe, or it can be defined more conceptually as multi-culturalism, European integration, globalisation or Islam. In the case of the LN, the principal alien out-group has changed over the years from the southern Italian to the immigrant. However, its strong territorial identity, its anti-immigrant stance, its Islamophobia, its hostility to gypsies and its anti-EU, anti-multicultural, anti-globalisation stances can all be interpreted as flowing from its essential nativism. Descriptions of it should not be reduced to any one of these political issues or negative stances. The emphasis in its discourse shifts according to whichever threat it sees as the most salient to its native constituency, or most politically profitable to focus upon in order to exploit emerging cultural opportunities.

For the populist radical right, the people are conceptualised as both *ethnos* and *demos*. For non-nativist populists such as Forza Italia, the emphasis is solely or mainly on the *demos* – the people as one. As noted in the conclusion to Chapter 5, this is a also distinction made by Tarchi in describing populism in Italy. Thus, while the LN has based its appeal on a notion of the people 'as both *ethnos* and *demos*', FI has concentrated solely on the latter, juxtaposing a popular heartland against a self-serving elite and concentrating on an 'anti-political, anti-party' message' (Tarchi 2008: 85–86).

Mudde distinguishes between the populist radical right and neo-liberal populists: while they share the one core ideological feature of populism, they differ in their other core ideological features:

> In essence, neoliberal populism is defined by a core ideology of neoliberalism (primarily in terms of economy) and populism. In contrast to the populist radical right, the ideological feature of nativism is either not present or not central to the neoliberal populist family, while the same applies to neoliberalism for the populist radical right.
>
> Mudde (2007: 30)

This seems apposite for distinguishing between the LN and FI. Indeed, Mudde places FI into the neo-liberal populist category (Mudde 2007: 47). Moreover, whereas the LN has previously been bracketed under a definition of radical right populist parties (RRPs), which combine economic neo-liberalism with xenophobia and populism (Betz 1994: 4), Mudde correctly highlights the secondary importance of economics to the populist radical right (Mudde 2007: 119–37). Economics is subordinate to both the populism and the nativism of such parties, and positions on the economy can change according to changing economic and political circumstances, as can be seen in the case of the LN, which was previously characterised as neo-liberal in the early 1990s (when a de-regulatory economic approach fitted well with its critique of the corrupt and inefficient Italian state) but has become more protectionist in recent years in relation to its northern heartlands (as exemplified by its championing of tariffs in relation to cheap Chinese imports viewed as threatening northern Italian producers).

Until 2008 at least, Forza Italia has been more consistent in its espousal of neo-liberalism, and it would be mistaken to put it in the same populist radical right category as the LN, particularly as it does not possess an essentially nativist core. However, although the party literature of FI and the speeches of Berlusconi (and latterly the PdL) are littered with neo-liberal proclamations, in practice, the actions of FI in government have fallen rather short of the stated objectives. While neo-liberal populism is a more apt classification for FI, problems remain in applying any such categorisation. As noted in Chapter 5, FI has is in some ways been more like a conventional political party, within which 'anti-political populism is entirely delegated to the leader' (Tarchi 2008: 86). While the LN's populism was clear in the analysis of its programmes and across all its activities, that of FI was confined more to the statements and communication style of its leader and founder, and did not always come across that clearly in its documents, which sought to present the party as a mainstream centre-right force.

In terms of the European right, FI appears as a rather *sui generis* formation. It was Italy's leading centre-right formation from 1994 to 2008, occupying the mainstream position in the Italian party system. Although at a European level it sat within the EPP with the French Gaullists, Spanish Peoples' Party and German Christian Democrats, the utilisation of an anti-political populist discourse made it quite distinct in the European centre-right context, as did the nature of its leadership and foundation in general. As explained in Chapter 5, it could be regarded as an extreme example of the electoral-professional model of political party also seen elsewhere in advanced democracies (Hopkin and Paolucci 1999). However, the role of its leader – as founder and leader by acclamation – appeared unique when compared with other leading European centre-right parties. While not alone among mainstream European leaders in his efforts to mobilise the kind of 'politician's populism' described by Canovan (1981), his Manichean demonisation of opponents, his outsider anti-elitist discourse and disdain for the trappings of liberal democracy (such as a robust and independent judiciary) and his appeals to the popular heartland that bypass constitutional procedure make him an exemplar of the modern anti-political populist zeitgeist as described by many authors (Canovan 1999; Mastropaolo 2005; Meny and Surel 2002; Mudde 2004; Taggart 2000).

At least initially, the characterisation of FI put forward in this book could also be applied to the new PdL formation, within which the dissolution of FI was announced at the end of November 2008. In the 2008 election, the PdL programme was similar in many respects to the programmatic documents of FI that preceded it, also reflecting many positions that could be characterised as mainstream centre right. At the same time, the anomalous leadership of Berlusconi persisted. Where this left the AN was also unclear. In agreeing to dissolve the AN into a new PdL party, its leader, Fini, was effectively consenting to the subordination of the party's distinct identity to Berlusconi's populist leadership, whereas Fini had previously sought to distinguish the AN from Berlusconi's idiosyncratic populism as well as from the radical right populism of the LN.

The path travelled by the AN since the early 1990s has been documented in Chapter 6. It has been a remarkable journey from the neo-fascist ghetto. Up to the 1990s, the categorisation of the MSI as a leading party of the European extreme right, or neo-fascist right, was fairly straightforward (Hainsworth 1992; Ignazi 2003; Ignazi and Ysmal 1992a). As suggested in the literature, other European parties with their roots in neo-fascism or Nazism, such as the FPO or FN, have also enjoyed electoral success by distancing themselves from their fascist heritage and adopting new forms of politics (Ignazi and Ysmal 1992a; Rydgren 2005a). However, these parties, taking the path of the populist radical right, have retained their extremist characterisation and remain shunned by mainstream politicians at the international level (and at the national level in the case of the FN). Although the electoral success of the FPO meant that it was able to secure a place in the Austrian governing coalition at the turn of the twenty-first century, its opponents on the centre left continue to denounce it as extremist, and its inclusion in government led to an international outcry and even short-lived sanctions by the EU. The AN, on the other hand, has generally been accepted into the mainstream, accepted as a legitimate actor by its opponents at the national level, accepted at the EU level through its membership of the UEN (former UPE) formation, and through the work of its leader in the European convention, as foreign minister and as president of the lower chamber. The AN has accomplished this by the employment of a very careful discourse and policy positioning. While populist themes have been exploited, it has avoided using the kind of xenophobic language that the LN can afford to use. Indeed, it would have been impossible for Fini to use the same kind of demagogic discourse that Bossi has deployed – he would soon have been re-labelled as fascist and consigned back to the fringes. Elements of ethno-nationalism or nativism persist, but do not characterise the whole party (or the leadership in particular). The party has dabbled with populism and has recently subordinated itself to Berlusconi's populist leadership, but Fini has more often eschewed anti-establishment discourse in an attempt to present himself as a responsible moderate post-fascist leader. Nevertheless, the party remains authoritarian – perhaps more so than FI and the LN – and retains a right-wing character. It cannot, however, be described as radical right populist or be bracketed with a broader radical right (Minkenberg 2003; Norris 2005), although it retains residual populist and nativist elements and is still marked by a widespread sympathetic view of the fascist past.

While exclusionist positions have been taken on immigration and multiculturalism, these are distinct from the ethno-populism employed by the LN and other parties of the European populist radical right. In many senses, the AN's positions have been very much in line with the European centre-right mainstream, from the French Gaullists to the German Christian Democrats to the British Conservatives. Where it differs from these parties is in its interpretations of the past and the historical heritage it struggles to deal with. Nevertheless, the path it has travelled resembles in some senses that of the Spanish Peoples' Party, which developed out of pro-Franco elements following the Spanish transition to democracy. Many of the latter's members and supporters also retain a rather unapologetic view of their country's fascist past.

The road travelled by the AN is certainly an example that could be followed by other European extreme right parties, although the role played by country-specific political opportunities remains a significant consideration. Without the rich fruit offered by the collapse of Christian democracy and the possibilities offered by the continuing uncertainties of the Italian political transition (which have engendered a more moderate strategy on the part of the AN), it may have preferred to follow a line more akin to that of the French FN or Austrian FPO, as indeed Fini appeared to favour prior to *tangentopoli.*

Given certain structural similarities, and leaving aside the particular circumstance of party system collapse that affected Italy, it remains notable that a populist radical or extreme right has not developed in the same way in other southern European countries. In his work on the radical right, Kitschelt links the absence of a significant radical right in certain western European states (i. e. Ireland, Spain, Greece and Portugal) to insufficient post-industrialisation (Kitschelt and McGann 1995: 56). He also suggests that, in Greece, Spain and Portugal, which only emerged out of authoritarianism in the 1970s, the extreme right is still fighting the old battles of the past (Kitschelt and McGann 1995: 72). Thus, one could argue that liberal democracy is older and perhaps more entrenched in the case of Italy and, moreover, that a process of post-industrialisation has occurred in the north, thus facilitating the rise of the LN and explaining the greater appeal of populism in general. In the under-industrialised south of Italy, on the other hand, a more traditional form of politics has continued, marked by a continuation of clientelistic practices and a demand for state assistentialism, and thus a different kind of right has continued to thrive. Thus, the AN continues to appeal to state-assistentialist sentiments in the south, while Berlusconi and FI have taken over some of the old clienteles of the DC, particularly in Sicily, and continue to promise ambitious state-funded infrastructure projects. Nevertheless, one could also argue that, in the case of countries such as Ireland and Spain, which have now overtaken Italy economically, such explanations are dated and that the potential for a populist right to develop in these countries is greater, although the Italian case still remains distinct in a number of ways, as explained below. Moreover, Kitschelt and McGann's thesis on the success of the radical right stressed a 'winning formula' of free-market economics and political and cultural authoritarianism, deriving from a right-wing backlash against left-wing post-materialism (Kitschelt and McGann 1995: vii). As

Mudde also argues, our findings indicate that neo-liberalism is not a core feature of such parties, or key to their success (Mudde 2007).

In contrasting the success of the right in Italy with its comparative failure elsewhere, one must stress a combination of political and cultural opportunities, combined with successful agency on the part of party leaderships. A number of authors have stressed the combination of such factors in explaining the differing performance of the extreme or populist right in Europe. For example, Rydgren sets out a framework based on the successful adaption and diffusion of framing strategies – linked to the agency of particular parties and their leaders – and expanding and contracting political opportunities (Rydgren 2005a: 417). More broadly, Carter, in her study of extreme right success and failure in Europe, stresses a combination of supply-side factors: in terms of the type of right-wing ideology embraced, the type of party organisation and leadership and the different patterns of party competition and institutional environment (Carter 2005: 2–8). Similarly, Mudde stresses a combination of external supply-side factors (i.e. political opportunity structures) and internal supply-side factors (the nature of the populist radical right parties themselves) in explaining their differing success (Mudde 2007: 232–76). As noted above, in Italy, we are analysing the success of a much broader right, in which the distinction between extreme, radical and mainstream right is blurred. However, the emphasis on the supply side in explaining its success remains valid, given that we assume that, across western Europe at least, the salience of issues that influence the demand for such parties, such as immigration, law and order, concerns about globalisation and economic change and anti-political sentiment, is broadly similar.

Explaining the success and failure of the populist right

As outlined above, in explaining the success of the Italian right in a more global context, we need then to distinguish between (1) political opportunities and (2) cultural opportunities, which will then be related to (3) factors pertaining to the structure of political communication and leadership and (4) agency factors related to parties' communicative strategies. We will conclude this section with a discussion on how all these factors have filtered the perception of policies. The Italian case illuminates the role of political opportunities that have emerged in similar ways in other EU countries.

Political opportunities

By political opportunities, we refer to factors stressed by political opportunity theory, which seeks to identify which contextual political factors empower political formations. The various strands of work on political opportunities have reached substantial consensus on a set of key factors. For instance, McAdam et al. (1996: 27) proposes a 'highly consensual list of dimensions of political opportunity' which consists of:

the relative openness or closure of the institutionalised political system; the stability or instability of that broad set of elite alignments that typically undergird a policy; the presence or absence of elite allies; the state's capacity and propensity for repression.

As for cultural and discursive opportunities, as mentioned, we emphasise opportunities relating to the role of the media (Gamson and Meyer 1996), to the agency of key individuals, such as charismatic leaders, or more broadly with reference to the distinctive and relatively stable constraints produced by countries' political cultures, ideological principles, institutional memories and political taboos (Polletta 1999).

Political opportunities from the collapse of the party system

Forza Italia's appearance and constant presence as the main centre-right party in Italy after 1994 was made possible by the rupture in the Italian party system created by the *tangentopoli* scandal and the collapse of the DC. This also applies in many respects to the LN, which was instrumental in promoting the political and cultural climate that made possible the prosecution of corrupt politicians, and of the then MSI, which benefited from its protracted exclusion from office and could present itself as immune from corruption.

The scandals provided for a re-opening of the institutionalised political system which, for the first time in decades, allowed new entrants credibly to compete for power. It re-fashioned the system of elite alliances requiring industrial and social elites to look beyond the forces of the *pentapartito* for political support.

Thus, the unfreezing of the Italian party system provided the conditions for, and indeed necessitated, the construction of a new mainstream centre-right party. Similar conditions would most probably be required for such a party to take form elsewhere in Europe, i.e. the collapse of a party system (as occurred in France in 1958), or indeed the establishment of democratic party competition following the end of an authoritarian dictatorship, as occurred in Spain, Portugal and Greece in the 1970s and in the former Soviet bloc at the end of the 1980s. In France, after the foundation of the Fifth Republic in 1958, a patriotic movement led by De Gaulle established itself as the leading player on the centre right. In the southern European cases, experimentation with new electoral–professional forms of party organisation did occur, although none was as successful as the populist business-form model pioneered by Berlusconi (Hopkin and Paolucci 1999). In the former communist countries of central and eastern Europe, a bewildering array of new parties has emerged, some employing populism successfully (e.g. the Law and Order party in Poland). However, it would require a combination of the kind of access to financial and organisational resources available to Berlusconi in 1994, and the kind of charismatic communication and leadership skills he possesses, for the Forza Italia model to be as successful and longlasting elsewhere. The increasing global importance of the media, and television in particular, with its emphasis on sound-bite politics, personal image and sensationalist reporting – when it comes to political campaigning – certainly makes it possible for the Forza Italia model to be aped with success, although cultural and historical factors will always mean that any such cases will take on their own national or regional peculiarities.

Political opportunities for the right also came from changes in the electoral law, which forced a previously unknown bipolar system and a political culture of bitter confrontation on to Italian politics. This political culture was more conducive to a coalition with a strong leader – perceived as such by both left and right (Barisione 2006: 20–26) – than to the fragmented leftist coalition. Nonetheless, it should be stressed that tactical advantages for the right have not resulted in the enabling of the political system as a whole to reach needed decisions. In recent years, under right-wing governments as well as under leftist governments, Italy has remained in a state of constant impasse – torn between anti-politics and immobility. The right under Berlusconi has certainly benefited from a greater ability to hold itself together for a full five-year term – an event unprecedented in Italian politics – but at the price of not achieving needed social and institutional reforms. This situation can be generalised to an extent.

In Italy, as was the case in the French Fourth Republic, governmental instability and citizen alienation from politics were connected to a highly conflictual multi-party system that was so internally divisive as to be in a frequent state of impasse. In Italy, but also in other EU member states (for example Austria under the *proporz* system of the post-war period), the institutionalisation of political parties within the state and their consequent isolation from society meant that overall the party system was viewed as a poor mechanism of interest aggregation. Disengagement from political parties reflected this increasing closeness to the machinery of the state, leaving open a space for a search for alternative channels (Deth 1997).

Cultural opportunities: anti-politics, nativism, cultural protectionism

In addition to political opportunities, cultural opportunities have also played a role. In Italy, the success of the right relied on its mastery of the values of social conservatism entrenched in Italian political culture by decades of Christian Democratic rule. It also utilised fears about migration, security and perceptions of ethnic rivalry for jobs and resources of the welfare state, which are widely shared in other European polities.

As in other European countries, a set of new grievances has characterised Italian politics and culture in recent years. Anti-political sentiments and immigration-related fears have particularly benefited the right everywhere. In Italy, the anti-political image of leaders such as Bossi – the ordinary 'villager' – and Berlusconi – the entrepreneur 'only temporarily lent to politics' – was crucial in explaining early successes. Reactions to immigration, concerns with changes in the structure of the welfare state and a perception of globa-lisation-induced economic vulnerability have been more relevant in recent years, without however any reduction in anti-political sentiments. Concerns for both these issues affect a growing set of social strata and permeate a dif-fused political culture that one can identify in several European member states. However, in Italy, anti-political attitudes have found a deeper echo than elsewhere. Critically – and differentiating Italy from other European experiences – an established party system collapsed – providing much greater space for political entrepreneurs and the conquest of mainstream centre-right voters by populist actors.

Italy is positioned on several indicators among the countries where politi-cians and political institutions are less trusted, and where political activity is less understood by the population. For instance, in 2002, only 40 per cent of Italians trusted their parliament and assigned a score higher than 5 on a 1 to 10 scale – a similar figure emerged in 2004; this is less than in most other western European countries – although more than ex-communist states (ESS 2002 data, http://www.europeansocialsurvey.org/ – variable trstprl5). They trust politicians even less, with only 6.5 per cent in 2002 and in 2004 assigning a score higher than 7 (on a 1 to 10 scale) – a lack of trust that is shared by other southern European countries (ESS 2002 data), although, as noted above, right-wing populism has not developed in the same way elsewhere in southern Europe. In 2002, 22 per cent of Italians found politics 'often too complicated to understand' – a similar figure of 20 per cent also emerged in 2004 – a figure in the highest quartile of EU countries.[1] It is also interesting to note that, in both years, the part of the electorate that found politics too complicated was on either the left or the right with the rest of the electorate in intermediate positions. This seems to indicate a rejection of how politics is conducted – the typically Byzantine style of Italian politics – particularly by the right and the left, which explains the frequency of anti-political and populist movements in both camps: as seen not only on the right, but also on the left through the recent activities of Beppe Grillo[2] and his circles.

In recent years, public disillusionment with politics has mounted further in Italy. As an issue, it is constantly debated in the Italian media. It concerns a set of related issues. Politics is often despised as a profession. Italians are concerned with the escalating cost of politics as a social activity, with the corruption and quasi corruption that it generates, with the pervasive extent of political patronage and with the inefficiencies and social injustice that can be directly attributed to the needs of the political system. The extremely suc-cessful books on the topic by politicians such as Salvi (Salvi and Villone 2005) and journalists such as Stella (Rizzo and Stella 2007) are recent con-tributions to this debate. And the debate on the consequences of corrupt politics is typically connected to the debate on the gross inefficiency of state services, for example on the much debated political intrusion and mis-appropriation of resources in the health services and public transport. Satis-faction with the performance of state services has been declining steadily since 2002, as documented by longitudinal studies with reference to schools, the health service, trains and other forms of public transport (Porcellato 2008).

Doubts about the mechanisms of representative democracy are not however limited to Italy. In this disenchantment with politics, Italy is not alone in Europe, although the phenomenon has different proportions in other countries. As Norris suggests, the decline in legitimacy of representative politics that has affected several European countries might well be small and part of a naturally fluctuating trend (Norris 2002). However, in recent years, several countries have been at the peak of this cycle, and a 'crisis of politics' has been diagnosed across Europe since the 1990s. While extreme versions of the thesis of a collapse of trust in governments are easily challenged, there is no doubt that some processes of erosion of conventional political interfaces between states and societies have occurred in recent decades. A general indicator of disaffection with politics lies in declining electoral participation, which has been related to processes of generational change and youth disengagement with electoral politics, a measurable erosion of trust in government and declining attachment to political parties (Dalton 2005: 39). Each of these factors is historically linked to others in a self-reinforcing constellation. In Europe, this has related to the process of European integration, resulting in anti-European sentiments that have found their voice in the rejection of the EU treaties in referendums in France, the Netherlands and Ireland, and the success of populist anti-European parties such as the United Kingdom Independence Party (UKIP) (Albertazzi and McDonnell 2008; Fella 2008).

European right-wing populism is not only united by an increasingly common enemy – the EU – it is also united by similar or comparable developments in member states. The impact of reactions against political corruption which has shaped recent Italian political culture might no longer be the episodic problem of only isolated countries. Episodes of political corruption have emerged in several countries, casting doubts on how the electoral process selects people for office, its incentive structures and its monitoring processes. This again has encouraged many citizens to advocate the presence of external controls on the political system – a monitoring role that the media – at least in some countries – has also come to play more thoroughly – which has further undermined the legitimacy of elected institutions.

The high level of distrust and dissatisfaction towards politicians is one reason why populism has been particularly successful in Italy. Anti-political sentiments are found throughout Europe and have resulted in notable successes for populist parties in many cases. However, these are usually fringe parties, which at best make it into government coalitions with existing mainstream parties (as in the case of the FPO in Austria and the List Pim Fortuyn in the Netherlands), or remain excluded from government but retain a significant impact on the political discourse of the mainstream (as in the case of the FN in France). In these cases, as in Italy, concerns about the implications of rising immigration, European integration and globalisation for economic and physical security and cultural cohesion have combined with a degree of hostility towards political elites in bringing success to populist movements. However, the difference in Italy is the degree to which populism has been utilised by the mainstream, by its leading centre-right formation Forza Italia.

As mentioned previously, as a weak ideology, beyond a general reference to 'the people' as a legitimising factor, populism tends to be vague and to become variably characterised by other ideological references. One such reference is localism and cultural protectionism or, more broadly, nativism, which is most typically represented by the LN. Cultural protectionism involves a negative reaction to the de-territorialising impact of globalisation. There is a re-discovery of local identities, local languages and dialects, local traditions and roots. As a relatively well-defined set of cultural values, it translates in political terms into policies that react against factors that engender territorial heterogeneity and mobility. It constitutes an important cultural opportunity for ethno-nationalist movements and parties such as the LN, but also, more broadly, other populist or nativist formations in Europe.

The LN's programme, particularly its utilisation of ethno-populist and anti-political frames, is similar in many respects to that of other populist radical right parties (using Mudde's classification). However, it differs in its use of the territorial dimension, and has been able to exploit a territorial grievance, combined with the collapse of a party system and an alliance with other non-traditional actors on the Italian right, in order to achieve a greater centrality to the party system than is the case with similar actors elsewhere in Europe.

In the context of established democracies in Europe, populists have taken for granted the main features of representative government, while at the same time often trying to subvert or limit them. Populist politics has often been characterised by a 'politics of the enemy', identifying key undesirable traits and locating them specifically in marginalised groups of the population. In most EU countries, there have been large migration flows in recent decades, and migrants have become one of the favourite scapegoats of populists. This said, European populism has varied according to the dominant institutionalised political values of different countries. Thus, in a generally liberal society such as the Netherlands, a homosexual populist would find electoral support, while in the more traditional Italian society, the homophobic LN emerged. In recent years, the debate on the European constitutional treaty gave populists an arena in which to reaffirm their allegiance to common European Christian values and, in a related context, to oppose Turkish membership of the EU. Thus, the EU context offers European populist parties chances to unite, while also leaving enough flexibility so that each can carve out a special niche that is congruent with different national cultures. The symbolic unity of European populism then takes place around values of cultural protectionism, nativism and anti-politics, with its different undertones in different countries.

More generally, the diffusion of populism in Europe goes beyond the success of the right and relates to an increased relevance for the media in agenda-shaping roles. There are several processes that account for this outcome. Some of these have already been pointed out with reference to the case of Italy but can be generalised: processes of social isolation where the media becomes one of the few socialising agencies, processes of media concentration and processes of decline in the role of parliaments and of politics increasingly becoming a spectacle (Eco 2007). Thus, what we have argued in the case of Italy could well be a harbinger of a more general trend, which studies of populism previously discussed have identified and which will need to be studied in a comparative framework in other contexts.

The role of the media

The growing importance of the media in politics has been noted by several observers (Livolsi 2006; Mazzoleni et al. 2003; Mazzoleni 2008). As Diamanti argues, at least in Europe, Italy is at the forefront of a 'mediatisation' of politics:

> Whilst the interconnection between media and politics has a long and global history ... in Italy this connection is stronger than elsewhere. It all happened so quickly that we almost did not realize it. It was the beginning of the stormy nineties. From the ideological mass parties with strong territorial rooting and grassroots organization, we passed to parties without an anchor society – organized at the centre but fragile in the periphery. And above all: personalised parties; parties influenced by marketing and communication models. A kind of media populism, whose undisputed and unsurpassed inventor is Silvio Berlusconi – the creator of a successful party, Forza Italia, but, at the same time, of the second republic – of which he has become the main reference point – to be accepted or rejected without reserve. He has 'sold' his party like a product, like Coca Cola or a chocolate. Following him television has become the main site of political participation and identity.
>
> Diamanti (2008a)

This portrayal focuses on the agency of Berlusconi. However, in the Italian case, there are broader processes involved. It is useful to consider the role of the media in Italy in terms of the political consequences of processes of concentration of media ownership and the growing role of the media in politics. Berlusconi's control of the media and the nature of media regulation in Italy help to explain the particularities of the Italian polity and the success of populism in Italy compared with the rest of Europe.

Because of the distinctive Italian patterns of media ownership, the right has been better able to exploit a general trend that several observers have noted towards a media-oriented re-definition of political competition (Mazzoleni 2008: 58). If there is a general European trend towards 'soft populism' whereby all political actors are increasingly aware of the role of the media, learn to use media outlets and prefer them to other political arenas, this knowledge and the ability to take advantage of media resources is differently distributed, and this is particularly the case in Italy. However, one needs to be cautious in explaining political behaviour with reference to television. While media strategies are increasingly and indisputably a major factor in politics, their impact should also be contextualised. In Italy, a survey study in 2007[3] showed that at least 60 per cent of Italians placed their trust in one of the main television news programmes, including those on Berlusconi's channels. In this survey, one finds clear support for the power of television in influencing opinion, but also of the relatively large number who are more sceptical. Nonetheless, it should be noted that, as Diamanti observes, the sector of the electorate that is most undecided – which is also less informed and less educated – is also the sector that relies on television more than others (Diamanti 2007). It can therefore swing the vote just before election time, as in part arguably happened during the 2006 election campaign with the last-minute substantial recovery of the CdL, and in 2008. Furthermore, the impact of the media is also cumulative and long term, as shown by the way popular views of the judiciary have evolved. During the 1994 election, Berlusconi campaigned as a supporter of the *mani pulite* team of judges and in favour of its most visible representative, Di Pietro. But during the 2008 election, he campaigned expressly against Di Pietro and more generally against investigating magistrates for whom he proposed mandatory 'tests of mental sanity'. Over a decade of negative portrayals of magistrates has altered public opinion to the point that the right could take for granted that the anti-elitist consensus also broadly regarded the judiciary as part of this elite.

Leadership, charisma and theatrical politics

The success of the Italian right has been marked by the emergence of a very strong polarisation of the electorate towards its leaders. Bossi has for years been seen as an uncultured buffoon by the left and as a skilled, straight-speaking politician by the right. Berlusconi has been seen as a corrupt and unreliable swindler by the left and as a brilliant entrepreneur by the right. At least for several years, Fini was viewed as a fascist in disguise by the left and as a moderniser by the right. The relevant literature has understood and emphasised the importance of leadership but, as Eatwell points out, there are major problems in operationalising and testing the leadership thesis, and results are still modest. Nonetheless, on the basis of our findings, some generalisations are possible. Eatwell's classification of types of leadership is useful as it illustrates significant differences between the different styles of leadership of the leaders of the right (Eatwell 2003).

Our findings point to the cultural specificity of leadership. Political symbolism is used by all leaders as a way of representing and idealising a mythology of their special bond with their 'people' – different symbolisms and an emphasis on widely varying personality features will produce vastly different leader behaviour. Leadership is a relational quality – a leader is generally only the leader of a specific type of electorate. He/she does not appeal to other electorates and, in fact, is often vigorously rejected outside his/her electoral pool. This is the case with all the leaders of the right, as we have noted previously and as survey research demonstrates (Diamanti et al. 2008). In addition, a slight majority of the electorate of the right believes that 'the leader is more important than parties' and does so more than other parties (Diamanti et al. 2008: 21).

However, there are significant differences among leaders. Berlusconi has strongly polarised the electorate, with large differences between left and right – much larger than for Fini (Diamanti et al. 2008: 25). These findings have emerged consistently over time. Similarly, Bossi is very popular among his followers, who express an almost mystical devotion to their leader, but rather unpopular in the rest of the electorate. His status is akin to the leadership recognition that typically took place in the social movements of the 1980s, where devotion to the leader and vilification of the enemy were part of the same psychological dynamic and justified the personally risky protest forms of the League's original action repertoires.

To Bossi, we could thus attribute Eatwell's category of *cultic charisma*, which is certainly not the case for Fini – often rather disliked within his own party and able to survive thanks to his electoral successes, and possibly to *centripetal charisma* – a general disposition of detached reasonableness that allows support to come from a variety of sources (Eatwell 2003: 153). Berlusconi also has broad recognition and popularity among his followers. Much discussion has taken place within the ranks regarding the way in which 'anti-Berlusconismo', the principled rejection of Berlusconi, is doomed to failure because it does not break the aura of *simpatia*, trust and admiration, among his followers. The popularity and trust in leaders such as Berlusconi and Fini has generally remained high in public opinion polls (Basso 2008).

This popularity is guaranteed by the personality of the leaders (see Eatwell 2003) who in different ways express shared traits and also individual traits. All three convey a *missionary vision*, a strong and moralised commitment to their objectives which, as mentioned, they reassert emphatically through a sense of symbolic belonging to the social categories they represent. Their ability to command is often emphasised. This comes across as a positive trait in both Berlusconi and Bossi. They also express both belonging and leadership of their constituency type through a language that mirrors the language of their constituency. They could thus be classified according to Eatwell's (2003) category of *symbiotic hierarchy* with their constituency. This is not the case with Fini whose decisionism is less frequently asserted and who does not represent the social style of much of his constituency – certainly not the nostalgic part of it.

Another aspect that characterises both Berlusconi and Bossi is, as mentioned, frequent processes of vilification of the enemy, which Eatwell (2003) classifies as *manichean demonisation*. Again this is not the case with Fini, who is generally more restrained for the reasons mentioned previously. Finally, one needs to emphasises that the *personal presence* of all three leaders is a quality that is greatly enhanced by the media ownership of Berlusconi, but also by the frequent use of symbolic politics.

Even more than in his/her policies, the leader needs to reassert symbolically and in public discourse the values of his/her electorate. In this perspective, one can thus explain the vulgar gestures of Berlusconi and Bossi as forms of anti-elitism, of symbolical representation of their anti-political stand, but also of self-validation of themselves as leaders. However, beyond this similarity, the language and gestures of Bossi express the rough exasperation and low educational status of his small-town base, while Berlusconi's double-breasted suits and courteous smiles express the bourgeois decorum, pride and sense of superiority of the successful Italian bourgeoisie. At the same time, his domineering style and insistence on reserving to himself all real decisions squares with the authoritarian tradition of Italian political culture. Fini, in contrast, has had to affirm a leadership style that distanced him as much as possible from this stereotype. One could argue that, while in Italian popular political culture a dictator such as Mussolini sadly still receives some discursive approbation for his 'ability to decide' and impose his decisions with speed, the Fascist party which he led was more universally rejected. For this reason, the leadership style of Fini had to be different to get his party legitimated, but this was not necessary for Bossi or Berlusconi, who could make statements that would not be acceptable if made by Fini. Thus, leadership means, on the one hand, interpreting and representing characters that are part of national culture but, on the other hand, differentiating them sufficiently to become specifically appealing to separate political cultures. In this sense, the differences between these different leadership styles confirm some of the issues discussed by Eatwell in his discussion of the cultural legitimacy theory of leadership (Eatwell 2004: 111–13).

The remaining differences between leaders are then bridged through symbolic action forms that can eliminate differences: the glossing over of conflicts through the use of vague and broadly appealing symbolism. Leaders of the right have symbolically bypassed electoral politics by staging large demonstrations even while in government. The political life of the Italian right has been punctuated by a set of theatrical mass demonstrations in which leaders have played a prominent role.

Mass initiatives have for instance ranged from the Security Day (16 October 1999) to the 'No Tax Day' (12 December 2004)[4] – in which all the right-wing parties of the coalition participated (but generally not the UDC) – and the many other similar large rallies, but also the smaller colourful protests of the LN such as the previously mentioned 'pig day' – the event staged to desecrate the ground on which mosques are to be built (Allam 2007; Fregonara 2007). Interviews with activists have pointed to the popularity of these events, the sense of identification with their party that comes from participating, the feeling of community and the positive value associated with the chance of meeting new like-minded people. But the use of symbolism is broader than even these political rituals. It includes unusual political posters that victimise particular social groups, such as immigrants or Italian southerners. It also includes gestures and actions often unusual in political contexts. One can think for instance of Berlusconi making mischievous gestures during the official photo of EU heads of state, or of Bossi and other leaders of the right giving the finger during official speeches.

Political symbolism provides at the same time an element of ambiguity in the political message conveyed and an amplification of its intensity that allows the creation of collective identities (Kertzer 1988). Its vagueness can be utilised to spur activists to action while avoiding any clarification of underlying ideological differences and therefore achieving effective mobilisation even among political actors who would dissent if their ideas were clarified (Ruzza 1997). The ample use of populist symbolism by the right-wing coalition has had precisely this function. It is a special kind of language that creates a vaguely defined but intensely felt sense of common interest. It glosses over ideological differences and it gives identity and cohesion to the three parties.

The agency of the three leaders, particularly Berlusconi, and their use of political symbolism and populist framing strategies has been critical to their success. While other leaders of the populist right in Europe may share their strategic and communication skills, and exploit similar issues, the leaders of the Italian right have been able to plunder the unique fruits offered by the transformation of the Italian party system that took place in the early 1990s. Moreover, the communication and financial resources provided by Berlusconi have given the Italian right a unique advantage.

The policies of the right and Italian society

If populism is an effective electoral strategy, and a means to structure links between the political environment and society, we cannot however conclude that its ideological use and the adoption of related symbolic practices necessarily permeate all policy-making activities. At a time of electoral battles increasingly fought with the weapons of political communication, saying populist things does not necessarily mean espousing populist policies. In politics, expressing ideas matters – especially expressing ideas in programmatic documents on what should be prioritised. However, such documents and manifestos are written with many intents. They do not constitute real promises, and it would be misleading to judge parties entirely on their programmes. In this volume, we have given relevance to public statements, but we have also contextualised them with reference to how they are translated to policies. Here, one needs to note that the relationship between different forms of public communication and policy-making differs substantially across systems with different institutional architectures. In Italy, the spectrum between ideas casually aired in the public sphere and law-making is particularly wide. In a country where a fragmented party system and a complex decision-making machinery prevent even governing parties from being held responsible, and often from even coming close to achieving the policy promises that are marketed to the electorate, policy proposals and even detailed legislative initiatives can be made as mere instruments of political communication. This however does not make political discourse less important. Policy proposals become a way of signalling shifting alliances to coalition partners and to the opposition, to test reaction from the base, to plan new alliances and to vilify enemies.

It is also necessary to reiterate that, at least for a portion of the right-wing electorate, the difference between signals and actual policies simply escapes recognition. The success of the right has been based on its popularity with an electorate that is less educated than average, watches more television and is less politically informed. Nonetheless, it would be misleading to explain away all the success of the right as a simple case of misrepresentation by a powerful media empire and astute populist strategies. The right is obviously successful first and foremost because a large portion of its electorate approves of its policies. This can be understood in terms of the wider political offering that has been available throughout the period.

Looking at the alternatives, the centre-left coalition has previously had to rely on a composite patchwork of small parties in which the radical left had a *de facto* veto power. This has produced a perception of immobility of centre-left government, which was particularly evident during the 2006–8 Prodi government. The left has often been perceived as utilising its veto power to protect employed workers from the rigour of the liberal policies advocated by modernisers in the moderate left and in the right. However, significant sectors of the population such as the young have often felt that protecting the already employed results in blocking the entry of new workers into stable employment and creating a dualism in the labour market between an elite of workers on permanent contracts and an expanding army of temporary workers. The left has been perceived as all too easily ready to utilise fiscal levers to move towards a balanced budget, or to accumulate resources for re-distribution. In a country where the state is notoriously inefficient and wasteful, many voters see all increases in taxation as ineffective or even detrimental. A justifiably wide-spread negative conception of the state underlies all recent elections and the success of the right. In recent years, security concerns might well have been exacerbated by the press, but the uncompromisingly inclusionist policies of the radical left have simply appeared unacceptable to sectors of the urban population. The advance of the LN in the 2008 election has been interpreted in these terms.

Similarly, the tax issue has also been magnified by the right-wing press and by the television. But even in this case, the centre left has probably paid a heavy price for the inclusion of the extreme left, which utilised counter-productive slogans such as 'even the rich must cry'.

Nonetheless, perceptions of threats to personal security related to immigration have certainly been accentuated by the media. So have perceptions of the re-distributive intents of the left coalition. Themes such as these have saturated the news on Berlusconi's channels, which points to the impact of the media. And the role of the media has not been limited to the selection of issues and their presentation but, particularly during electoral campaigns has also involved an over-proportional coverage of the leaders of the right and of Berlusconi in particular (Campus 2006).

One might observe that these issues are reflective of Europe-wide concerns that have forced the European left into retreat on issues such as employment protection, taxation, welfare expenditure and immigration policy (or to embrace the agenda of the centre right on these issues – as has been the case of New Labour in the UK). These questions have been exploited to the full in the Italian populist right, but have also proved fruitful for more conventional centre-right politicians such as Sarkozy in France – although his leadership style has earned comparisons with Berlusconi (Musso 2008) – and Merkel in Germany.

Going back to the question we asked at the beginning of this chapter: how relevant is the Italian case for analysing broader European trends? In short, factors such as the collapse of an entire party system, and a personalised ownership of the media and massive control of political resources reflect a set of contingencies that are not likely to be replicated elsewhere. However, several other factors that have contributed greatly to the success of the Italian right might very well emerge elsewhere in Europe, or are actually already under way. We are referring to processes of personalisation of politics and the implication this carries for the 'soft populism' of many European political leaders. Second, the institutionalisation of parties within the state, episodes of political corruption and the related increasing anti-political sentiments are also emerging in comparable fashion in other European democracies. Anti-immigrant feeling and broader nativist reactions to real and imagined threats posed by outsiders are mounting throughout Europe. Localism, cultural protectionism and anti-globalisation feelings are emerging and becoming politicised in several European countries. All these factors contribute to a constellation of political factors that favour the European right. It is however a constellation whose mix is different in different countries and, in Italy, it has crystallised in such a way as to create distinctive synergies.

In summary, we have distinguished between political opportunities and discursive opportunities. As mentioned, the former relate to variations in alignments of political elites and to issues relating to openness or closure of the institutionalised political system, and therefore to the developments that opened up access to mainstream politics to right-wing forces that were previously consigned to the fringes. Discursive opportunities relate to the framework of ideas and meaning-making institutions in society (Ferree et al. 2002: 62).

In terms of political opportunities, we have thus emphasised the impact of the collapse of the previous party system, the renewal and transformation of political elites and the role of the new electoral law. Notably, we emphasised the formation of new elites who could incorporate fringe parties such as the LN and MSI. As for discursive opportunities, we emphasised the role of the generalist commercial media. We have also included in this category the role of charisma, which we find acts as a mediator between the dominant framework of ideas already present in society and specific perspectives and goals of key political actors. In the case of the right, the congruence between the two on key themes identified in the frame analysis is therefore a key finding in our work. Overall, we have assessed the comparative relevance of different factors in political and discursive opportunities.

We have argued that each of these two orders of factors have differentially benefited the entire coalition and specific parties within it. The initial victory of the right was made possible by a set of new political opportunities mainly coming from the acquisition of elites from crumbling First Republic parties and from business, together with the leadership of Silvio Berlusconi who re-framed in terms of his coalition programme the dominant anti-corruption and liberalising ethos emerging in the population. Subsequently, an alignment has been successfully pursued between populist and traditionalist values and the parties of the right.

Italian politics and European democracy

Analysts of Italy have often been uncertain as to how to assess its democratic credentials. The prominence of parties in Italian life has frequently been cause for concern about democracy, and in the same way, the transition from the first to the second Italian republic has been scrutinised in terms of the country's democratic credentials (Newell 2000). Buffachi and Burgess discuss the Italian transition since the early 1990s in terms of an absence of liberal culture in Italian politics. While Italy was a democracy of sorts, it was not built on liberal foundations, and was not a liberal democracy. Liberal democracy would have required the establishment of equal rights for individuals, but this was sacrificed to power-based patronage, with governmental resources assigned on the basis of personal relationship and clientelism: 'Democracy is flawed by the mismanagement of power that arises from the false conception of the state as a vehicle for personal or factional advantage' (Buffachi and Burgess 2001: 9). Prior to *tangentopoli*, parties had expropriated state instruments for their own particular ends. Rather than universalism, state policies were characterised by clientelism. However, the transition to a 'Second Republic' has not brought a transition to a more liberal democracy. Rather, we have the patrimonial clan-based policies of Berlusconi and a populist form of politics that shows disdain for liberal constitutional norms and the rights of certain minority groups.

Connections have been made in the literature between poor institutional performance in Italy (Putnam et al. 1993) and earlier scathing critiques of widespread political corruption and particularism (Banfield 1958). However, other authors have praised the virtuous performance of some regions and their structures for enhanced political participation at the local level. Against negative portrayals of politics in the Italian south, some *meridionalists* – observers of the southern problem – have reacted vigorously, pointing to the importance of un-institutionalised examples of social capital in society and its virtuous economic and political impact on local development (Piselli 2007; see also Huysseune 2006). However, exploring the democratic credentials of a country whose prime minister controls a vast media empire, has a massive conflict of interest and is constantly under investigation for corruption and other offences that appear incompatible with holding office seems to point at least to a cautious answer as to the quality of Italian democracy and its prospects. One could of course observe that there is a Berlusconi exceptionalism because there is an Italian exceptionalism that prevents social life being conducted with the same certainties one might expect in other industrial democracies. Thus, normal checks and balances in the country's institutional structure are prevented from functioning normally and stopping abuses to democratic procedures, while trials are never concluded in a reasonable amount of time. In the same vein, regardless of how one assesses it politically, Berlusconi's success has been possible because of a political system that, in over a decade, has not been able to produce a credible legal regulation of conflicts of interest by office-holders. This is if one does not count as sufficient the internationally criticised Gasparri law on media ownership (see, for instance, Haraszti 2005) and the 2004 Frattini law, which was also criticised for regulating the conflict of interest by essentially only denying him the right to retain the presidency of AC Milan football club.

However, the menu of political activity that one would consider *prima facie* incompatible with a western democracy is broader than the Berlusconi phenomenon, and often specifically concerns the parties that we have examined in this volume. In any other European country, the leader of a party in government would not state that his followers have rifles ready to be unearthed, as Bossi stated recently (Trocino 2008), while no other ex-fascist parties are in power in other western democracies. After the split within the AN and the formation of the new right-wing La Destra party, it became clear that a sizeable number of old-style fascist nostalgics had operated within the ranks of the AN, at least until recently, only to migrate to a party that indulges public displays of Roman salutes and other fascist paraphernalia. One could also argue that the incorporation of extreme parties in government has not been limited to the right. The Prodi government also relied on the radical left for support, and witnessed the continuation of the interconnection between government activities and protest activities exhibited by right-wing parliamentarians and ministers. While these events might be compatible with a modern democracy, they seem once again to point to an Italian exceptionalism that makes it difficult to use Italian findings to illuminate other European experiences.

If a viable democracy requires acceptable standards in a set of social and political institutions and viable state services, no obvious trend of improvement can be observed from our survey of Italian politics. Political corruption is still endemic. The state's ability to control the territory has possibly diminished in some areas, and the impact of organised crime has grown and expanded to regions such as Campania and Puglia. The judiciary is constantly under political attack and its functioning is unacceptable, with chronic underfunding and trials lasting several years. Furthermore, the historical problem has not been solved of a second chamber that duplicates the first and thus imposes long delays and additional veto points to decision-making. In brief, a dysfunctional political system is made possible by a poorly functioning state, and the interaction between the two make any reform difficult to achieve.

Yet, as many observers have noted with surprise, the quality of institutional, economic, social and political life is, at least in some respects, acceptable and even occasionally satisfactory. A country whose political modernisation can still be regarded as incomplete shows signs of positive innovation in some localities. One can for instance make reference to practices of successful participatory democracy at city level, or to the positive and growing role of the third sector in delivering state services and replacing an inefficient and corrupt state. In an epoch of smaller states and involvement of non-state actors in governance activities, Italy could be said to have been obliged to stimulate civic virtue out of necessity, and thus to be at the forefront of changes happening everywhere. The literature on industrial districts or on territorial pacts seems to run counter to negative forecasts on the future of the country (Amendola et al. 2005; Ramella et al. 2002).

Italy is then coming to terms with the many changes that the transition from government to governance is engendering in several EU countries. As some observers have noted, the surprising element in relation to Italy is its ability to endure if not prosper, despite its failing politics and state (Ginsborg 1990). Despite at least a decade of comparatively poor economic performance, the country has shown a significant ability to respond to the economic challenges of globalisation in some sectors. Furthermore, it has been able to circumvent the impasse that the absence of institutional reforms is causing. In its ability to survive within a framework of weak political institutions, Italy could become a positive model for the present challenges in other European countries. Nevertheless, these positive aspects are outweighed by several negative traits in which the Italian case is again a leading European example.

Italy is also a democracy that is more than elsewhere shaped by *media-cracy* – a system where political choice is shaped by manipulated information. Moreover, it is a system in which the political offering itself is conditioned by a logic of marketing and the anticipatory use of surveys to select policies and decide how to package them. On the basis of our findings, Italy could well also be a model, albeit a negative one, for other European democracies. In particular, FI has been characterised as an extreme example of the electoral–professional model of political organisation (Hopkin and Paolucci 1999; Panebianco 1988). Similar tendencies have been notable elsewhere. For example, a similar debate has characterised the development of New Labour in the UK, and the professionalised techniques it used to manipulate information and market its political product in the 1990s (Jones 1999).

Berlusconi has taken this process a step further – he does not manipulate the media, he owns and controls at least a relevant part of the media. As mentioned, this situation is unlikely to replicate itself elsewhere, as it came about in the context of a state unable to ensure compliance with the law, and where political patronage is more important than elsewhere (remembering that Berlusconi's dominance of the Italian private TV networks was aided and abetted by Bettino Craxi). Because of this situation, Italian democracy appears uniquely weak in Europe. But similar dynamics are taking place in the political communication of other European countries. This has been identified as a new broader phenomenon in France and elsewhere – the 'Sarko-Berlusconism' – which has characterised the strategy of both the Italian prime minister and the French president (Musso 2008). With this neologism, Musso refers to the ability of the two leaders to speak directly to the people through the media and bypass the electoral process (Musso 2008: 32–33). He also refers to the 'anti-political installed within the political' (Musso 2008: 13), and this is another aspect on which Italy can provide a lesson – or a warning – to other European democracies.

The political success of the right in Italy has come with a seeming refusal to acknowledge its political character – these are political parties seemingly populated by non-politicians. Berlusconi and others present themselves as political neophytes, even a decade and a half after entering politics. His style remains that of the political outsider, the man of the people – the successful entrepreneur who can now bring success to Italy. Similarly, Bossi's contribution to a new, simplified and bombastic use of the language amounts to a rejection of the political class – a rejection in which Italy has again anticipated the politics of other European leaders.

Finally, among the many innovations that the parties of the Italian right have produced and that might well find an echo in Europe is the structure of political parties. Freed by the collapse of the previous party system, they were able to innovate more than elsewhere. Two winning models emerged, even if opposing. On the one hand we have the 'light' or 'virtual' party – FI – with little in the way of internal democracy and politicians chosen by the party elites, distributing the electoral kits which advised political candidates on dress styles, and paid for their dentistry needs. On the other hand, we have the territorial party, the LN, that has re-discovered the model of face-to-face propaganda and social network ties. Several successful European ethno-nationalisms are inspired by the latter model, while the former model has also found its echo elsewhere, although usually employed by traditional parties burdened with weightier organisational models. Among European centre-right leaders, Berlusconi has a unique dominance over his party, with a capacity to direct, re-invent and dissolve that is most likely the envy of his counterparts who have to deal with less compliant and flexible party models.

The leaders of the Italian right have been instrumental in engineering innovative models and pathways of party development, exploiting a unique set of political and cultural opportunities to the full, while dealing with a political environment that is in other ways still traditional and marred by inefficiency, corruption and widespread political patronage. Moreover, they have taken ownership of a number of issues of particular salience to the Italian public, such as immigration, law and order, taxation and state efficiency, through the employment of communication and framing strategies that the centre left has been unable to respond to in an effective manner, providing a broader lesson on the effective use of populism, which has masked their own divisions, contradictions and failings.

Now, for them and for the country, the greater challenge will be their ability to deal with the short- and long-term consequences of an unprecedented economic crisis and, above all, their ability to plan their own succession. Age and illness have previously threatened and will in the future challenge the strong leadership of Bossi and Berlusconi at least. Their ability to manage a leadership transition and pave the way for a new generation of leaders will be the ultimate challenge for what has been – at least in their own terms – the establishment of a creative, longlasting and successful Italian right.

Appendix A

Election results 1994–2008

Table A.1 Election results 1994–2008

	1992	1994	1996	2001	2006	2008
PDL						37.4
FI		21	20.6	29.4	23.7	
LN	8.9	8.4	10.1	3.9	4.6	8.3
MPA						1.1
MSI–AN	5.4	13.5	15.7	12.0	12.3	
MS–FT			0.9	0.4		
La Destra–FT						2.4
AS					0.7	
PLI	2.7					
PSDI	2.5					
PRI	4.3					
DC	32.7					
CCD–CDU/UDC			5.8	3.2	6.8	5.6
DC+PSI[1]				1.0	0.7	
Udeur[2]					1.4	
DE					2.4	
Lista Pannella/ Radical Party	1.1	3.5	1.9	2.2		
La Rosa nel Pugno[4]					2.6	
IDV (Di Pietro)				3.9	2.3	4.4
PSI	14.6	2.2				1
PPI		11.1				
Patto Segni		4.7				
La Rete	1.9	1.9				
AD		1.2				
RI (Dini)			4.3			
Ulivo/PD					31.2	33.2
PDS/DS	17	20.4	21.1	16.6		
Margherita				14.5		
PPI–SVP–PRI			6.8			
Rainbow Left						3.1
RC	5.6	6	8.6	5	5.8	
PDCI				1.7	2.3	
Verdi	2.5	2.7	2.5		2.1	
Girasole[8]				2.2		

Note: [1]New PSI only.
[2]Was part of Margherita in 2001.
[4]United list of Radicals and ex-Socialist SDI.
[8]United list of Verdi (greens) and SDI.

Appendix B
Frame analysis

Political analysis has often faced the problem of assessing the contents of political texts. Politics communicates through texts of various kinds, which have different formats, genre, styles and address different audiences. To identify the main points of a political text is a difficult but crucial task. There are several content analysis techniques, and each has advantages and disadvantages. Typically, there are techniques that infer the contents of texts from the frequency of words and the context in which they appear, and techniques that infer contents from the categorisations conducted by culturally competent observers. The first approach is highly replicable, but often cannot satisfactorily identify meaning from the occurrence and frequency of words, as the same meaning can be expressed in an almost endless variety of linguistic expressions. The second approach – often described as 'semantically based' – is more difficult to replicate but often more fruitful in categorising texts whose meaning is subtle, as political texts often are (Donati 1992). One example of the first type is the numerous studies of the Manifesto Research Project (Budge et al. 1998). An example of the second tradition is the studies of the critical discourse analysis tradition (Wodak and Meyer 2001).

Closer to the second tradition, frame analysis techniques are one of the most popular means of categorising texts. Over the years, several variants of this technique have been proposed and tested (Johnston and Noakes 2005). We have utilised a frame analysis technique to identify the values emphasised by the political communications of the three parties analysed. The concept of the frame has its origins in the work of Goffman, but it now varies greatly in terms of how the approach is systematised and to which data it is applied (Fisher 1997). The concept of frame analysis refers particularly to a rich tradition of empirical research on social movements (Gamson and Meyer 1996; Johnston and Noakes 2005; Snow and Benford 1988; Snow et al. 1986) and policy analysis (Rein and Schon 1994) – (for a discussion of the concept of the frame, see Ruzza 2006). Data examined range from cartoons (Gamson 1992) to newspaper articles (Reese 2001) and websites (Ruzza and Bozzini 2006). In recent years, several computerised techniques have become available, which make the work easier to carry out and replicate. There are several approaches that vary in the extent to which quantification is utilised (Johnston 1995).

We utilised the text analysis program Atlas ti (http://www.atlasti.com/) and the statistical software SPSS for the quantitative elaborations. A small group of five analysts selected relevant texts, read them carefully and dialogically identified key ideological elements. A few trials were conducted on the sample materials to ensure sufficient reliability. Then more extensive trials were performed on the actual materials to be analysed. New frames were added to accommodate instances of discourse not previously unequivocally coded within the scheme proposed. A total of sixty frames emerged. While the initial scoring of texts was conducted using the list of codes that all researchers had agreed typified the discursive universe of the Italian right, each researcher could also add additional codes that uniquely characterised a specific document, therefore producing both a standardised comparison of contents but also an individualised and contextual reading. In other words, of the sixty frames considered, most are applicable to all the parties, and a few only to one party where no instances of such frames were found in the documents of other parties.

Each concept was then crystallised in an example sentence and given a label. After attributing a label to these elements, texts were scored to quantify their occurrence.[1] Each time a sentence in a document could in principle be substituted with the example sentence, one instance of the ideological frame was recorded. Computerised analysis allowed quantitative manipulation of the results. But, more importantly, it allowed the researchers to retain immediate access to the relevant texts and compare them rapidly for consistency, and to identify differences in political discourse of different parties and over time. This approach assumes that the more a code is recurrent, the more it is relevant in the ideology that is being analysed. Thus, a concept that is expressed twice in two different paragraphs is recorded as a double occurrence of a frame. The two authors also reviewed the text analyses conducted by different researchers for consistency and congruence with their own reading. The presentation of materials was conducted bearing in mind that texts differ in length and this influences the number of frames identified. Thus, for instance, the frame 'law and order' would be more prominent if it emerges ten times in a document in which overall fifty frames have been counted (20 per cent) than if it emerges fifteen times in a longer document in which a hundred frames have been identified (15 per cent). In order to compare frame frequency across texts, we then calculated and presented in our tables the percentage of each type of frame over the total number of frames identified. However, when we investigated the distribution of frames for each party during the entire period, we conceived their entire textual production as our unit of analysis and reported the absolute number of frames.

In practice, the method utilised consists of a structured reading of documents in which specific thematic issues that characterise a document are identified. Their presence is then compared over time and across political formations. To illustrate the different types of ideological framing, excerpts that typify the most recurrent frames are presented and discussed in the party chapters.

The documents analysed were the founding document of the AN in 1995 and the texts of its programmatic congresses of 1998, 2001 and 2006, the electoral programmes (or guides for candidates) of the LN for the 1994, 1996, 2001 and 2006 elections. For Forza Italia, and in view of its dominant role in the entire coalition, we considered the FI election manifestos of 1994 and 2004 (European elections) and joint manifestos of the Polo or CdL for 1996, 2001 and 2006, as well as the FI *Carta dei Valori* (Charter of Values). We also analysed the PdL *Carta dei Valori* and programme for 2008. After we completed the identification of the key and secondary elements in the party ideologies, we could identify constant and changing elements within and across the parties, and relate these to historical and organisational developments in Italy. The assessment of the respective positions of the parties also incorporated a particular focus on the increasingly salient issue of immigration in Italy, illustrative as it is of the way in which these parties seek to frame their identity. The documents selected reflected distinct phases in which the varying shifts and counter-shifts undertaken by these political actors in order to respond to changing political circumstances could be broadly identified: (1) the collapse of the post-war party system and the foundation phase of the new parties 1991–95; (2) the right in opposition, consolidation and radicalisation 1995–99; (3) the reconstitution of the right-wing coalition and the return to government 2000–2005; (4) the 2006 election; and (5) the 2008 election.

The reason we chose this technique is that it approaches the texts without imposing the categories of the researcher, but rather lets the categories emerge from the interaction between the text and a group of competent observers of a specific political culture. Their opinions are elaborated discursively and practised on sample texts before the analysis is conducted. Differences are reconciled and a common set of categories, scoring standards and identification of implicit contents is allowed to emerge over time from the actual practice of empirical research. As with other approaches, there are problems with this approach. Being ultimately the outcome of the interaction of a text with a specific individual with his or her sensibility, it is difficult to achieve high reliability which can be achieved with automated methods, but it is much more sensitive, allowing for a reading 'between the lines'.

The main value of the method should not be seen as limited to a transformation of 'words into numbers' but in its ability to retain access to specific contents and give the reader a feel for each category through a necessarily random selection of some instances of the most frequent categories. The reader is then able to judge the actual political meaning of the categories we identified and quantified. A second limitation of this method is that many categories with a small number of occurrences risk being generated. Thus, if one provides a numerical summary of the outcome of our analysis, a category that is fragmented into several subcategories risks disappearing from the analysis. We are aware of this risk and have tried in some cases to re-aggregate texts that obviously fit together to retain their analytical visibility.

However, this is another reason why the reader should also concentrate on the actual excerpts rather than only on the quantification of the findings. The method is thus essentially a form of structured reading and as much as possible a competent summary of the materials – it is a way of providing a reaction of culturally competent observers and should not be interpreted in a mechanical fashion. We think it is a useful and distinctive approach, but it should be interpreted as one piece of empirical evidence along with our other approaches – interviews, monitoring of media reports and statistical analysis of attitudinal questionnaires.

As for the selection of materials analysed, our decision to concentrate on electoral materials needs to be clarified. Parties speak with different voices to different audiences. We are aware that an analysis of popular media texts or of the quality press would probably have produced somewhat different results. However, concentrating on electoral materials offers several advantages. We concentrated on electoral programmes because they offered texts that have a special representative value, having resulted from an often lengthy mediation between the different factions in the parties and, being clearly dated, they can be compared across time. Furthermore, it can be argued that, at least to an extent, the texts utilised constitute the raw materials that are often used by political communicators at election time. Being the official voice of the parties, they crystallise views that often trickle down in other kinds of texts. They are in this sense the essence of party ideologies. Since *tangentopoli*, electoral programmes have acquired a special relevance. One of the recurrent criticisms of the DC was the lack of clearly stated promises to the electorate, of vague and convoluted political language. After the demise of the old *partitocrazia*, the language of politics acquired special relevance, and all the parties were forced to produce programmes that were clearer, if not concise. Thus, for historical reasons, we also felt that it was appropriate to focus on these materials. However, we also monitored other kinds of materials and did not find obvious contradictions between other sources and electoral materials – just occasional differences of emphasis that would be difficult to summarise and generalise. Finally, in terms of timing, it was useful to concentrate on electoral materials because election time is when political discourse matters the most. One may argue that ideologies change slightly all the time, but the electorate tends to respond to the ideological offering at election time.

Notes

2 Right and centre right in the post-war party system

1 This was the puppet regime set up by the Nazis in northern Italy in 1943, under Mussolini's leadership, after the latter was dismissed by the king and the new Italian government had signed an armistice with the allies.

2 Paradoxically, some neo-fascists, such as the more 'revolutionary' factions, have preferred to disassociate themselves from the 'right wing' label. To them, the term has connotations with the backward conservative preservation of institutions, while they claim that their fascism transcends traditional left–right boundaries, echoing the claims of the original fascists. De Felice's distinction between fascism in power and fascism in movement is highly relevant here (De Felice 1976).

3 The PCI participated in the design of the republican constitution and had been present in government from 1945 until 1947, when the onset of the cold war made its exclusion necessary in the eyes of the DC.

4 Although provided for in the 1948 constitution, regional government was not enacted until 1970.

5 These coincided with the revelations concerning the Gladio network – a clandestine network, set up with CIA help, to direct resistance and sabotage should Italy come under communist rule. Although ostensibly the network was intended only to be operationalised should Italy be invaded by the Soviet bloc, there were suggestions that the network had also been mobilised to combat internal subversion – from the communist left. It has been suggested that Cossiga's interventions were intended to detract attention away from his involvement in the Gladio affair (Buffacchi and Burgess 2001).

6 It is a controversial issue whether the north–south dimension could be properly defined as a cleavage. Some authors argue that all attempt to politicise it in a permanent and recognised political divide have failed, and that even the LN, by increasingly emphasising its right-wing character, has given up on identifying this dimension as its major identity (Gangemi 1996).

7 He had previously moved to the centre-stage as the promoter of the referendum on the abolition of the multiple preference vote in 1991. This was aimed at diminishing the power of the faction leaders by preventing electors from expressing a preference for a number of candidates belonging to one faction. The new system after 1991 would allow electors to express a preference for only one candidate. While it resulted in a concentration of votes for the nationally important names from the factions, it made it impossible for their supporters to be guaranteed seats.

8 A broader reform was necessary given the Italian system of perfect bicameralism (whereby the powers of the parliamentary chambers are identical).

9 The new government included five AN ministers of cabinet rank. Two of these, Fisichella and the former Christian Democrat Publio Fiori, were external to the

MSI. The remaining three were trusted Fini loyalists from the conservative moderate wing of the MSI, as were the twelve MSI undersecretaries appointed to the government. The most important cabinet appointment was Giuseppe Tatarella as deputy prime minister.

10 Led by Mario Segni.

11 Siniscalco resigned because of the failure of Berlusconi to back him over his demands that the governor of the Bank of Italy, Antonio Fazio, resign for improperly favouring the interests of the Banca Popolare Italiana against a Dutch consortium in its attempt to takeover the Banca Antonveneta.

12 Nevertheless, there was a degree of unease within the AN about support for devolution. Indeed, Domenico Fisichella – one of the few non-MSI 'independent conservatives' who had founded the party with Fini – voted against the reform and later left the party.

13 The four tax rates were 23 per cent for the first €26,000, 33 per cent between €26,000 and €33,500, 39 per cent for €33,500 to €100,000 and 43 per cent over this.

14 Napolitano was a former leading member of the reformist wing of the PCI. He was president of the chamber of deputies from 1992 to 1994, and minister for the interior in the first Prodi government 1996–98.

15 Di Pietro was one of the leading investigating magistrates in the *mani pulite* investigations. He later quit the judiciary to form his own party, Italia dei Valori (Italy of Values, IDV).

3 Populism and the right – an explanatory model

1 Mudde builds on the definitions of Adorno et al. of 'a general disposition to glorify, to be subservient to and remain uncritical toward authoritative figures of the ingroup and to take an attitude of punishing outgroup figures in the name of some moral authority' (Adorno et al. 1969: 228) and of Altemeyer (1981: 147–48) of a belief that certain authorities should be trusted to a relatively great extent and are owed obedience and respect.

2 This is conceptualised in opposition to an 'agrarian populism' type.

3 Interviews have been undertaken in a variety of contexts over a number of years. These include interviews with LN representatives and activists at a number of party events, and around forty interviews with political actors including representatives of the CdL government of 2001–6, and prominent civil society actors, undertaken in the context of two EU-funded research projects, CIVGOV (Civil Society and European Governance), 2002–5 – co-ordinated by the Department of Sociology and Research, University of Trento, and XENOPHOB (The European Dilemma: Institutional Patterns of 'Racial' Discrimination), 2003–6 – co-ordinated by the Centre for Multiethnic Research of the University of Uppsala, Sweden. Both projects were funded by the EU 5th Framework Programme for Research.

4 The authors wish to thank the Cattaneo Institute for giving access to the ITANES data sets.

5 Selected editions of right-wing party newspapers together with selected parliamentary debates on immigration and other political speeches, and some of the party programmes analysed, were collected in the context of the EU 5th framework research programme sponsored project 'The European Dilemma: Institutional Patterns of "Racial" Discrimination' (XENOPHOB).

4 The Northern League

1 For a discussion of the role of institutional activists, see Santoro and McGuire (1997).

2 For additional data see Diamanti (2003a).

3 Strong differences in voting outcomes within regions are discussed by Diamanti (1996: 86). These differences are explained through an 'ecological' approach by Cento Bull and Gilbert (2001: 71), who correlate the LN's success with the presence of industrial districts. One should also note that there is a significant overlapping between catholic areas in the north during the First Republic and LN areas in the Second Republic (Diamanti 1996). An economic approach to explain different voting patterns among areas is utilised by Diamanti (2003a) and by Deas and Giordano (2003) to explain differences between cities and metropolitan areas.

4 This and the following data on the LN electorate were produced by original authors' elaboration of data provided by the Istituto Cattaneo of Bologna in the context of the ITANES research programme.

5 For a discussion of this see Tambini (2001).

6 The main organisations are Sindacato Padano, Scuola Padana, Orsetti Padani, Donne Padane, Padanassistenza, Co.Pa.M., Cattolici Padani, Umanitaria Padana, Padani nel Mondo, Artenord, Padania Bella, Padania Ambiente, Volontari Verdi, Guardia Nazionale Padana, Associazione Alpini Padani, Medica Padana, Padas, Automobile Club, Autisti Padani, Eurocamp. However, often even these remain staffed by only a few members and without real significance.

7 He argued that they needed to be made to walk 'barefoot', which would be done through the abolition of the tax provision that allows Italians to indicate that 0.8 per cent of their income should be directed to the church and deducted from their income tax. The AN senate leader, Domenico Nania, threatened that the AN would block Bossi's cherished federal reforms should he continue 'to attack the values and symbols of Catholicism and the role of the Italian capital' (Staff Reporter 2004e).

8 In 2001, the LN did not present a formal programme, endorsing as it did the Piano di Governo (Plan of Government) of the CdL. However, it did publish a 'guide for candidates', which read like an electoral programme.

9 In response to a government initiative to establish a consultative forum for Muslim migrants in Italy in 2005, Calderoli stated: 'An Italian Islam does not exist' and 'can never be integrated' (Staff Reporter 2005a).

5   Forza Italia

1 In 2000, the centre-left government would introduce a new law, the so-called *par condicio*, regulating the airtime that parties would receive in electoral campaigns, ensuring equitable access to airtime in the run-up to all elections. Berlusconi has repeatedly campaigned against the law.

2 Berlusconi's membership of P2 came to light in 1981. His name was on a list found by a Milan magistrate investigating a banking scandal. The list included several members of parliament, officers in the armed forces and the heads of the secret services, as well as magistrates, police chiefs, bankers and businessmen. The stated aim of P2 was to combat communism through the infiltration of political parties, trade unions, the media and other key institutions (Ginsborg 2004: 30–32).

3 These allegations were made by two leaders (Maria Antonietta Cannizzaro and Andrea Fabbri) of another extreme right group, Movimento Sociale, who claimed that they had been to a meeting with Storace, in which he sought to persuade them to join his new party, claiming that Berlusconi had already donated €2 million to help with the launch (Carmelo Lopapa, 'Sulla Fiamma l'avance di Destra. "Per comprarla li aiuta Silvio"', *La Repubblica*, 14 November 2007, p. 20).

4 Following her nomination, a dissident centre-right parliamentarian, Paolo Guzzanti, suggested that her nomination was a sad example of *mignottocrazia* ('whore-ocracy') and dismissed Carfagna as a 'calendar girl'. In August 2008, Carfagna took legal action against his daughter, Sabina Guzzanti, a well-known left-wing

stand-up comedian, who had publicly attributed her appointment to her sexual relations with Berlusconi. Despite the stir caused by Carfagna's appointment, her poll ratings as a minister remained high at the end of 2008, much to the frustration of the government's critics. Subsequently, Paolo Guzzanti resigned from the PdL. In spring 2009, Ms Lario filed for divorce, lamenting her husband's consorting with 'minors'. This referred to his attendance of the 18th birthday celebration of a would-be actress (... or politician, as she stated), Naomi Letizia. Widespread coverage in the Italian and international media focused on the unclear nature of his relationship with Ms Letizia, and how he came to meet her. More broadly, coverage referred to an apparent misuse of military aircrafts to transport his personal guests.

5 Fini had been critical of Berlusconi's continuation of a strategy based on a belief that the centre-left government would collapse quickly and that there was therefore no need to rethink the objectives of the centre-right coalition or to engage with the government on the pressing questions of electoral and broader constitutional reform. Fini had also expressed anger that Berlusconi's Mediaset channels had been focusing excessively on his private life (Fini had recently separated from his wife and his new partner was expecting his child). The initiative for a new party appeared to be an attempt by Berlusconi to bypass the AN. Indeed, Berlusconi was quoted as stating that he had 'brought Fini from the sewer (referring to his role in bringing the MSI–AN out of the political ghetto in 1993–94) and would send him back there'. Berlusconi then expressed a desire to deal directly with the new centre-left formation (the Democratic Party, formed out of a merger of the DS and Margherita) in talks on electoral reform, in order to bring back a purer form of proportional reform, which would render the need for broad alliances of the right (or left) unnecessary. Berlusconi reportedly stated that bipolarism was dead, as was the CdL.

6 The MSI–AN

1 For a 2002 description of the main factions, see Damilano (2002).

2 Once in possession of the *Carta di soggiorno*, which is obtainable after six years of continuous employment and residence in Italy.

3 He made this proposal at a CNEL (National Economic and Labour Council) meeting on 7 October 2003.

4 At the same time, the LN tabled a rival bill in order to make it obligatory that immigrants wishing to obtain Italian citizenship pass tests not only on knowledge of Italian culture and language, but also on the local dialect of the region in which they live (Staff Reporter 2003d).

5 Gasparri declared that, within the AN, 'everyone was opposed, even those that say they are not'. The party's national co-ordinator, Ignazio La Russa, was involved in physical altercations with hard-line party militants who were jeering Fini as he explained his position at a party meeting in November 2003.

6 For example, Storace has argued that pardons for the right-wing terrorists who were convicted in relation to the Bologna train station massacre in 1980 should also be discussed if Sofri is to be pardoned (Jerkov 2004).

7 For accounts of the REP rise, see Westle and Niedermayer (1992) and Minkenberg (1992).

8 In 2007, the news would break that Fini was separating from his wife and had fathered a child with another woman.

9 This was at a conference on immigration held in Rome on 5 June 1990 reported in *Il Secolo*.

10 The meeting was a manifestation organised by the AN on 9 November 2003 to celebrate the anniversary of the fall of the Berlin Wall. It was at this meeting that La Russa was involved in physical altercations with hard-line party militants who were jeering Fini.

11 Fini made this point on the TV discussion programme, *Porta a Porta*, Rai Uno, 1 December 2003.

7 Sources of success of the Italian right

1 On this, see Panebianco (2007).
2 See Hooper (2007).
3 *Girotondi* roughly translates as ring of roses and refers to a movement that sprang up in opposition to the second Berlusconi government and was led by prominent artists and intellectuals, notably the film director, Nanni Moretti. The movement organised circles of protest (forming human rings) and vigils in public places to draw attention to Berlusconi's conflicts of interests and the threat to democratic norms represented by his government (Andrews 2005).
4 See Staff Reporter (2007a).
5 This was a large rally organised on 11 May 2007 by Savino Pezzotta, a catholic ex-trade unionist, and well attended by the right (Staff Reporter 2007b).
6 For instance, a survey conducted by Demos-coop in November 2007 showed that, while over 87 per cent of Italians acquire information daily through television, only 30.2 per cent acquire it through newspapers. Even counting occasional weekly readings of newspapers, the total figure is only 63.4 per cent. While the global level of trust is fairly limited, it is however much higher for television news. See Bordignon and Ceccarini (2007).
7 For instance, a set of television reports entitled W l'Italia – Pane e Politica (Let's go Italy – Bread and Politics), co-ordinated by Riccardo Iacona and broadcast on 4, 11 and 18 March 2007, demonstrated widespread corruption at local level in Calabria. The reports are available at http://www.media.rai.it/mpplaymedia/0, RaiTre-witalia%5E17%5E20291,00.html.
8 Another issue that needs to be at least mentioned is that in Italy electoral change is often the consequence of a swing vote by an electorate relatively disinterested in politics, which decides very near election time and is therefore difficult to identify and study. This issue emerged with the rapid late improvement in the vote for the CdL just before the 2006 elections. Polls were often off the mark because they failed to identify this problem. Thus, although statistics based on large surveys of the electorate are useful, they might under-represent the undecided vote.
9 The stand-up comedian Beppe Grillo has for years represented a powerful voice in criticising governments and in his popular blog (www.beppegrillo.it) has expressed strong negative views of Italian politicians. On 8 September 2007, he organised a protest in Rome dubbed the ' V Day' (V for *Vaffanculo*, roughly translated as 'go f*** yourself'), attendance at which was estimated at nearly one million participants. For comment on and description of the event, see Serra (2007).
10 Figure 7.1 shows the results of a one-way ANOVA (test F of difference between groups: significance = 0.007). The anti-politics index was created with the following questions (possible answers from totally disagree to completely agree on 1 to 4 scale: '*Che governi la destra o la sinistra, le cose non cambiano*'; '*I politici sono in maggioranza corrotti*'; '*Negli ultimi vent'anni, la classe dirigente italiana ha completamente fallito*'. ('Things do not change whether the right or the left rule', 'The majority of politicians are corrupt', 'In the last twenty years, the Italian political class has completely failed'). The one-dimensionality of the index has been evaluated by means of principal component analysis (percentage of variance explained from the first component extracted: 53.5 per cent). According to these questions, a score ranging from 0 to 9 was assigned to each respondent.
11 Figure 7.2 shows the results of a one-way ANOVA (test F of difference between groups: significance = 0.000). The index of xenophobia was created with the following questions (possible answers from totally disagree to completely agree on 1

to 4 scale: '*E' giusto permettere ai musulmani di costruirsi delle moschee sul territorio italiano*'; '*Gli immigrati, se sono regolari e pagano le tasse, dovrebbero votare alle elezioni amministrative del comune dove abitano*' ('It is right that Muslims should be allowed to build mosques in Italy', 'If legal residents and paying taxes, immigrants should be able to vote in local elections'). The one-dimensionality of the index has been evaluated by means of principal component analysis (percentage of variance explained from the first component extracted: 69.6 per cent). According to these questions, a score ranging from 0 to 6 was assigned to each respondent.

12 ITANES data, 2006.

13 Among those who voted for the left in 2001, 22.9 per cent considered religion very important in their lives and 42 per cent rather important against, respectively, 35.8 per cent and 45 per cent on the right.

14 Figure 7.3 shows the results of a one-way ANOVA (test F of difference between groups: significance = 0.000). The index of religiosity was created with the following questions: '*Quale posto occupa la religione nella sua vita?*'; '*Escluse le cerimonie (come matrimoni, funerali e battesimi) con quale frequenza partecipa alla messa (se non cattolico: a funzioni religiose)?*' ('What is the place of religion in your life?'; 'How often do you go to mass? (excluding ceremonies such as funerals and baptism) (if non-catholic, to religious functions?)'. According to these questions, a score ranging from 0 to 7 was assigned to each respondent. The one-dimensionality of the index has been evaluated by means of principal component analysis (percentage of variance explained from the first component extracted: 81.4 per cent).

15 Irene Pivetti, the youngest ever president of the lower chamber, was heralded by the LN as symbolising the link between traditional catholicism and attention to the values of federalism and devolution. Observers described her as representing the iconography of a 'Jean d'Arc' with loyalty to her cause and strong territorial attachment. After substantial dissent with the leadership, she left the LN and has worked as a TV light entertainment host in recent years.

16 Buttiglione suggested that the inability of Muslims to integrate was also a cause of criminality among their number: 'if one takes into account the level of criminality that emerged from different national groups and their capacity to integrate, one discovers that the group that causes the least problems are Catholic or Christian. This is the case because these groups have a culture more similar to ours and can count on a network of reference such as the parishes' (Staff Reporter 2000).

17 As noted previously, the internal differentiation of the AN was larger than in other parties, more institutionalised and changed gradually over time, with tensions emerging and disappearing on the basis of political, but often also personal, conflicts.

8 Conclusions: populism and the right

1 ESS 2002 and 2004 data. Question: 'Politics too complicated to understand' (variable polcmpl). Significance: 0.00.

2 Information on the activities of Beppe Grillo and his circles is available in English on his blog (see http://www.beppegrillo.it/).

3 Data reported in the 16th report of the Demos-Coop observatory on social capital released on 26 November 2007 and discussed in Diamanti (2007b). For a discussion of the data that assess the influence of television on politics somewhat differently and play down its influence, see Bordignon and Ceccarini (2007).

4 For a recording of the 'Security Day', see http://www.radioradicale.it/scheda/172298/berlusconi-al-security-day-di-forza-italia; and for a recording of the 'No Tax Day', see http://www.radioradicale.it/scheda/221025/no-tax-day.

Party materials

Alla Ricerca del Buon Governo. Appello per la Costruzione di un'Italia Vincente (November 1993).

Alleanza Nazionale (1995a) Pensiamo Italia, Il Domani c'e gia: Valori, Idee, e Progetti per l'Alleanza Nazionale – Tesi Politiche per il XVII Congresso Nazionale del MSI–DN, Fiuggi, January 1995.

Alleanza Nazionale (1995b) Statuto di Alleanza Nazionale.

Alleanza Nazionale (1998) Alleanza Nazionale – Un Progetto per l'Italia del Duemila – Verona 27 Febbraio–1° Marzo 1998, Verona.

Alleanza Nazionale (2001) Un Patto di Programma con gli Italiani per la Prossima Legislatura, Seconda Conferenza Programmatica di Alleanza Nazionale – Napoli 23–25 Febbraio, Naples.

Alleanza Nazionale (2006) Alleanza Nazionale Statuto, Approved by National Assembly.

Alleanza Nazionale (2006) Le Proposte di AN – Terza Conferenza Programmatica (Onorevole Maurizio Gasparri), Rome.

Berlusconi, S. (2000) L'Italia che ho in mente: i discorsi 'a braccio' di Silvio Berlusconi, Milan, Mondadori.

Borghezio, M. (1997) Speech for the Northern League, 30 September, Chamber of Deputies, Rome.

Bossi, U. (1991a) Discorso della Lega Nord. Pieve Emanuele.

Bossi, U. (1991b) Intervento al congresso della Lega Nord. Lega Nord, Milan.

Bossi, U. (1996) Il mio progetto: discorsi sul federalismo e la Padania, Milan: Sperling & Kupfer.

Bossi, U. (1998) 'Per una Padania libera e antagonista all'omologazione', Tesi congressuale (speech to Party Congress), 1998.

Bossi, U. (2000) Speech at Pontida.

Dussin, L. (1997) Speech for the Northern League, 23 October. Chamber of Deputies, Rome.

Fongaro, C. (1997) Speech for the Northern League, 28 October. Chamber of Deputies, Rome.

Fontan, R. (1997) Speech for the Northern League, 19 November. Chamber of Deputies, Rome.

Forza Italia (1994) Electoral programme.

Forza Italia–Contratto con gli italiani (1996) Electoral programme.

Forza Italia–Casa delle Libertà (CdL) (2001) Piano di governo, 2001.

Forza Italia–Contratto con gli italiani (2001) Puntata del 7 Maggio di Porta a Porta.

Forza Italia per il Partito popolare europeo (2004) Programma per le elezioni europee 2004 (Forza Italia per il Partito Popolare Europeo).

Forza Italia (2004) Idee chiave del nostro progetto. Carta dei Valori.

Forza Italia (2008) Carta dei Valori: il popolo delle Liberà.

Gasparri, M. (1997) Speech for the National Alliance, 23 October, Chamber of Deputies, Rome.

Lega Lombarda (1982) Manifesto della Lega Lombarda. *Lombardia Autonomista.*

Lega Lombarda (1983a) Impedire l'uso della Lombardia come sede di soggiorno obbligato e per l'allontanamento definitivo degli immigrati che commettano gravi crimini o risultino implicati in rapimenti, estorsioni, spaccio di droga. *Lombardia Autonomista.*

Lega Lombarda (1983b) Statuto della Lega Lombarda, *Lombardia Autonomista*, n.14, September 1983.

Lega Lombarda (1984) Programma per elezioni europee 1984, *Lombardia Autonomista* n. 19, 1984.

Lega Lombarda (1986) Lo sfrattato vale più di un immigrato. *Lombardia Autonomista.*

Lega Lombarda (1989) Programma per elezioni europee 1989, *Lombardia Autonomista* n. 6, 1989.

Lega Nord (1994) Programma per le elezioni politiche del 1994. Milan, Lega Nord.

Lega Nord (1996) Programma politica, Lega Nord Programma Elettorale per la Padania Elezioni Politiche del 21 Aprile 1996.

Lega Nord (1999) Per una Padania libera in una libera Europa, programma per le europee, 1999.

Lega Nord (2001) Programma per le elezioni politiche del 2001. Milan, Lega Nord.

Lega Nord (2002) 'Ragionare sull'immigrazione: la nuova legge Bossi', testo specificatamente dedicato alle politiche della Lega per l'immigrazione, 2002.

Lega Nord (2004) Programma per le elezioni Europee del 2004. Milan, Lega Nord.

Lega Nord (2006) Programma per le elezioni. Milan, Lega Nord.

MSI (1983) L'avanzata del MSI–DN. Un voto per la nuova Repubblica, Programma per le Elezioni 26, 27 giugno 1983.

MSI (1984) Dalla protesta alla proposta, XIV Congresso Nazionale MSI, Rome, 29 November–2 December 1984.

MSI (1987) XV Congresso Nazionale MSI, Sorrento, 10–13 Dicembre 1987 (documenti congressuali).

MSI (1990) XVI Congresso Nazionale MSI–DN, Rimini, 11 Gennaio 1990 (Tesi politiche e programmatiche orientative a carattere nazionale).

PdL (2008) Il programma del Popolo della Liberta - Sette Missioni per il Futuro dell'Italia, Rome 2008.

References

Accornero, A. & Como, E. (2003) The (failed) reform of article 18 in the second Berlusconi government. In Blondel, J. & Segatti, P. *Italian Politics: The Second Berlusconi Government*, Oxford: Berghahn Books.

Adam, A. J. & Gaither, G. H. (2004) *Black populism in the United States: an annotated bibliography*, Westport, CN, and London: Praeger.

Adorno, T. W., Frenkel-Brunswick, E., Levinson, D. J. & Sanford, R. N. (1969) *The authoritarian personality*, New York: W. W. Norton.

Albertazzi, D. & McDonnell, D. (2005) The Lega Nord in the Second Berlusconi Government: In a League of its own. *Western European Politics*, 28, 952–72.

—— (2008) *Twenty-first century populism: the spectre of western European democracy*, Basingstoke: Palgrave Macmillan.

Altermeyer, R. (1981) *Right-wing authoritarianism*, Winnipeg, Canada: University of Manitoba Press.

Amadori, A. (2002) *Mi consenta. Metafore, messaggi e simboli. Come Silvio Berlusconi ha conquistato il consenso degli italiani*, Milan: Libri Scheiwiller.

Amendola, M., Antonelli, C. & Trigilia, C. (2005) *Processi innovativi e contesti territoriali*, Bologna: Il Mulino.

Andrews, G. (2005) *Not a normal country – Italy After Berlusconi*, London: Pluto Press.

Baker, D., Gamble, A. & Seawright, D. (2002) Sovereign nations and global markets: modern British Conservatism and hyperglobalism. *British Journal of Politics and International Relations*, 4, 399–428.

Baldini, G., Bellucci, P., Caciagli, M., Cartocci, R., Corbetta, P., D'Alimonte, R., Diamanti, I. & Legnante, G. (2001) *ITANES: perchè ha vinto il centro-destra*, Bologna: Il Mulino.

Bale, T. (2003) Cinderella and her ugly sisters: the mainstream and extreme right in bipolarising party systems. *West European Politics*, 3, 67–90.

Banfield, E. G. (1958) *The moral basis of a backward society*, New York: Free Press.

Bar-On, T. (2007) *Where have all the fascists gone?*, Aldershot: Ashgate.

Bardi, L. & Morlino, L. (1994) Italy: tracing the roots of the great transformation. In Katz, R. S. & Mair, P. (eds) *How parties organize: change and adaption in party organizations in western democracies*, London: Sage.

Barisione, M. (2006) *L'immagine del leader*, Bologna: Il Mulino.

Barisione, M., Bellucci, P., Biorcio, R., Caciagli, M., Cartocci, R., Corbetta, P., D'Alimonte, R., Diamanti, I. & Legnante, G. (eds) (2006) *ITANES: dov'è la vittoria – il voto del 2006 raccontato dagli Italiani*, Bologna: Il Mulino.

Bell, J. (1992) *Populism and elitism: politics in the age of equality*, Washington, DC: Regnery Gateway.

Belucci, P. (2007) Changing models of electoral choice in Italy. *Modern Italy*, 12(1), 57–72.

Benhabib, S. (1996) *Democracy and difference: contesting the boundaries of the political*, Princeton, NJ, and Chichester: Princeton University Press.

Berlet, C. & Lyons, M. N. (2000) *Right-wing populism in America: too close for comfort*, New York and London: Guilford Press.

Betz, H.G. (1994) *Radical right-wing populism in western Europe*, New York: St. Martin's Press.

Bigot, G. & Fella, S. (2008) The Prodi government's proposed Citizenship Reform and the debate on immigration and its impact in Italy, *Modern Italy*, 13(3), 305–515.

Biorcio, R. (1997) *La Padania promessa*, Milan: Il Saggiatore.

—— (2002) Forza Italia and the parties of the centre right. In Newell, J. (ed.) *The Italian general election of 2001 – Berlusconi's victory*, Manchester: Manchester University Press.

Bobbio, N. (1996) *Left and right: the significance of a political distinction*, Cambridge: Polity Press.

Bosworth, R. (1993) *Explaining Auschwitz and Hiroshima*, London: Routledge.

Brock, P. D. B. (1973) *Nationalism and populism in partitioned Poland. Selected essays*, London: Orbis Books.

Buckley, R. (2005) *Winds of change in Latin America: populism versus US imperialism*, Cheltenham: Understanding Global Issues Ltd.

Budge, I., Klingemann, H.D., Volkens, A., Bara, J. & Tanenbaum, E. (1998) *Mapping policy preferences: estimates for parties, electors, and governments 1945–1998*, Oxford: Oxford University Press.

Buffachi, V. & Burgess, S. (2001) *Italy since 1989: events and interpretations*, Basingstoke: Palgrave.

Bull, M. (1991) Whatever happened to Italian communism? Explaining the dissolution of the largest communist party in the west. *West European Politics*, XIV, 96–120.

Bull, M. & Newell, J. (2005) *Italian politics: adjustment under duress*, London: Polity Press.

Caciagli, M. (1988) The MSI–DN and neofascism in Italy. *Western European Politics*, 11, 21.

Campus, D. (2006) The 2006 election: more than ever, a Berlusconi-centred campaign. *Journal of Modern Italian Studies*, 11, 516–31.

Canovan, M. (1981) *Populism*, New York: Harcourt Brace Jovanovich.

—— (1999) Trust the people! Populism and the two faces of democracy. *Political Studies*, 47(1), 2–16.

Caprara, M. & Semprini, G. (2007) *Destra estrema e criminale*, Rome: Newton Compton Editori.

Carter, E. (2005) *The extreme right in western Europe: success or failure?*, Manchester: Manchester University Press.

Catanzaro, R., Piselli, F., Ramella, F. & Trigilia, C. (2002) *Comuni Nuovi*, Bologna: Il Mulino.

Cento Bull, A. & Gilbert, M. (2001) *The Lega Nord and the northern question in Italian politics*, Houndmills, Basingstoke, and New York: Palgrave.

Cheles, L. (1995) The Italian far right: nationalist attitudes and views on ethnicity and immigration. In Hargreaves, A. G. & Leaman, J. (eds) *Racism, ethnicity and politics in contemporary Europe*, Aldershot: Edward Elgar.

—— (2006) From ubiquitous presence to significant elusiveness: Berlusconi's portraits, 1994–2005. *Journal of Contemporary European Studies*, 14, 41–67.

Conniff, M. L. (1981) *Urban politics in Brazil: the rise of populism, 1925–1945*, Pittsburgh, PA: University of Pittsburgh Press; London: Feffer and Simons.

—— (1999) *Populism in Latin America*, Tuscaloosa, AL, and London: University of Alabama Press.

Conti, N. (2006) Party conflict over European integration in Italy: a new dimension of party competition. *Journal of Southern Europe and the Balkans*, 8, 217–33.

Dalton, R. J. (2005) *Citizen politics: public opinion and political parties in advanced democracies*, Washington, DC: CQ Press.

Daniels, P. (2000) The 1999 elections to the European parliament. In Gilbert, M. & Pasquino, G. (eds) *Italian politics: the faltering transition*, Oxford: Berghahn Books.

De Felice, R. (1975) *Intervista sul fascismo*, Bari: Laterza.

—— (1976) *Fascism, an informal introduction to its theory and practice*. New Brunswick, NJ: Transaction Books.

De Winter, L. & Tursan, H. (eds) (1998) *Regionalist parties in western Europe*, London: Routledge.

Deas, I. & Giordano, B. (2003) Regions, city-regions, identity and institution building: contemporary experiences of the scalar turn in Italy and England. *Journal of Urban Affairs*, 25, 225–46.

Della Porta, D. & Vannucci, A. (1999) *Un paese anormale. Come la classe politica ha perso l'occasione di Mani Pulite*, Bari: Laterza.

Deth, J. V. (1997) *Private groups and public life: social participation, voluntary associations and political involvement in representative democracies*, London: Routledge.

Diamanti, I. (1993) *La Lega: geografia, storia e sociologia di un nuovo soggetto politico*, Rome: Donzelli.

—— (1994) Forza Italia: il mercato elettorale dell' imprenditore politico. In Ginsborg, P. (ed.) *Stato dell'Italia*, Milan: Il Saggiatore.

—— (1996) *Il male del Nord: Lega, localismo, secessione*, Rome: Donzelli.

—— (2003a) *Bianco, Rosso, Verde e … Azzurro*, Bologna: Il Mulino.

—— (2003b) *La sicurezza in Italia: significati, immagine e realtà. Seconda indagine sulla rappresentazione sociale e mediatica della sicurezza*, Padova: Demos & PI.

Diamanti, I. & Lello, E. (2005) The casa delle libertà: a house of cards? *Modern Italy*, 10, 9–35.

Diamanti, I. & Vassallo, S. (2007) Un paese diviso a metà. Anzi, in molti pezzi. Le elezioni politiche del 9–10 aprile. In Mastropaolo, J.L. (ed.) *Politica in Italia – I fatti dell'anno e le interpretazioni – edizione 2006*, Bologna: Istituto Cattaneo.

Diamanti, I., Bordignon, F., Ceccarini, L. & Porcellato, N. (2008) *Rapporto: gli Italiani e lo stato – Edizione X 2007*, Venezia: Demos & PI.

Donati, P. (1992) Political discourse analysis. In Diani, M. & Eyerman, R. (eds) *Studying Collective Action*, London: Sage Publications.

Dornbusch, R. & Edwards, S. (1991) *The macroeconomics of populism in Latin America*, Chicago, IL, and London: University of Chicago Press.

Drake, P. W. (1978) *Socialism and populism in Chile, 1932–52*, Urbana, IL, and London: University of Illinois Press.

Durden, R. F. (1965) *The climax of populism. The election of 1896*, Lexington, KY: University of Kentucky Press, pp. xii. 190.

Eatwell, R. (1989) The nature of the right: the right as a variety of 'styles of thought'. In Eatwell, R. & O'Sullivan, N. (eds) *The nature of the right*, London: Pinter, pp. 62–76.

—— (1995) *Fascism: a history*, London: Chatto and Windus.

—— (1996) On defining the 'fascist minimum' the centrality of ideology. *Journal of Political Ideologies*, 1, 303–19.

—— (2003) Ten theories of the extreme right. In Merkl, P. & Weinberg, L. (eds) *Right-wing extremism in the twenty-first century*, London: Frank Cass.

—— (2004) Charisma and the revival of the European extreme right. In Rydgren, J. (ed.) *Movements of exclusion: radical right-wing populism in western Europe*, Hauppauge, NY: Nova Science.

Eatwell, R. & Mudde, C. (2004) *Western democracies and the extreme right challenge*, London: Routledge.

Eco, U. (2007) *A passo di gambero. Guerre calde e populismo mediatico*, Milan: Bompiani.

Edelman, M. (1973) *Politics as symbolic action*, Chicago: Markham.

—— (1988) *Constructing the political spectacle*, Chicago, IL: University of Chicago Press.

Edwards, P. (2005) The Berlusconi anomaly: populism and patrimony in Italy's long transition. *South European Society and Politics*, 10, 232–33.

Fabbrini, S. (2006) The Italian case of transition within democracy. *Journal of Southern Europe and the Balkans*, 8(2), 145–61.

Fava, T. (2000) Veneto: una regione democristiana. *Le Istituzioni del Federalismo*, 21 (3,4), 631–34.

Federici, M. P. (1991) *The challenge of populism: the rise of right-wing democratism in postwar America*, New York and London: Praeger.

Fella, S. (2006) From Fiuggi to the Farnesina – Gianfranco Fini's remarkable journey. *Journal of Contemporary European Studies*, 14, 11–23.

—— (2008) Britain: imperial legacies, institutional constraints, and new political opportunities. In Albertazzi, D. & McDonnell, D. (eds) *Twenty-first century populism: the spectre of western European democracy*, Basingstoke: Palgrave Macmillan.

Fella, S. & Ruzza, C. (2006) Changing political opportunities and the re-invention of the Italian right. *Journal of Southern Europe and the Balkans*, 8(2), 179–200.

—— (2007) The National Alliance and Northern League in Italy: rivals in power, enemies in defeat. In Poirier, P. & Delwit, P. (eds) *Identités, politiques, sociétés, espaces: extrême droite et pouvoir en Europe/ The extreme right parties and power in Europe*, Bruxelles: Université de Bruxelles.

Ferraresi, F. (1988) The radical right in post war Italy. *Politics and Society*, 16(1), 71–119.

Ferree, M. M., Gamson, W., Gerhards, J. & Rucht, D. (2002) *Shaping abortion discourse: democracy and the public sphere in Germany and the United States*, Cambridge: Cambridge University Press.

Fini, G. (1999) *Un'Italia civile*, Milan: Ponte alle grazie.

Fini, G. & Francia, P. (1994) *Fini: la mia destra*, Rome: Viviani Editore.

Fisher, K. (1997) Locating frames in the discursive universe. *Sociological Research Online*, 2.

Fouskas, V. (1998) *Italy, Europe and the left*, Aldershot: Ashgate.

Freeden, M. (1996) *Ideologies and political theory: a conceptual approach*, Oxford: Clarendon Press.

—— (1998) Is nationalism a distinct ideology? *Political Studies*, 46, 748–65.

Furlong, P. (1991) Government stability and electoral systems: the Italian example. *Parliamentary Affairs*, 44(1), 50–59.

—— (1992) The extreme right in Italy: old orders and dangerous novelties. *Parliamentary Affairs*, 45, 345–56.

Gamson, W. A. (1988) Political discourse and collective action. *International Social Movement Research*, 1, 219–44.

—— (1992) *Talking politics*, London: Cambridge University Press.

—— (1998) Social movements and cultural change. In Giugni, M., McAdam, D. & Tilly, C. (eds) *From contention to democracy*, Lanham, MD, Boulder, CO, and New York: Rowman & Littlefield.

Gamson, W. & Meyer, D. (1996) Framing political opportunity. In McAdam, D., McCarthy, J. D. & Zald, M. N. (eds) *Comparative perspectives on social movements*, Cambridge: Cambridge University Press.

Gangemi, G. (1996) *Meridione, nordest, federalismo da Salvemini alla Lega Nord*, Catanzaro: Soveria Mannelli; Messina: Rubbettino.

Gomez-Reino Cachafeiro, M. (2002) *Ethnicity and nationalism in Italian politics: inventing the Padania: Lega Nord and the northern question*, Aldershot and Burlington, VT: Ashgate.

Gilbert, M. (1995) *The Italian revolution: the end of politics, Italian style?*, Boulder, CO, and Oxford: Westview Press.

Gilbert, M. & Pasquino, G. (2000) *Italian politics: the faltering transition*, New York and Oxford: Berghahn.

Ginsborg, P. (1990) *A history of contemporary Italy*, London: Penguin.

—— (2003) The patrimonial ambitions of Silvio Berlusconi. *New Left Review*, 21 (May/June), 21–64.

—— (2004) *Silvio Berlusconi: television, power and patrimony*, London: Verso.

Giordano, B. (2001) The contrasting geographies of 'Padania': the case of the Lega Nord in northern Italy. *Area*, 33, 27–37.

—— (2003) The continuing transformation of Italian politics and the contradictory fortunes of the Lega Nord. *Journal of Modern Italian Studies*, 8, 216–30.

Griffin, R. (1996) The post-fascism of the Alleanza Nazionale: a case study in ideological morphology. *Journal of Political Ideologies*, 1(2), 123–46.

Griffiths, D. B. (1992) *Populism in the western United States, 1890–1900*, Lewiston and Lampeter: Edwin Mellen.

Hainsworth, P. (1992) *The extreme right in Europe and the USA*, London: Pinter.

Haraszti, M. (2005) Visit to Italy: The Gasparri Law: observations and recommendations. Report no. 15459. Organization for Security and Co-operation in Europe – The Representative on Freedom of the Media.

Harris, G. (1994) *The dark side of Europe*, Edinburgh: Edinburgh University Press.

Harrison, T. (1995) *Of passionate intensity: right-wing populism and the Reform Party of Canada*, Toronto and London: University of Toronto Press.

Harvie, C. (1994) *The rise of regional Europe*, London: Routledge.

Hine, D. (1993) *Governing Italy*, Oxford: Clarendon Press.

Holmes, W. F. (1994) *American populism*, Lexington, MA: D. C. Heath and Co.

Hopkin, J. (2005) The Berlusconi government at mid-term: a miracle just around the corner? *Mediterranean Politics*, 10, 109–15.

Hopkin, J. & Paolucci, C. (1999) The business firm model of party organization: cases from Spain and Italy. *European Journal of Political Research*, 35, 307–39.

Husbands, C. (1992) The other face of 1992: the extreme right explosion in western Europe. *Parliamentary Affairs*, 45(3), 407–25.

Huysseune, M. (2006) *Modernity and secession. The social sciences and the political discourse of the Lega Nord in Italy*, Oxford: Berghahn.

Ignazi, P. (1993) The changing profile of the Italian social movement. In Merkl, P. H. & Weinberg, L. (eds) *Encounters with the contemporary radical right.* Oxford: Westview Press.

—— (1994a) *Postfascisti? Dal Movimento Sociale ad Alleanza Nazionale,* Bologna: Il Mulino.

—— (1994b) Alleanza Nazionale. In Diamanti, I. & Mannheimer, R. (eds) *Milano e Roma: guida all'Italia elettorale del 1994.* Rome: Donzelli Editore.

—— (1998) MSI/AN: a mass party with the temptation of Fuhrer-Prinzip. In Ysmal, Ignazi, P. & C. Ysmal (ed.) *The organization of political parties in southern Europe,* Westport, CT: Praeger.

—— (2003) *Extreme right wing parties in western Europe,* Oxford: Oxford University Press.

—— (2005a) Le varie anomalie del centrodestra. *Il Mulino,* 6, 1083–94.

—— (2005b) Legitimation and evolution on the Italian right wing: social and ideological reposition of Alleanza Nazionale and the Lega Nord. *South European Society and Politics,* 10, 333–49.

Ignazi, P. & Ysmal, C. (1992a) Extreme right wing parties in Europe. *European Journal of Political Research,* 22, 1–2.

—— (1992b) New and old extreme right parties: the French Front National and the Italian Movimento Sociale. *European Journal of Political Research,* 22, 101–21.

Inglehart, R. (1971) The silent revolution in Europe: intergenerational change in postindustrial societies. *American Political Science Review,* 65, 991–1017.

—— (1990) *Cultural shifts in advanced industrial societies,* Princeton, NJ: Princeton University Press and Oxford University Press.

Isser, S. (1996) *The economics and politics of the United States oil industry, 1920–1990: profits, populism, and petroleum,* New York and London: Garland.

Johnston, H. (1995) A methodology for frame analysis: from discourse to cognitive schemata. In Johnston, H. & Klandermans, B. (eds) *Social movements and culture,* London: UCL Press.

Johnston, H. & Noakes, J. A. (2005) *Frames of protest: social movements and the framing perspective,* Lanham, MD: Rowman & Littlefield Publishers.

Jones, N. (1999) *Sultans of spin: the media and the New Labour government,* London: Gollancz.

Katz, R. &Ignazi, P. (1996) Introduction. In Katz, R. & Ignazi, P. (eds) *Italian politics: the year of the tycoon,* Oxford: Westview Press.

Kazin, M. (1995) *The populist persuasion: an American history,* New York: Basic Books.

Kertzer, D. I. (1988) *Ritual, politics & power,* New Haven, CT: Yale University Press.

Kirkheimer, O. (1966) The transformation of the western European party systems. In Weiner, J. L. M. (ed.) *Political parties and political development,* Princeton, NJ: Princeton University Press.

Kitschelt, H. & McGann, A. J. (1995) *The radical right in western Europe: a comparative analysis,* Ann Arbor: Michigan University Press.

Koopmans, R. &Olzak, S. (2004) Discursive opportunities and the evolution of right-wing violence in Germany. *American Journal of Sociology,* 110, 198–230.

Koopmans, R. & Statham, P. (1999) Ethnic and civic conceptions of nationhood and the differential success of the extreme right in Germany and Italy. In Giugni, M., McAdam, D. & Tilly, C. (eds) *How social movements matter,* Minneapolis, MN: University of Minnesota Press.

Laclau, E. (1977) *Politics and ideology in Marxist theory: capitalism, fascism, populism*, London: Atlantic Highlands Humanities Press.

Legnante, G. & Maino, F. (2000) Lombardia: il consolidamento di Formigoni e la debolezza del centro-sinistra. *Le Istituzioni del Federalismo*, 21(3,4), 599–613.

Leonardi, R. & Wertman, D. (1989) *Italian Christian Democracy: the politics of dominance*, New York: Macmillan.

Lipset, S. M. & Rokkan, S. (eds) (1967) *Party systems and voter alignments: cross national perspectives*, New York: Free Press.

Little, W. & Herrera, A. (1995) *Populism and reform in contemporary Venezuela*, London: University of London, Institute of Latin American Studies.

Livolsi, M. (2006) *La società degli individui: globalizzazione e mass-media in Italia*, Rome: Carocci.

Locatelli, G. & Martini, D. (1994) *Duce addio – la biografia di Gianfranco Fini*, Milan: Longanesi.

Love, P. (1984) *Labour and the money power: Australian labour populism 1890–1950*, Carlton and Ashford: Melbourne University Press.

Lukacs, J. (2005) *Democracy and populism: fear and hatred*, New Haven, CT, and London: Yale University Press.

Luther, K. R. (2002) *The self-destruction of right-wing populism?: Austria's election of 24th November 2002*, Keele: School of Politics, International Relations and the Environment, Keele University.

Maier, C. (1987) *Changing boundaries of the political: essays on the evolving balance between the state and society, public and private in Europe*, Cambridge: Cambridge University Press.

Majone, G. (1989) *Evidence, argument, and persuasion in the policy process*, New Haven, CT: Yale University Press.

Mannheimer, R. (ed.) (1991) *La Lega Lombarda*, Milan: Feltrinelli.

Mannheimer, R. (1994) Forza Italia. In Diamanti, I. & Mannheimer, R. (eds) *Milano e Roma: Guida elettorale del 1994*, Rome: Donzelli Editore.

Mannheimer, R. & Sani, G. (1987) *Il mercato elettorale: identikit dell'elettore italiano*, Bologna: Il Mulino.

Maraffi, M. (1996) Forza Italia: from government to opposition. In Caciagli, M. & Kertzer, D. (eds) *Italian politics: the stalled transition*, Oxford: Westview Press.

Mastropaolo, A. (2005) *La mucca pazza della democrazia: nuove destre, populismo, antipolitica*, Torino: Boringhieri.

—— (2008) Populism and democracy. In Albertazzi, D. & McDonnell, D. (eds) *Twenty-first century populism: the spectre of western European democracy*, Basingstoke: Palgrave Macmillan.

Mazzoleni, G. (2008) Populism and the media. In Albertazzi, D. & McDonnell, D. (eds) *Twenty-first century populism: the spectre of western European democracy*, Basingstoke: Palgrave Macmillan.

Mazzoleni, G., Stewart, J. & Horsfield, B. (2003) *The media and neo-populism: a contemporary comparative analysis*, Westport, CT, and London: Praeger.

McAdam, D., McCarthy, J. D. & Zald, M. N. (eds) (1996) *Comparative perspectives on social movements*, Cambridge: Cambridge University Press.

McCarthy, P. (1996) Forza Italia: the overwhelming success and the consequent problems of a virtual party. In Katz, R. S. & Ignazi, P. (eds) *Italian politics*, Vol. 10 – *The year of the tycoon*, Oxford: Westview Press.

McDonnell, D. (2006) A weekend in Padania: regionalist populism and the Lega Nord. *Politics and Society*, 26, 126–32.

—— (2007) Beyond the radical right straitjacket. *Politics*, 27, 123–26.

McGuigan, J. (1992) *Cultural populism*, London: Routledge.

McMath, R. C. & Foner, E. (1993) *American populism: a social history 1877–1898*, New York: Hill and Wang.

Mény, Y. & Surel, Y. (2001) *Populismo e democrazia*, Bologna: Il Mulino.

—— (2002) *Democracies and the populist challenge*, Basingstoke: Palgrave.

Minkenberg, M. (1992) The new right in Germany. *European Journal of Political Research*, 22, 55–81.

—— (2000) The renewal of the radical right: between modernity and anti-modernity. *Government and Opposition*, 35, 170–88.

—— (2003) The west European radical right as a collective actor: modeling the impact of cultural and structural variables on party formation and movement mobilization. *Comparative European Politics*, 1, 149–70.

Morlino, L. (2001) The three phase of Italian parties. In L. Diamond & R. Gunther (ed.) *Political parties and democracy*, Baltimore, MD: Johns Hopkins University Press.

Mudde, C. (2000) *The ideology of the extreme right*, Manchester: Manchester University Press.

—— (2004) The populist zeitgeist. *Government & Opposition*, 39, 541–63.

—— (2007) *Populist radical right parties in Europe*, Cambridge: Cambridge University Press.

Munro-Kua, A. (1996) *Authoritarian populism in Malaysia*, Basingstoke: Macmillan.

Musso, P. (2008) *Le Sarkoberlusconisme*, Paris: Editions de l'Aube.

Newell, J. (2000) *Parties and democracy in Italy*, London: Dartmouth Publishing.

—— (2006) The Italian elections of May 2006: myths and realities. *West European Politics*, 29, 802–13.

Norris, P. (2000) *A virtuous circle: political communications in postindustrial societies*, Cambridge: Cambridge University Press.

—— (2002) *Democratic phoenix: reinventing political activism*, Cambridge: Cambridge University Press.

—— (2005) *Radical right: voters and parties in the electoral market*, Cambridge: Cambridge University Press.

Novelli, E. (2006) *La turbopolitica. Sessant'anni di comunicazione politica e di scena pubblica in Italia: 1945–2005*, Milan: BUR Biblioteca Univ. Rizzoli.

Ociepka, B. (2005) *Populism and media democracy*, Wydawn: Acta Universitatis Wratislavensis.

Panebianco, A. (1988) *Political parties: organisation and power*, Cambridge: Cambridge University Press.

Paolucci, C. (2006) The nature of Forza Italia and the Italian transition. *Journal of Southern Europe and the Balkans*, 8, 163–78.

Pasquino, G. (2001) The Italian national elections of May 13, 2001. *Journal of Modern Italian Studies,* 6, 371–87.

—— (2003a) The government, the opposition and the President of the Republic under Berlusconi. *Journal of Modern Italian Studies*, 8, 485–99.

—— (2003b) A tale of two parties: Forza Italia and the Left Democrats. *Journal of Modern Italian Studies*, 8, 197 – 215.

—— (2005) What is right in Italy? *South European Society and Politics*, 10, 177–90.

—— (2007) The five faces of Silvio Berlusconi: the knight of anti-politics. *Modern Italy*, 12.

—— (2008) Populism and democracy. In Albertazzi, D. & McDonnell, D. (eds) *Twenty-first century populism: the spectre of western European democracy*, Basingstoke: Palgrave Macmillan.

Piattoni, S. (2003) Le clientélisme revisité. Politique clientéliste et développement économique dans l'Italie de l'après-guerre. *Pole Sud*, 19, 155–74.

Piselli, F. (2007) Social capital and civil society: governing outside the state at the local level. In Ruzza, C. & Sala, V. D. (eds) *Governance and civil society: policy perspectives*, Manchester: Manchester University Press.

Poli, E. (2001) *Forza Italia: strutture, leadership e radicamento territoriale*, Milan: Il Mulino.

Polletta, F. (1999) Snarls, quacks, and quarrels: culture and structure in political process theory. *Sociological Forum*, 14, 63–70.

Porcellato, N. (2008) Il pubblico e il privato. In Diamanti, I., Bordignon, F., Ceccarini, L. & Porcellato, N. (eds) *Rapporto: gli Italiani e lo stato – edizione X 2007*, Venezia: Demos&PI.

Putnam, R., Leonardi, R. & Nanetti, R. (1993) *Making democracy work*, Princeton, NJ: Princeton University Press.

Quaglia, L. (2005) The right and Europe in Italy: an ambivalent relationship. *South European Society and Politics*, 10(2), 277–91.

Raby, D. L. (1983) *Populism: a marxist analysis*, Montreal: Centre for Developing-Area Studies, McGill University.

Reese, S. D. (2001) Prologue – framing public life: a bridging model for media research. In Reese, S. D., Gandy, O. H. & Grant, A. E. (eds) *Perspectives on media and our understanding of the social world*. Mahwah, NJ: Lawrence Erlbaum Associates.

Rein, M. & Schon, D. (1994) *Frame reflections*, New York: Basic Books.

Rizzo, S. & Stella, G. A. (2007) *La casta. Così i politici italiani sono diventati intoccabili*, Milan: Rizzoli.

Ruzza, C. (1996) Collective identity formation and community integration in the Lega Lombarda. In Breakwell, G. M. & Lyons, E. (eds) *Changing European identities: social psychological analyses of social change*, London: Butterworth Heinemann.

—— (1997) Institutionalization in the Italian peace movement. *Theory and Society*, 26, 1–41.

—— (2000) Language and nationalism in Italy. In Barbour, S. & Carmichael, C. (eds) *Language and nationalism in Europe*, Oxford: Oxford University Press.

—— (2004) The Northern League: winning arguments, losing influence. *Current Politics and Economics of Europe*, 13, 309–34.

—— (2006) Frame analysis. In Scott, J. (ed.) *Sociology: the key concepts*, London: Routledge.

Ruzza, C. & Bozzini, E. (2006) Anti-Americanism and the European peace movement: the Iraq war. In Fabbrini, S. (ed.) *The United States contested: American unilateralism and European discontent*, London: Routledge.

Ruzza, C. & Schmidtke, O. (1992) The making of the Leagues. *Telos*, 90, 57–70.

—— (1993) Roots of success of the Lega Lombarda: mobilization dynamics and the media. *West European Politics*, 16, 1–23.

—— (1996a) Changing conceptions of the enemy in the Lega Lombarda. In Foolbrok, M. & Cesarani, D. (eds) *Citizenship, nationality and migration*, London: Routledge.

—— (1996b) Towards a modern right. In Gundle, S. & Parker, S. (eds) *The new Italian republic*, London: Routledge.

Rydgren, J. (2005a) Is extreme right populism contagious? Explaining the emergence of a new party family. *European Journal of Political Research*, 44, 413–37.

—— (2005b) *Movements of exclusion: radical right-wing populism in the western world*, New York: Nova Science Publishers.

Saloutos, T. A. H. & Hicks, J. D. (1961) *Twentieth-century populism. Agricultural discontent in the Middle West, 1900–1939*, Lincoln, NE: University of Nebraska Press.

Salvi, C. & Villone, M. (2005) *Il costo della democrazia*, Milan: Mondadori.

Santoro, W. A. & McGuire, G. M. (1997) Social movement insiders: the impact of institutional activists on affirmative action and comparable worth policies. *Social Problems*, 44, 503–19.

Sarti, R. (1990) Italian fascism: radical politics and conservative goals. In Blinkhorn, M. (ed.) *Fascists and conservatives*, London: Unwin Hyman.

Sassoon, D. (1995) Tangentopoli or the democratization of corruption: considerations on the end of Italy's First Republic. *Journal of Modern Italian Studies*, 1, 124–43.

Schmidtke, O. (1996) *The politics of identity: ethnicity, territories, and the political opportunity structure in modern Italian society*, Sinzheim, Germany: Pro Universitate Verlag.

Shin, M. E. & Agnew, J. A. (2008) *Berlusconi's Italy*, Philadelphia, PA: Temple University Press.

Sidoti, F. (1992) The extreme right in Italy: ideological orphans and counter-mobilisation. In Hainsworth, P. (ed.) *The extreme right in Europe and the USA*, London: Pinter.

Snow, D. A. & Benford, R. D. (1988) Ideology, frame resonance, and participant mobilization. From structure to action: comparing social movement research across cultures. *International Social Movement Research*, 1, 197–217.

Snow, D. A., Rochford, E. B., Worden, S. K. & Benford, R. D. (1986) Frame alignment processes, micromobilization and movements participation. *American Sociological Review*, 51, 464–81.

Sznajder, M. (1995) Italy's right wing government: legitimacy and criticism. *International Affairs*, 71(1), 83–102.

Taggart, P. A. (1996) *The new populism and the new politics: new protest parties in Sweden in a comparative perspective*, Basingstoke: Macmillan.

—— (2000) *Populism*, Buckingham: Open University Press.

Taguieff, P.A. (1994) *Sur la Nouvelle Droite: jalons d'une analyse critique*, Paris: Descartes & Cie.

Talshir, G., Freeden, M. & Humphrey, M. (eds) (2006) *Taking ideology seriously*, London: Routledge.

Tambini, D. (2001) *Nationalism in Italian politics: stories of the Northern League in Italy, 1980–2000*, New York: Routledge.

Tarchi, M. (1997) *Dal MSI ad AN*, Bologna: Il Mulino.

—— (2002) Populism Italian style. In Mény, Y. & Surel, Y. (eds) *Democracies and the populist challenge*, Basingstoke: Palgrave.

—— (2003a) *Fascismo*, Bari: Laterza.

—— (2003b) The political culture of the Alleanza Nazionale: an analysis of the party's programmatic documents 1995–2002. *Journal of Modern Studies*, 8, 135–81.

—— (2008) Italy: a country of many populisms. In Albertazzi, D. A. D. M. (ed.) *Twenty-first century populism: the spectre of western European democracy*, Basingstoke: Palgrave Macmillan.

Tassani, G. (1990) The Italian social movement: from Almirante to Fini. In Nanetti, R. & Cantanzaro, R. (eds) *Italian politics: a review*, London: Pinter.

Tremonti, G. (2008) *La paura e la speranza. Europa: la crisi globale che si avvicina e la via per superarla*, Milan: Mondadori.

Trigilia, C. (1986) *Grandi partiti e piccole imprese: Comunisti e Democristiani nelle regioni a economia diffusa*, Bologna: Il Mulino.

Valentini, C. (1994) Alleanza nazionale: la componente 'storica' del Polo della libertà. In Ginsborg, P. (ed.) *Stato dell'Italia*, Milan: Donzelli Editore.

Van der Brug, W. & Fennema, M. (2003) Protest or mainstream? How the European anti-immigrant parties developed into two separate groups by 1999. *European Journal of Political Research*, 42, 55–76.

Vassallo, S. & Baldini, G. (2000) Sistemi di partito, forma di governo e politica di coalizione nelle regioni italiane. *Le Istituzioni del Federalismo, Elezioni, assemblee e governi regionali, 1947–*2000, 3–4, 534–72.

Vignati, R. (2001) La memoria del fascismo. In Chiarini, R. (ed.) *La Destra allo specchio*, Venice: Marsilio Editori.

Weinberg, L. & Eubank, W. (1987) *The rise and fall of Italian terrorism*, Boulder, CO: Westview Press.

Westle, B. & Niedermayer, O. (1992) Contemporary right wing extremism in Western Germany: the 'republicans' and their electorate. *European Journal of Political Research*, 22, 83–100.

Wodak, R. & Meyer, M. (eds) (2001) *Methods of critical discourse analysis*, London: Sage.

Zaslove, A. (2004) The dark side of European politics: unmasking the radical right. *European Integration*, 26, 61–81.

—— (2007) Alpine populism, Padania and beyond: a response to Duncan McDonnell. *Politics*, 27, 64–68.

Zimmerman, J. F. (1986) *Participatory democracy: populism revived*, New York and London: Praeger.

Zincone, G. (2002) Immigrazione. In Tuccari, F. (ed.) *Il governo Berlusconi, le parole, i fatti, i rischi*, Bari: Editori Laterza.

—— (2006) The making of policies: immigration and immigrants in Italy. *Journal of Ethnic and Migration Studies*, 32, 347–75.

Press articles

Allam, M. (2007) Il 'maiale day' non fa ridere. *Corriere della Sera*, Milan, 14 September, p. 1, 15.

Batista, P. (1994) Freedom and fascism. *The Guardian*, Manchester, 9 June 1994, p. 15.

Bei, F. (2006) Neofascisti, Berlusconi ci ripensa. *La Repubblica*, Rome, 16 February, p. 2.

—— (2008) Leggi razziali, fascismo e male assoluto: Scontro tra comunità ebraica e Alemanno. *La Repubblica*, Rome, 8 September, p. 10.

Berizzi, P. (2008) Bossi: dialogo io con Veltroni e a Silvio dirò di darsi una calmata. *La Repubblica*, 30 June, p. 2.

Bordignon, F. & Ceccarini, L. (2007) Indagine sulla televisione: tutti la guardano, pochi si fidano. *La Repubblica*, Rome, 26 November, p. 34.

Borghezio, M. (2000) La Lega da sempre afferma che, al contrario, l'immigrazione è un fenomeno che si può e si deve governare. *La Padania*, Milan, 14 September, p. 1.

Basso, F. (2008) Sondaggio IPSOS: Boom di fiducia per Napolitano. *Corriere della Sera*, Milan, p. 13.

Buzzanca, S. (2007) Fisco, la minaccia di Bossi Si può tirare fuori il fucile. *La Repubblica*, Rome, 27 August, p. 2.

—— (2008) La Russa: omaggio ai soldati di Salò, Napolitano: un simbolo chi rifiutò la Rsi. *La Repubblica*. Rome, 9 September, p. 6.

Cremonesi, M. (2002) Immigrati nel mirino, Europa e centristi i nemici: Un militante con la scritta «secessione»: è sempre sotto la cenere. *Corriere della Sera*, Milan, 24 June, p. 5.

Caporale, G. (2008) Abruzzo, l'autogol del candidato Pdl "offriva lavoro in cambio di voti" *La Repubblica*, Rome, 25 November, p. 10.

Casadio, G. (2003a) Alle urne ma senza candidarsi, ecco il ddl sugli extracomunitari. *La Repubblica*, Rome, 12 October, p. 8.

Cavalera, F. (2003) Basta rinvii, cacciare i clandestini con la forza. *Corriere della Sera*, Milan, 16 Giugno, p. 5.

Damilano, M. (2002) AN: dietro le quinte del congresso di Bologna – Alleanza diagonale: Fini e i suoi fedelissimi. Le fronde di Storace e Gasparri. I nostalgici. E le pasionarie. Tutti assieme litigiosamente *L'Espresso*, n. 15, 11 April 2002, p.73.

De Luca, M. N. (2004) Dieci spinelli e si rischierà il carcere. *La Repubblica*, Rome, 18 November, p. 28.

Diamanti, I. (2003c) 'I fini ambigui del voto agli stranieri', *La Repubblica*, 1 October, p. 1.

—— (2007) Bipolarismo mediatico: in quel teatrino si decide il voto. *La Repubblica*, Rome, 26 November, p. 1, 35.

—— (2008a) Il regime mediocratico. *La Repubblica*, Milan, 13 July, p. 1.

Di Caro, P. (2007) Fini: impossibile integrarsi con chi ruba. *Corriere della Sera*, Milan, 4 November, p. 5.

Fregonara, G. (2007) Maiale day anti-moschea. *Corriere della Sera*, Milan, 14 September, p. 15.

Fusani, C. (2007) Denuncia – choc di un senatore Berlusconi mi voleva nella Cdl. *La Repubblica*, 13 November, p. 12.

Giannini, M. (2008) L'ultimo passo della nuova destra. *La Repubblica*, Rome, 1 May, Repubblica Online http://www.repubblica.it/2008/04/sezioni/politica/camere-riaprono /nuova-destra/nuova-destra.html.

Hooper, J. (1995) In the shadow of Mussolini. *The Guardian*, Manchester, 6 February 1995, p. T6.

—— (2007) Violence as Italy expels migrants. *The Observer*, Rome, 4 November 2007.

Incerti, M. & Polli, G. (1999) Resistenza linguistica, nuovi suggerimenti. *La Padania*, Milan, 10 January, p. 5.

Jerkov, B. (2004a) Soldi alla Chiesa, bufera su Bossi: ha superato la decenza. *La Repubblica*, Milan, 12 January, p. 2.

Jerkov, B. (2005) Se vince la sinistra miseria, terrore e morte. *La Repubblica*, Rome, 17 November, p. 2.

Lopapa, C., (2007) 'Sulla Fiamma l'avance di Destra. "Per comprarla li aiuta Silvio"', *La Repubblica*, Rome, 14 November 2007, p. 20.

Luzi, G. (2004) Morale evadere dopo il 33%. *La Repubblica*, Rome, 12 November, p. 12.

Luzi, G. (2004) Bossi: 'Togliere soldi alla Chiesa' Fini: 'Ha superato la decenza'. *La Repubblica*, Rome, 1 Marzo, p. 2.

—— (2008) Inno, Fini ammonisce Bossi non puoi offendere gli italiani. *La Repubblica*, Rome, 22 July, p. 6.

Meli, M. T. (2008) Fini riceverà gli omosessuali "olimpici". *Corriere della Sera*, Milan, 4 August, p. 11.

Meloni, M. (2008) La svolta: il malessere del Nord. *La Stampa*, Torino, 16 April, p. 10.

Messina, S. (2003) Immigrati, AN lancia la sua legge – la Lega replica con un DDL: test di Italiano per gli stranieri. *La Repubblica*, Rome, 17 October, p. 8.

Panebianco, A. (2007) L'inevitabile resa dei conti. *Corriere della Sera*, Milan, 11 November, p. 1

Passalacqua, G. (2003) Milan, Bossi spara su An e immigrati. Con Fini leader elezioni perse. *La Repubblica*, Rome, 5 December, p. 6.

Picchio, N. (2006) Il contratto del premier con gli Italiani – Il giudizion complessivo. Gli economisti: alcuni elementi positivi, ma le clausole non sono pienamente rispettate. 'Obiettivi centrati a metà' *Il Sole 24 Ore*, Milan, 15 January, p. 11.

Polchi, V. (2008) Contrordine, la paura è svanita. *La Repubblica*, Rome, 22 November, p. 1.

Polidori, E. (2003f) Non affonderemo il governo ma litigheremo fino al 2006. *La Repubblica*, Rome, 12 October, p. 8.

Polli, G. (1999) L'Italia sotterra i nostri idiomi. *La Padania*, Milan, 16 May, p. 4.

—— (2000) Milan: nella lingua i suoi valori morali. *La Padania*, Milan, 14 January, p. 3.

Rognoni, A. (2004) Stretta di mano poetica tra Lombardi e Sardi. *La Padania*, 25 May, p. 2.

Salvia L., Zuccolini R. (2008) Le periferie del Sud votano Pdl. *Corriere della Sera*, Milan, 18 April, p. 1, 12–13.

Serra, M. (2007) La piazza di Grillo tra politica e populismo. *La Repubblica*, Rome, 9 September, p. 1.

Staff Reporter (2000) La miopia della sinistra contro Biffi. *Il Secolo*, 30 October.

Staff Reporter (2001) "Ha offeso il tricolore" Bossi condannato. *La Repubblica*, Rome, 23 May, La Repubblica Online http://www.repubblica.it/online/politica/vincitoritre/bossi/bossi.html.

Staff Reporter (2002) Lega e immigrazione: le opinioni di Borghezio. *La Repubblica*, 23 June.

Staff Reporter (2003b) Fini avverte Berlusconi. *La Repubblica*, Rome, 10 November, p. 8.

Staff Reporter (2003c) Fini: corteo contro l'Occidente. *La Repubblica*, Rome, 21 March, p. 6.

Staff Reporter (2003d) Immigrati, AN lancia la sua legge. *La Repubblica*, Rome, 17 November, p. 8.

Staff Reporter (2004b) Immigrati, sul voto il si di Strasburgo, AN contro FI. *La Repubblica*, Rome, 16 January, p. 21.

Staff Reporter (2004c) No alla grazia per Priebke, tutti d'accordo con Ciampi. *La Repubblica*, Rome, 7 March, p. 5.

Staff Reporter (2004d) Si al corteo bipartisan. *La Repubblica*, Rome, 14 March, p. 11.

Staff Reporter (2005a) Via alla consulta islamica, Lega in trincea: Pisanu firma il decreto istitutivo. *La Repubblica*, Rome, 10 September, p. 1.

Staff Reporter (2005b) Pisanu vara la consulta per l'Islam la Lega: serve la legge del taglione. *La Repubblica*, Rome, 11 September, p. 8.

Staff Reporter (2006) L'ambasciatore di Francia contro Calderoli. *La Repubblica*, Rome, 11 July, p. 4.

Staff Reporter (2007a) Blitz leghista alla camera: Garibaldi non fu un eroe. *La Repubblica*, Rome, 7 November, p. 20.

Staff Reporter (2007b) Family Day, anche Berlusconi in piazza. *Corriere della Sera*, Milan, 12 May, p. 3.

Staff Reporter (2007c) Gli ebrei romani contro Berlusconi. *La Repubblica*, Rome, 13 November, p. 14.

Staff Reporter (2007d) Berlusconi va all'attacco "La CdL un ectoplasma" "Gli alleati mi fecero perdere le elezioni nel '96" *Corriere della Sera*, Milan, 25 November, p. 8–9.

Staff Reporter (2007e) Storace: non malediremo mai il fascismo. *Corriere della Sera*, Milan, 11 November.

Staff Reporter (2008b) Focus: il boom del Carroccio – La Lega si fa rete. *Corriere della Sera*, Milan, 16 April, p. 12–14.

Staff Reporter (2008c) Fondazione Nord-Est: non è più un voto di protesta. *Corriere della Sera*, Milan, 16 April, p. 13.

Staff Reporter (2008d) I flussi elettorali. *La Repubblica*, Rome, 17 April, p. 20.

Staff Reporter (2008f) Mani pulite secondo Berlusconi 'Mise fine a 50 anni di progresso'. *La Repubblica*, 23 November, Repubblica Online http://www.repubblica.it/2008/11/sezioni/politica/berlusconi-varie/conf-laquila/conf-laquila.html.

Traynor, I. (1994) Neofascists push Italy into Balkan row. *The Guardian*, Manchester, 28 June, p. 12.

Trocino, A. (2008) Bossi: fucili contro questa canaglia romana. *Corriere della Sera*, Milan, 7 April, p. 7.

Vecchi, G. G. (2008a) Federalismo, i timori della Lega. Bossi avverte i "traditori" nel Pdl. *Corriere della Sera*, Milan, 24 November, p. 13.

Verderami, F. (2008) Berlusconi e il decisionismo "imbrigliato". *Corriere della Sera*, Milan, 14 June, p. 1, 8.

Zuccolini, R.(1995) Immigrati, le espulsioni della discordia. *Corriere della Sera*, Milan, 15 November, p. 5.

Index